MANAGEMENT OF CORPORATE COMMUNICATION
From Interpersonal Contacts to External Affairs

MANAGEMENT OF CORPORATE COMMUNICATION
From Interpersonal Contacts to External Affairs

Robert L. Heath
University of Houston

LAWRENCE ERLBAUM ASSOCIATES, PUBLISHERS
1994   Hillsdale, New Jersey   Hove, UK

Lawrence Erlbaum Associates, Inc., Publishers
365 Broadway
Hillsdale, New Jersey 07642

Cover design by Jan Melchior

Library of Congress Cataloging-in-Publication Data

Heath, Robert L. (Robert Lawrence), 1941–
    Management of corporate communication : from interpersonal
contacts to external affairs / Robert L. Heath.
        p. cm.—(LEA's communication series)
    Includes bibliographical references and index.
    ISBN 0-8058-1551-1 (c).—ISBN 0-8058-1552-X (p)
    1. Communication in management. 2. Communication in
organizations. 3. Public relations—Corporations. I. Title. II.
Series.
HD30.3.H4   1994
658.4'5—dc20   93-48157
                                            CIP

Books published by Lawrence Erlbaum Associates are printed on
acid-free paper, and their bindings are chosen for strength and dura-
bility.

Printed in the United States of America
10 9 8 7 6 5 4 3

Contents

Preface

The term *management* is synonymous with guidance, conduct, control, and actions taken to bring something about, to achieve goals. As used in this book, management is thought of as joint enactments by people as they coordinate efforts and interact with stakeholders outside of the company with the intention of achieving mutual benefit. This view assumes that managers cannot control, but can guide employees. Employees influence and sometimes control managers. The key to understanding how companies operate is to realize that joint efforts are required to bring them to life. Enactment is an excellent metaphor for grasping this dynamism. It emphasizes how companies result from joint (joined) efforts, between persons inside the organization, and between the organization and people outside of it. The central theme of this book, trying to balance the dynamic influence between management and personnel, is that successful organizations exhibit joint enactment. Managers are best when they enact a drama with employees rather than attempt to direct the actions of employees.

Chapter 1 provides an overview of enactment theory. It discusses how the meanings people have of their company, market, environment, customers, themselves, and jobs affect their job performance. They enact their jobs as actors enact the scripts in plays. The difference, however, between people in companies and actors on a stage is that members of companies help write the scripts they enact. How people think of their job, their company, their management, and themselves can determine whether they believe themselves to be empowered. The assumption is that the culture of the company empowers or disempowers employees, which in turn affects their productivity and the quality of their work. The upshot of this analysis is to argue for a view of organizational communication that combines information, rhetoric, and dialectic. Chapter 2 argues that the expectations people have of one another and communicate to each other affect what they do together and how they act toward people outside of the company. What happens during enactment depends on the extent to which the meaning of people involved is compatible enough to allow them to coordinate their efforts and attain harmony instead of disharmony. The chapter sets forth principles that are explored in the book and poses a model of enactment that features the organization as shared reality, persona of employees and company, identities of employees and customers, messages, and relationships. What people do becomes the Voice of the company. To the extent that these acts express a Voice that is coherent and coordinated, as well as supports the goals of the company, the members of the organization are likely to be successful. Performance is guided by what people think others expect of them.

Chapter 3 reasons that all of what people know makes sense to them as a narrative. The big Narrative is the large picture of their society, company, industry, product, service, market, and customers. The content of that Narrative constitutes the context for the enactment of each company and each person's work as a narrative. Employees tell stories about their work and workers. From these stories, they learn about the culture of the company, its form and content. In that way they learn the roles, persona, scripts, principles, assumptions, norms, and dramas that guide their work.

Chapter 4 examines an information model of organizational communication. Information affects people's feelings of certainty regarding what they do, what others expect them to do, and the effects of their efforts toward satisfying goals—personal and corporate. In addition to seeking and processing information, people interpret it. Their interpretations are not only individual, but depend on the information-processing and decision-making systems of which they are part. The extent to which people have the information they need to make decisions (personal and corporate) and interpret them in similar and useful ways leads to a feeling of satisfaction that can affect job performance.

Chapter 5 looks at organizational identification and management options. It discusses how the dominant themes of a company are likely to exert unobtrusive control over the actions of employees and considers how the identifications employees have with the company and management affect their work decisions. One view of this principle is that management can control employees by shaping the meanings that they enact. The contrary view is that employees respond by shaping meanings that challenge or conform to those of management. Therefore, management and all acts on behalf of a company can be treated as symbolic action.

Based on discussions in previous chapters, chapter 6 features the negotiation of meanings and the stakes that accompany them. Each group plays out (gives and withholds) stakes based on its view of the value of its stakes, the risks associated with giving and withholding them, and the gains that can be made by giving and withholding them. Through these means, power and coordination are enacted. Managers are advised to think less about how to direct the efforts of their employees and to concentrate more on enacting appropriate narratives with them. This view encourages management to identify with subordinates and become involved in their work effort.

Chapter 7 pays close attention to the meaning that is shared at the superior–subordinate level, the effect of that meaning on those relationships, communication styles, work performance, and work satisfaction. Interpersonal contact, especially between workers and managers, is the basis for coordinating actions and expressing expectations.

Instead of adopting a view of networks as patterns of information flow throughout a system, chapter 8 deals with those subunits as zones of meaning. Each department has different views of its roles in the company, itself as a part of the organization, its power and position in the organization. The chapter argues that interactions between departments are frustrated or enhanced to the extent that their unique jargons and perspectives are compatible with one another.

Chapter 9 examines the communication that occurs regarding products, services, company image, and public policy issues. Marketing people, advertising people, and public relations experts try to create zones of meaning that customers enact in their buying behavior and public policy preferences.

Chapter 10 addresses the challenges public relations people face as they seek to create zones of meaning, in response to zones created by outside stakeholders, such as environmental groups. The zones that exist in the external environment affect what a company can do (as constrained by community values, regulations, and legislation). Companies try to influence this meaning in order to rationalize their actions. If what the company does fits with the expectations of outsiders, the company will be in harmony with them. In that sense, external communication requires the creation and enactment of narratives with persons outside of companies.

Robert L. Heath

1

Managing Communication in Companies: An Enactment Point of View

A century ago companies began to increase in size. Many of them became large, complex, and bureaucratic, often employing thousands of workers. Whereas workers had once toiled alongside a boss who participated in and directed their efforts, the advent of large companies—especially investor-owned corporations—required that employees' work be supervised to bring success to their employer if not to themselves. Whether by art or science, managers in large businesses were required to plan and coordinate these operations. As is true of all instances when humans band together to amplify their individual efforts, communication was instrumental in the endeavor of managers to direct activities needed to create, produce, and sell products or to provide services.

Early management theories assumed bosses should be dominant, paternal, and rational in the use of communication to direct employees' work. The body of knowledge relevant to that managerial philosophy can be reduced to one directive: Give instructions clearly and firmly. From that limited beginning, research and theory progressed to explain the impact organizations have on how people communicate and why communication helps or harms organizations (Morgan, 1986; Redding, 1985; Richetto, 1977).

Management philosophy advanced when researchers demonstrated that human relations help employees feel good about their work, themselves, and the organization. Building on that advice, the human resources approach resulted when managers and researchers recognized the importance of involving employees in the design and execution of work; it acknowledged that bosses cannot control workers. Revolutionizing management theory, human resources shifted the locus of control from the exclusive domain of managers toward a cooperative balance between bosses and employees. A recent version of this approach reduces organizational excellence and productivity to the axiom "Work smarter, not harder." That approach to management treats employees and organizational processes as being thoughtful (Jablin, 1982a; Morgan, Frost, & Pondy, 1983; Pacanowsky &

O'Donnell-Trujillo, 1983; Pondy & Boje, 1980; Sackmann, 1990; Weick, 1979a; Weick & Browning, 1986).

Even though people who enact companies are thoughtful, they are not always rational. As Shrivastava, Mitroff, and Alvesson (1987) reasoned, "The assumption that organizations are rational entities is an unnecessary and mystifying limitation that obscures important aspects of organizing" (p. 90). Organizational behavior is thoughtful even though people do not continually and "consciously select a set of means to achieve predetermined ends with optimal or at least satisfying results" (p. 90).

This brief overview highlights two goals that motivate organizational studies. One is to make organizations effective, productive tools by which people achieve personal, collective, and societal ends. An understanding of communication can help managers and their personnel coordinate efforts needed to achieve their company's mission. In the past two decades, productivity improvement has been a catchword in the struggle to invigorate U.S. companies' ability to deliver quality goods and services at prices that compete domestically and internationally. The Malcolm Baldridge National Quality Award symbolizes a renewed commitment to improve individual, corporate, and national competitiveness.

A second goal of organizational studies is to increase people's happiness in organizations—to empower them and give them the personal satisfaction that their time is well spent. The study of organizational communication should rivet on the fact that companies are tools by which people do what they cannot do by themselves. To avoid the personal side of organizational life ignores a dominant motive for studying human communicative behavior: to understand how people make choices and act in ways that benefit them and affect the success of organizations in which they work.

The challenge facing the savvy manager and employee is to work smart and get others to do the same. This daunting challenge requires insight into organizational communication performance, skills, and processes. The prize for such insight, as Sypher and Zorn (1986) discovered, is greater likelihood of success in companies. Upward mobility is associated with superior cognitive skills and communication abilities: self-monitoring, perspective taking, and persuasiveness. Self-monitoring refers to self-awareness, thinking of what one is doing and how. Perspective taking is the ability to see an issue, situation, another person, or oneself from other people's points of view. Persuasion consists of the ability to influence thoughts and actions—to make requests that others grant.

The focal point of organizational communication analysis is the acts people perform that are meaningful for themselves and others, along with their thoughts about organizing and working. To that end, this book integrates theory, research, and commonplace observation needed to help persons work smart on behalf of themselves, their work units, and an organization. Scholarly inquiry can help people become empowered with attitudes and skills needed to lead rewarding organizational lives—a worthy goal, because at least one third of many people's lives is devoted to work.

Research and theory featured in this analysis draw on empirically derived conclusions and on interpretative insights into organizational rhetoric. Although some writers stress the differences between these lines of analysis, they are treated here as partners for what each can contribute to our understanding. That blend of inquiry lets us understand how, why, and what people communicate, what they communicate about, what they think, and how communication relates to productivity and quality of performance. To appreciate the dynamics of organizational life, we must understand the skills, processes, and meaningful impact of communication in companies. At the heart of this analysis is an interest in knowing how people in companies create and enact meaning, a sense-making approach to the study of organizational performance. This chapter provides rationale for that approach to the study of organizational communication.

TOWARD EFFECTIVE ORGANIZATIONS THROUGH COMMUNICATION

People who manage and work in companies and other complex organizations are expected to be productive and achieve high quality outcomes. *Productivity* entails the ratio of input to output; as material and human resources expended to achieve individual and organizational output decline, productivity increases. *Quality* deals with levels of performance outcome measured in ability to meet or exceed customer and other stakeholder expectations. It responds to the current indictment that U.S.-made products are inferior to those of foreign competitors. Improving organizational effectiveness centers on factors that increase employees' ability and willingness to be effective.

People are the heart, soul, and sinew of companies; through communication and the creation of meaning, they coordinate and focus their efforts. Each company results from what people think and do—in the sense that what they do has communicative force. People use communication as a tool to accomplish individual and collective goals and obtain rewards. In addition to using communication to influence others, people are affected by it in how they perceive themselves, the expectations they have regarding work and rewards, and their opinion of the company.

What the organization is and becomes—how it thinks and operates—is the product of collective efforts. A company is the manifestation of individual and collective needs and efforts. Thus, the study of organizational communication examines how each company constitutes a context that affects people's personal and organizational lives. Organizational research makes people the focal point of analysis and reasons that each company is the product of individual interactions and relationships.

Members of companies want to be efficacious, to be rewarded for their effort, and to feel that what they do is of value. People may have their own peculiar notions of what efficacy entails, and their definition may differ from that of their boss.

Persons outside of companies want to be efficacious, to associate with companies—as customers or vendors for instance—in ways that lead to positive outcomes. People increase their efficacy by creating or joining organizations; they "buy" their way into organizations through what they do and say. Success is communicated as rewards or punishments, outcomes more likely to be favorable if people act as expected.

Communication is a variable taken for granted so that much of what employees do each workday may not seem to depend on their ability to communicate but rather on their performance of work tasks, such as operating machines, making architectural designs, selling hamburgers, or creating and storing information. However, even when people do not overtly and intentionally engage in communication, what they do—such as operate a machine—and how they do it serves as information and has impact on other people, internal and external to each organization. Actions are meaningful and speak loudly; communication occurs when the actions of one person affect another.

Rather than assuming organizational effectiveness is achieved by advising managers on ways to communicate with employees, this book seeks insights that can be used to help individuals cooperate strategically to achieve mutually satisfying outcomes on behalf of themselves and the companies in which they work. Such analysis must acknowledge that people have different goals and values, and negotiate relationships fraught with conflict that demands resolution.

This realization forces us to consider whether a company can be designed properly so that employees—like rats in a maze—will be happy and productive. Rather than being manipulated or controlled, people—regardless of their level within a company—must feel encouraged to operate effectively on its behalf. If a person works correctly to help an organization, the individual expects to be rewarded appropriately and fairly. Distribution of rewards constitutes communication. In addition to material rewards, a sense of achievement can be communicated to employees in many ways, often so subtle that they are hard to identify. Rewards are subject to individual interpretation and, although they should, may not be mutually recognized throughout the company.

Given these assumptions, where should we look in our search to explain organizational effectiveness? Recent studies have argued that meaning—the sense people make of themselves and their circumstances—has an enormous impact on how people come to know which acts to perform on behalf of themselves and their organizations. Stressing this point, Eisenberg (1986) reasoned that organizations are best understood "as the ongoing evolution and negotiation of meaning" (p. 88). Language affects behavior—that of each person and of those he or she influences—and it is a key part of cognition. How actions and events are interpreted is vital to organizational communication. For instance, persons' reaction to stress depends on their interpretation of which events are stressful. They are more tolerant of events they believe they have cognitive or behavioral control over, a belief they will not face an event beyond their limits of endurance. Coping also depends "on the meaning of control for the person undergoing the aversive event" (S. C. Thompson, 1981, p. 98).

A communication-oriented approach to understanding human thought and behavior in organizations must analyze dynamic interaction processes and feature language and meaning as the materials about which people think and with which they make judgments and know which enactments to make. This point is brought into focus by realizing that enactments cannot be random or without meaning if they are to allow people to engage in the activity of organizing. On a day-by-day basis, as people interact, they gain insight into what is going on in each organization—its priorities and expectations often expressed in reward systems. This information is presented in countless conversations, memos, meetings, and corporate communication vehicles, such as employee newsletters. Each organization comes alive and becomes meaningful through communication.

How do successful organizations differ from unsuccessful ones? Ability to control, plan, coordinate, and direct actions are some of the reasons, along with mental factors needed to perform insightful, astute observation, and innovative analysis. Taking that view, Weick (1979a) argued that companies are thinking organisms, obtaining and interpreting information correctly and wisely to maximize opportunities and minimize costs. Thoughtfulness culminates in the creation and execution of organizational and departmental missions. Articulation of thoughts results in shared meaning that guides actions of managers and employees. However, thoughtful planning fails to result in proper execution of business strategies unless organizational members are supportively interlocked with one another. The quality of relationships determines how well the people obtain and use information for planning, strategic management, and operations.

Drawing conclusions about quality organizations is easy, but knowing how to implement them is difficult because explanations of why people act as they do can become a tangle of variables and generalizations. Attempts to derive research-based conclusions people can use to guide their behavior, including communication activities, are frustrated by qualifications; what works under one condition may not work under all circumstances. One objective of organizational studies, then, must be to reduce complex issues to manageable observations that are theoretically sound, testable through research, and built around variables that truly make a difference. This reduction, however, must avoid the kind of simplicity characteristic of lists of "do's and don'ts" of effective management.

Useful generalizations about organizational performance have resulted from the growing interest in organizational culture (Kelly, 1985; Pacanowsky & O'Donnell-Trujillo, 1982). Culture influences behavior because it contains the *social reality* people use to know what they are expected to do—the expectations others hold—and what rewards and punishments result from individual and collective efforts. Members join together to perform activities needed to achieve their goals, to do what they cannot accomplish by themselves. Not all activities in an organization are equally appropriate and rewardable. Culture defines which act is appropriate and which is not so that people can coordinate their efforts.

Culture leads people to share a vocabulary that carves reality—physical and social—into meaningful units. Thus, they hold similar views. By adopting the idiom (including specialized jargon) unique to each organizational culture, employees take on the social reality of culture and think in its terms. In that way, they come to know what is expected of them, what they should expect of others, and how relationships are defined and rewarded. Themes unique to each company give its members a sense of structure and mission.

Members do not need to have identical thoughts or know the same information for a company to function properly, but they must share key principles and themes. As Morgan (1986) advised, "Any realistic approach to organizational analysis must start from the premise that organizations can be many things at one and the same time" (p. 321). Each culture reflects the unique traits of each company—its information systems, politics, ideology, machine-like quality, and ability to produce social change. Each company consists of subcultures that are adequately blended into a unifying culture. Subcultures may complement one another, or lead to conflict and confusion. This realization led Van Maanen and Barley (1985) to point out that "structural ironies and normative tensions between groups are facts of life in most organizations" (p. 48). To be productive and achieve excellence, individuals who make up a company must blend their differences into a coherent and focused whole. Enactment theory explains how this is accomplished.

ENACTMENT THEORY

To capture the dynamism of the people who bring companies to life, enactment theory treats life in general and organizations in particular as an undirected play (Pearce & Cronen, 1980). Noting this dynamism, Deetz (1982) concluded: "Individuals and organizations are constantly in the process of self-formation" (p. 141). To form themselves into an organization, personnel "achieve stability through the enactment of interaction cycles and the subsequent development of rules and recipes for appropriate behavior" (Eisenberg, 1986, p. 89). In this way, enactment theory captures the thoughtful processes that people require to achieve continuity and coordination. It makes explicit the roles and rules that grow from expectations people share to predict and coordinate their activities with one another. This metaphor embraces the strategic and routine actions that typify efforts employees make on behalf of companies, as well as the responses to them by outside stakeholders.

Enactment theory treats companies as theater. As is true of a theatrical production, members of each company must create and enact shared perspectives, scripts, and themes. Narratives and metaphors, the stuff of theater, serve this purpose. Enactment offers a powerful explanation of this activity because it "allows us to use all that theatre, as a performing art, implies. It allows us to think about creativity, to consider the craft of actors playing characterizations, it provides considerations of tragedy and comedy, it suggests all the constraints of situation and history which affect any live performance, it allows for inquiry about the link between performance and what goes on backstage" (Mangham & Overington, 1987, p. 3).

At first glance, the metaphor of business as theater is alluringly simple and, perhaps for that reason, compelling, but it is fraught with difficulty. One oversimplification is the assumption that employees enact a play that management creates, a perspective that may discount the importance of employee empowerment by overemphasizing the directive role of management. To coordinate their efforts, people need a playbook, containing scripts and a plot. But how are these created?

To understand enactment theory requires insights into the way people think and act in organizations. On this matter, Weick (1979b) reasoned that they cannot separate themselves from how they think about and make sense of their environment. They are reflected in their views of that environment. Through their employees, companies engage their environment and become part of it, and the environment reflects their presence. "The external environment literally bends around the enactments of people, and much of the activity of sense-making involves an effort to separate the externality from the action" (Weick, 1979b, pp. 130–131). For example, members of a car manufacturing company see the possession and use of automobiles as a dominant theme in their discussion of their industry, plant operations, identities, and society. That view dominates their planning, operations, and marketing. These people see themselves, their customers, and society through the perspective of manufacturing, selling, repairing, financing, and owning automobiles. Reflecting on Weick's theory of enactment, Bantz (1989) agreed that organizing results when employees enact change in an environment that is ambiguous and equivocal. People select an interpretation designed to reduce the equivocality and retain a sense of the causal relationships expressed in that interpretation. This approach to enactment has reshaped organizational research.

By using enactment as the paradigm of organizational behavior, Weick (1979b) refuted the conclusion that organizational structure is static. He argued that a company is not an organization, but is engaged in the *process of organizing*. It undergoes constant change. The structure that exists occurs because of what people in the organization do and think together, as a unit. Viewed this way, people enact structure through the process of forming, maintaining, and dissolving relationships. Enactment results because people are conscious of relationships. Thus, Weick (1979b) conceptualized organizations as a continual state of falling apart and rebuilding.

In Weick's (1979b) view, enactment transpires through communication processes that occur in stages: act, interact, and double interact. One person, as an individual or representative of a company, does something (*act*) that is meaningful to another person. The second person reacts; this is an *interact*—an act followed by a reaction. Reaction to the interact is a *double interact*. Persons involved in these relationships read each other's behavior and make attributions to comprehend what each person and the situation means. The meaning of each act is defined by reactions—symbolic action—persons make to it, to themselves, and to the persons who commit it.

Weick's (1987) analysis requires an understanding of the processes people employ as they collectively attempt to interpret their environment: enactment, selection, and retention. *Enactment* is "a bracketing activity" (p. 153). *Selection* refers to what people focus on as they observe themselves and their environment. *Retention* entails remembering events, concepts, and scripts, as individuals and as groups in a company. Through interaction, people achieve sufficient collective interpretations to lessen the equivocality in information about themselves, one another, and their environment.

Enactment involves perception and attention. People focus on some elements of their environment as they interact with one another about it, and they ignore other aspects. Recurring selections transform into schemata—patterned and predictable ways of perceiving and thinking. Information derived from this process becomes retained in individual and collective memories. Each schema, Weick (1979b) reasoned, is "an abridged, generalized, corrigible orientation of experience that serves as an initial frame of reference for action and perception. A schema is the belief in the phrase, 'I'll see it when I believe it.' Schemata constrain seeing and, therefore, serve to bracket portions of experience" (p. 154).

Believing that people perceive reality selectively through perceptual filters, Weick (1979b) reasoned that they see what their orientations and assumptions— even biases—allow them to see or prevent them from seeing. Such is the case because each "person's idea is extended outward, implanted, and then discovered as knowledge. The discovery, however, originated in a prior invention by this discoverer" (p. 159). Individuals are part of the environment they perceive and they cannot see it independent of their interest and presence in it.

For instance, managers of fast food or soft drink companies make sense of their environment in terms of a narrow, focused interest in their product and customers. Members of such companies think of people external to the companies as purchasers and users of their product. They use those schemata when they think of and act toward them. Enactment is a self-fulfilling prophecy. People see what they expect to find. For this reason, Weick concluded, enactment is not merely perception: "Enactment emphasizes that mangers construct, rearrange, single out, and demolish many 'objective' features of their surroundings. When they unrandomize variables, they insert vestiges of orderliness, and literally create their own constraints" (p. 164). People can share views of reality by having common experiences and assigning similar interpretations to them. Enactment occurs when "people, often alone, actively *put* things out there that they then perceive and negotiate about perceiving. It is that initial implanting of reality that is perceived by the word *enactment*" (p. 165).

What enables individuals to achieve collective effort? Weick's (1987) answer featured two concepts: thought and interaction given form through the idiom unique to each industry, company, and work discipline. Scripted in business idiom, "measures of profitability, debt to earnings ratios, reports of capital investments and the like are vital information about any enterprise" (Mangham & Overington, 1987, p. 3). Interpretations of these "facts" arise from perspectives employees and mangers share—or should share. The "language trappings of organizations such as strategic plans are important components in the process of creating order. They hold events together long enough and tightly enough in people's heads so that they act in the belief that their actions will be influential and make sense" (Weick, 1987, p. 98). Language makes public the assumptions, expectations, justifications, and commitments that people use to "span the breaks in a loosely coupled system and encourage confident actions that tighten systems and create order. The conditions for order in organizations exist as much in the mind as they do in the rationalized procedures. That is why culture, which affects the mind through meaning, is often more important than structure" (p. 98).

Culture, as Morgan (1986) defined it, is "a process of reality construction that allows people to see and understand particular events, actions, objects, utterances, or situations in distinctive ways" (p. 128). It helps people to hold views that they share and know that they share with other members of their organization. Culture consists of jargon unique to each company, its subunits, and its industry. It contains knowledge of the company (expressed as beliefs and attitudes), as well as its values, roles, and rules—those relating to communication activities, work, and interpretations. Culture defines which behaviors and judgments are appropriate and rewardable. Because it focuses on some alternatives to the exclusion of others, it influences the actions of organization members.

As meaning changes so does organizational structure because people enact the scenes they know and expect to be rewarding. Therefore, to change organizational structure requires altering the definition of scenes or the actions that are appropriate to each scene. Smircich (1983a) reasoned that management relies on "the systems of knowledge that make up the basis for organized action" (pp. 240–241). For that reason, she advised managers to maintain "the sense of organization by working to achieve interpretive schemes that are shared widely enough to allow for organized action. This means attending not only to tasks, objectives, and deadlines, but to concentrating on the means by which people make sense of their situation." A major task facing supervisors and senior officers is to lead their personnel by "the management of meaning in ways oriented toward particular purposes. Much power lies in the capability to define and shape social reality" (p. 241).

Premises that become widely accepted throughout a company influence the judgments and actions of employees, supervisors, and senior management. Such premises provide "unobtrusive control" over the performance of personnel (Tompkins & Cheney, 1985). From management's point of view, premises are crucial to coordinating successful operations. Premises can define products, services, operations, or lifestyles and exert influence in the marketplace and public policy arena. However, despite the influence managers may appear to have through the manipulation of symbols and culture, C.A. Ray (1986), for one, doubted that management could control employees through symbols; even if such were the case, management would have to worry about the consequences of achieving a singular set of thoughts, because a "homogenization of employees is potentially threatening" (p. 295). As potent as premises are for shaping organizational activities, Morgan (1986) was concerned that efforts to influence personnel through culture could devolve into ideological warfare. He mused: "The fact that such manipulation may well be accompanied by resistance, resentment, and mistrust, and that employees may react against being manipulated in this way, receives scant attention" (p. 138).

An executive view of the management of meaning presumes that employees do not contribute to the culture of their company by their statements and actions. However, an informed approach to management philosophy recognizes that all members of companies not only contribute to their organization's culture, but also monitor it to learn how to maximize gains while minimizing losses. Although personal interpretations of culture are similar to one another, they are also idiosyncratic in ways that allow individuals to hamper collective, cooperative efforts. Members exert strains on their company's culture in an attempt to alter definitions of the scene in which they work; they may seek to rationalize behavior that management might not prefer.

Given these differences of opinion, we may wonder how much management and employees must agree for an organization to be productive and achieve excellence. If commonality exists, is that because of actions and statements by management? Or is management merely voicing what it senses to be sentiments expressed by employees? A good answer to these questions is that employees and management both influence the culture of their organization (Martin, Sitkin, & Boehm, 1985). Efforts of all members of a company culminate in its organization; individuals influence one anothers' opinions and behaviors. Whether leading or following this wave, managers seem to need to at least appear to be vital to the process. Their success depends, as contingency theory predicts, on performing acts that achieve desired outcomes in light of prevailing circumstances. Such is the case, for example, in a sales region when a manager is able to establish a few key themes that become recognized and used by salespersons to guide their efforts and influence their customers' judgments (Siehl, 1985).

Discussions of this kind—which feature meaning, culture, management, and employee activities—have fostered the rise of interpretivism as an approach for diagnosing and changing organizational and personnel performance. "The interpretive perspective, with its emphasis on context," Smircich (1983a) observed, "forces examination of purpose." In contrast, functionalist theory "considers organizations as ends in themselves and management as the pursuit of efficiency. . . . The interpretive perspective recognizes that managers are enactors of their situations; they often contribute to patterns of action that are unnecessarily limiting. Thus managers informed by the interpretive view would develop reflexivity and consciousness of the ways they create their organizational worlds" (p. 241). For that reason, managers may be more able to take perspectives and communicate more effectively and persuasively among themselves and with personnel.

If Smircich is correct, managers become more able by gaining insight into the meaning created by their behavior and statements that affect themselves, as well as the meaning created by other members of their company. What is communicated and how it is communicated advances or hinders each company's efforts. What employees in a company do is influenced by what they think is expected of them, including how to dress, preferences in personal grooming, what to say, and to whom to say it. Based on their study of the culture of Disneyland, Smith and Eisenberg (1987) concluded, "The park or 'show' is the enactment of Walt Disney's utopian vision; it is 'the happiest place on earth'" (p. 372).

Enactment occurs when people perform roles and use strategies appropriate to each role. It results when relational partners know how and are willing to enact complementary strategies by employing compatible communication plans, styles, and message design logics. Applying this rationale to understand how performance relates to role-specific communication styles, Putnam and Jones (1982) found that "management representatives relied on defensive tactics while labor negotiators specialized in offensive maneuvers; these strategies emerged in the interaction structure of negotiators, especially in their use of attack–defend and offensive-information giving patterns. Impasse dyads, as compared with agreement pairs, exhibited a tightly-structured, reciprocal pattern of attack–attack or defend–defend, with management initiating this cycle" (p. 170). This finding suggests that negotiations can occur because participants know how to interact—act and counteract.

What people experience and what they communicate about those experiences becomes a way of having something in common on which to base their coordinated enactments. By sharing experiences and adopting idioms unique to work activities, people identify with each other. To explain that process, Tompkins (1987) agreed with Burke (1966b), who argued that people see reality through a fog of symbols— "terministic screens" (p. 105). The featured term, Tompkins asserted, is Burke's concept of identification (1969b); because people use similar terms and define themselves in similar ways they identify with one another and thereby can act together. Thus, Tompkins reasoned, "If there is to be hierarchy there must be division; if there is to be organization there must be communication (rhetoric, persuasion, identification) and *symbolism* by which to compensate for and occasionally transcend the division" (p. 83).

Information increases identification. Employees identify with an organization and become committed to it if they feel they have sufficient information to make decisions (Penley, 1982). Another means for increasing identification is to enlarge the number of relationships people have with one another in the organization. Persons who believe they have a rich array of relationships with other organizational members identify more with the organization (Bullis & Bach, 1991).

Sharing idioms is another factor in the identification people have with other members of the organization and with the organization itself. People's understanding of reality is never free from the words they use to talk and think about it. Therefore, their experiences may not be as important as the terms they use to discuss them. The terminology people use to enact that reality is crucial to the enactment whether they have engaged in actions or merely have terms that refer to those actions. Thus, "language is a way of acting together by living the substance of the perspectives captured in each idiom" (Heath, 1986, p. 121). This view of enactment is based on the principle, as Burke (1965) reasoned, that "a motive is not some fixed thing like a table, which one can go and look at. It is a term of interpretation, and being such it will naturally take its place within the framework of our Weltanschauung as a whole" (p. 25). How people enact roles on behalf of and in response to each other and their work depends on the perspectives they hold. They enact their perspectives as though they were "dancing an attitude," the essence of symbolic action (Burke, 1973, p. 9).

Not only do words stand for things, but they also give people the means to act in collective ways. Words define, but more importantly they express attitudes and prescribe actions. Because people enact their behavior according to what they believe is normative and rewarding, their actions express attitudes because they appear to prefer some actions and avoid others. In that way, symbolic action is attitudinal action—enactment of attitudes (Burke, 1961).

At this point in our analysis, an important distinction must be considered. Is reality only what people think it is and do they find themselves in that reality, as Weick (1979b) argued? Answering that question, Pilotta, Widman, and Jasko (1988) reasoned: "Not only are human beings capable of altering their environments, they also are capable of creating that environment. The creation of an environment, as distinguished from sheerly inhabiting an environment, is precisely the capacity for culture" (p. 331). Pilotta et al. (1988) reasoned that "enactments determine the contours and character of an organization, defining at the same time external organizational borders. The cultural 'text' is the totality of the guidelines employed for the interpretation of all organizational action; it grounds the 'hows' and 'whys' giving meaning to the already enacted 'what'" (p. 331).

Distinctions raised by this analysis are not so much a matter of choosing between opposites as of determining degrees of difference. Whether inside an organization or through the assertion of an organization into its environment, people affect their environment. Inside, as well as outside of a company, employees shape their environment by how they enact it. For example, through communication about products, attitudes, and public policy, the car industry created a *car environment*. Employees react to themselves as auto workers, an identity that can limit their employment options—"I am an auto worker." Likewise, if a person submits to sexual discrimination that act results in a different environment than if that person opposes it. Although people enact their organizational dramas in scenes partially created by others, how they enact those dramas defines the scene (the act should fit the scene and if it does not the scene may change). No clearer or stronger evidence of that point exists than that provided by observing the ideological battle between businesses and environmentalists regarding which acts are preferred given their definitions of the scene—our environment—they are enacting.

This analysis brings to mind an important question regarding the boundaries of each company. Where does the company stop and its environment begin? This question is tantalizing because in a real sense the consuming public (of soft drinks or fast food, for instance) is an extension of the company as well as its environment. Are consumers not simultaneously external to the company and *part* of it, engaging as partners in the consumption of its products? For this reason, organizational boundary is not merely the property line of the organization (Cheney & Vibbert, 1987; Dutton & Duncan, 1987; Dutton & Ottensmeyer, 1987; Huber & Daft, 1987). A company extends beyond its four walls, but how far and in what ways? Its boundaries are physical. But more important, they are also symbolic.

Interpretative frames used by people inside and outside each company are as important to defining its boundaries as is its physical perimeter. The boundary of each company is symbolic—constituting the interpretations outsiders share with insiders. This conclusion encourages persons who want to understand and operate companies to seek to comprehend the key words people use to interpret reality, which in turn allows them to join with others in the performance of connected, interlocking activities. Morgan (1986) pointed to some items to which meaning is essential: "Organizational structure, rules, policies, goals, missions, job descriptions, and standardized operating procedures perform a similar interpretive function." These are "primary points of reference for the way people think about and make sense of the contexts in which they work" (p. 132).

Managers have a great deal of control over these organizational documents and statements, but the search for "points of reference" should not overlook informal means of communication such as stories, the grist of everyday conversations, and definitions employees impose on company documents through their actions and comments about them. Understood this way, cultures inside and outside of a company can contradict one another, be variations of a common theme, or complement one another (Rose, 1988).

This approach to organizational communication assumes that each company—co-defined by all participants engaged with the organization—constitutes meaning, actions that are interpreted by those participants. This reasoning emphasizes that a company results from (a) enactments—overt, observable actions and the visible products of those actions—and (b) the meaning (perceptions and interpretations) that those enactments have for participants. Actors perceive their own enactments, as well as those of others, and attribute meaning to them and interpret the context in which they occur. The definition of each company results from enactments by its members, interpretations of those enactments by persons affected by them, and reactions to those enactments and interpretations.

This analysis is brought into focus by realizing that plays (or any dramatic event) are rarely the product of single individuals. They result from the actions—interactions—by many actors, and are reacted to by audiences—outsiders. Moreover, the meaning of the play does not stop at the edge of the stage. The audience participates in the play by responding to it and by taking away residual thoughts and feelings derived from it. Each company is the product of what people do and say as well as the thoughts and feelings they have about it. People act toward themselves, other members of the company, the company as a perceptual entity, and external individuals based on interpretative perspectives. Through their interpretations, people know how to merge their interests with some people and divide themselves from others. The jargon used by persons involved with an organization defines it and its role in society—as well as roles of people who serve it and people it serves. These interpretations prescribe identities, relationships, performance expectations, rewards, punishments, evaluations, and ethics.

Enactment theory gives a rationale for distinguishing between strategic and routine behavior. Much enactment is scripted. During normal business routines, recurring statements are made with slight variation, but some enactments are performed without scripts. People periodically engage in conversations and make decisions that demand that they use new scripts and decision heuristics; or, and as is true of periods of personal, organizational, or environmental turbulence, scripts that once sufficed may now be inadequate. People employ routine communication plans when they can; when they cannot, their ability to devise new plans is crucial to their success as company members.

Because it features the processes of how people share interpretations, enactment theory is a powerful explanation of organizational behavior. By sharing meaning, individuals obtain and interpret information and expectations in ways that guide their judgments and behaviors. For this reason, managers may seek to exert leadership by communicating interpretations that they want employees to enact (Mumby, 1987; Smircich, 1983a). Enactment theory can accept, but does not assume, that managers play a dominant role in the creation of interpretative perspectives; this theory assumes that the meaning that guides organizational performance is subject to negotiation and persuasive influence by *all* members of a company. Although much of what they do is defined by a playwright, actors are not controlled by the playwright. They can change scripts and ad lib. So do employees.

These distinctions are crucial because writers on corporate activities love the word *strategic*—as in strategic planning, strategic management, or strategic behavior. A strategic perspective on organizations can lead us to assume that managers and employees are smart, strategic, and dynamic. That thinking suggests that every effort people make on behalf of a company is thoughtful and designed to achieve specific goals. Dozens of texts explain how to improve strategic communication skills and improve strategic performance and thereby to be useful to a company and acquire social and monetary rewards. Despite the prevalence of such assumptions, we must be realistic in our understanding of collective and individual performance. To do so, we must acknowledge that companies—and their personnel—are not always strategic or smart; they may be quite narrow and myopic; they may not plan very much or very well. A lot of what occurs on behalf of a company is routine, scripted, and random rather than strategic.

Enactment theory embraces all of these perspectives. Whether as strategic and planned or routine ritual, it views organizational efforts as symbolic action, the dancing of an attitude.

EMPOWERMENT

One innovation of management and organizational communication theory is the concept of *empowerment,* which assumes that quality and productivity increase as people use power constructively. Discussions of empowerment focus on the sense of power people believe they exert in companies. Their performance tends to increase as they see that their self-interest is positively affected by what they and others do to achieve ends in support of their personal and their company's interests. Sophisticated views of empowerment assume that people have power and are not "given" it by management. Whether they feel empowered affects how they use the power they have and whether they experience self-efficacy as a member of a work unit and company. From each organizational member's point of view, empowerment arises from knowing the appropriate act in each scene, those that are collectively rewarding.

Do people work harder to enact a drama they help to create? Many people think so. Each person is an individual as well as a member of organizations; identities—the ways they deal with themselves—involve organizations. Inherent in such relationships, Burke (1973) reminded us, is the tension between being an empowered individual (doing what we can on our own) and being empowered through membership in organizations. We are "just a person" until we get to work; then we become an "Acme employee." How people think of themselves and what they learn from stories of others' successes and failures can predict whether they feel empowered. An important aspect of empowerment is the desire to protect and advance self-interests through collective activities. Involvement theory suggests that people become physically and cognitively active when they believe their self-interests are affected by what is happening around them (Petty & Cacioppo, 1981, 1986).

Asserting that "empowering subordinates is a principal component of managerial and organizational effectiveness," Conger and Kanungo (1988) challenged managers to look for ways to convince employees that they can effect outcomes (p. 471). Empowerment can be enhanced by training employees and managers, by implementing appropriate policies and procedures, and by designing effective work routines. Empowerment is likely to occur and increase organizational effectiveness when superiors help their subordinates to obtain and use power.

How is this done? Conger and Kanungo (1988) concluded that "most management theorists have dealt with empowerment as a set of managerial techniques and have not paid sufficient attention to its nature or the processes underlying the construct" (p. 471). This has led to assumptions "that empowerment is the same as delegating or sharing power with subordinates and, hence, that the construct requires no further conceptual analysis beyond the power concept" (p. 471).

To correct this mistake, Conger and Kanungo asserted that empowerment is a relational construct "used to describe the perceived power or control that an individual actor or organizational subunit has over others" (p. 472). This view of empowerment draws on social exchange theory, which "interprets power as a function of the dependence and/or interdependence of actors. Power arises when an individual's or a subunit's performance outcomes are contingent not simply on their own behavior but on what others do and/or in how others respond" (p. 472). This conception of empowerment features the double interact, the basis of relationships, and the enactment of complementary, supportive, competing, or destructive dramas. The power each individual has is proportional to his or her "ability to provide some performance or resource that is valued by the organization or the actor's ability to cope with important organizational contingencies or problems" (p. 472).

Empowerment is not something given to employees by managers, but rather it is enacted by members of each organization. Pacanowsky (1988a) described an empowering organization as one in which power and opportunity are distributed; an empowering organization exhibits open communication, fosters integrative problem solving, establishes an environment of trust, and encourages employees to achieve high levels of performance and self-responsibility. Culture and climate result from the dialectic between persons, regardless of level, who compose each organization. Culture is a product of the shared interpretations of each organization, its operations, personnel, and environment. Climate results from interpersonal relationships, expressed in concepts such as control, trust, and intimacy.

Some companies attempt to create an empowering culture by making appropriate statements in their charter, the mission of the organization. Real culture, however, is not what a charter says but interpretations of it, what it means in action. Pressing this issue, Pacanowsky (1988a) mused, "The charter is the *explicit,* organizationally sanctioned set of statements about a company, its vision of itself, what it does, why, and how" (p. 361). The operant organizational culture "is much broader than its charter; it is the totality of sense-making practices and resultant 'sense made' of the organization. Ideally, the charter and the culture should be largely in sync with one another, although it is unreasonable to assume that organizational practices will never deviate from the charter" (p. 361). Members of an organization may disagree with or disregard its charter; the true charter of an organization is what is enacted collectively, rather than what a single document says.

Based on his case study of W. L. Gore & Associates, Pacanowsky reasoned that employees are empowered by positive possibilities rather than fixed limits. He argued that Gore empowered employees by following six principles:

1. *"Distribute power and opportunity widely"* (p. 372). Power is defined by each individual and each organization's collective sense making. It is defined by what people think, do, and understand others to be thinking and doing. At Gore, empowerment arose from the opportunity "to pursue accomplishments cooperatively, which increases the resources to take on additional problems" (p. 373).

2. *"Maintain a full, open, and decentralized communication system"* (p. 374).

3. *"Use integrative problem solving"* (p. 374). Through integrative problem solving, responsibility is distributed rather than concentrated, and individual definitions of power and performance are de-emphasized in favor of collective definitions. For instance, task forces may foster empowerment if employees have full and open access to information and if they are expected to think in terms of the entire organization as they solve problems. Having information and thinking broadly can help managers and personnel to cast problems and solutions in terms of the total organization rather than as vested interests of individuals or subunits.

4. *"Practice challenge in an environment of trust"* (p. 375). Organizational culture provides members with information about the operating principles and processes of the organization. If they believe that competing points of view are melded into one coherent policy, they are empowered.

5. *"Reward and recognize people so as to encourage a high-performance ethic and self-responsibility"* (p. 376).

6. *"Become wise by living through, and learning from, organizational ambiguity, inconsistency, contradiction, and paradox"* (p. 376). Chaotic lack of definition can lead to frustrations that disempower employees. A healthy examination of premises and operations can increase identification with the company, spark

concern for its well-being, and foster development of shared perspectives that guide enactments.

Set against this ideal is the disempowering organization, which Pacanowsky (1988a) reasoned, "tends to encourage office politics, a careerist or cynic mentality, and obscene individualism clothed within an 'other-oriented' personality. Incapable of directly initiating action, the individual gives up hope or tries to ferret out the clues behind the mysterious and incomplete information all around and thereby provide a way by which the flow of action can be foretold or perhaps even influenced. The cynic sees no possibility in relating to others; the careerist sees possibility in using others" (p. 378). Given these guidelines, can managers and employees determine which statements empower? Are these disempowering statements: "Who the hell does this guy think he is?"; "Why did she do that when I told her not to?"; "I will give you the details regarding your job on Monday; until then you are on your own." Statements such as these have the potentiality of disempowering employees. Whether they are disempowering depends on individual interpretations based on the prevailing organizational climate and culture, which give members a sense of what is expected of them, how much personal control they have, and how other members appreciate their efforts. These statements are the kinds employees use to clarify what others expect of them.

Supporting this point, Albrecht (1988) approached empowerment from "a personal control framework" (p. 380). Perceived control is an individual difference construct grounded in each person's "belief that his or her actions have desirable causal effects on the environment" (p. 381). This approach to empowerment relies on an attribution paradigm that postulates that individuals attribute causality for outcomes based on heuristics that (a) emphasize either internal personal traits or external environmental traits, (b) are stable or unstable over time, and (c) are specific or global. In this sense, members of organizations employ hypotheses about power that they test by seeing whether they have power *as they define it*. This interactional approach to empowerment features the dialectic of superior-subordinate relationships.

Attribution operates out of sets of hypotheses embedded in decision heuristics regarding what people expect of themselves and what they think others expect of them. Through personal experience and communication, employees develop hypotheses, which they test. However, people are more "naive" than "scientific" in the way they explain outcomes by attributing them to the character and behavior of persons they encounter and to themselves (Sillars, 1982). Decision heuristics are attribution patterns people have tested through experience. In work situations, people bring to bear well-established assumptions about people and organizations as they attempt to figure out what makes the organization tick and whether they have personal control in it and can effect positive or negative outcomes.

Personal control results, Albrecht (1988) reasoned, when employees realize they "can affect others (even if it is an admittedly exaggerated estimation of one's ability). . . . Knowledge that one has personal control in the workplace is created within the opportunities the manager or nonmanager has to test the causal impact of behaviors. Having sufficient job latitude to modify personal constraints and participate in company decision making activities are among the best situations for exercising personal influence" (p. 384). Albrecht (1988) reasoned that her approach agreed with Pacanowsky's that "a sense of personal control develops among members of the organization when opportunities are afforded for the individual to attain rewards in sensible ways. This circumstance enables members to better predict reward contingencies and understand the requirements for success. Information and resources are adequate for reducing uncertainty, solving problems, and decision making, thereby maximizing one's influence capabilities" (Albrecht, 1988, p. 385). For these reasons, Albrecht asserted that the personal control model requires consideration of three variables: interdependence, uncertainty, and strategic ambiguity. Interdependence requires that individuals be coordinated to the extent that freewheeling does not become disruptive and counterproductive. Uncertainty is "the lack of attributional confidence about cause–effect patterns" (p. 387). Organizations are stronger when they reduce uncertainty. Strategic ambiguity empowers individuals when it increases their coping powers and does not limit their creative efforts.

Instead of viewing power as something management has and can distribute, we should think of it as something that exists—is enacted—within relationships between members of each company. They exert power over one another; they experience self-efficacy by testing whether what they do is satisfying to—meets expectations of—themselves and others. The crucial question is not only whether they feel empowered, but also whether they use the power they have and have the power they need to operate in constructive ways that increase their sense of self-efficacy and support the company's need to operate productively and achieve the desired level of quality.

Members of a company obtain information about the power they have and how it is used toward other members of the company. An expectancy-value, social exchange model predicts that people respond positively when they believe their efforts produce collectively desired outcomes (Ajzen & Fishbein, 1980; Roloff, 1981). Efforts to feel empowered can be harmed by information uncertainty that surrounds significant organizational change, poor communication, and an impersonal, bureaucratic atmosphere that does not yield to individual influence and the need for strategic variety. Supervisors can fail to provide needed information if they use an authoritarian managerial style, voice negativism, and do not explain the reason for actions and consequences. Reward systems hurt empowerment when they are arbitrary and do not reward what key employees believe to be competence and innovation. Job design can lessen self-efficacy when role definition is unclear, training is inadequate, rules are too rigid, goals or tasks are not meaningful, and people are not included in work design or lack needed resources.

Empowerment results from cognitive factors, such as reduced uncertainty and proper attribution, behavioral processes including interdependent decision making, and tolerance for strategic ambiguity that results because people realize they cannot communicate so clearly or extensively that all members understand and agree on all points.

Viewed as enactment, empowerment is the result of persons' perceptions of the effect they and their organizational unit have on their own outcomes, as well as those of other persons or units. Power results from action and reaction. In an effort to "share" it, a manager can dissipate a unit's power by not helping to use it to produce desirable results. To empower workers, a manager must create collective enactments through which employees exert their collective efforts. To avoid a managerial bias, we should recognize that subordinates empower their superiors when they act in ways that foster rather than impede directions, policies, and guidelines. Power is something people enact rather than have, and it assumes that all organizational members have power that they can enact constructively or destructively.

COMMUNICATION AS THE RATIONALE OF ORGANIZATION

What is an organization according to an enactment point of view? One response to this question could feature concepts such as structure, order, management, and division of work into task roles members are expected to perform. This paradigm of an organization features functional tasks and structures as focal points of analysis. An enactment view defines organization as a collectivity of persons who have specific interlocking role expectations that result from shared organizational meaning, the enactment of which can satisfy individual and collective goals by obtaining stakes. Viewed this way, enactment is not trivial; it is used to obtain stakes, something of value—tangible or intangible. Through communication, a company comes alive and takes form to serve many interests.

All that people do and say is communication; communication influences relationships and is influenced by relationships. The scope of analysis ranges from individuals engaged in cognitive processes (self-talk and intrapersonal communication) through contact with others on a one-at-a-time basis (interpersonal communication) through group processes, all of which add up to what one would think of as an organization. At all points of this process, communication is the means by which people make themselves and their opinions known to one another, through which they shape mutual meanings sufficient to coordinate goals and activities, and to enact them as a collective, even though each act is an individual act.

One of the dramatic forces reshaping the definition of organizations has been the work of researchers such as Morgan (1986), who argued that the nature of any company resides in the impressions people have of it in particular and of organizations in general. According to this reasoning, people manage their actions within and in regard to each company based on their opinions of it—its people, management philosophies, and code of social responsibility (business ethics). Further attempting to cut the definition of an organization loose from its managerial moorings, Pacanowsky and O'Donnell-Trujillo (1982) defined it as "the interlocked actions of a collectivity" (p. 122). Based on this rationale, they argued that organizations are "places where people do things together, to the extent that what they do together involves communication" (p. 122). When reflecting on this definition, it is interesting to speculate on the view of organizational communication that results from changing "*involves* communication" to "*is* communication." Keep in mind that this conception does not mean that the end of the organization is to communicate. The purpose of the organization is to do work, which is accomplished through communication.

With some notion of what an organization is, it is time to define communication. The definition of communication should be broad rather than narrowly focused on message exchange. Featuring interaction, Gerbner (1967) concluded that communication is "interaction through messages. Messages are formally coded symbolic or representational events or some shared significance in a culture, produced for the purpose of evoking significance" (p. 430). Carrying the concept of sense making further, Cronen, Pearce, and Harris (1982) defined communication as "a process through which persons create, maintain, and alter social order, relationships, and identities" (pp. 85–86). Both definitions acknowledge the importance of shared meaning, but the latter underscores how it is created through interaction. Defined broadly, communication exists when one person affects another (Hewes & Planalp, 1987). The effect of communication is meaning.

Do members of organizations share ideas? Do they feel encouraged to formulate and execute plans needed to move their company forward? Do they withhold ideas that could be used to improve it? Are employees encouraged to creatively solve problems or routinely perform functions in scripted ways that ignore or make problems worse? Do relationships between members help a company to be flexible, dynamic, and adaptive? Do relationships lull managers into a false sense of orderliness that masks the reality that dynamism and creativity have been replaced with mindless routine and scripted performance typical of the "8-to-5" and "regular pay" syndrome?

The theme that should come to mind in considering these questions is that communication is not only a means for organizing, but is also a *rationale*—the basis—for organizing. Organization is the result of communication; communication is the result of organization. Companies are such that people frequently enact routines and experience inertia rather than engage in calculated efforts to perform most effectively or engage in constant change. Relationships sustain organizations; employees spend huge amounts of time joined in repeated, collective efforts to achieve individual and collective goals. In periods of turbulence, relationships are crucial when an organization, department, or individual needs to act strategically, thoughtfully, creatively, and proactively.

Relationships result as people make themselves known to each other by using relational messages, messages that define relationships (Burgoon & Hale, 1984). Language shades the interpretations interactants make of their relationships, their relational partners, themselves as relational partners, and these relationships in the "scheme of things." Enactments of relationships are episodic; they exhibit dramatic form (Gergen & Gergen, 1988). For this reason, people describe their organizational activities in narrative form: "Let me tell you what happened at work today."

Narrative form provides continuity for each organization, its subunits, and the activities of individual members, because it gives a sense of structure by defining episodes of actions as events in a drama presented by a cast of characters over time. People know how to enact this play because meaning defines the company as scene and the acts appropriate to it. The drama comes to life through acts by organizational members.

Thus, communication is not merely a tool for giving directions, regulating performance, sharing information, and making decisions. What an organization is and does is made possible through the creation, maintenance, and dissolution of relationships. This emphasis on communication is not intended to ignore the technical skills and knowledge individuals must have to perform their work. Engineers must be properly schooled in their disciplines, as are lawyers, accountants, secretaries, information management experts, and other employees. Trade and craft people must know the skills necessary to perform their jobs. But communication holds this knowledge and talent together and focuses it through relationships. Analysis of communication should not obscure the fact that the goal of each company is to do that for which it was created—to manufacture and sell products, to provide a service, to pay dividends. But what would happen to a company if it could not communicate? How long would it continue to operate?

Viewed that way, each organization exists as communication. As people communicate with one another they create the organization. How they communicate—with whom and for what reason—defines the organization and gives it a sense of coherence. It becomes meaningful to customers and others outside of it by what its personnel do. One way to capture the individual and collective levels of enactment is through the concept of *voice*. At least two levels of voice exist within an organization. One Voice—the macro-level—consists of all of the statements and actions made by members of an organization, by the organization as a single entity, or by a person who represents the organization. What this voice "says" *is* the organization. The other voice consists of statements and actions that culminate in the macrolevel Voice. The goal, whether for individuals or the organization as a single entity, is to manage multiple identities (Cheney, 1991).

Voice refers to all of the actions one entity makes that are meaningful to itself and to others. Quality of a product is voice. What the product is, what it does, where and when it is delivered, and how well it works—these are voice. What companies do to provide service is voice. Their voice is the quality of service and the way it is performed. How employees work, what management does and says, success or failure of goals and projects: All of these are an organization's Voice. If companies manufacture products that are believed to be worth their cost, that is Voice, as is the opposite. If a company makes products, such as asbestos or tobacco, that are widely believed to be harmful, but not illegal, that company speaks to its publics. If management implements benefits programs tailored to the unique needs of its employees, it voices concern for them.

One concern addressed by this paradigm is the extent to which voices of individuals correspond to and support the organizational Voice of management, or whether individual voices express such conflicting views of the organization and the efforts being made on its behalf that it is difficult to tell what the Voice of the organization actually is, or what it is saying. Individual employees wonder whether their voices are heard as they want them to be, and some companies pay fortunes to have their Voice heard on public policy issues or in regard to product or service quality or availability. An organization (or any part of it) comes to life through actions of its members. It is made known to others by what is done—verbal and nonverbal acts by each member as interpreted or recalled by persons affected by it.

One view of the organization's Voice is that it is the same as the organization's culture. Management's voice results from its strategic plan, its managerial philosophy, and its mission. To the extent that these are part of its culture, voice and culture are the same. But rather than thinking of them as the same, it is best to think of them as complementary. What each individual does contributes to the Voice of the organization. How that action is interpreted is culture, not voice. Voice is enactment; culture is the narrative memory of the organization, what is done and said.

Each act or statement by an employee is part of the Voice, a *synecdoche* (a part for the whole or the whole for a part). An organization does not speak or act, individuals speak for it. An organization has no essential substance or voice other than what is presented by its members. The same is true for departments and divisions within an organization. When personal or professional standards do not coincide with, or even contradict, those of an organization, employees are confronted with speaking their voice *or* that of the company. In this event, Voice can be a jangle at odds with itself. In contrast is the Voice that is clear and consistent, such as a car manufacturer's warranty that is stated in its product advertisement and enacted just as it is stated (as the customer understood it and expected it to be) by the service writers and mechanics who repair the automobile.

Where do employees obtain the points of view they express as they work in a company? Do these come from the company, or from some other source? A view of organizational communication that exhibits a managerial bias assumes that this influence is top down. Featuring the concepts of identification and identity, Cheney (1983a) demonstrated that some employees respond to their own sense of ethics and to a set of ethics and standards drawn from a source external to the company, such as professional standards typical of engineering or medicine. People often identify more with either self-imposed or an external source of premises rather than those prescribed by management. Recognizing that employees have multiple identities, Cheney (1991) reasoned, "*Identity* is a preoccupation of contemporary Western society, and the *management of multiple identities* is a preoccupation of contemporary organizational life" (p. 23).

As employees enact a company, their actions are interpreted by people who encounter the company. If employees who work in one department are friendly and cooperative toward personnel of other departments, the department is likely to be viewed as friendly and cooperative. Employees are prone to say, "I would not like to work in X department because it is too stuffy and formal, at least that is the impression I get by the people I meet from it." Terms such as *stuffy* or *formal* are often used to characterize the climate that exists—or is thought to exist—in an organization, or a unit of it. Terms of this kind are also used to refer to the quality of relationships. To say that bosses are stuffy and formal indicates that the way they act leads to the conclusion that they possess those traits.

How can companies' efforts to communicate be measured? Communication effectiveness depends on the extent to which a company speaks with a coherent Voice and the extent to which the Voice creates positive relationships. This Voice should attract and keep the best employees and help them assimilate into the company. Assimilation requires taking on the Voice of the company along with perceptions of role/task expectations and reward–cost matrices. The Voice includes scripts and interpretative schemata unique to the company. It involves character-izations and attributions unique to the company and its industry.

A company's success does not rest exclusively with high-level communication devoted to strategic planning and implementation of management decisions. Achieving a company's mission requires statements and actions that are repeated each day. People who act on behalf of a company or one of its departments learn its unique scripts. This requires not only knowing how to use them and when, but also for which ends. In organizations across the nation, employees repeatedly voice phrases such as: "May I help you?"; "In this company, we...."; "Can I take your order?"; "I can't answer that for you, only Mr./Ms. ... can give that answer and he/she is out and will have to get back to you—may I have your name and number?"; and "The design specifications that we have used in the past are no longer appropriate." Employees coordinate actions and express expectations of each other by using statements that are no more dramatic than, "We need to order 3,000 XYZ bolts today so they will be here by Friday." Such statements can suffice to enact a relationship between the warehouse manager and a buyer in a purchasing department. With that request the buyer can set into operation a series of events that, if they work as planned, will lead to delivery of the bolts by the required time, in the quantity needed, and at the price quoted.

The Voice of a company is the expression of a collective effort to create meaning that extends to roles, activities, values, and attitudes needed on a moment-by-mo-ment, daily, quarterly, annual, short- and long-term basis to operate the organiza-tion. This Voice is similar to what is meant when people use the terms *party line*. It does not mean that all employees need to be thinking and doing the same things at the same time for an organization to be successful. The concept of the party line need not imply a tyrannical management that dictates that everyone be on the same page, saying the same thing at the same time each day.

Chances are that employees do not and will not speak in one voice, but variations of Voice are decreased by open discussions that empower employees. One concern is that so many voices emerge in a company that they do not express a common, desirable theme, but express competing and conflicting themes that lead away from unity of purpose and effort. Another concern is innovation that necessarily implies different voices is suppressed in favor of a bureaucratic routine.

It is difficult to strike the proper balance in regard to how similar thoughts need to be for people to coordinate their efforts. Some management philosophies address this issue by assuming that organizations function more effectively if they are operated so that clarity and similarity prevail over ambiguity and constructive differences. Each person needs to know, according to this paradigm, a substantial amount of what each other person knows. This view assumes that clarity outweighs ambiguity; people of an organization are thought to be poorly organized if they do not share meaning to a high degree. This view could advocate the importance of creating many control mechanisms and performing careful training so that individual voices speak as one on behalf of an organization. Such a view assumes that *similarity* of thought and statement is preferred to *difference*, and that clarity is inherently superior to ambiguity. To tolerate difference is not to reject similarity. Some companies thrive on similarity of product and service customers encounter. For example, fast food establishments try for as much uniformity as possible to avoid unpleasant surprises. However, given the diversity that exists in most organizations, all people cannot possibly know what everyone else does.

In contrast to the single voice paradigm, a competing view is that ambiguity is not only inherent because of the nature of language and the meanings attached to it, but to some extent, several voices—some ambiguity—actually make an organization more dynamic and adaptive. The notion of several voices—or is it slightly different versions of the same voice—is paradigmatic. Addressing this point of view, Eisenberg (1984) pronounced as dysfunctional the standard of achieving a level of understanding and clarity free from ambiguity. Not only are language and perception such that people have differences for those reasons alone, but also if a company had to achieve clarity, without ambiguity, it would accomplish nothing else because that task is so difficult and time consuming. Ambiguity helps people deal with many situational requirements and develop and pursue multiple or even conflicting goals.

Stressing this thesis, Eisenberg concluded, "Strategic ambiguity is essential to organizing in that it: (1) promotes unified diversity, (2) facilitates organizational change, and (3) amplifies existing source attributions and preserves privileged positions" (p. 227). He continued, "Particularly in turbulent environments, ambiguous communication is not a kind of fudging, but rather a rational method used by communicators to orient toward multiple goals. It is easy to imagine the ethical problems that might result from the misuse of ambiguity. In the final analysis, however, both the effectiveness and the ethics of any particular communicative strategy are relative to the goals and values of the communicators in the situation" (Eisenberg, 1984, p. 239). He acknowledged that his "definition of ambiguity is a direct outgrowth of the relativist view of meaning" (pp. 228–229).

Building a philosophy of meaning, Eisenberg (1984) reasoned that all action is symbolic and therefore potentially communicative. "Unfortunately, the concept of an ideally clear message is misleading in fundamental ways. Clarity (and conversely, ambiguity) is not an attribute of messages; it is a *relational* variable which arises through a combination of source, message, and receiver factors. Clarity exists to the extent that the following conditions are met: (1) an individual has an idea; (2) he or she encodes the idea into language; and (3) the receiver understands the message as it was intended by the source" (p. 229). This view adopts a coorientational, rather than referential theory of meaning and clarity. "While organizations must generate sufficient consensus to survive, it is not always necessary or desirable to promote high levels of consensus among individual attitudes and goals" (p. 230). This view of meaning assumes that through interaction people develop the interpretation and expectations they need to coordinate their activities. Meaning is conventionalized through interaction.

A referential view of meaning assumes that people think of the same referent as they interpret the definition of a term or phrase. A coorientational view of meaning acknowledges the presence of ambiguity, and assumes that one person can understand the other by knowing how that person interprets a word or phrase even if the two people hold different interpretations. You have probably had that experience many times. You know what someone else means by a term or experience, even if you hold a different interpretation of it. A person engaged in a communication episode might signal the occurrence of this situation by saying to an interactional partner, "I know what you mean by that even though I interpret it differently." Such a phrase does not mean that the two people experience conflict, merely difference. It assumes that meaning resides in conventionalized interpretations of words quite independent of the objects or experiences to which they refer.

One dimension of a coorientational model is *accuracy*, the extent to which each person knows what the other person means. Another variable is *agreement*, which, different from accuracy, assumes that people may disagree even though they understand. The third variable is *satisfaction*, the extent to which a relationship produces positive rather than negative outcomes. In this way, a coorientational model gives critical and analytical insights needed to explore where shared meaning breaks down and to ascertain whether that is a problem (McLeod & Chaffee, 1973).

People have different experiences and therefore may see the world differently. People may lessen or increase that lack of sameness. A boss can withhold information from employees, thereby increasing the difference between what each knows. Subordinates can also withhold information (even by giving distorted reports). Some distortion and withholding is intentional, and some is accidental—a matter of perception, interpretation, or omission. Convergence theory assumes that as people discuss issues and share experiences they converge in their meaning (Bormann, 1983; Rogers & Kincaid, 1981). However useful that model is, it presupposes that just because people share experiences they see them in the same way. Even though people have similar experiences, they may interpret them differently.

This dialectic of voices, Burke (1973) believed, results "whereby a difference becomes converted into an antithesis" (pp. 138–139). "You have noted," he continued, "that when two opponents have been arguing, though the initial difference in their position may have been slight, they tend under the 'dialectical pressure' of their drama to become eventually at odds in everything" (pp. 138–139). How do we know when people make incorrect identifications? Burke reasoned incorrect identifications result from the variety of meanings possible in the first person pronoun we. Bosses like to say "We are...". *We* is a pronoun that can express a collective will, or it can imply relationships that are either a lie or falsely assumed. Does a boss use *we* as the shepherds do with their sheep? ("We are going to pasture and then coming home to market.") As individuals, people engage in a tug of war to maintain their self-identity while serving a collective end. This relationship is frustrated when terms of identification mask division. Do the CEOs really mean it when they say, "We (this company—Acme X) had a successful year"? One cause of a demoralized work force is the salary increases executives vote themselves while laying off employees, closing divisions, suffering losses, and denying employees fair benefit packages and salary increases. That enactment declares loudly that executives are more important than employees.

Each organization emerges through communication; individual acts (voice) culminate in a collective Act (Voice) whether coherent or discordant. This dialectic entails a search for order, control, coordination, and shared interpretation. How a company operates results from enacted relationships and meanings that emerge from and guide those relationships. Such is the case whether Voice is coherent, unified, focused, and clear or fragmented, divisive, incoherent, and unfocused. Once we view a company as communicator, certain assumptions and conclusions follow. The quality of goods and services is an act, a statement. If a company cares about its reputation and customers, it provides a level of quality of goods and services to foster positive regard by its customers. It tries to match the quality of its product or services to the expectations of its consumers, some of which result from marketing and advertising sponsored by the organization. Shoddy goods and services communicate that the organization does not care about its customers.

Promptness is another instance of communication. How many times have we been told that something would be done by Friday, only to have the service or delivery postponed until Tuesday, for instance? Behavior by individuals and groups is communication. Some groups convey a sense that they think themselves superior to members of other groups. They are in no hurry to "get back" to the other group. They issue condescending statements and blame mistakes on others. Arrogance may be an aspect of climate that one group (or individual) communicates to another. Receptionists are a vital part of the Voice of a company. If they sound bright, cheerful, and helpful, customers are likely to view the company (its Voice) that way. If the receptionists sound as though they are on the brink of death, the company may be in trouble. Each of these examples focuses on personae and the relationships between members or between the company, enacted by its members, and external stakeholder publics.

INFORMATION, RHETORIC, AND DIALECTIC

Brought to life through acts of their members, organizations are interpretative, adaptive systems that survive by making sense of information about themselves and their environment (Daft & Weick, 1984; Huber & Daft, 1987; Weick, 1979b). For that reason, information is a dominant concept in organizational studies. In the process of making sense of their environment and gaining acceptance, organizations influence opinions and thereby assert themselves into the community around them. These interpretative frames are confirmed or disconfirmed by how people respond to them—what others believe to be true and proper, a dialectic of action and counteraction.

An information paradigm alone fails to explain the power dynamics and negotiated relationships vital to organizations. It treats organizations as thinking entities that make cybernetic adjustments to environments based on data regarding how well they are achieving their ends, but it misses the rhetorical and dialectical assertiveness of people and organizations. Enactment theory embraces all three dimensions: information, rhetoric, and dialectic.

Through rhetoric, people take on identifications consisting of identities, expectations, and interests that allow them to work together. Making that point, Burke (1969b) reasoned that people identify with one another when they believe their interests and identities are the same. People assimilate into an organization and become representatives of it by coming, in varying degrees, to reflect it. The process entails adopting technical jargon and perspectives needed to interact with others.

Instead of being transformed by organizational rhetoric, some people strive to remain independent of or oppose the company in which they work, but most people accept what it says to them as modified by what they say to themselves about it and their place in it. Merger results when individuals are persuaded to refer to the organization as *we* rather than *they*. Communication in an organization (as well as between it and its external stakeholders) is characterized by rhetorical and dialectical tensions between the congregated voice of *we* versus the segregated voice of *they* (Cheney, 1983b). Part of the success of an organization is the ability of its members to blend *I* or *they* into *we*. New members of a department are outsiders (*they*) until they take on and enact the terminology of the department (*we*).

Rhetoric and dialectic constitute the adjustive processes that people use to negotiate relationships and organizations use to adjust to their economic and sociopolitical environments. Thus, Benson (1977) challenged researchers to develop a dialectical view of organizations because what one person does leads to dialectic adjustments by others, much as the ball goes back and forth between tennis players. That view of organizations is based on a key principle: "The social world is in a continuous state of becoming—social arrangements which seem fixed and permanent are temporary, arbitrary patterns and any observed social patterns are regarded as one among many possibilities" (Benson, 1977, p. 3). Participants in this dialectic make sense of it because principles guide each episode. For instance, an organizational member progresses from first-job, new-hire status through a series of transformations to become department manager. This advancement results from acts—enactments—that follow the principle of upward mobility. "People are continually constructing the social world. Through their interactions with each other social patterns are gradually built and eventually a set of institutional arrangements is established. Through continued interactions the arrangements previously constructed are gradually modified or replaced" (p. 3). A dialectical perspective views organizational relationships as dynamic, changing through series of episodes.

Relationships that occur in these episodes exhibit at least two dialectical patterns: merger (we) and division (they); or both/and ("I am *both* an employee *and* a customer of this company.") (Burke, 1969a). People negotiate rules and rewards of entering and maintaining relationships. The *we* of a people in a department can be so strong that they see themselves against others—*they*. Anyone who has worked during a holiday sale in a department store can quickly recall the terror of the *we* of the department being "attacked" by the customers—*they*. "Here *they* come." Sales meetings may have the voice of salespeople conspiring against customers. Whether employees communicate that customers are *we* or *they* makes a crucial statement about relationships between a company and its customers. That dialectic influences whether employees enact cordial or hostile customer relations.

According to the both/and dialectic, people can enact different roles simultaneously. At the company picnic, the boss is *both* "the boss" *and* a participant in the sack race. Salespeople can think of customers as *both* persons who are making a purchase *and* partners in the design of products that become increasingly popular with customers. That latter dialectic entails listening to customers as though they were partners.

Enactment theory depends on interpretations shared by members of an organization and between it and its external stakeholders. The meaning of a term is the dialectical reaction others make to one another's meanings—and actions based on those meanings. The definition co-workers hold for a term, such as *procedure* or *power tool*, also reflect the definitions those people know are held by others with whom they interact. For example, imagine what a boss thinks about a policy requiring employees to be at work at a specific time. Bosses capable of perspective taking know that policy is needed but they also realize that employees do not like it when it cramps their personal activities. Both sets of meanings constitute the meaning of "tardiness policy." Employees may realize the dual meanings, and enact one rather than the other. How the boss responds defines the term from the company's point of view. If meanings for both parties are more similar than different, implementation of the policy is likely to be harmonious.

Believing that members enact organizations through the dialectical tensions of relationships, Benson (1983) challenged the *rational structuring* model of organizations. The rational structuring model assumes that an "all-knowing" boss creates a rational structure by which to guide the activities of others. Reflecting on this model, Benson observed, "The old forms of organization theory focusing on the rational structuring of unitary organizations were invented within the context of competitive capitalism consisting ... of internally rational organizations within irrational societies" (p. 45). He continued his criticism: "The conventional wisdom of organization theory has featured the rational organization adjusting to a hostile and sometimes turbulent environment. The relations between organizations have been consigned to other disciplines, especially economics, with assumptions appropriate for a world of competition, exchange, and bargaining, a world beyond purposeful control" (p. 45).

People adjust to themselves and their relational partners in ways that are strategically enacted to maximize rewards and minimize costs. This dialectical process, expressed in social exchange theory, operates on the premise that "rewards beget rewards. If rewarding behavior is absent, the relationship is placed in jeopardy" (Roloff, 1987, p. 11). What constitutes a reward in the views of partici-pants involved in a relationship and how does each participant know when a reward is sufficient? Relationships are enacted through limits and obligations participants impose on one another through rules of exchange. According to Roloff (1987), "Rules of exchange represent acceptable methods of operationalizing the norm of reciprocity. They are more precise than the norm of reciprocity but provide flexibility by noting *ranges* of acceptable exchange behavior rather than a single option: The recipient of a benefit feels some obligation because of the norm of reciprocity and from a set of actions specified by exchange rules devises a strategy for repaying the debt" (p. 14).

Exchange rules define what a reward is and when it is sufficient. At what point in the exchange are sanctions appropriate if a reward is not given or is insufficient? Expanding on this point, Roloff (1987) noted that "the function of communication is to facilitate the acquisition of resources needed to control one's environment. Specifically, communication serves as a means by which resources are offered, transferred, or shared between individuals, and it is also an instrument for negoti-ating the exchange of resources" (p. 25).

Not only do rules govern each relationship, but the kind of relationship that exists between people influences which rules are used. Some rules are relatively explicit. Others are subtle. The quality of relationships, particularly the degree of intimacy, is a predictor variable of the recognition of the need for a reward and willingness to give it. Discussing social exchange processes unique to intimate relationships, Roloff (1987) observed, "In more intimate relationships, individuals will generally work harder to ascertain, disclose, and meet each other's needs" (p. 30). In less intimate relationships, Roloff (1987) reasoned, "individuals may have to educate partners and convince them to provide resources. Such is the stuff of *interpersonal negotiation*: A process wherein needy individuals try to conclude exchange agreements with relational partners" (p. 30). Principles such as these explain the dialectic between co-workers, superiors and subordinates, and members of organizations and external stakeholders. This explanation accounts for why guidelines, either created by management, negotiated between workers, or imposed by persons outside of an organization, are essential to coordinate relationships by defining the exchanges that are needed for a relationship.

Why is social exchange motivational? Greenberg (1980) addressed this question by featuring indebtedness as a key concept in social exchange theory. "*Indebted-ness* is defined here as a state of obligation to repay another" (pp. 3–4). Greenberg preferred the concept of indebtedness to inequity as the focal concept underpinning social exchange. Both are motivational because of dissonance that results from the difference between what people receive from another and what they think they should have received.

Equity may only be one factor affecting a relationship. As Leventhal (1980) reasoned, "Equity theory in its present form has serious limitations as a framework for studying perceived fairness in social relationships. The theory must be incorporated into a larger framework that takes account of problems that equity theory does not consider." This is so because "perception of fairness is governed by two types of justice rules—distribution rules and procedural rules. Distribution rules dictate that rewards, punishments, and resources should be allocated in accordance with certain criteria. The relative importance of distribution rules changes from one situation to the next. The weights assigned to them depend on the social setting, and the individual's role in that setting" (p. 53). In estimating equity, "An individual evaluates not only distributions of rewards, but also the mechanisms in the social system that generate those distributions. A complex sequence of procedures often precedes the final distribution of reward, and an individual usually develops a cognitive map of the allocative process. Any component of this cognitive map may become the focus of a judgment sequence that evaluates procedural fairness" (p. 54). These dynamics involve information, rhetoric, and dialectic.

Enactment of relationships requires individuals to influence each others' definition of a satisfying relationship and to decide whether a relationship is satisfying. These relationships include those between co-workers, between superior and subordinate, between company and customer, or between company and external group. Relationships are based on a cost–rewards matrix whereby participants act to maximize rewards and minimize costs.

CONCLUSION

This chapter demonstrates why enactment theory should be used to study organizations:

• It reasons that communication between organizational members and between organizations and their external stakeholders is vital, the means by which the organization comes into being and is known.

• It assumes that words create terministic screens that lead to coordinated efforts because people enact shared views of reality. Sense making influences what persons mean to one another—the attitudes they "dance" collectively.

• It reasons that individuals seek and interpret information because uncertainty is unpleasant.

• Enactment uses a dramatistic paradigm, which features narrative form, to explain how people know how to enact their roles. Because stories thrive on action and central themes, narrative can guide behavior. An information paradigm of organizational communication can explain how people know one another, but it does not account for interaction rituals or relationships.

• The theory features relationships requiring that people define expectations and rewards or sanctions as the basis for deciding whether relationships are satisfying. People enact relationships by establishing boundaries and constraining or rewarding one another. Each enactment suffers counter enactment, a dialectical of behavior, role definition, relationship development, and understanding.

• Enactment emphasizes rhetorical influence whereby people define the meaning they and others use to enact coordinated activities.

Communication is a means by which people join to achieve goals that require interaction. What we think an organization is, what we perceive it to be, is the result of persons—individual and collective—who enact it.

2

Coordination Through Meaningful Expectations

Our minds are full of thoughts about companies, job duties, products, services, personnel, and companies' roles in society. Our thoughts dwell on communication acts, episodes, plans, styles, and processes that occur on behalf of companies. The interpretations we and others have of such events predict what we will do to enact a company and how well we do it—the quality and productivity of our effort. We have a sense of what we and others should do as we work; as customers, we expect the products and services we buy to be of a certain quality.

This chapter reasons that meaning leads to, results from, and guides the actions people use to enact companies. The perspectives employees hold are not dictated by managers but negotiated by the players inside and outside of the company—by what each person says and does. These perspectives become embedded in idioms people use to interpret each other's actions, to know how firmly they hold opinions, and to know what they expect of one another. By sharing themes and premises, they coordinate activities and achieve individual and collective goals.

What people do depends on what they think others expect them to do—and their ability and willingness to meet those expectations. Companies perform services and provide products, at least ostensibly to meet or exceed customers' expectations. They use advertising and marketing to shape customers' expectations. How do expectations become established and made known to the parties involved in enacting an organization? How do people reward and sanction themselves and others for meeting or failing to achieve these expectations?

Expectations feature management concepts such as responsibility, authority, standards of performance, and goals that are used to focus activities. Other management concepts include quality, quantity, time, and cost–return ratios. In the abstract, these terms are not very meaningful. Translated into specifics, they express performance expectations people need to enact organizations.

PERSPECTIVES FOR STUDYING ORGANIZATIONS
AND THEIR COMMUNICATION

A meaning-centered approach to understanding organizational performance is one of several that can be used to study and improve the performance of people in companies. One version of that approach views companies as being management or supervision intensive—featuring activities by managers or supervisors who design, coordinate, and monitor employee performance. In addition to this view is a product- or service-intensive orientation that magnifies the importance of organizational activities needed to provide products or perform services. These views of organizational performance are important, but we also need to consider how communication intensive companies are. Pressing this issue, Pilotta et al. (1988) reasoned that "the field of human communication needs to develop a more clearly communication-based perspective of formal organizations and organizational behavior" (p. 311). To understand each company's performance, we must understand the communication used to enact it.

Many thoughtful observers of the dynamics of companies have begun to reconsider the management point of view that has dominated organizational research. That bias led to some relatively static models designed to explain and guide organizational operations in general and communication in particular. Such models presumed that organizations would be improved if studies revealed how workers could efficiently and effectively do what they do, implying that managers and supervisors could use such knowledge to guide and improve workers' performance. Among the traditional factors governing performance is motivation, which assumes that workers need to be spurred on and guided by management, which doles out rewards and punishments. One managerial answer to the problem of motivating performance is to create structure—arrange people into work groups, assign them tasks, monitor performance of those tasks, and use rewards or punishments to motivate and guide performance. According to that view, managers communicate by giving clear instructions along with accurate and timely performance feedback.

A review of seminal managerial philosophies offers an opportunity to consider the accuracy and usefulness of that view of the role communication plays in organizations. For instance, Max Weber (1947) characterized an organization as a bureaucracy exerting control through the application of rational rules. According to that view, a company is a machine that should operate efficiently; communication is used not only to present routine messages but also to convey the message that the organization favors routine. Mayo (1949) challenged the bureaucratic model by stressing how organizational atmosphere and informal groups influence members' productivity. In his view, communication was assumed to contribute to an organization's atmosphere—its climate. Stressing the importance of complex networks of decision processes, Simon (1957) reasoned that organizational effectiveness derives from the quality of decisions made by key figures in the organization. Communication, in this view, is important to decision-making processes.

Will communication—especially at the group level—foster or hamper quality decisions? McGregor (1960, 1968) contended that how people manage and communicate depends on their view of workers. Those assumptions are reflected in what managers communicate, to whom, when, and with what intended outcomes. One kind of manager, Theory X, assumes that employees must be guided and directed because they work only for monetary rewards and lack initiative to complete their work. The other kind of manager, Theory Y, believes employees are capable of self-direction and, therefore, manages by fostering work rather than directing it. The managerial style that each person prefers will shape how that individual communicates, and with whom, in the effort to achieve the purposes of the organization. Likert (1961) expanded this two-part model into four parts and based it on the same assumptions regarding how managers' perceptions of employees affect their managerial style.

This brief review demonstrates how managerial perspectives govern studies of organizational performance. Some perspectives feature structure, whereas others stress motivation–need (physical, social, or psychological), task, or economic reward systems. Some views of corporate performance are driven by assumptions unique to disciplines such as finance, marketing, manufacturing, or logistics. The managerial point of view—which emphasizes structure, control, and motivation—has come under serious attack over the last several years. This attack was motivated in part by ideas that invaded the U.S. from abroad as other countries, particularly Japan, appear to have become successful in being more productive and achieving higher quality performance than of U.S. managers.

What has emerged is a process-oriented approach that acknowledges that goals can be achieved by strategic means. According to this paradigm, process rather than structure is crucial to achieving the goals of the company and its members. Not one method—but many—can be used by organizations to operate successfully. This process approach assumes that management philosophies and strategies need to be contingent (Morgan, 1986). Contingency theory predicts that management functions and styles are best when they are carefully tailored to outcomes desired, circumstances facing the organization, tasks involved, and abilities of personnel; conversely, maladapted management styles lead to dysfunctional organizations. Translating this orientation into metaphors, Morgan (1986) described various management types: organizations as machines, organisms, brains, cultures, political systems, psychic prisons, instruments of domination, and flux and transformation. But how do we know when to use which plan? How do we coordinate our plan with other members of our team? Answers to these questions involve developing and making known the expectations and plans needed for collective enactments.

If structure and rigid policy lead to a stifling bureaucracy that prevents employees from doing their best work, then models of organizational planning, management, operations, and communication need to concentrate on how to maintain maximum fluidity, adaptability, purpose, and control. This must be done in ways that are meaningful to the persons who collectively enact an organization through what they do and say. Viewed this way, approaches to organizational communication need to be broad enough to account for communication processes, functions, and styles unique to each company, each subunit, or each person.

PERFORMANCE EXPECTATIONS

Enactment assumes that people (and organizations enacted by them) present themselves in ways that affect understanding, evaluation, and agreement. Action, whether verbal, written, or nonverbal, is symbolic and therefore meaningful especially when expressed as themes or premises. Because enactment cannot be random, members of organizations must share meaning. People in companies can operate together insofar as they know what is expected of them and are willing and able to act as others expect. What employees know is influenced by management, as well as other employees, customers, competitors, and members of other organizations.

As predicted by contingency theory, people in organizations engage in strategic activities, including those designed to communicate, to achieve outcomes; strategy selection is based on an interpretation of which actions are preferred and rewardable given the circumstances in which people find themselves. By this logic, people will use different strategies in a sales presentation than in a job interview. Different strategies are used to sell goods than to buy them. Employees are likely to act differently among themselves than in the boss' office. They establish norms of behavior, standards of performance, and sanctioned and unsanctioned opinions. By this logic, some meanings foster quality, increase productivity, and empower employees, whereas other meanings limit the quality and productivity of what employees do and make them feel disempowered.

People have lots of opportunities to think about their jobs and learn how to enact them. They think and talk about their work, both while they are on the job and while they are not. They read newspapers and magazines and view television programs that describe and portray people at work—in fact and fiction. People not only receive this information about their own work, but also about companies with which they interact. In this regard, a company exists as meaningful to people who encounter it. Because of what it means to them, they can enact it in coordination with one another. How they enact it will be different—either compatible or not—depending on the interpretations they make of it. In that way, enactment theory explains how the meaning people have regarding organizational life and company activities translates into coordinated efforts. For example, if people think working conditions are unsafe, they may enact their routines differently than if they think they are safe.

This overview should lead us to realize that most employees' efforts on behalf of their company are devoted to routine activities—enacting meaning instead of making decisions. Indeed, organizations "commit a relatively small proportion of their temporal and material resources to making decisions and a relatively large proportion of their resources to defining and accounting for 'What's going on here?'" (Browning & Hawes, 1991, p. 35). Thus, we should study organizations as the enactment of perspectives, being attentive to the fact that on occasion people make decisions. Shared expectations lead to routine, repetitive, stable, and predictable thoughts, decisions, and behaviors that allow people to enact companies. Meaning characterizes and rationalizes each company as well as its subunits, its people, its place in society, responses others make to it, and actions and decisions its members make in coordination with one another. Through communication "meaning is created and, over time, sedimented" (Mumby, 1988, p. 14).

Organizational events, what people do and say, are meaningful because individuals need to interpret them as the basis of their organizational world. People seek and give instructions; they use persuasive messages to gain compliance from co-workers, supervisors, subordinates, and customers. People decide whether to comply with others' requests. Episodes, such as meetings, interviews, and negotiations, can occur only because people know how to coordinate activities; episodes involve giving and receiving instructions, explaining and justifying processes, creating and implementing procedures, promulgating policies, appraising employees, and making sales presentations. All of this activity has to make sense to the people who must enact it in coordinated and predictable ways. Some of what occurs in companies is the artifact of what a group, such as management, means. For instance, a policy document may specify how employees should handle chemicals in the workplace. The meaning of that document is modified by the cues given by management or assumed by employees regarding how serious management is regarding the policy.

Communication serves many functions in organizations: informing, persuading, seeking information, coordinating, including, rewarding, and punishing. Some functions carry negative connotations: lying, cajoling, controlling, misinforming, disinforming, distorting, and misrepresenting. Some organizational communication functions are carefully implemented and highly formalized efforts to influence what the organization means to others; such functions include public relations, product or service advertising, investor relations, customer relations, sales presentations, safety meetings, and training and development programs. Although oriented toward the accomplishment of key functions, whether it occurs at individual, interpersonal, small group, organizational, or macrosocial (mass mediated) levels of analysis, communication is about meaning. Because it has meaning, it allows people to work together.

Studies of organizational communication are designed, at least in part, to determine which communication plans, skills, and tactics people need to be successful in their jobs: supervision, customer relations, sales, project coordination, advertising, public relations, and day-by-day activities such as writing memos, making telephone calls, and participating in meetings. These activities may require substantial communication planning and control. In this array of activities, one might expect communication effectiveness to result from precision, such as giving clear and exact instructions. For example, in a major utility company hundreds of telephone service representatives (TSR) take dozens of calls each day regarding customer service, bill complaints and inquiries, service installation, and service termination. Each TSR response is highly scripted; supervisors monitor TSR responses to assure that the Voice preferred by management is maintained and that customers are presented with the meaning preferred by the company.

Such precision, a legitimate criterion for communication, is offset against ambiguity, a perplexing but predictable aspect of communication in companies, because the people who enact them have different thoughts, opinions, experiences, and judgments. Organizations at times require substantial amounts of precision, such as specifications stated in contracts, procedures for operating and maintaining equipment, safety procedures, and guidelines for ordering parts or assigning tasks. These documents make explicit the expectations one person has of another.

Despite the need for precision (low ambiguity) under such circumstances, organizations often tolerate a great deal of ambiguity due to the fact that words are subject to alternative interpretations and because people have different experiences; some persons have firsthand experiences that other members of the organization can only assume or struggle to understand. Such is the case when operations personnel report on activities to other company personnel far removed structurally from those operations. This bewildering set of events would seem to be chaotic and lack coherent shared meaning.

To be able to enact each episode, employees use communication plans that depend on their expectations of *objectives* (outcomes) that are sought, *persons* who are engaged in communication episodes, *strategies* that are appropriate to achieving the objectives given the persons involved, and the *circumstances*. This relationship of communication elements, as explained by contingency theory, is inherently rhetorical and guided by interpretations actors make regarding the events, tactics, and outcomes. If people have different meanings regarding which action is appropriate, they will enact episodes differently. People influence one another's interpretations of organizational events and the appropriateness of actions in light of those events. Because they have been persuaded to do so, people use routines they believe are appropriate to the circumstances and relevant to their desired outcomes.

Another problem related to coordinating meaning is people's tendency to act toward one another based on the assumption that they actually know what the others are doing and why. To interpret comments and actions of others, people attribute motives to them and to themselves. As well as making attributions about individuals, they think of companies and industries as though they were actors and personify them as such: "My company is making great strides." A company does not actually stride, and it is not a single entity, but an amalgamation of buildings, processes, messages, images, and people. Nevertheless, people think and speak as though an organization were an entity, and they attribute motives to it.

As people assign meaning to others' actions (including management's), they interpret the purpose behind those actions. Attributions help people make sense of the company for which they work, the actions of persons in it, and their own behavior. People make attributions because they like to think that events that occur and actions by people are rational, the result of known and predictable causes (Kelley, 1972, 1973). Shared attributions give a sense of order to encounters people have. If they make attributions similar to the people they encounter, they will be able to coordinate meaning and enactments that are appropriate to that meaning.

Similar attributions are essential if people are going to create and share meaning needed to routinize and coordinate organizational activities. Persons can engage in collective behaviors if their interpretative frames allow them to make similar attributions. The ability to make similar attributions results from shared reality (collective meaning).

Attributional processes predict how people will respond to events. When outcomes are good, people tend to attribute success to themselves, as in "we did it," but when outcomes are bad, attribution is placed on external forces, such as "an unfavorable turn of the economy" (Bettman & Weitz, 1983; Conrad, 1992). *I* takes credit for good outcomes; *they* are responsible for bad ones.

Knowing how they make attributions can help people adjust to one another during communication episodes. For instance, managers are prone to attribute success to themselves and blame external circumstances as a strategy for giving the appearance of being in control (Bettman & Weitz, 1983). Such attributions may be inaccurate and are self-serving. To the extent that management and personnel have markedly different interpretative frames, they will make different attributions of what is going on in a company and probably will enact different versions of the organization. People enact their interpretations to the extent that they have no other interpretations of what to do. When competing interpretations exist, people enact those that are most rewarding.

These conclusions demonstrate how companies exist because their members share meaning and coordinate actions based on the expectations these meanings contain. The meanings that arise in a company are the products of statements and actions by management along with other personnel; meaning is not something managers can predictably use to control employees. It is negotiated by the dialectic of what people do and say. Improving organizational performance requires insights into what people in organizations do and say that helps them coordinate their efforts. This analysis assumes that people only know one another by what they do and by what that action means for them—especially in terms of performance expectations.

A COMMUNICATION APPROACH TO ORGANZATIONAL STUDIES

Perspectives used to improve the performance of organizations must be sufficient to help scholars, consultants, and members of each company to understand its internal dynamics and how to situate it in its environment—the trends, events, and policies to which it must adapt. To be useful for the study of organizations, communication must be conceptualized as an essential part of the activities that foster the relationship between the company and internal and external people whose stakes it needs to achieve its mission. Given this requirement, organizational communication must embrace all of what members of an organization do that affects people who have a stake in it. This is the case because an organization itself does not actually "speak" but "speaks" through its members whose statements and actions are interpreted by others, including colleagues, customers, vendors, stock analysts, regulators, special-interest activists, or reporters.

Advancing a meaning-centered approach to understand organizational behavior acknowledges the need people have to make sense of what they experience and to be able to define and measure their own competence as a member of organizations. It also suggests that people become known to one another and affect one another through the meaning each uses to interpret actions, relationships, and expectations. Building on the analysis advanced in chapter 1, the rationale of an organization is that it is known only through what its members do and say.

Through meaningful, interpretative frames, people define their circumstances. As they think about something, so do they tend to act toward it. This "something" could include their work roles and how to perform them, as well as relationships with others in the organization—or with the company. This meaning arises from the motivation people have to reduce the uncertainty they experience in their encounters with physical and social reality (Krippendorff, 1977). The desire to reduce uncertainty motivates people to make and employ communication plans to present themselves in ways they think are appropriate (Berger, 1987; Berger & Calabrese, 1975).

Each person working on behalf of a company performs many *roles*, whether successfully or not. Each role constitutes an identity; in this sense, if employees enact several roles, they must reconcile the problem of multiple identities, each of which is enacted with others who also have multiple identities (Cheney, 1991). Roles involve thoughtful, learned behavior that is prescribed by idioms unique to society at large and to the company and subunit in which they are performed. More than narrow sets of expectations of behavior prescribed by role-specific rules, each role entails enactment of ideas, a definition of behaviors intimately entwined with behavior of other members. Definitions of these expectations result from culture inside and outside of the company.

In this sense, the role teacher is not merely one who stands in front of classes giving instruction (as prescribed by role-specific rules). The role entails meaning of what being a teacher involves, what teachers do and how they are expected to relate to one another, to serve members of society, and to be rewarded for that service. The role of teacher has a history, present, and future; it has status and purpose in society. It assumes behaviors, self-expectations, societal expectations, identifications, and rituals. How well people are thought to perform their roles depends on the expectations other members of an organization have (other teachers, administrators, or students, for instance) as well as the expectations of people (especially parents) outside of the organization.

Roles prescribe a *persona*, the enactment of character, how people want others to perceive them. Persona refers to the communicative styles people use to manage the impressions others form of them. It results when company members enact roles that can be interpreted by others. Enactment involves scripts and communication styles relevant and unique to each role. Whereas some of the scripts that people learn are quite routine (such as patterned statements used by receptionists), others are extemporaneous as a consequence of adapting to situations that are not routine.

Scripts consist of predictable statements, whether elements of conversation (such as what is said during an interview) or extended presentations (such as a sales pitch). Enactments are motivated by the need to establish relationships with and affect other members of the organization, as well as people outside of it. Relationships are necessary for people to work with one another in spatial, reward, and psychological proximity. Organizations operate through the initiation, maintenance, and dissolution of relationships.

Enactment entails *communication plans* and *message design logics* that involve routine and strategic selection or creation of scripts, *themes* or *premises*, *interpretative schemata*, and *decision heuristics* that influence how people make sense of information and respond to persuasive messages.

Each these factors that constitute this organizational communication model provides a focal point for analysis. Enactment theory integrates them into a coherent framework by examining communication at all levels: intra-individual, interpersonal, group, macro-organizational, and macrosocietal. This approach to organizational communication relies on theory and research regarding uncertainty reduction, involvement, social exchange, and self-presentation (self-efficacy).

The search to discover which concepts, variables, and themes are most appropriate for research and theory regarding organizational communication can be focused around several propositions that guide the analysis in this book.

1. *Through communication, members of an organization—as well as external stakeholders—enact their views of the social reality that is relevant to themselves, others internal and external to the organization, and each organization.* Each of us participates in the drama of life, by employing scripts as well as creating and utilizing extemporized communication plans. Through enactment with others, people really do make up their lives as they go along (Goffman, 1959). If this behavior is meaningful, it communicates, and has effect on other persons.

2. *Through communication, members of a company—as well as its external stakeholders—enact personae; the expectations of these personae are the products of the social reality persons hold in regard to each persona.* Social reality is a concept used to describe the perspectives people have in regard to the physical and social phenomena they encounter. The concept assumes that views of reality are shared with others who have similar views based on shared idioms and experiences. This social reality is reflected in personae expected by key members of the company. As people encounter one another, they monitor the behavior of each other, as well as themselves.

3. *Enacted through communication, the personae, stakes, structures, and relationships that constitute an organization are negotiated by individuals who seek to define the limits, rewards, costs, constraints, and obligations that are needed for personal and organizational success.* This negotiation takes two forms. As predicted by social exchange theory, people negotiate to determine which rewards and constraints are appropriate for establishing and maintaining relationships, including those between superiors and subordinates. For instance, fellow employees decide which actions foster their relationship as do superiors and subordinates. The

second form of negotiation occurs in the adjustments in meaning that transpire as people define and redefine their relationships. For instance, as employees mature into job positions, they may come to be more expert in their performance than the boss is. One result of that level of expertise is that the boss recognizes it and honors it by allowing the employees maximum autonomy. The other result is the boss fails to recognize the expertise or doubts the employees' ability and continues to treat the employees as "ignorant" and needing close supervision. Members of an organization negotiate their relationships by defining them and persuading others to accept and enact those definitions (Cheney & Vibbert, 1987). As Duck (1985) contended, relationships are maintained or destroyed through persuasion; individuals persuade each other to enact relationships in a particular manner.

4. *Information is a primary means by which one person gets to know another and define the organization and its environment.* For this reason, an organization is a mechanism suited for information exchange (Farace, Monge, & Russell, 1977). Information is not inherently meaningful or predefined; it is interpreted through the terministic filters of culture unique to each organization and is enacted through communication. People within and outside of an organization use persuasion to influence each others' interpretations of what bits of information mean. For instance, a response typical of people in a meeting who have just received some data is to ask, "What do these data mean?" During that episode, those people might discuss, argue, and agree on the appropriate interpretation of the data.

5. *A major part of the assimilation process through which each organizational stakeholder passes consists of learning the climate and culture—social reality of the organization—which includes definitions of personae, relationships, performance expectations, and reward–cost ratios.* Old members enact this social reality for new members. For example, new members learn how hard to work, the intricacies of office politics, and other vital information by observing others' actions as well as communicating directly with them.

6. *Organization enactment results in relationships based on expectations that are negotiated through communication and embedded in shared meaning.* Relationships constitute the structure of the company. One assumption—typical of a static model—is that structure is defined in the organizational chart. A process, enactment orientation treats structure as the product of relationships between people (McPhee, 1989; Poole & McPhee, 1983). According to this model, a boss might have less control over the department than do the employees. Or, members of a department may use friends in other departments to obtain valuable information more quickly than it can be acquired via channels prescribed in the organizational chart.

7. *How people use communication to enact the social reality unique to each organization will be reflected in their message design logics, communication goals, scripts, schemata, relationships, message content, and stakes.* This proposition argues that each organizational member's communication behavior results from the individual's views of the situation and the behavior that is appropriate to it. The resultant behavior, an enactment of that social reality, is interpreted by others based on their sense of social reality and their belief of the social reality held by persons with whom they interact.

Each act in a relationship is based on assumptions related to how the partners involved in it define its boundaries and decide which enactments are appropriate to it. Which acts are needed for a relationship to succeed? How do participants know what these acts are in light of each relationship? How do interactional partners know the limits and responsibilities of their roles in the relationship? Why do people comply or refuse to comply with those expectations?

ORGANIZATIONAL ENACTMENT OF MEANING: MESSAGE DESIGN

As a vital part of understanding organizational communication processes, increased attention is being directed to understanding message variables and meaning (Hewes & Planalp, 1987; Seibold & Spitzberg, 1982). As Hewes and Planalp (1987) observed, "Effective communication requires not only that people share knowledge (intersubjectivity) but also that they know they share knowledge" (pp. 165–166). As people make themselves known to one another, they compare and negotiate the meaning and interpretations. Shared awareness of message design logics needed to create, convey, receive, and interpret messages in an organization gives people some sense of what they must do in the design and use of messages (O'Keefe & McCornack, 1987). Not only do people use rules to guide their interpretations and interactions, but they also need to know the rules others use and have a sense of how both sets of rules are appropriate and interlocked. Only by using protocols of interaction can people enact organizations as undirected plays.

This approach to organizational communication is justified because actions— verbal and nonverbal—have meaning due to the significance each person assigns to them. How well people understand one another depends on the "significance" they share. As Eisenberg (1986) concluded, "With few exceptions, researchers have argued that a primary function of communication in organizations is to facilitate the development of shared meanings, values, and beliefs" (p. 90). But, Eisenberg (1984) cautioned, attempts to understand organizational communication must acknowledge that ambiguity is the norm, and openness and clarity are nonnormative. In addition, "a communicator's goals are not assumed to be unitary or even consistent; rather, individuals have multiple, often conflicting goals which they orient toward in an effort to satisfy rather than to maximize attainment of any one goal in particular" (p. 227). Message design logics are a way of knowing which message and presentation sequences to use to obtain a desired outcome. The selection of satisfactory interlocking message design logics begins with awareness of interlocking goals. For instance, a secretary need not know anything about repairing locks on doors to arrange to have them repaired. The goals of having locks repaired and repairing locks become focal points from which the interactants' message logics start.

On one hand, it is scary to realize that communication is conducted by people who have many goals, as well as goals they have not thought through very well. We prefer an approach to communication that maximizes precision and minimizes ambiguity. The key, however, is the realization that organizations function adequately because of strategic ambiguity. Ambiguity can be planned and it can also occur because personnel simply cannot communicate sufficiently and experience enough to know what all other members know. But they can share common idioms that serve as predictable scripts and cues needed for enactment. What people need is a shared set of premises to orient their efforts so that differences do not prevent collective, focused enactment.

To advance this discussion of strategic behavior and ambiguity, we should acknowledge the value of requisite variety, the benefits of which result when enough points of view and message design logics exist in a company so that all relevant points of view are incorporated into the culture, the sum of the subcultures. To some extent, this requisite variety assumes that many people can work together adequately, and even in a superior fashion, if they can tolerate reasonable but limited differences of strategic behavior, interpretative perspectives, and performance expectations. Everyone need not know and do everything in the same way to be effective. Expecting people to do so is dysfunctional.

Much of what people do is routine and therefore the message design logics are widely known and predictable, even if not optimal. Not only do people know that different types of messages are appropriate in certain contexts, but they also follow knowable and shared design logics that are sensitive to message content, context, and interlocked communication goals. However, the design logic that is appropriate for talking to a fellow employee, for instance, might be inappropriate for interacting with the president of the organization. Although much of the communication in an organization is scripted and maybe even fairly mindless, some of the most important transactions require the use of message design logics that are not routine.

In this regard, two kinds of goals, primary and secondary, appear to be essential to the communication process. The first gives focus to interaction by constituting the outcomes each person has in mind for engaging in communication. Secondary goals become the substance of the first. Secondary goals—including those regarding the social appropriateness of strategies such as use of threats or being topic relevant—are employed to achieve primary goals. Once individuals determine what their primary goals are, they can consider which secondary goals are likely to achieve them. This relationship between primary and secondary goals constitutes the individual's communication plan under each set of the circumstances (Dillard, Segrin, & Harden, 1989). Individuals assume that their behavior can affect desirable and predictable responses in other persons. Part of the success of that outcome is knowing the other person's goals, knowing the strategies that are relevant to those goals, and knowing what is expected in such circumstances, including which alternative responses are sanctioned and which are not.

As we reflect on message design logics and the affect of one person on another, we realize that what meaning "means" for people engaged in communication is not static—not a dictionary definition carved in stone, but one that arises through interaction. What does the word *quality* mean as an abstraction? Contrast that definition against the one derived as superiors and their subordinates negotiate the specific quality of the product—the work—the subordinates are expected to produce. Or consider the meaning of the term *work*, for instance that of the janitor as opposed to the chief financial officer poring over a company's records in search of good news to recommend to stockbrokers. How do message design logics employed by boss and employee interlock to discuss quality? How do the logics of evaluating the work of a janitor compare to those of the CFO? When is a logic merely expressive, used for blowing off steam, or evaluative, intended to alter the performance of a fellow employee?

Message design logics either maintain and enact routine behaviors and thereby confirm established approaches, or they are new and unique, thereby requiring change in response or interpretations. For instance, employees of an American automobile manufacturing company might believe that their products are superior to imported cars. Thus, they might employ a rhetorical message design logic to argue that the federal government should protect the domestic automobile industry from foreign imports produced by people who are underpaid and exploited by their bosses. The members of this organization are likely to have a shared social reality regarding the design and construction of an automobile. They may even carry this social reality into goal-directed activities outside of the company. Stories abound that personnel who work for domestic automobile companies will punish—a message design logic—fellow workers who buy imports; thus, "build American, buy American." Likewise, you have probably experienced the definition of "enough work" in one company or department as contrasted to its definition in another company or department. Such standards are enacted by statements such as "That's enough for today," or "What do you think I'm paying you for?"

As individuals enact design logics, they attribute motives to their interaction partners and to larger units, such as executive management, as they interpret the meaning that results from those logics. Attribution processes are fraught with misperception and bias. Attributions are likely to reflect metaphoric or archetypical observations such as "He is a bully," or "She is open and supportive." If attributions are correct, the messages interpreted in light of them will differ from messages that result from incorrect attributions.

This analysis of message design logics has emphasized three important points. First, people enact design logics that are routine and extemporaneous. Both are likely to be effective to the extent that participants operate out of compatible and shared goal orientations. Second, motives that are attributed to logics of people and organizational units with whom we interact are instrumental to interpreting the meaning of their enactments. Third, variations in meaning and message design logics are tolerable, even preferred, as long as they do not prevent coordinated activities.

People in different departments in a company can have markedly different social realities about the company and still play productive, supportive roles on its behalf. Employees' views may differ slightly or substantially in what they know and how they interact. Through interaction, individuals learn which parts of that reality matter and which do not. They decide the latitudes of acceptable or unacceptable variation regarding what they believe about the company and which message strategies are acceptable. They learn which norms are important to their organization, their department, and themselves. A survey designed to disclose social reality would reveal individuals' views of political economy, business practices, the company, its industry, the product or service, and their work. It would also reveal opinions regarding which actions are inappropriate to the enactment of the company. Thus, it would discover that organizations consist of zones of meaning.

ORGANIZATIONS AS ZONES OF MEANING

Even casual understanding of organizations reveals that although a lot of social reality is shared, individuals as well as entire departments have social realities that are only partially shared with others. Some are not shared at all. One need not have much contact with a company to realize that at times, and perhaps on crucial matters, people in one department do not understand what people in other departments are talking about. An organization consists of *zones of meaning*, different social realities. Because this is true, how do people communicate across departmental lines, and to what extent must members of an organization, department, or interpersonal relationship have similar social realities to be able to coordinate their activities? Without a shared social reality, people have no way to detect deception, conflict, or failure to coordinate efforts (Hewes & Planalp, 1987).

The key to comprehending this relationship is not to dwell on understanding as much as on coordination. People can coordinate efforts without having the same knowledge or understanding, and merely because they understand does not mean that they can coordinate their activities. For example, not all spectators at a sporting event understand the sport equally well or even support the same team. We can imagine people playing on the same team but not speaking each other's language— as long as they know the logic of the game and what is expected of them to play it. How can people perform different actions for similar goals, and similar actions for different goals—and coordinate their activities in a meaningful way? Part of the answer results from the realization that they enact organizations through a dialectic and a rhetoric whereby they define, influence, sanction, and reward each others' behavior insofar as it is vital to coordination. The dynamics of enactment are fluid, depending on the people involved, their goals, their commitment to achieve mutual outcomes, and their sense of interdependence. For instance, people who attend a sporting event have a mutual interest in seeing it to its conclusion—to the point that winners and losers are decided.

The models Eisenberg (1986) suggested to support this analysis of zones of meaning include coorientation, symbolic convergence, and culture. Coorientation assumes that two people can understand the same phenomena in the same way (accuracy) and be equally satisfied by what they experience; based on that assumption, corrective actions could increase understanding (which may involve getting data or altering interpretative frameworks) or the standards of judgment used to estimate degrees of satisfaction. The culture of an organization can be crucial in this regard because it carries evaluative frameworks that people obtain and negotiate as part of acting together. If people are enacting scripts that have quite different meanings—at least on crucial issues—they may not be sufficiently coordinated to join their activities into one focused effort. Lack of coordination—if the goal is to achieve coordination—should motivate personnel to clarify and negotiate the relationship to achieve sufficient agreement to coordinate their efforts.

Many opinions are embedded in culture, which employees learn as they become assimilated into a company or one of its subunits. Part of the assimilation process by which people enter and learn a new company or department occurs through conversations during which people realize that they have had similar experiences, through *group fantasies* (Bormann, 1983). As people share these fantasies, a social reality develops that gives them the basis to understand one another and coordinate activities. "The basic communicative dynamic of the theory is the sharing of group fantasies that brings about symbolic convergence for the participants" (Bormann, 1988, p. 394). As people talk and tell stories, they realize they "share a number of fantasies, inside cues, and fantasy types" that may lead them to share a rhetorical vision. "A *rhetorical vision* is a unified putting together of the various scripts that gives the participants a broader view of things" (p. 396). These perspectives may be expressed in key premises captured in one or more master metaphors.

Carried on enough, such talk can lead to a level of group agreement that Janis (1972) called groupthink. He believed that an organization, whatever its size, can be driven to achieve consensus, which stifles individual thoughts and creativity. Any organization that denies individual thoughts and creativity is likely to become a closed system, no longer receiving information from the environment and therefore suffering decline—entropy. Groupthink occurs when people do not want to disagree with what is said early in a meeting. They limit rather than increase the number of alternative ideas, issues, problems, or solutions they consider. If the members of a group favor an issue, it is difficult or impossible to introduce criticism of that proposal. If the majority of a group does not favor alternatives early in the decision-making process, those alternatives are likely not to receive consideration later in the deliberations. Highly cohesive groups are likely to resist information from the outside that conflicts with the positions they hold, and they are likely only to accept outside opinions if they confirm the opinion shared by the group.

Suffice it to say that speaking in one voice can be dangerous if it denies innovation and growth—characteristics essential to an open system. Dissent and debate do not mean that people are not speaking with one voice; the legal system is a good example of how precedents and vocabulary unite a profession in the conduct of its business, even though the essence of the profession is disputation. The disputation is voiced within standards, procedures, and goals that keep it focused.

As meaning and design logics begin to shift, change that may be radical or trivial occurs (Daniels & Spiker, 1987). New voices emerge to challenge old ones. Innovation is a new voice—a new way of looking at and expressing reality. For instance, the voice of MCI emerged to change the telecommunications industry by destroying AT&T's monopoly on long-distance telephone service.

How then can meaning be handled, given that zones of meaning exist naturally and properly, even in ways that are contradictory and destructive. One answer to that problem is to realize that macrolevel meaning is a vehicle by which people can organize and make sense of microlevel meaning and actions. Message design logics are guided by an awareness of macrolevel meanings regarding unifying themes and norms that occur at a microlevel. Moreover, what people do—voice (microlevel)—combines to become the macrolevel Voice. Also, their view of the macrolevel Voice is reflected in their own messages. Supporting this reasoning, Eisenberg (1986) called attention to the short-term meaning that is the product of one person receiving a message from another. That single encounter is limited in its scope and meaning given the ongoing dynamics of organizational encounters. As a consequence, he recommended "considering the practical force of messages to be a function of incremental, cyclical effects" (p. 88). This view abandons the orientation that organizational communication is instrumental and aimed only at getting work done; it examines the importance of all of the communication that transpires in the organization, and does so by seeing communication as essential to "the ongoing evolution and negotiation of meaning" (p. 88). Each episode adds some increment of meaning to what the persons involved know about themselves, their relationship, and work efforts. The immediate meaning results from the message designs used in each episode. There is also the long-term meaning—one that is the residue from other events and that frames the event into the context of other events, all of which add up to the ongoing dynamics of each relationship and work event in particular and the organization as a context.

The sufficiency of the commonality of meanings between the persons involved in an episode is tested through the cybernetic principle that if too little meaning is shared, coordination of goal-oriented activity is difficult, perhaps impossible. Such a criterion deemphasizes agreement in favor of understanding. It places actions in context with one another by asking what all of them amount to in concert. Simply put, one person can understand where the other is "coming from" without agreeing with what the other is saying. For that reason, people enact misunderstanding and disagreement in quite routine and predictable ways. The degree to which meaning is shared is proportional to the extent to which it allows participants to enact mutually recognizable goals.

As predicted by social exchange theory, people reward and sanction one another as ways of negotiating goals and the meaning needed to obtain them. Therefore, if a person or persons do not know the meaning and use the appropriate interaction styles needed to coordinate their efforts with persons in other zones of meaning, their failure or the sanctions each is likely to impose on the other become the motivation to correct the lack of shared meaning.

Zones of meaning are not limited to differences between departments or other units of an organization. What each zone contains and how it is communicated may depend on factors such as status, rank, and position, as well as demographic traits such as age, gender, and race. Older workers may not share zones with younger members, or they may mentor them. Do women have special difficulties in their attempts to assimilate into organizations, departments, or organizational hierarchy—especially because they may lack mentors? Should they take on "male" meaning or communication styles to be successful? Research on matters such as these is complicated by not knowing whether success is due to gender, adeptness, or assumptions made by and introduced into the situation by the researchers. Many concerns need to be solved in regard to such issues, for instance those regarding gender—male–female—relationships in organizations (Fairhurst, 1986).

The importance of zones was central to a case of alleged sex discrimination brought before the U.S. Supreme Court in 1989. The plaintiff, Ann Hopkins, asserted that she was denied a partnership in an accounting firm because she was perceived to be too macho and assertive. She also alleged that some partners were offended by her profanity. The court decided that she had been treated unfairly because "feminine" standards had been applied to the evaluation of her candidacy for partnership.

What can be called "female" managerial styles and message design logics can produce different results than do "male" managerial styles and message design logics. At least this was the case for nurses who reported having higher morale and job productivity when their managing nurses exhibited female rather than male managerial styles. The preferred styles were characterized by more receptivity to new ideas, happier relationships, encouragement, concern, attentiveness, friendliness, and approval (Camden & Kennedy, 1986).

Analysis of topics such as sex discrimination emphasizes the need to generate and use research findings to resolve such issues, perhaps through training that enhances communication skills and fosters cooriented meaning. Such analysis heightens the importance of using zones of meaning as a focal point for analysis. That approach demonstrates that differences are overcome by shared principles and themes. These differences are negotiated into shared zones of meaning as the rationale for achieving sufficient coordination to achieve mutual goals. Adequate similarity can result in coherent and coordinated effort because people interpret the available information so as to enjoy the same social reality.

Society, as well as internal operations and culture of an organization, can become fractured—at odds with itself—to the extent that conflicting versions of social reality occur and to the extent that communication norms and styles exhibit too much variance from shared expectation. Each company should communicate in ways that help people, internally and externally, obtain and adopt corresponding or compatible versions of social reality. If the people within an organization sufficiently share social reality, they have the foundation for making similar interpretations and evaluations of information and opinion. It increases the likelihood that actions will be sufficiently or maximally coordinated. If people who have a stake in an organization have social realities that differ markedly from the one held by the management of the organization, friction is likely. Such differences manifest themselves, in the case of external audiences, when critics challenge corporate actions that management believes are normal and not deserving of criticism. To minimize differences in social reality inside and outside of the organization, companies are advised to communicate with key stakeholders to create zones of meaning that are as favorable as possible to the interests of all parties (Cheney & Vibbert, 1987).

PRESENTING DIFFERENT FACES AND SPEAKING
WITH DIFFERENT VOICES

This view of organizations stresses the importance of realizing that each act by a person on behalf of a company communicates and results in meaning. Manufacturing quality or accounting accuracy, for instance, is as much a communicative act as is a presentation by a sales representative or coordinated actions between a crew leader and warehouse personnel. Each act, regardless of the organizational level of the person committing it, provides persons, whether inside or outside the organization, with information they use to interpret the company (or a department of it), its relationships with them, and what is likely to be rewarding behavior. Members of a company enact their views of that organization, its mission, its structure and reward system, and their roles and self-interests on behalf of it.

If employees comply with management expectations, that is the preferred Voice; if they do not comply, another Voice results that may be at odds with itself. The dialectic between employees and management is a vital part of organizational Voice. How coordinated that Voice is determines whether the company presents different personae and speaks with different voices.

For example, we would assume that airline personnel attempt to convey to customers a persona of efficiency, safety, and promptness. The company culture may stress a key premise: Customer satisfaction is the first and only goal. Given that premise, we might expect cabin crew personnel to undergo extensive training to learn the skills and communication style needed to enact the preferred persona, under routine *and* emergency circumstances. A great deal of coordination is required for hundreds of flights to occur each day in dozens of airports in ways that move people across countries and around the world with relative exactness and substantial safety. Equipment must be purchased, maintained, operated, and scheduled. Employees are required to know how to interlock their efforts with those of other persons; the result is collective effort to satisfy travelers and achieve an attractive bottom line. This quick review of one industry suggests that a great deal of managerial time and effort are devoted to routinizing enactments by voicing expectations—rather than making decisions that lead to organizational changes (Browning & Hawes, 1991).

Others know us (and our company) by what we do and say, and we only know others by what they do and say. If people do not interact with one another as they actually are, then they deal with one another as though they are something other than what they are. Sometimes they may be dealing with others as they are but wish they were something else. Differences between expectation and actuality can destroy clarity, coordination, and trust.

Consideration of some scenarios help make this point. For instance, you go through several interviews for a job. One interviewer says, "The job will be exciting and only the brightest young person will qualify." Another interviewer remarks, "Most college graduates are not nearly as well prepared as they need to be." And the third observes, "Most people in this company are afraid to hire truly qualified employees who might challenge their position." Each statement presents a different version—Voice—of the company and may influence how you see yourself if you are hired, or turned down.

Another example occurs when you call a department in your company and find the personnel friendly and helpful. They say the part you need will be delivered by Friday; it arrives on your desk Thursday morning. In contrast to this happy example, you call another department and ask that some information be sent to you; you get neither it, nor a call explaining why not. One more example: Each time you approach your bosses with what you believe to be an innovation they become argumentative and quickly put you down, giving you the feeling that innovation is not appreciated. Another example: Members of one department act in ways that make them appear to be more important than personnel in other departments. They are slow to respond to the needs of people from other departments, but quick to scold those people if they are not quick to respond. One last example: You make a service appointment. The service representative calls to confirm the appointment time and location and arrives 5 minutes before the scheduled time. The service person is clean and pleasant and listens to you as you explain the problem. The person does not smirk as you explain the "strange" sound that comes from the copier. The repair is made promptly, then the service person explains the problem, shows you why the part was defective, and tells you how to lessen the likelihood of the problem resulting again.

These illustrations address the coherence of the Voices of companies by considering how communication influences them *and* they influence communication. By moving beyond the conception of communication as a tool managers use to administer their organization, we can more accurately view it as a means by which people in a company coordinate their efforts. Thus, companies are a complex balance between what is thought, what Morgan (1986) calls images of the organization, and what is done that fosters or frustrates the effort to achieve organizational goals.

As a communicator, each company seeks to combine many efforts so that they speak as one, with one persona in one Voice that management enacts in coordination with its personnel. That outcome assumes that what employees do and say will be similar and complementary, thereby becoming the desired Voice. To assure its Voice is appropriate to its mission, a company may devote substantial effort to maximizing uniformity. Open, dialogic meetings and discussions that empower employees support collective goals. Training programs designed to enhance communication skills and styles, employee selection processes, guidelines and policies, and procedures for monitoring and reviewing employee performance can increase uniformity. Such programs employ exercises to improve employees' enactments. One program by Arthur Andersen & Company has managers jump from a flagpole to a trapeze, pass buckets of water between participants, and scale walls. These exercises are intended to improve confidence and teamwork—to enhance enactments.

Employee empowerment efforts can increase the extent to which the company achieves its desired Voice although many managers have trouble working with their employees in ways that let them share in organizational decisions and build organizational identification. Several factors predict the extent to which people will learn and enact a voice that supports the Voice preferred by management. These factors include awareness of what management wants, locus of identification, the reward system as defined by corporate culture, coherence among the premises embedded in the organizational culture, climate, ability to perform the preferred enactment, and feeling of empowerment. For managers to empower employees, they need to listen to them, to look at what is said to learn their subordinates' perceptions of key similarities and differences. This requires that managers be attentive to the stories employees tell and metaphors they use, which indicate whether they feel empowered. They need to consider whether a symmetrical or asymmetrical relationship between management and employees exists.

A company may be ineffective in its efforts because its messages are incoherent or inconsistent or fail to foster the self-interests of those whose lives are affected by it. Corporate communication requires systematic development and presentation of messages, the meaning of which organizes and guides efforts of employees, by conforming to the reward system. This meaning can influence external stakeholders' opinions and actions in regard to buying products or services, as well as supporting or opposing public policy positions that relate to each company's interests. Examining that principle by looking at what makes an information campaign successful, Hill and Cummings (1981) discovered that effectiveness depends on the degree of cooperation between persons who make decisions and those who explain them. Supervisors are more satisfied with efforts of people who design and enact information campaigns when what is said corresponds to what the supervisors want to have said.

Recognizing that it needed to build rapport with customers to survive in a highly competitive marketplace, Chrysler Corporation devoted $30 million to improve the way dealership personnel—salespeople, service department, and support staff—talk and listen to customers. Chrysler realized that customers dread buying automobiles because they do not trust pushy salespeople and service department personnel who work on commissions and have incentives to be untruthful and dishonest. Chrysler created a new persona for itself and contributed to the formation of a new persona for its industry, one that was more appealing to its stakeholding customers.

Viewed this way, communication is not merely a means by which work is directed, it is the work. It creates views of work, responsibility, and performance in the minds of organizational members. New members use communication to assimilate and enculturate into the organization; they learn the meaning and performance styles expected to be assimilated and enculturated (Jablin, 1984). Employees manage impressions of themselves by presenting a persona they think to be appropriate to their bosses, colleagues, and customers.

Looked at purely as a management tool, communication used in an employment interview might be studied to determine which kinds of questions are most useful in ferreting out the best candidate, perhaps by being able to spot deception. Such studies miss the dynamics of organizational communication if they do not acknowledge that prospective employees use communication to manage their impressions, as well as to reduce uncertainty about the company and begin the process of assimilating into it. Communication during the interview can be used by prospective employees to calculate risks and advantages of assimilation into the organization.

Enactment theory offers a major justification for superiors to appraise employee performance. By evaluating performance by comparing it against reasonable and known expectations and in the context of useful reward systems, managers can increase the likelihood that the voices of employees contribute to the desired organizational Voice. That effort, however, needs to avoid a managerial bias, one that disempowers employees. The criteria by which organizational performance is measured should not be derived by management who coerce employees to comply with traditional rewards and punishments. Employee empowerment assumes that superiors and employees work together to set goals and agree on performance criteria that are mutually clear and relevant to the company and the individual's role in it. Management must enact its role responsibly by being involved with employees, cooperating with them to solve problems, and not becoming an impediment to organizational success. When employees, supervisors, and management share expectations and coordinate activities, that goes a long way toward explaining how companies speak with similar voices and present one face internally and externally.

COMMUNICATION AS SELF-PRESENTATION AND SELF-EXPECTATION

According to self-perception theory, people believe that others do what they do because they want to be doing it; otherwise they would not be doing it or would be doing something else (Bem, 1972): "Joan must like to work hard because she works so hard"; "I must like this company because I work here"; "John must like being lazy because he does so little work." These statements indicate that we assume that people's behavior corresponds to their attitudes. Because we can see behavior, but cannot see attitudes, we use the former to infer the latter. Given that reasoning, people tend to enact themselves—sometimes strategically and sometimes not—as possessing certain attitudes or dispositions.

Although people at all levels in a company are assumed to reflect its attitudes by what they do, executives have an inordinate amount of importance in this regard. For instance, reporters and stock analysts often believe that they get better information—a better sense of the company—if it is provided by the president (or chief executive officer or chief financial officer) of a company. Investor relations specialists often try to get the attention of stock analysts to tout quarterly earnings that are "better than average." Their efforts may be met with yawns. But let the president or chief executive (or chief financial) officer say the same thing and heads turn and word processors light up. During its crisis with Tylenol, Johnson & Johnson public relations people realized that eventually the company president would have to speak for the company; so the crisis management plan featured the president as the chief spokesperson. Some corporate leaders reach the status at which their personality is inseparable from that of their company. Frank Lorenzo did that for Texas Air, the small, upstart airline company that came to own and operate Eastern and Continental Airlines. T. Boone Pickens became the persona of Mesa Petroleum (legendary for its corporate takeover attempts) as Lee Iacocca did for Chrysler, or Dave Thomas has done for Wendy's.

As you ponder these examples, you may consider the importance of persona, the character that is created as the company speaks, whether through the voice of management or its individual members. Members of a company portray its persona, as you might expect a sales representative of IBM or Xerox to exhibit the persona of the company. Individuals may present their unique persona, which other people use to infer what the company is, or the persona might be tailored by the company so that we do not think of the person as an individual. In either case, an individual may exhibit a persona that in our mind becomes or constitutes the Voice of the company. A rude sales representative or customer service person can speak with a persona that tarnishes your opinion of an entire company. The same can be said for people within a company. As they go about routine activities, you are likely to use individual contacts to infer what a department is like, as well as the people who work there.

The persona would be different if the company were trying to exude precision and innovativeness as a leader in the development of high technology as opposed to a business trying to appear friendly in its marketing effort. Much of what we know and think about a company comes to us through actions and statements by people we encounter who present the company to us. Customers' experience with a major automobile company is not through the president or CEO, but through the salesperson who sells cars, for instance, touting the comprehensiveness of the warranty. The persona changes when the sales manager explains that a $300 repair is not covered by that warranty, which is not as comprehensive as originally portrayed. The Voice of the company becomes shattered, divided, and its persona is tarnished.

An excellent example of this problem was reported in *The Wall Street Journal* on March 17, 1989. A major trust company had enticed patrons with the claim that it would "always" pay high dividends. Several months later, the company sent out letters pulling the rug from beneath those patrons by announcing that its dividend calculations would be revised and the promise was revoked. One persona was abandoned and a new one was asserted by the company or attributed by its customers.

Earlier, we mentioned Frank Lorenzo. Let's go further with that example. In the late winter of 1989, a bitter struggle occurred between corporate headquarters— particularly through the person of Frank Lorenzo, chairman of Texas Air—and striking machinists for Eastern Airlines, a subsidiary. One irony of the battle was that for some years the concept of the "Eastern family" had been ballyhooed in consumer advertising and inhouse publications. The theme was that Eastern provided excellent service because it was a close-knit family. Participants in the strike recalled how the company *had been* a "family," which now was feuding. The Voice of the company had become discordant. The family was washing its linen in public. This example shows how communication within a company is one matter, but what is said inside can affect what is said outside. During the Eastern strike, comments within the organization were not always cordial or well accepted.

In response to others' accounts of the Eastern strike, its management resorted to a full-page ad in *The Wall Street Journal* (March 20, 1989) in which it hoped to set the record straight. The ad asserted: "The fact that a dramatic, big story is being played nationally does not mean that the *whole* story is being told." The theme of the ad was: "We're going to build a better Eastern for you." The ad observed, "We've come to a kind of frustrated resignation that a lot of the real facts and real issues are bound to be drowned out in the shouts of slogans and accusations." Many audiences were addressed in the ad: shareholders, investors, customers, and employees. The message was that Eastern was rebuilding. To do so would require, "consolidating our strength," "marshalling our resources," "re-establishing trust," and "building on our most important resources." This latter item spoke directly to a select segment of its employees: "a small but growing team of professionals of extraordinary pride and dedication—sharing common goals and a common spirit of an underdog fighting back to the top of the industry. These people, truly our most valuable resource, will grow and succeed with us." This thought seemed incongruously warm and cordial given the fact that part of the incentive for the strike (perhaps a large part) was dislike for Lorenzo, a man recognized for not being employee oriented. Was this the true Voice, an old one that had not been heard, or a new one prompted by the strike?

Organizations speak outwardly, not only to sell products and services, but also to shape the political economy. Until the end of the last century, most public policy in this country was created as the product of individual people discussing the values that should guide that policy and debating which alternatives would work best to guide society. Emergence of large corporations about 100 years ago dramatically changed the public policy process. Major economic entities began to foster adoption of policies in their interest. Through mergers and other means, some repulsive to us today, giant organizations came to dominate basic industries, such as railroads, steel, meat, tobacco, and oil. They became dominant forces in society because they were run by people who were powerful enough to create public policy in their self-interests. These companies spoke as individuals and collectively as industries.

In response arose the muckraking journalists who alerted the public and goaded legislators to constrain business. The Sherman and Clayton Antitrust Acts were created to curtail the business activities of industrial giants. The Interstate Commerce Act created a commission that was intended to regulate interstate commerce, as the Pure Food and Drug Act attempted to protect people from unsafe foods, drugs, and cosmetics. This era brought into being the activist group—collectives of people who band together to acquire sufficient power to pressure companies and legislators or regulators into adopting and implementing policies in the "public interest." The clash among corporations, governmental agencies, and activist groups that occurred in the 1960s and 1970s created the most robust period of regulation in the history of the United States. In that short period, 26 major pieces of regulatory legislation were passed. This figure is made more important when it is realized that only nine other pieces of similar legislation had been passed in the previous 80 years that corporations had been in existence. The 1960s and 1970s not only saw the implementation of many pieces of legislation but also witnessed the creation of many new terms, such as *biodegradable, toxic waste management, ozone levels, equal opportunity employer,* and *corporate social responsibility.*

As these examples demonstrate, companies communicate inwardly and outwardly. They operate through communication and they cannot operate without it. Communication transpires inside of them as employees strive to accomplish the tasks needed to achieve their personal goals, which in turn are expected to support departmental and company goals. Companies not only require communication among their employees, but also outwardly to persons who have a stake in their operations: customers, shareholders, neighbors, regulators, legislators, journalists, bureaucrats, advertising agencies, suppliers, and many others. The key to understanding organizational communication is to realize that it is motivated by the desire people have to make favorable self-presentations and thereby to achieve rewards and avoid losses. Expectancy theory predicts that people present themselves as they do on the assumption that they can know what produces rewards and what avoids punishments. They seek to negotiate relationships by enacting reward and punishment scenarios. Key elements are self-presentation, attribution, and self-expectation.

Some companies and other organizations are well known for their ability to conduct a truly integrated communication campaign designed to get the same message across even thought it is tailored to various stakeholders. Not only is the matter one of providing a coherent and consistent message that fosters an understanding of the company as its management and employees want it to be understood, but it also means that key audiences are addressed in terms of the stake each of them holds with regard to the organization. Prominent examples are GTE Corporation and Ford Motor Corporation. They conduct their corporate communication effort with the intention of conveying the same messages, although tailored to the needs and interests of each audience reached by their product service advertising, investor relations, employee communication, image/corporate advertising, and public policy stances (MacEwen & Wuellner, 1987).

Terms such as *quality* and *innovation, service* and *commitment* are quite general. If they are associated with key activities and policies throughout the company, employees and customers begin to think in those terms. Terms like those become meaningful because they are repeated and associated with decisions, policies, and standards relating to products and service as well as to performance expected of employees as expressed in the organizational reward system. If a company addresses the world by making a commitment to building quality into products, that becomes a social reality that its employees use to define and interpret information about their work—the expectations others have of it. This kind of evaluative schemata not only defines and confirms the social reality, but it also allows organizational members to evaluate their performance and that of their company.

Those who have stakes that an organization seeks to obtain will negotiate their interests through dialectical processes. In this sense, an organization is "a whole with multiple, interpenetrating levels and sectors" (Benson, 1977, p. 9). The relationship between each member of a company and the organization itself is dialectic. Applying this logic to the analysis of superior-subordinate relations, Weick (1979b) observed that "subordinates ultimately determine the amount of influence exerted by those who lead" (p. 16).

One way to explain this relationship is by applying Burke's (1969a) notion of the thing (the company) and the thing contained (organizational member). Actions of each member of an organization take on meaning in the context of that organization. Members have an identity that is flavored by their membership in an organization. As they communicate and perform functions related to their organizational membership, what they do and how they do it takes on meaning because of the scene created by the company. Members of the marketing department, for instance, are likely to have a different persona if they work in a company that stresses marketing rather than deemphasizing it. In the first organization, ambitious employees seek passage through the marketing department as one of the best means for rising into the ranks of executive management. The same could be said for engineering, accounting, or other departments, based on the unique culture of each organization.

The notion of the container and the thing contained constitutes what Burke (1969a) called an act–scene ratio. According to this logic, acts performed by organizational members are governed by and interpreted in the scene where they occur. Thus, the scene is not only likely to serve as a motivational framework for individual actions, but it is also likely to be used as the basis by which others in the organization, as well as outside, interpret the action. Any act that occurs suggests to the person seeing that act the kind of scene that would permit that act and the kind of person who would commit that act given that scene. As Burke (1969a) reasoned, "there is implicit in the quality of a scene the quality of the action that is to take place within it. This would be another way of saying that the act will be consistent with the scene" (pp. 6–7).

What people do and say in an organization is shaped by their perceptions of the scene and acts it requires. This conclusion emphasizes the importance of the expectations personnel and managers have of their own performance, as well as what they think others expect of them internal and external to the company. This logic is pretty simple. Once members of an organization have progressed through the assimilation process, they acquire a corporate social reality that contains expectations and the accompanying communication behaviors that they predict will allow them to function in ways that lead to rewards. If the scene calls for a highly scripted behavior, they tend to follow that norm (or leave or be unhappy because the act does not fit the scene). If the scene calls on them to understand the requirements of a certain work discipline and the presentation of a persona on behalf of it, members adopt—to the best of their ability—these requirements. The same can be said for managerial philosophy; an autocratic scene would require different acts than would a scene that placed a premium on employees making suggestions and being self-directed.

This relationship leads to an important kind of interaction between the individual, other individuals, subunits of an organization, and the total organization. It occurs between companies. Burke (1969a) captured this theme with the notion of "the competition of cooperation or the cooperation of competition" (p. 403). People can compete only through cooperative compliance with the rules of competition. Within an industry, each company speaks with its unique Voice—perhaps interpreting information differently—but shares the jargon and idiom unique to the industry. Each organization relies on what is said and thought about its products and services. Within an organization, each department competes with each other one for the resources available—material and intangible. Companies within an industry work together in cooperative competition to define the way in which the industry does business. These relationships are a matter of levels and interlocking relationships. Companies within an industry band together by forming trade associations to oppose legislation that would harm the industry. Even while banding together, they seek individual advantage in the marketplace. Alliances, according to this paradigm, take many permutations, but the dynamics of the system lead people and organizations to speak with different voices, depending on the advantage being sought at the moment.

Within the organization, this also is true. The reward system of a company is part of its communicated meaning. By rewarding individual members and departments in different ways, the organization speaks. The executives get different rewards than do the mail clerks, for instance. But management and the mail clerks are bonded into an alliance because of mutual need and mutual interest. Burke (1973) said, democracy is "a device for institutionalizing the dialectic process, by setting up a political structure that gives full opportunity for the use of competition to a cooperative end" (p. 444). Extending this point, Burke (1966b) reasoned: "A character cannot 'be himself' unless many others among the dramatic personae contribute to this end, so that the very essence of a character's nature is in a large measure defined, or determined, by the other characters who variously assist or oppose him" (p. 84). This orientation gave Burke (1969b) evidence that rhetoric is clash: "Rhetoric is thus made from fragments of dialectic" (p. 175). This theme is echoed by Morgan (1986), who concluded: "A dialectical view of reality suggests that tension and contradiction will always be present, though they will vary in their degrees of explicitness and will take different forms according to the oppositions that are drawn. The choice that individuals and societies ultimately have before them is thus really a choice about the kind of contradiction that is to shape the pattern of daily life" (p. 267). What each person does and says communicates some meaningful information, to self and to others. Part of what is said is based on the interpretation the receiver gives of the individual as an individual. Part of that interpretation is governed by that individual's perception of how that communication fits into the larger Voice of the company. Bringing these interpretations together is a crucial part of corporate self-presentation.

What each company does is communication, including the quality of its goods and services. The same can be said for individual members and departments. If they produce high-quality goods and services, that is a different statement than if they do not. If they are prompt and share information with other units in the organization, that is communication. If they exert power in regard to others, that is a statement, their Voice.

Each day as people go about their activities on behalf of an organization they look for reason to guide their actions. If they are fully assimilated into the organization, they speak its Voice and understand the world, themselves, and their role expectations and activities in terms of the Voice of the company. Thus, they are more likely to be comfortable, and the organization may enjoy increased productivity. If the people of a company communicate without concern for its Voice, they may create a discordant voice that confuses and muddles their efforts and those who have a stake in its activities, and who may also become a voice for or against the organization.

Companies express their goals and guidelines in various degrees of specificity and exactness. Goals and guidelines permeate the culture of each company. Each unit and each person should know how personal and professional goals integrate with the corporate goals and when they are contrary to those goals. In this context, one of the major issues is control and bureaucracy. Some companies make employees worry so much about not making a mistake that they stifle creativity and originality. The company assumes that individuals cannot and will not learn from mistakes. So the operating factor is not to make a mistake; do nothing rather than do something wrong. If managers use positive approval in dealing with subordinates, employee performance is likely to increase. If subordinates are empowered to discover for themselves ways to correct their mistakes, the length of time increases before the problem recurs (Fairhurst, Green, & Snavely, 1984). Regard is enacted by how superiors interact with subordinates. Regard is not only a message but also a scene that shapes the kinds of acts that subordinates feel encouraged to perform in that scene. In response, employees communicate acceptance of this regard and reward it with high performance—a message to their superiors.

So many controls can be integrated into an organization that they impede decisions or actions. For instance, dozens of signatures may be required for individuals who want to purchase items they need to do their business. In such a case, the bureaucracy may disempower the individual who has little control over the acquisition of goods. If many controls are implemented to assure that employees make no mistakes, that policy or procedure communicates that the company assumes employees are prone to make lots of mistakes. High control convinces employees that they cannot have a useful, efficacious self-presentation without conforming to a bureaucracy.

Under such conditions, a kind of diffusion of responsibility principle can begin to operate, whereby each member of the organization assumes that everyone else is responsible for catching errors. In this situation, more errors may occur than would otherwise be the case. Actions, such as everyone being a check on everyone else, can communicate low regard and distrust. How people act toward each other establishes the boundaries of freedom and control, the tightness of constraints. All of this meaning is negotiated and enacted in ways that define the expectations people have of those with whom they must enact the organization.

CONCLUSION

The paradigm of the corporation as communicator reasons that through communicative acts meaning that eventually governs how people act toward one another and the organization is generated and shared. Meaning is an important outcome of individual efforts to reduce uncertainty in regard to why others do what they do. Once people share meaning, they define work-related situations, interpret and attribute meaning to the behavior of others, and establish the basis for control, motivation, and role performance. Meaning establishes the schemata that are used to interpret information. It affects relationships. Not only does meaning define relationships, but it also suggests the kinds of message design logics, communication plans, and scripts that are appropriate to those relationships.

As they enact organizations, people need to know what is expected of them. By what they do, they communicate what they expect of others. By knowing what is expected and being willing and able to comply, people can enact a company properly. Chapter 1 began by directing attention to quality and productivity. The standards of excellence of an organization serve as expectations that people enact—and thereby reinforce or refute—by their actions. If they demonstrate that they expect increased quality and productivity, that becomes part of the criteria each person uses to assess his or her enactment.

Each day hundreds of conversations occur. Some result in new sales; others lead to lawsuits. Employees share insights about how people fit into the company; employees advise one another on such matters. Meetings transpire. Reports are written; some are read. Oral presentations are made. In these ways and many more, companies create the understanding members need to coordinate their efforts with one another and with external audiences.

3

Narrative, Enactment, and Organizational Discourse

How do personnel know how to coordinate their efforts so that their actions and opinions integrate in a meaningful, goal-oriented manner? The answer, "employees do what they are told," suffers a managerial bias that assumes that they cannot figure out or know better than their bosses how their work should be done. A top-down bias fails to explain how managers know how to manage—know what is expected of them and what they should expect of their employees. A sense of what the company is and what organizing means shapes what members at all company levels do, say, and remember. As this chapter demonstrates, stories contain information and premises that members use to coordinate their activities. Narratives offer organizational frames of reference that "include methodological, epistemic, ontological, and ideological assumptions that enable organizational members to make consensual meaning out of social events" (Shrivastava et al., 1987, p. 95).

If we eavesdrop on people discussing their work or managers explaining "why we do things as we do," we find that these presentations entail storytelling. These stories are more than idle chatter. They give insights into how people enact and recall relationships and policies as episodes—details of organizational activities and opinions. Persons' knowledge of the company is captured in myriad stories that are told and retold: "Let me tell you what happened at work today"; "Last year we dealt with customers in a much different way because"; "Over the years we have seen a steady decline in management support because employees were treated better then than now"; "When management found out what the folks in plant safety were doing heads rolled."

A story told by a person who received a special raise might begin "Once upon a time," and end "lived happily ever after," giving listeners a sense of the sequence of events needed to achieve a reward by modeling their attitudes and behavior after those of the successful person. The time frame that runs throughout a story is not merely metaphorical. "Time is critical because transactions have no meaning outside of their historical contexts; the expectations attendant upon an interaction moment are crucial for understanding the meaning of that interaction" (Eisenberg, 1986, p. 89). Key moments in narratives include themes or "morals of the story," sequences of events leading to the moral, thematic linkages between events, and demarcation signs ("Once upon a time"; "and then I responded") that highlight main points.

This sense of structure gives shared meaning and coherence to facts that would otherwise be subject to idiosyncratic interpretations by each hearer or reader. Organizational stories create a framework that instructs people on how to interpret the events of their work lives. Emphasizing this point, Gergen and Gergen (1988) observed:

> Narratives are, in effect, social constructions, undergoing continuous alteration as interaction progresses. The individual in this case does not consult an internal narrative for information. Rather, the self-narrative is a linguistic implement constructed by people in relationships and employed in relationships to sustain, enhance, or impede various actions. It may be used to indicate future actions but it is not in itself the basis for such action. In this sense, self-narratives function much as histories within society do more generally. They are symbolic systems used for such social purposes as justification, criticism, and social solidification. (p. 20)

To appreciate the importance of organizational narratives as means for understanding personnel's performance, we need an organizing rationale and researchable focal points that can explain how myriad stories become meaningful, how they give an encompassing view of the organization and the environment beyond it, and how they translate into coordinated actions, as well as shared beliefs, attitudes, and values. To serve our interests, a narrative view must embrace the meaning contained in company documents such as policies, procedures, and nonnarrative memos and instructions.

Stressing the role narrative plays in people's ability to enact an organization, Kelly (1985) concluded that organizations are cultures. Culture is the heart of organizational sense making; it provides the knowledge each person has of how things are done. Stories do not grow out of culture; rather, culture is the product—the residue—of meaning captured and repeated in stories (Smircich & Morgan, 1982; Weick & Browning, 1986). Stories portray characters and actions unique to each organization; supply its attitudes, beliefs, and values; and describe its practices and operations. Stories are thematic, interpreting values such as equality, security, and control (Kelly, 1985). Narratives undergird organizational culture "as meaningful orders of persons and things" (Goodall, 1990, p. 70). Narrative gives order and perspective to enactments between members as well as with external players. Viewed this way, culture makes sense because it states which actions company members are expected to perform to enact episodes, routine or not. For this reason, narrative analysis can be used by managers, organizational development experts, and employees—all of those who strive to improve company performance.

That analysis raises the issue of the relationship between thought (expressed as attitudes and beliefs) and action. Although it is easy to believe that actions follow opinions, in truth, this equation is often elusive. For instance, Bem (1972) argued that attitudes follow behavior; when people act they form attitudes to justify what they do. When they think about their behavior they rationalize why they act as they do by forming attitudes that are congruent with that behavior. Stories rationalize the attitudes that are associated with successful and unsuccessful actions. According to Pacanowsky (1988a), culture is embedded in "rituals, oft-told stories, key symbols, and so on as the indicators of the cultural beliefs and values of organizations" (p. 358).

Narrative structure is vital to performing enactments because they occur over time and with varying degrees of coordination, similar to episodes in a play. This line of reasoning satisfies the requirement that studies of organizational communication must account for routine work and communication activities, as well as those that are not routine. Work is often routine, and conversations are scripted. But sometimes the otherwise placid fabric of behavior and thought becomes turbulent. How do people know how to enact episodes during turbulent and poorly structured occasions? To answer that question, we note that narrative structure occurs in tightly *and* loosely coupled organizations (Orton & Weick, 1990). This structure can explain why loosely coupled organizations (those lacking apparent structure and coordination) can operate as successfully as their tightly coupled, highly coordinated counterparts. People learn through narratives what performance options are available and appropriate and which are not.

Narrative form is a structural undercurrent in all organizational events and thereby guides actions and structures ideas of any group of people (W. R. Fisher, 1985, 1987, 1989). This view of narrative encompasses phenomena that range from strategies corporate managements employ to (re)present their companies' images or personae to internal and external publics (Cheney, 1992) including archetypes of organizational identity (Heath, 1988b), and "as an instantiation of the deep structure power relations in an organization" (Mumby, 1987, p. 125). Narratives are used to describe and analyze complex ideas, particularly those that require expressions of value and personal tone (Pacanowsky, 1988b). "Ideology is the structural force that frames reality, holding the coherent picture of one's world view in place" (Guerro & Dionisopoulos, 1990).

Narrative analysis supports the conclusion that organizational communication and behavior are thoughtful (Jablin, 1982a; Pacanowsky & O'Donnell-Trujillo, 1983; Pondy & Boje, 1980; Sackmann, 1990; Weick, 1979a; Weick & Browning, 1986). Tellers and hearers share narrative themes as unquestioned assumptions even though stories are told and received idiosyncratically (Shrivastava & Schneider, 1984).

In companies, meaning—as shared reality—is the product of interaction (Bormann, 1983; Pacanowsky & O'Donnell-Trujillo, 1983; Rogers & Kincaid, 1981; Weick, 1979b). As Gergen and Gergen (1988) concluded, "Not only do we tell our lives as stories, but there is a significant sense in which our relationships with each other are lived out in narrative form" (p. 18). Burgoon and Hale (1984) wrote: "As communication episodes are enacted, the nature of the relationship between participants is defined. At the core of this definitional process are the relational messages exchanged between participants" (p. 193). The role one person enacts and the scene of the act set the stage for corresponding enactments by other characters. For instance, if a customer wants to fight, but a sales representative does not enact the corresponding fight narrative, that fight is difficult or impossible for the irate customer to sustain.

Thus, narratives are vital to employees' and customers' efforts to reduce uncertainty, achieve identification, and engage in company politics. Narrative analysis embraces the elements of the organizational communication model featured in Chapter 2: role persona, scripts, relationships, communication plans, message design logics, communication styles, themes and premises, and schemata (decision heuristics). This perspective of organizational communication incorporates the role of thought and idea in organizational behavior, makes culture a manageable construct, and fosters insights into organizational communication that allow applied research and human resource development to promote company and personal quality and productivity.

To expand these generalizations, this chapter discusses narrative by examining assumptions that incorporate but move beyond a rhetorical view of narrative as information shared and influence wielded. The view advanced here features narrative as action and thought—an ontology. Narratives are not merely rhetorical devices but offer participants in organizations the content and form of the company. This ontology suggests that central principles (which can also be called *ideology* or *deep structure* in organizational culture) emerge from narrative enactment. These principles guide judgments, behavior, and choices by organizational members. Narrative form structures enactments over time and places them within the hierarchy of metaphoric symbols unique to each organization.

From a managerial perspective, the heart of this analysis is that management cannot lead or control employees by merely using stories for rhetorical effect, but must enact appropriate narratives in conjunction with employees. Narratives improve quality and productivity of companies when they create the appropriate culture to guide action and the climate needed to motivate employees.

STORIES AS ORGANIZATIONAL RHETORIC

One approach to organizational stories treats them as rhetorical devices by which managers increase the impact of their messages. In this regard, research has discovered that information presented in stories has more impact than when it is not presented in story form. One explanation of this phenomenon is that stories present information vividly (Taylor & Thompson, 1982). They have persuasive impact because they enliven discourse, thereby increasing attention and retention (Martin & Powers, 1983). In a similar fashion, Pratt and Kleiner (1989) concluded that stories are powerful because "the information passed by a story is better retained than policy definition" (p. 12). Managers' communication styles differ in the number, type, and intensity of the metaphors they use. Each organization has its unique set of metaphors, and metaphor usage correlates with subordinates' perception of managers' effectiveness (Coffman & Eblen, 1987).

To be effective, M. H. Brown (1990) reasoned, stories must have (a) a ring of truth (conform to actions and events), (b) relevance, (c) story grammar (start, development, and finish), and (d) a sense of temporality. They should meet criteria such as *veracity*—the extent to which they accurately (or at least credibly—another criterion) present facts that people perceive to conform with what they think is true. In addition to supplying facts, narrative form should be coherent and present events in a manner that is coherently sequential. A story has more impact when it relates to participants' interests; people use stories to learn which rewards and stakes others want and can withhold.

Stories are part of organizational rhetoric. For instance, Pettegrew (1988) concluded that people learn a lot of information and behavior relevant to health care from stories. People tell stories about those who suffered (avoided, or survived) some ailment: "And that is the point of the story"; "Uncle Fred lived to be 97 and smoked two packs a day"; "Uncle Fred died of a massive heart attack at age 47 because he smoked two packs a day." Through stories, people provide and obtain information that they use to reduce organizational uncertainty (M. H. Brown, 1990; Wilkins, 1984). Managers are expected to explain and legitimize their organization's social reality in ways that influence and coordinate subordinates' actions and reinforce the organization's definition of leadership and its attributional schemata (Pfeffer, 1978, 1981). Managers' effectiveness depends on their ability to use metaphors to elicit enthusiasm and goal-seeking behaviors on the part of employees (Coffman & Eblen, 1987).

Such conclusions might lead managers to assume that they can guide, even control, employees' behavior by using stories to increase the impact during the presentation of information and policy. That assumption is likely to be invalid for two reasons. First, managers are not the only ones who present information in story form; other employees may refute, modify, or confirm the presentations made by managers. Second, what individual managers do and say is compared against larger narratives that prevail in the organization.

For these reasons, a more encompassing explanation of why stories increase the impact of messages is that organizational culture indicates which detail is important or unimportant. For instance, during presentation of a policy, a story invokes interpretative schemata regarding the degree to which the policy should be taken seriously and serves as a means for obtaining reward or avoiding punishment. "Excellent" companies "have a clear set of concrete examples of past management actions (passed on informally from employee to employee as stories) which make the philosophy come alive to participants who are far removed from the executives who write the philosophy statements" (Wilkins, 1984, p. 42). Stories supply significant symbols and indicate legitimate, preferred modes of action (Pilotta et al., 1988).

This analysis explains why we should not focus exclusively on the narrative content of individual messages to determine why they are effective. Impact of stories is enhanced because organizational culture is narrative and rhetorical.

"Culture is most powerful when it both captures the imagination with broad symbols and, at the same time, guides action with concrete scripts" (Wilkins, 1984, p. 47). Because stories use temporal, progressive form to present information about rewardable and punishable actions, organizational researchers use them to disclose organizational culture. Culture comes to life in bits and pieces, such as artifacts, verbal and nonverbal activities, metaphors, myths, rituals, and stories. Organizational stories are told and retold about people, departments, activities, and products, as well as the past, present, and future of each organization. Perspectives become lived and bureaucratized as they are portrayed in stories.

Employing narrative analysis, Wilkins and Dyer (1988) defined organizational culture as "socially acquired and shared knowledge that is embodied in specific and general organizational frames of reference" (p. 523). Stories, a vital expression of culture, perform many functions: (a) "reduce uncertainty by providing information about organizational activities," (b) "manage meaning by framing organizational activities in terms of organizational values," and (c) "bond members together by presenting points of shared identity" (M. H. Brown, 1990, p. 163).

Organizational rhetoric involves power; in the rhetorical contest of power, persons vie to give their preferred narrative interpretation to facts and guidelines for enacting episodes. Each narrative implies a sense of drama that justifies some actions and denies others—favors some principles and makes others irrelevant or unacceptable. If one person gets another to accept a particular narrative view of a situation, that person has exerted power by determining which facts, principles, and roles are appropriate. The other person involved in the episode now plays—enacts—a role based on that scenic definition.

Taking a broad rhetorical view, Wilkins (1984) emphasized the impact stories have. Some have totemic or mythic importance for the organizational "clan," because they ostensibly account for key perceptions and assumptions shared by organizational members. Examples to support this conclusion include: (a) the 3M story of how transparent cellophane tape was innovated—"Never kill a new product idea," (b) Bank of America—"laying pipe" (anticipating and preparing for events), and (c) Northrup—"Everyone at Northrup is in marketing." Taking this view of stories, Wilkins reasoned that they are most useful when they "symbolize the overarching purpose and philosophy [of the company] in a way that inspires and teaches" (p. 44). All stories are not created equal; totemic stories voice a company's culture.

When they feature totemic stories, organizational studies may exhibit a management, sender-oriented bias, which can incorrectly assume that managers use the stories to prescribe company members' behavior. That orientation features managers as creators of stories that are told to employees to define their sense of the organization. Even when they contradict management's preferences, narratives are rhetorically powerful because they are concrete, contain common knowledge, are believable, and grow out of, as well as portray, social contracts. Emphasizing this point, Wilkins (1984) suggested that stories "provide concrete context to abstract philosophy and suggest specific behaviors without becoming inflexible rules" (p.

45). This analysis assumes that individuals who encounter stories learn from them because they convey organizational "truth."

How organizational members use stories to interpret corporate social reality and its preferred behaviors has a telling effect on each company. Repeated stories become summative even though they may be told and interpreted in ways that are idiosyncratic to individuals and departments. Management portrays a sense of reality that may influence members' judgments and behavior, but subordinates also tell their stories, some of which describe when managers are to be taken seriously. In this sense, stories told by management and subordinates rhetorically vie to present views of the company, policies, and employees that constitute a power struggle to define which thoughts and actions should be followed and whether managers deserve employees' respect.

NARRATIVES AS ORGANIZATIONAL POWER

To examine organizational rhetoric, Mumby (1987) explored the ways ideology, story, and power interrelate. "Power," Mumby (1988) concluded, "is exercised in an organization when one group is able to frame the interests (needs, concerns, world view) of other groups in terms of its own interests" (p. 3). In this sense, power arises from sense making. The group that "makes sense" exerts power.

Examining stories for their informational content, Mumby (1987) concluded, leads to the realization that "power is exercised when ambiguous or equivocal information is interpreted in a way that favors the interests of a particular organized group; or, alternatively, when organizational ambiguity is utilized and amplified to disguise the exercise of power" (p. 116). As rhetoric, stories do more than inform; they "help to *constitute* the organizational consciousness of social actors by articulating and embodying a particular reality, and subordinating or devaluing other modes of 'organizational rationality'" (p. 125). Mumby acknowledged that narrative is "a material social practice by means of which ideological meaning formations are produced, maintained, and reproduced" to legitimize the hegemonic interests of some groups and privilege "certain practices over others" (p. 118). This occurs because narrative can "articulate a form of social reality that is accepted by all organizational groups, regardless of their position in the organizational hierarchy" (p. 118). Narratives are "an ideological force that articulates a system of meaning which privileges certain interests over others" (p. 114). This analysis is an advance over the informational theory of culture as sense making, because it explains "the process through which certain organizational realities come to hold sway over competing world-views" (p. 113).

Power groups, Mumby (1987) explained, influence organizational structure because they create ideologies that justify the power of some groups and deny that of others. This view explains part of the dynamics operating in superior–subordinate relations. The ideology of the power group narratives "provide members with accounts of the process of organizing. Such accounts potentially legitimate dominant forms of organizational reality, and lead to discursive closure in the sense of restricting the interpretations and meanings that can be attached to organizational activity" (p. 113). Ideology, power, and narrative are interrelated because "narratives not only evolve as a product of certain power structures, but also function ideologically to produce, maintain, and reproduce those power structures" (p. 113).

This dialectic of narrative, ideology, and power demonstrates how the three interact to support each other. For this reason, "story-telling is not a simple representing of a pre-existing reality, but is rather a politically motivated production of a certain way of perceiving the world which privileges certain interests over others" (Mumby, 1987, p. 114). This view of narrative sees ideology as "materially grounded in the organized practices of social actors. Ideology constitutes subjectivity (consciousness) through its ordering of these practices into a coherent lived-world for the individual" (p. 119). Through narrative, power groups continually reproduce "the structure of social practices that best serves them" (p. 119).

Mumby's analysis reasons that individuals who are influential in an organization achieve privilege by interpreting events in particular ways. Although managers may shape their company's narratives, less organizationally prominent employees provide counterinterpretations. Therefore, dominance resides in the themes and meanings portrayed through narratives that are widely accepted and thereby become the basis of shared meaning and identification. For these reasons, narrative can legitimate or delegitimate political structures and meanings prescribed by dominant groups. Competing narratives can prevail in subcultures and produce friction between them and other ostensibly dominant cultures. This wrangle can lead to an incoherent, uncoordinated Voice.

Narratives are political because "they are produced by and reproduce these relations" between organizational members and subunits by positioning them "within the historical and institutional context of the material conditions of existence. A politically informed interpretation of institutional narrative must therefore explicitly take up this duality of structure, and uncover its 'strategies of containment'" (Mumby, 1987, pp. 125–126).

Stating a managerial view, C. A. Ray (1986) observed that "the top management teams aim to have individuals possess direct ties to the values and goals of the dominant *elites* in order to activate the emotion and sentiment which might lead to devotion, loyalty and commitment" (p. 294). This view holds that employees are "emotional, symbol-loving, and needing to belong to a superior entity or collectivity" (p. 295), a view that may reflect the hopes of management rather than the reality of common practice. Narratives have rhetorical power because they can (a) represent "sectional interests as universal," (b) deny or transmute contradictions, (c) reify structure by eliminating alternative views of social reality, and (d) "control through active consent rather than through passive acceptance of pre-given social formations" (Mumby, 1987, pp. 118–119). Despite the appearance of what could be managerial control through symbols, C. A. Ray (1986) acknowledged that "there is no persuasive evidence, however, that the manipulation of U.S. corporations' cultures really functions as a form of control" (p. 295).

This interpretation of organizational influence constitutes the rhetoric of definition. Creation and acceptance of one perspective can eliminate or mute alternative ways of thinking and acting. Those who create narratives that others adopt thereby achieve power. Those narratives create and disseminate corporate ideology that defines the players and their relationships. In this way, stories establish, reproduce, disseminate, and maintain power relationships because they give a view of the world that the receivers of the story accept and enact. "Organizational members inhabit a symbolic environment in which they create the rules, norms and values that frame the process of organizing" (Mumby, 1987, p. 120).

As tantalizing as this explanation of the political and interpretative impact of stories is, we must not assume that only one interpretation of a story or event is likely to occur, or that any group is likely to prevail and achieve power for long. Although important "rituals, oft-told stories, and key symbols" are employed by management, Pacanowsky (1988a) concluded, "the interpretation a grunt on the loading dock might give of a story, say, might be very different from the one management might intend" (p. 358). Each version supplies a perspective that privileges one group, but that does not mean that both groups inevitably adopt the same version.

For confirmation of that claim you need only to talk to human resource personnel who work tirelessly, and perhaps without much success, to create a single culture in an organization. Or talk to human resource personnel who deal with the personnel who survive a merger, or worse, a hostile takeover. They experience a clash of cultures. When companies go abroad, they may blunder substantially in their efforts to impose a culture, as General Electric did during training programs for French and other European managers. Each person involved in the training program was given a T-shirt carrying the GE slogan, "Go for One." The French viewed these shirts in the same light they did Hitler who required them to wear uniforms and exhibit unshaken loyalty. GE concluded that company cultures are always different.

The following narrative demonstrates the problem of a "one story" interpretation of organizational narrative and shows how interpretations are political because they seek adherents to adopt one organizational "structure" in preference to another:

> In a large Southwestern electric utility company, a third attempt is under way to implement a computerized work order management system. Two previous attempts to implement the system failed. During breaks throughout training sessions (where a consultant heard them) on the use of the system, personnel told three stories about this project. Story 1 emphasized that previous attempts had failed and therefore this one would; persons who told that story appeared dedicated to making the project fail by impeding its implementation. Story 2 consisted of accounts of why the first two efforts failed, but emphasized that the circumstances and quality of the new work order system were superior to the first two and that this version would succeed. Persons who told that story vowed to make this trial work. Story 3 stressed problems that had occurred with the first two attempts and approached the third with a mixture of caution and indifference; persons who told that version seemed uncommitted to support this iteration but made no effort to subvert it.

> All three stories were "true" insofar as they contained facts about previous attempts. Each interpreted the facts regarding the quality of the third attempt to implement a

computerized work order system. Moreover, each story predicted a different future—success or failure of the project. That each group of individuals sought to enact its version of the story led to friction among the employees regarding amounts of dedication and the wisdom of their commitment and efforts. Beyond the surface story is the deeper narrative of the company's attempts to use automation to increase productivity, a policy that would lead to a loss of autonomy for how work is done and increasing accountability for the effective completion of work. Embedded in the stories were competing characterizations of the personnel who worked on previous attempts.

By listening to persons muse about the efforts to implement an automated work order system, the consultant got the impression that substantial uncertainty, well-defined subcultures, and important political struggle prevails among the three parties—each of which has its identification on the line. What is true of all three versions is that a drama is being enacted, the form of which portends resolution, the outcome of which is unclear, a truly "undirected play." The drama contains participants and symbols that occur at all levels of the organization, from management with its commitment to productivity, down through supervisors charged with implementing the system, across to the computer assistance department, which is required to consult on such projects, and eventually to the foremen and schedulers who either buy into the new system or continue the use a "back of the envelope and bellow" style of maintenance crew scheduling and supervision.

The presence of the three versions produced friction between training workshop participants, as each faction attempted to have its version of the drama prevail. In enacting this conflict in the context of training sessions, members competed to dominate, to exert power. Despite managers' efforts to exert power over members' interpretation of the situation, these powerful narratives remained incompatible. Although the plot in that narrative is unresolved, its form predicts that resolution will occur—of one outcome or another. Each version constitutes a rhetorical perspective that has political implications. Each version of the story contains a hypothesis about the project and managerial leadership qualities that its adherents test as they gather data about the project.

That narrative provides insights into stories' place in organizational change. Emphasizing the importance of definitions in this process, Wilkins and Dyer (1988) noted four types of organizational change: "(a) one general frame is replaced by another, (b) an existing specific frame becomes the pattern for a new general frame, (c) old specific frames are replaced with new ones, and (d) new specific frames are learned without replacing old ones" (p. 524). They suggested that the movement in and out of different frames of reference (frame switching) is an inherent part of organizational culture, but does not induce change in the culture. This line of analysis corresponds with the "two voice" model of organizational order. That is, the general culture articulates the large Voice of the corporation, whereas a specific culture is an individuation of the corporate Voice, a subculture. Some of the frames that exist correspond to the sphere of knowledge that exists in various parts of an organization.

Frame change will be influenced by the amount of contact people have with alternative frames, as well as the success and stability of the company history. Wilkins and Dyer (1988) suggested that stability is more likely "if the history has been codified in organizational stories through which members are told how the organization has survived past challenges by using the general frame, even when it seemed difficult to do so" (pp. 525–526). Frames can be changed by management, organizational circumstances, or self-monitoring. When alternative frames exist, the current frame is likely to be fluid. "Specific frames also can make general frames more fluid because switching between frames requires self-monitoring by members. Hence, participants who are comfortable with switching specific frames may learn to value adaptation, and this may increase their willingness to adapt the general frame in new situations. Moreover, this also may indirectly lead to lower commitment to the general frame" (p. 528). As in the example of the computerized work order controversy, the expression of different versions of the story during the training session made specific frames public. Self-monitoring individuals may switch frames, demonstrating their willingness to adapt to, as well as change, their level of commitment to the general frame.

This version of organizational culture corresponds with the view that each story is judged against what each teller and hearer knows about other narratives or versions of narratives. The power of narrative analysis is its ability to compare each narrative with other narratives. Encompassing narratives set the scene against which each immediate story is interpreted. Culture results when individuals share knowledge through stories and interpret events.

This brief review of narrative in organizations suggests five prominent themes: (a) narratives are rhetorically potent devices for increasing message impact, (b) narratives are devices of control and influence through dominant organizational themes, (c) narratives contain information that may increase and decrease uncertainty, (d) narratives provide a means for expressing and capturing the interlocking layers of culture and subculture in an organization, and (e) narratives have an impact on commitment levels. These conclusions provide exploratory insights into the functions of organizational narratives. Insight into the functions of narratives offers substantial potential for advancing organizational analysis because it gives a means by which to analyze each narrative in a context of other narratives. Such analysis gives insights into how perspectives create and reflect the order required for coordinated social behavior.

SUBSTANCE AND FORM OF ORGANIZATIONAL NARRATIVE

As Mumby (1987) reasoned, "Political reading of narrative draws attention to the relationship between narrative structure and the process of interpretation" (p. 113). The narrative paradigm offers the rationale to connect structure or form and content or substance of organizations as undirected plays. This concept emphasizes how interaction through communication episodes occurs as organizational members enact their narrative view of their company as development of relationships through series of episodes that transpire over time and organize around shared themes. Narrative content and form explain how organizational members comprehend and translate thoughts into activities over time. People, who are familiar with the principles central to their narrative plots, enact roles in response to enactments by others who also know those themes and plots. This narrative framework explains how company members attribute motives to one another, episode by episode and scene by scene.

Because narratives privilege certain interests and practices, we must be able to unlock the way this occurs. People throughout an organization tell stories, often quite unintentionally, and perhaps for no other motive than ventilation ("You won't believe what happened") and amusement ("John/Joan did X again"). Several stories may exist about the same event, providing different versions of it. To advance the scope of narrative analysis, we need to be able to explain how myriad stories interlock into a coherent narrative fabric so that the order of the company is made apparent and enactable, even though individuals may disagree and experience conflict.

Narratives provide perspectives through which people coordinate behavior. Their content informs "tellers" and "hearers" about the cost–reward ratios that exist for each effort they consider undertaking or avoiding. Stories predict the rewards or punishments expected to result from actions that comply with or differ from behavioral intentions that result from employees' attitudes toward actions and their willingness to comply to norms—expectations—within the company (Ajzen & Fishbein, 1980). Tellers, as well as hearers, use each story as a mirror by which to see themselves in contrast to others. The grammar of such narrative form is reflective, transitive, or intransitive. Stories are means for thinking aloud. Some stories moralize, whereas others are told to imagine and examine certain conditions of the organization. In this way, the meaning contained in stories is a fabric of thought, a constellation of symbols by which each organization exerts its uniqueness. This meaning expresses performance expectations.

Interpretation of the relationship between symbols, thought, and action begins by approaching narratives as perspectives, terministic screens (Burke, 1966b). The assumption is that if people share perspectives embedded in symbols made meaningful by narrative content and form, they will think and act in predictable, interlocking ways. Such is the case even if the coordination results in conflict and uncooperativeness. Even competition requires cooperation. The dialectic of war requires persons who know how to engage in combat. Democracy is "a political structure that gives full opportunity for the use of competition to a cooperative end" (Burke, 1973, p. 444).

What W. R. Fisher (1985, 1987, 1989) called the narrative paradigm allows us to look beyond individual stories. It assumes that "there is no genre, including technical communication, that is not an episode in the story of life (a part of the 'conversation') and is not itself constituted by *logos* and *mythos*" (W. R. Fisher, 1985, p. 347). Even technical discourse contains myth and metaphor, and aesthetic communication has "cognitive capacity and import" (p. 347). People are valuing and reasoning animals who examine and express thoughts in light of large, dominant Narratives against which each specific narrative is compared and interpreted. Making this point, W. R. Fisher (1987) concluded that knowledge "is ultimately configured narratively, as a component in a larger story implying the being of a certain kind of person, a person with a particular worldview, with a specific self-concept, and with characteristic ways of relating to others" (p. 17).

This analysis suggests that discourse in a company can be interpreted as narrative, even though it does not "tell a story" in the literal sense of the word. Exchange of correspondence (such as memos, letters, conversations, and telephone calls) occurs as episodes in a drama; if a person were to describe these events, chances are they would be presented narratively: "I said...."; "He said...."; "She said...." Some documents, such as policies and procedures, constitute scripts: "Do this and say this." Procedures are often narratively based on temporal progression of steps: "Do this."; "Next do this." Meetings transpire temporally as episodes of engaging actors. Not only is each meeting an episode, but the discussion of each meeting is episodic. Meetings, as is true of other kinds of discourse, progress as players enact what they think to be appropriate roles (personae) as they contribute to the discussion. A sense of theme—shared social reality and shared development of a reality—guides the discussion as each person's comments shape the progression of some theme, a guiding principle in the narrative enactment. Narrative development of themes gives continuity to the enactment of these episodes.

Annual reports are ideal places to look for the kinds of stories companies tell. These stories have narrative qualities, particularly a drama (a sense of plot), accounts of reality, form that is chronological, characters, and circumstances. In its 1984 annual report, Tenneco Corporation, for instance, reported on its Newport News Shipbuilding Division, saying: "The Yard was the successful bidder on three construction contracts for *Los Angeles*-class attack submarines awarded by the U.S. Navy in November." In this narrative, the persona of the company entails helping to maintain a quality navy while doing business successfully. In this vein, the accounts in the Tenneco report continued: "In 1984, the Shipyard delivered its 11th and 12th *Los Angeles*-class attack submarines, *Salt Lake City* and *Olympia*. The attack submarine *Chicago* was launched in October, and the keels were laid for two other attack submarines, *Newport News* (SSN750) and SSN723, as yet unnamed" (Tenneco, 1984). These passages are a small portion of the extended narrative used by Tenneco to report on one of its operating divisions.

Stories often contain archetypal characters and events. Consequently they predict enactments vital to the reward/cost system. In this sense, they exhibit rhetorical presence of "nonpresent" persons, who influence others' behavior without being present. Stories often use the nonpresent persons as the basis for examining appropriate actions, rewards, and costs. For instance, commenting on the portrayal of business persons through television characters, Theberge (1981) concluded that they are presented as crooks, con men, and clowns.

Stories that account for the origin of something, such as a company, department, major idea, product or service, are totemic. They are devoted to the theme of origination. The ideology of our society is a totemic narrative that contains stories of dominant business transactions and developments. This narrative fabric is institutionalized in museums, some of which present the history of a specific industry or company. Work and workers are portrayed totemically. Capitalism is a narrative that differs from socialism or state-run business. Narratives in companies or industries, as well as those related to work activities, are captured in statements typical of "we used to do that this way" or "we've always done that this way."

The narrative paradigm assumes that meaning is interpreted and enacted in temporal, progressive form. What occurs each day in each organization is framed as part of the narrative of the development of business transactions. Each transaction has meaning in the context of the narrative "doing business." Doing business has meaning that exhibits a continuity with the past, is set in the present, and can be projected into the future. This kind of meaning is embedded in the society in which doing business is learned and enacted. People learn how to do business from hearing stories others tell, as well as from the media in the form of situation comedy, drama, news, feature story, and documentary.

This kind of perspective on narrative is important as we consider the scope of narrative analysis and wonder whether the paradigm is too broad. One critic of this perspective, Rowland (1989), has contended that it is too broad because it goes beyond what makes narrative rhetorically interesting—"that storytelling is an essential part of the human condition" (p. 39)—and he claimed that all forms of discourse are not narrative. In response to this challenge, W. R. Fisher (1989) clarified and amplified his work by noting three interdependent levels of narrative: narration,[1] which includes individuated forms; narration,[2] which includes generic forms; and narration,[3] which includes "a conceptual framework, like dramatism, for understanding human decision, discourse, and action" (p. 55). This hierarchy of narratives occurs in companies because each organizational story is an instance of its type (narration[1]), generic stories abound (narration[2]), and all judgments and enactments in an organization are meaningful because they can be interpreted through encompassing terministic screens (narration[3]). At this last level of generality, any act in a company, any thought or judgment, has meaning because of the narrative of all organizations—what the interpreters know about the past, present, and future of doing business and the enactments that bring the narratives to life.

If stories are means by which organizational members share reality, what happens when many stories and their various interpretations are present for the same phenomenon? Part of the answer is supplied by W. R. Fisher (1985), who pointed out that his narrative paradigm "provides principles—probability and fidelity—and considerations for judging the merits of stories, whether one's own or another's" (p. 349). Some stories might have more rhetorical impact because of their probability and fidelity. *Narrative probability* refers to the extent to which a story holds together and is free from internal contradiction, whereas *fidelity* refers to the weight of values, good reasons, consideration of fact, consequence, consistency, and the degree to which a story has a bearing on relevant issues. Organizational narratives give internal and external audiences the chance to know (test hypotheses) which thoughts and actions are reliable and what good reasons are operational in a company, and not just by what is said but also by what is done.

Is narrative used in organizational rhetoric because it enlivens and dramatizes tales about employees, as well as provides anecdotes regarding corporate policies and actions, or because it gives them order and coherence, leading individuals to be able to enact collective stories? The latter answer seems to be best. Narratives live in companies because they convey information and dramatize the clashes and power struggles that define the ideas, rewards, and players to be followed and avoided by savvy organizational members. Their form suggests the preferred enactments. Narratives configure routine behavior and lead people to have some sense of what to do when routine breaks. They combine substance and form to supply a sense of order, which people enact.

As Burke (1969a) argued, *"Our instruments [of thought and analysis] are but structures of terms, and hence must be expected to manifest the nature of terms."* For this reason, any method of examining reality *"reveals only such reality as is capable of being revealed by this particular kind of terminology"* (p. 313). The essence of the dramatistic metaphor is the actor on the stage—the dialectic of the scene–act ratio whereby scene (the terministic screens) determines which act is appropriate, and the act that is performed defines the scene in which the actor is performing.

Stories can be analyzed as presenting meaning that can be used by people at various levels of the organization; this meaning can also be enacted in a temporal frame, with a past, present, and future. Burke's ideas on form and order reveal the connection between thoughts and the symbols in which they are embedded. Because organizational symbols have unity across zones of meaning throughout a company and are instructive of behaviors that transpire over time, narrative analysis can be used to understand the meaning that prevails throughout the organization.

NARRATIVE FORM: ORDER AS ULTIMATE PRINCIPLE

Stories guide enactments because they portray episodes in narrative form, which is temporal and progressive as are day-by-day activities in companies. Each act with its responding acts expresses one or more principles (voice) that becomes meaningful in the context of the Narrative of the company (Voice). The narrative paradigm is powerful largely because it explains the form in which meaning is enacted: if narrative content, then narrative form; if form, then order. The point is that meaning contained in narratives is more than details about a company, such as its rewardable behaviors and political perspectives. The interaction between the form and content of narratives constitutes order, whether temporal or hierarchical.

The key to this analysis is the way each person enacts the episodes of his or her life—one step at a time. Each step is meaningful in the context of an ultimate principle, as Burke (1969a) reasoned:

> [I]f the fate of our hero is developed through a succession of encounters, each of these encounters may represent a different "principle," and each of these principles or stages may so lead into the next that the culmination of one lays the ground for the next....If

one breaks down a "dramatic idea" into acts of variously related agents, the successive steps of the plot could be reduced to corresponding developments of the idea; and the agent or scene under the aegis of which a given step was enacted could be said to represent personally the motivational principle of that step. (p. 197)

Each plot has the sense of being ultimate, featuring a principle that guides and motivates each act. "Ultimate vocabularies of motivation aim at the philosophic equivalent of such narrative forms, with a series of steps that need not precede one another in time, but only 'in principle'" (p. 197). The narrative paradigm gives rationale for an enactment approach to understanding the formal structure and operations in a company as the expression of its unique idea of doing business (Tompkins, 1987).

Summarizing the efforts of researchers to understand enactment, Jablin, Putnam, Roberts, and Porter (1987) emphasized their interest in "the nature of emergent, enacted patterns of interaction in organizations. Frequently treating communication as an independent variable, these scholars have attempted to provide a view of how patterns of interaction create and shape organization structure and how individual and organizational goals are achieved through enactment processes" (p. 297).

The narrative model captures the long-term development of corporate culture (Voice) and each employee's enactment of it (voice). Culture has characters, personae, relationships, plots, and principles or themes. Employees come to understand the company as the performance of activities (events in a narrative) guided by principles embedded in culture. Enactment of each person's drama occurs in the scene of the larger drama—narrative—of the company, and industry.

Principles that guide each person's enactment are negotiated through interaction with other organizational members. Individuals negotiate relationships in the context of encompassing narratives that portray roles, plots, and principles or themes. For this reason, enactments are the working out of ideas. The order that permeates these ideas gives structure at individual, departmental, and organizational levels and over time (the joining of actors in narratives and the working toward ultimate resolution or consummation).

To explain order as an ultimate principle, Burke (1966b) discussed how people use claims of origin: *In the beginning of the organization was the word, and the word was order*. Origination is vital to companies: founders, history (in business since 1974), introduction of products or services, and commencement of employment ("been here since 1983"). Such statements feature the centrality of origin and order in human experience. The goal is to determine how words in a company narrative exhibit form and present or command order. This discussion recognizes, according to Burke (1966a), that form is exhibited in all discourse: "Classical principles of dramatic form are implicit in political, historical, philosophical, metaphysical, and theological systems" (p. 55) because they are dramatistic. Thus, any document is a "structure of interrelated terms" that we experience "*in terms of these terms*" (p. 55). Narratives are experienced in terms of higher terms, the content and form of which are crucial to the sense of order embedded in them.

On the topic of form, two phases of Burke's thought are worth considering because his theory of form ultimately features the act of developing an idea, rather than mere excitation and satisfaction of expectations (Heath, 1979). The first phase culminated in the argument that the effect of form results when some work—a document—arouses and fulfills desires: "A work has form in so far as one part of it leads a reader to anticipate another part, to be gratified by the sequence" (Burke, 1968, p. 124). He featured three major categories of form—progressive, repetitive, and conventional—as well as minor forms such as metaphor, paradox, reversal, and contraction (Burke, 1966a, 1968, 1976). In his view, progressive form (syllogistic and qualitative) involves "the use of situation which led the audience to anticipate or desire certain developments. 'Repetitive' form involves the ways in which a work embodies a fixed character or identity, the ways in which a work however disjunct, manifests some kinds of internal self-consistency. 'Conventional' form involves the kinds of expectation which an audience brings to the theatre as an established institution" (Burke, 1966a, p. 54).

Building on this view of form, Burke came to stress how the teleology of terms compels people to work out implications of the principle central to them. The fact that a person is a *worker* compels him or her to enact that meaning. In this way, terms progress through *transformation* (change) to *consummation* (resolution). Transformation results from action between symbols, or between individuals and the symbols for scene, act, agent, agency, or purpose. Organizational narrative can be viewed as "a *development* or *transformation* that proceeds *from* something, *through* something, *to* something" (Burke, 1942, p. 15).

Transformation is captured in the cycle of terms implicit in the idea of order. Burke's (1966a) point was this: "In such a cycle of terms that imply one another, there is no one temporal succession. You can go from any of the terms to any of the others. For instance, you can with as much justice say either that the term 'order' implies the contrary term 'disorder,' or that the term 'disorder' implies the term 'order'" (p. 59). The structure of narrative results from transformation of ideas, which consists of an "arc" achieved by moving from *A* to *I* made possible by the unifying theme *O*. For this reason, "narrative form (as in a play) in its necessary progression from one episode to the next is like the stages from *A* to *I* along the arc. But as regards the principle of internal consistency, *any* point along the arc is as though generated from Center *O*. And the various steps from *A* to *I* can be considered as *radiating* from generative principle *O*, regardless of their *particular* position along the arc of the narrative sequence" (p. 59). Although Burke's analysis was not originally intended to shed insights into organizational discourse, we can see that it applies to that discourse insofar as it is narrative.

To characterize differences that resulted after an organization had changed, Sanford (1990) focused on how the old culture—the central principle *O*—of an organization had promoted the values of "individuality, freedom, and fun" that led the employees to be "a close-knit group working together toward a goal—success" (p. 111). After the change, she felt the organization had lost its commitment to excellence and to hiring and keeping the best employees. Scene and culture changes produced different concepts of *O* as the organizing principle of the company.

Applying this thematic analysis, Kelly (1985) found that the stories told in high-tech organizations addressed three issues central to the managing process: equality, security, control, and the characters who portray these themes. Core terms, such as *quality*, are important to customers, companies, and personnel (coorientation model), and have a variety of interpretations that may vary according to the person's relationship to the product or service. Recurring emphasis on quality by managers focuses employees' attention on that concept (Gorden & Nevins, 1987). Srivastva and Barrett (1988) found that root metaphors express themes that groups follow in the social construction of reality.

Meaning in companies must be shared sufficiently for personnel to coordinate their behavior, but can never achieve consensus. Each member can never understand every other member exactly, without any strategic ambiguity. How is the reality created and known by people in ways that instruct and prescribe their thoughts and behaviors? Core meanings in culture—what some would call deep structure—constitute key ideas or *O*. Awareness of organizing principles lessens the impact of ambiguity that could otherwise be debilitating to employees' need to coordinate their efforts.

A narrative episode is a transformation of symbols that stand for each person and work activities; the key episodes constitute the development of an idea as stages of transformation and "the unfolding of each transformation prepares for the next, as the removal of one card from a deck reveals the next one immediately beneath it" (Burke, 1966a, p. 62). "It is only by some measure of *uniformity* that a structure of expectation can arise at all" (p. 63). Uniformity results from the theme that runs through the interlocking enactment of each episode and from episode to episode.

Seen against this background, the three dominant forms (progressive, repetitive, and conventional) take on importance. Progressive form entails the advancement of an idea through syllogistic or qualitative development. In a narrative, syllogistic progression of premises forces conclusions: "Jones relied on Boss A's instructions. Jones was punished for how he did his job. Therefore, one should not rely on Boss A's instructions." A qualitative progression would deal with attributions made about character: "Only persons of low character who are willing to lie and cheat get ahead in this company; therefore to get ahead in this company I must be willing to lie and cheat, or if I do not get ahead it is because I do not lie and cheat." Repetitive form relies on maintenance of principles under new guises: "Persons in this company are promised many rewards for performance, and those rewards are never (always) forthcoming." Conventional forms feature development of standard themes, for example: "In American management schemes, the relationship between superior and subordinate is Y leading to X outcomes." People know how to enact their organizational dramas (routine work activities) because of conventional forms, but not every organization is conventional. Many situations are unresolved, leaving company members with unfulfilled expectations that are based on extrapolation from current story bases: If X characters and Y plots then Z outcomes. The importance of this analysis is not story content per se, but the form of that content because the form gives meaning and logic to the content.

NARRATIVE STRUCTURE: ORDER THROUGH
TRANSFORMATION

Order is more than form. Order implies principles that can be used to determine the hierarchy of ideas present in one or many narratives. This analysis is sharpened by realizing that narrative is inherently dialectical; it is achieved through transformation that moves toward consummation. Narrative is enactment; interaction and self-presentation are dialectical. One character's enactment is in dialectical relationship with the scene and the other actor(s) in the scene (Gergen & Gergen, 1988). Scene, act, and actor are symbolic (capable of being meaningful) and therefore interpretable as symbolic action.

To understand the order that exists among levels of terms, as Burke (1969b, 1970) explained, requires carefully drawn distinctions between positive, dialectical, and ultimate terms. Positive terms stand in reference to things, experiences, and such. They require no opposite in order to be understandable. In a sense, the most basic word–thing relationship exists between a positive word and the thing for which it stands. We find distinctions of that kind between company and the name for the company, work or job activities and the name for work or job, worker and the name for worker, product or service and the name for product or service. A basic positive term in an organization is each employee, with his or her name and number.

Dialectical terms are meaningful because of contrasting or opposite terms. The term *quality*, for example, is meaningful because of its opposite: *inadequate* or *unacceptable*. In a company, dialectical pairs include labor/management, superior/subordinate, productive/unproductive, and union/nonunion. Ultimate terms become elevated so that they constitute motives with far-reaching importance. Acts are done in the name of ultimate terms because they are so potent that they can rationalize the lower level terms. In this sense, the ultimate term *profit* can rationalize the presence of all *work* and *workers*. Work is done in the name of profit. Order results from the upward struggle to establish (and therefore to know) ultimate terms. This effort entails "the linguistic drive toward a Title of Titles, a logic of entitlement that is completed by thus rising to ever and ever higher orders of generalization" (Burke, 1970, p. 25). Likewise, a company as a title of titles explains each "thing": workers, products, equipment, company cars.

This sense of order counterbalances the ambiguity of meaning and structure typical of companies. One can argue that companies that enjoy a significantly larger amount of personnel loyalty exhibit a stronger sense of order, which gives employees a way of knowing what is expected of them and how they fit into the company. At the positive level is worker—a specific person with an employee number. The dialectical level results in "field" workers/"office" workers. At the ultimate level is the archetypal worker ("employee of the month," "member of the 20-year club," or "an IBM professional"). Each member of the company "participates" in the substance of that generality (Burke, 1966b). How the levels of meaning coalesce is important for identifying (by each employee or by those diagnosing and studying organizations) the ideology of the organization.

Burke (1966b) can apply form as the development of a principle because an ideology, such as Marxism or its dialectical counterpart capitalism, is "an ultimate vocabulary" (p. 195). In this sense, individual acts—moments in a narrative whether lived or told—reflect the principle of order of each organization, and each act is transformed or transforms the unifying principle. The ultimate term is the Voice of the organization; each act is a statement (voice) of that order. How each act modifies each other act creates or reflects the organizing principle of the organization.

In this sense, what each person does is set in the context of principles of the Narrative. Justifying this point of view as the underpinning for enactment, Burke (1969b) concluded that "the fullest kind of understanding, wherein one gets the immediacy of participation in a local act, yet sees in and through this act an over-all design, sees and feels the local act itself as but the partial expression of the total development" (p. 195). Organizational stories transform details into meaningful order. Details of stories are relevant only to the extent that they reveal form and order; or, conversely, details become meaningful once their form and order are discovered.

Dialogue is narrative, "a process of *transformation* whereby the position at the end transcends the position at the start, so that the position at the start can eventually be seen in terms of the new motivation encountered enroute" (Burke, 1969a, p. 422). Dialectic takes the form of the upward and the downward way so that stories take on order because they embody ultimate principles of an ultimate Narrative. "Beginning with the particulars of the world, and with whatever principle of meaning they are already felt to possess," dialectic "proceeds by stages until some level of generalization is reached that one did not originally envisage, whereupon the particulars of the world itself look different, as seen in terms of this 'higher vision'" (Burke, 1969a, p. 306). Stories are dialectical—the act, the reaction, and the thing learned (Burke, 1969a). Their structure is a dialectic for working out a principle, an order. Over time, many stories told and retold in a company or one of its subunits establish themes that seem enduring, and are treated as such, because they are repeated.

Narrative characters—job titles and individual personnel—become meaningful and useful to the extent to which they embody and enact the substance of principles that have a place in the form and order of the Narrative of the company. In this sense, individuals—as characters—are not particulars; they are ideas representing principles. What they say and do becomes meaningful when their actions transform the principles of the organization, and are transformed by those principles. Progression—basic to form—is the working out of an idea through symbolic action.

One way to gain insight into the interpretative schemata of individuals in companies is to observe how they attribute characteristics to one another. As people name one another, that name predicts how they act toward one another. J. Solomon (1989) reported that employees give names to one another based on salient attributes. Such characterizations fit comfortably with narrative form. For example, in one company a fastidious executive was nicknamed "Little Lord Fauntleroy" and a chief executive officer was called "The Prince of Darkness" because of his intimidating managerial style. In a similar way, Mitroff (1983) examined the archetypal attributions made of managers, such as "drill sergeants" or "wet blankets," and Heath (1988b) made a similar study of attributions external publics can make of companies, "rocket innovators," or "can't make an omelette without breaking an egg." Each archetype fits its appropriate narrative. Knowing the characters—given standard narrative plots—people can complete the narratives because enactments follow the form and order of the principles of the Narrative of the company. Comments in a company evidence the presence of the narrative form. "So, what's her story this time," might be a statement appropriate between two supervisors discussing the repeated tardiness of an employee. The "story" has narrative quality, plot, characters, and principles.

Narrative content and form are the grist of interpretivist analysis. Interpretivists, Goodall (1989) concluded:

> Must present the contexts of his or her prose as extensions of self and identity the products not of neutral methods but of a lifetime of lessons, insights, judgments....Second, this telling about oneself must be done in narrative form within the context of the observations presented, a blending of self and scene into a rendering that takes into account not only what is being seen and experienced but also why this detective was induced to recognize and respond to these symbols....The detective, then, searches for those meaningful orders....Locating meaning in an organization's culture requires paying attention to parts of the story that, while seemingly unrelated, are in fact very much part of the plot. (pp. xiv–xv)

Such analysis assumes that stories do more than report details. They are the living of principles. They lead to and guide enactments because they have form and order.

This analysis can be brought to life by examining the following narrative about buying a battery. This analysis begins with a reminder that enactments are made in the name of guiding principles. Routine purchases require enactment and archetypal stories, which are repeated. Each of us knows the archetypal story of buying a product. Salespersons teach one another how to sell by living and telling "selling stories." Customers teach one another buying by living and telling buying stories. These two activities are interlocking; buyer and seller are loosely coupled but nevertheless capable of enacting appropriate scripts, interactions, relationships, episodes, and order.

With this reminder in mind, let us examine what can happen when this archetype does not work as predicted. Transformations fail and thereby fall short of consummation of the organizing principle, "exchanging money for goods." The story speaks about the organization (and perhaps the society) in which it transpires. The form—expected resolution of an idea—becomes meaningful in the context of the order of the Voice of the organization saying "Be customer oriented." The societal Voice says "Buy from a customer-oriented company."

The narrative began innocently and routinely when a customer started having battery problems and decided to buy a battery at a nationwide department store. The old battery had been purchased from that store, had served well, and was reasonably priced—principles that would predict repeated buying behavior. The customer decided to buy a new battery because the old one had twice failed to start the car after it had not been started for 3 or 4 days in a row. So off to the store went the customer. This episode lead to the routine check-in, "Leave the keys and we'll check the car." After some time the salesperson said that a mechanic reported that tests indicated the battery was okay, but that a part in the car's electrical system—a voltage regulator—was bad and needed to be replaced. The store did not have this part. The service of checking the electrical system was done for free as a customer service, and the store kept the battery to charge it free of charge. (The operating principle was "Be customer oriented"; the buyer was confident in the principle, "Buy from a customer-oriented store.") The task of recharging the battery would take 3 days; during that time the customer was loaned a battery and set out to buy and replace the part. The story seemed to be leading through transformation to "happily-ever-after" consummation.

The plot became problematic because the technician who worked on the car was incapable of reinserting the bolt that held the battery in place, a simple procedure. This inability, however, when witnessed by the owner of the battery, weakened the credibility of the personnel. Another problem was that instead of taking the predicted time ("Come back in 1 hour and your car will be ready"), the task of reinstalling a battery took over 2 hours. By now, the department and the shop were speaking with several voices; incompetence was outweighing competence.

The owner of the car replaced the voltage regulator and at the appointed time returned to have the recharged battery installed. This time he was instructed that because of the number of customers the wait would be 2 hours. After a leisurely dinner, the customer returned—2 hours later. The car had not been worked on. A mob of customers was waiting for service, and several were angrily muttering that they had "been waiting forever." The mood worsened. "Management types" were unavailable or oblivious to the problem. No one was working with the crowd, which was talking itself into a lynch mob. One salesperson became aware of the problem, but most of the complaints were voiced to or in the vicinity of the polite and efficient young woman who was busily processing payments. She was getting the majority of information that the manager could have used to comprehend the problem of handling customers, but she said she was not responsible for solving it. At least she was not contributing to the problem.

Finally, the recharged battery was installed and the car was ready. Its owner had a mechanic check the electrical system to be sure that the repair had solved the problem. This was, in true scientific style, a pre- and posttest of the system to verify that the repair worked. The test was performed, and the readout indicated that the battery (newly recharged) was good. "But the voltage regulator is bad," said the mechanic in a professional tone. The customer left believing that the new "voltage regulator was bad." Days later, a mechanic in a dealership said, "There is nothing wrong with that voltage regulator, the battery is bad." Back to the store went our weary customer. Again, chaos existed. Two hours before closing, customers were being told that if they wanted a new battery they would have to install it themselves. Some customers left. Some began to borrow tools from the mechanics in the shop and from one another. Our intrepid customer, fearing the worst, had been strategic enough to take his tools and was smug when a salesperson said, "Wait at your car and a new battery will be brought to you in 10 minutes." A few minutes later, a mechanic in passing said, "I'll be right back, but you know that we have to check your battery to see if it needs replacing." The customer replied, "I want a new battery. I'm satisfied that it needs replacement. I am willing to buy it without discount, and I will install it myself." "Okay," replied the mechanic, "I'll be right back." Thirty minutes later the customer gave up in bewilderment, turned in the sales sheet, and went home to call Customer Relations.

Prompted by this call, Mr. Service Manager called our weary customer and got the whole story. The Manager said, "Please forgive us. Come in tonight. Mr. Evening Manager will take care of you." That evening—so the plot continues (note the narrative structures and dramatic subtleties to this explanation)—the customer returned and said, "I need to see Mr. Evening Manager. He is expecting me." The salesperson said, "Can I help you? What do you need?" "I need a new battery. I don't want the old one checked. It has been. You say it is fine. Okay. I will pay full price. I was here last night. I am ready to install it myself. I have my tools. If Mr. Evening Manager will sell me a new battery, I will be on my way." At that point the salesperson efficiently began to write up a sales slip and politely paged Mr. Evening Manager. He arrived, and said, "Can I help you?" The customer replied, "I was sent to see you by Mr. Service Manager." And the customer repeated the whole story—checks, voltage regulators, trips back to the store, tools, frustration, and so on. At that point Mr. Evening Manager's mood changed. He "grabbed" the sales slip and said, "Give me the keys." The customer assumed that a new battery would be installed. One hour later the salesman who had written the sales slip came to our customer and said, "We have checked the battery. It is okay, the problem is your voltage regulator." This statement stunned the customer. What incompetent mechanic—one who could not even replace a battery—was running what tests and producing what results that seemed to go on forever?

During the interim, our customer had talked with other customers who had been waiting "forever." Again all of this conversation occurred to and in the vicinity of the competent and polite young woman who was busy routinely and efficiently processing sales slips for payments. Finally, the new battery was installed. The salesperson insisted that the old one did not need to be replaced but they would do so, and at discount, to keep harmony with valued customers. The new battery worked without any difficulty and solved the problem.

The consummation of this long story: Even though buying/selling narratives are simple (archetypal) efforts to enact, this one took on a new life, new transformations that tested the actors' ability to keep principles central to both enactments. Each set of enactments (company and customer) was sufficiently unrelated that the drama was difficult to enact. The customer had thoughts about the ultimate principles that made the company what it was. Speculations were made about the characters in terms of how each act exhibited a statement that developed a principle that became the Voice of the entire organization.

Let us take up the young woman, the efficient payment processor, as the first point of additional analysis. Conversation between the customer and her revealed that she did not participate in department meetings where she might share the information she acquired in regard to customer dissatisfaction. In that sense, she did not participate in a zone of meaning shared by the manager of the department. She was outside of that narrative—that zone of meaning. She did not see it as "her place" to report that information because she did not want to "get anyone in trouble." Until it was pointed out to her, she did not recognize that these complaints constituted "information" that needed to find its way through the network. She said she thought all customers in automotive departments "acted that way." In that regard, she was enacting a different story from that of the customers and managers. Had she been involved in department meetings, even random comments about customer satisfaction could have prompted her to voice the complaints that could have been used as information to make management decisions that would lead to strategic changes designed to lessen the complaints. She was inside of the work network of the department, but outside of the information network. The people in the department seemed so intent on doing what they had been told to do that they lacked the ability to step back and analyze their operations. Indeed, they may have been given no incentive to participate in the thinking and planning of the department.

This analysis leads into that of the voice. The members of the department spoke with one Voice: "Here is how we do business. Bear with us and we will treat you systematically and routinely—perhaps even mindlessly, loyal to machines in preference to people." Three times the car of the customer was put through the same tests, with the same report of results. At no point did any of the characters doubt the machine, its operation, or the reports it provided. When the customer said, "Let's enact this drama differently," the members of the department were unprepared (or prevented by management) from doing so. Overreliance on technology and confidence in products stifled individual discretion. Following procedure seemed more important than knowing what the theme (plot) of the department was and enacting it with variation to satisfy customers. Instead of being a department capable of creative problem solving, it was highly scripted, univocal, and inflexibly bureaucratic. The network was functioning as a virtually closed system, oblivious to external influences. It was a drama without a sense of the larger drama or narrative in which it occurred. Members of the store narrative were induced through identification to act one way, regardless of "good reasons" to the contrary.

AN ONTOLOGICAL VIEW OF ORGANIZATIONAL NARRATIVE

An ontological view of narrative reasons that it is not as much a vehicle for conveying shared reality in a company as it is a means for bringing that reality to life through enactment. Describing organizational communication as cultural performance, Pacanowsky and O'Donnell-Trujillo (1982) concluded that shared reality is "the residue of the communication process. It is the resultant structure—the sense that is made or the account of reality—that body of knowledge that is drawn on as a resource for explaining and making sense of new experiences" (p. 123). In this view, organizational meaning is enacted by what people in an organization do. Knowing and making known are the essence of organizational communication.

As W. R. Fisher (1987) reasoned, "the narrative paradigm sees people as storytellers, as authors and co-authors who creatively read and evaluate the texts of life and literature. A narrative perspective focuses on existing institutions as providing 'plots' that are always in the process of re-creation rather than existing as settled scripts" (p. 18). This is possible because "people's symbolic actions take the form of stories" (p. 19). W. R. Fisher (1987) agreed with Campbell (1970), who advocated an ontological view of rhetoric based on her assessment of three competing views of rhetoric (a) as rational judgment-rational influence, (b) as influence resulting from "basic, unlearned drives," and (c) as the result of people being "the symbol-using or signifying animal" (p. 97). The ontological view emphasizes symbols and symbol using. W. R. Fisher (1987) agreed and took a symbolic interaction interpretation that "one of the decisive dimensions of rhetorical experience when persons interact symbolically is their perceptions of the others' perception of them. These perceptions they read from what and how the other persons communicate" (p. 17). Clarifying his case, Fisher cautioned, "I do not mean to say that knowledge is unimportant in communication. I do mean, on the other hand, that it is ultimately configured narratively, as a component in a larger story implying the being of a certain kind of person, a person with a particular world view, with a specific self-concept, and with characteristic ways of relating to others" (p. 17).

Rationale for treating stories as enactment came from Burke (1967), who studied language and thought as action rather than as means of conveying information. The view of narrative as enactment rather than transmission of ideas calls for an ontological, rather than epistemological justification. Ontology is the philosophy of being. As such, symbols are symbolic action, modes of being; they are vehicles by which people present themselves and become meaningful to one another. Whereas an epistemological view of organizational discourse assumes that one person knows something that is conveyed through messages to another person, an ontological view assumes that meaning is made available through interpretations of that enactment. Narrative analysis of organizational culture rests with the difference between discourse as action and discourse as conveying knowledge from source to receiver.

Stressing the ontological underpinnings of interpretivism, Pacanowsky and O'Donnell-Trujillo (1983) compared their version of enactment to that of Goffman (1959), who described communication in theatrical terms: actors performing roles on various stages unique to each situation. This theatrical model constituted a major advance over the mechanical model of organizational behavior. The theatrical model treated organizational members as choice-making individuals rather than people driven by organizational forces. Agreeing with the theatrical perspective of organizations, Pacanowsky and O'Donnell-Trujillo (1983) asserted, "Organizational members do not 'conform' to behavioral laws but rather *act* (or more precisely, *choose to act*) in ways which reflect (or flout) the social conventions of other organizational members" (p. 130). They acknowledged the presence of scripts, but argued that "even these scripts do not bind the organizational members to an inflexible performance" (p. 130). For that reason, "the notion of theatricality not only suggests a break from more mechanistic views of organizational communication [but] it additionally suggests that organizational communication is situationally relative and variable" (p. 130). Employees make choices, within latitudes of each organizational narrative, of what enactments, including scripts, are appropriate. Appropriateness is based on the extent to which enactments in each episode conform with a central principle (*O*).

This view supports the conclusion that each company is brought into being by what its members do and say. The view of Pacanowsky and O'Donnell-Trujillo (1983) progressed beyond Goffman's theatrical approach because they reasoned that organizational "performances are those very actions by which members constitute and reveal their culture to themselves and to others. Performances are not inauthentic nor superficial; they are the very things which bring to completion a sense of reality" (p. 131). For that reason, organizational researchers must consider "the notion that reality is brought 'to life' in communicative performances" (p. 131). This view of companies treats role enactment as genuine, the basis for creating shared meaning and coordinating behavior, rather than as distanced, artificial performance.

Using an ontological view of narrative analysis to increase insight into the decision-making and advocacy processes that occur, Weick and Browning (1986) reasoned that a sizable portion of organizational communication is devoted to reasoned discourse. Whereas many people who operate in organizations are endowed with the capability of presenting and analyzing logical, rational arguments, even more people are capable of understanding and presenting evidence and reasoning in the form of narratives. Such discourse adheres to tests of probability (extent to which a story appears to be true) and fidelity (extent to which a story adheres to facts), as does argumentation. Narrative also makes values more a part of corporate decision making than is the case with purely rational discourse. "The narrative paradigm takes the position that values are ultimately persuasive and that to evaluate nonformal arguments, soundness is the essential standard of reasoning" (Weick & Browning, 1986, p. 249).

A view of organizational discourse as reasoned argumentation can have an epistemological bias. In contrast, Weick and Browning (1986) concluded, "The narrative paradigm is grounded in ontology rather than epistemology and presumes that ordinary discourse consists of symbolic action that creates social reality. In other words, stories are everything" (p. 249). Agreeing with Smircich and Morgan (1982), Weick and Browning (1986) reasoned, "Stories, in the context of the narrative paradigm, have ontological significance and may not just carry the culture but may also create it" (p. 250).

Communication, viewed ontologically, is a mode of action rather than a means for conveying knowledge. Emphasizing that point, Burke (1983b) observed,

"There was no story before we came, and when we're gone the universe will go on sans story" (p. 859). Story began as people learned to talk and thereby introduced words, symbolic action. In this way, "when Story comes into the world there enters the realm of the true, false, mistaken, the downright lie, the imaginative, the visionary, the sublime, the ridiculous, the eschatological..., the satirical, every single detail of every single science or speculation, even every bit of gossip" (Burke, 1983b, p. 859). Because of this line of reasoning, Burke (1983a) cautioned that our "vocabulary hypnotizes" us (p. 10). The ontological basis of narrative is enactment—the realization and individuation of meaning through others' enactments (lived stories as well as purely symbolic ones in the form of told stories).

Burke's (1955) approach centers on "the *substantiality* of the *act*" (p. 259). Behavior and opinions are made real and meaningful through what others say and do. Meaning results from interpretations made based on acts and acquisition of terministic screens that account for coordinated actions over time. This point can be established, Burke (1983a; Deetz, 1982) reasoned, because knowledge is dialectical: "(a) one acts; (b) in acting, one encounters the *resistance to one's purpose*; (c) *one learns* by suffering the punishment dealt by such resistances" (pp. 22, 26). By taking on a story, people take on action rather than information and knowledge of action. The action is unified by the theme that is its essence; for instance, acts expected to achieve rewards. In this way, enactment of rewardable behavior is captured in symbolic interaction.

This analysis provides rationale to progress beyond a view of narratives as organizational discourse used to convey knowledge, to establish an ontological view of organizational enactment. An epistemological view of discourse assumes that messages, including those contained in stories, convey information and shape perspectives used to interpret that information. In contrast is the preferred view that a company is enacted as people bring meaning to it through what they do. Meaning includes more than interpretations of what is said; the entire enactment is message.

FOCAL POINTS OF NARRATIVE ANALYSIS

Persons who seek to understand and change organizations can treat stories as "repositories of organizational intelligence" with which to assess what is needed for organizational development (Kreps, 1990, p. 191). Using stories to generate information about an organization, Glaser, Zamanou, and Hacker (1987) estimated that the degree of congruency between management and employees is measured by the degree to which company Voice corresponds to individual voice. These researchers asked groups of subjects to give their perceptions of their organization by using stories. The results indicated that management thought the climate of the organization was more positive than the employees did. It felt more involved in the organization and believed that communication was better than subordinates did. It perceived supervision to be more effective than employees did.

The following list indicates focal points for narrative analysis and offers questions that can illuminate the nature of each organization:

- *Narrator(s)*: Who tells the story? In what context? For what reason(s)? What personae are presented in the story?
- *Auditor(s)*: To whom is the story told? In what context? For what reason(s)? How do the auditors interpret the story in light of Narrative?
- *Plot*: What plot and theme are central to the story? How do they fit the plot and theme of the encompassing Narrative of the company, industry, or work discipline? Do different narrators tell the same story but with different plots or themes? Do the actors enact the same story in the same way? Does the enactment achieve consummation?
- *Moral*: What is the moral of the story? Do people use the same story to make different points? Are the morals compatible or incompatible? Does the point to be made drive the progression of the story to consummation?
- *Characters*: Who are the characters of the story? How are they featured? Do some narrators tell the same story, but feature the characters in different ways? What archetypal characters emerge? Who enacts the story?
- *Location of the story (internal to the organization or external)*: Is the story related to persons at work—a work-related story—or is it related to their personal time activities—home, children, social activities, financial problems, spouse, relationships, etc.)? How does the scene of the story define the enactment it presents?
- *Relationship*: What relationship is enacted by the actors? What metaphor describes this relationship? How does it contribute to and reflect the climate of the company?

These diagnostic questions treat stories as the residue of enactments. They capture stories that are carefully manufactured and propagated—such as those presented by senior management through public relations, advertising, employee relations, and investor relations—as well as those told daily by employees to one another or to persons outside the company.

Stories told in a company reveal themes employees use to make sense of it. They create and convey arguments and conclusions. Employees use this reasoning to make sense of their circumstances, especially the principles from which they operate.

It is natural to interpret events and enactments in terms of rewards and costs. Narratives help people grasp the sense of themselves and others in the enactment of a company. Evidence of this narrative form and content is revealed in how events are recalled and reported: "I went into the boss today to get that raise I deserve. I said.... The reply was...." Similar accounts are given by persons external to a company who are affected by it and consider how to play the stakes they hold: "I thanked the clerks for their kindness."; "That store earned my business."

Analysis of the meaning in companies takes at least two orientations. One is called *critical interpretivism*, an orientation that examines which organizational practices and meanings are contrary to the human spirit and therefore undesirable. This analysis differentiates between company practices and policies that foster happiness or unhappiness and recommends the former in lieu of the latter. A second interpretativist orientation, called *analytical*, assumes that people seek useful attitudes and opinions in their calculation of which opinions and actions lead to rewards and avoid punishments.

This orientation is supported by social exchange theory, which reasons that people trade rewards and sanctions and meet expectations as they enact relationships (Roloff, 1981, 1987). The orientation reasons that people adopt behavior and opinions as they take on the jargon of each company, culture, and trade or profession. By direct experience, observation of models, and role playing, individuals test which opinions and actions produce rewards and avoid punishments (Bandura, 1977). The culture of a company results from dialectical tensions between members who attempt collectively to achieve a reasonable and predictable shared reality that can lead to collective, coordinated, and predictable behavior, useful for the individual and the organization to achieve their goals. The assumption is that people act in similar ways because they think in similar ways.

This relationship takes on a different perspective when it is reversed. People infer opinions based on the behavior they observe. If an employee moves slowly and seems unmotivated then that person is thought to be lazy. If that is the only employee a person external to the department or the company encounters, the tendency is to infer that the culture of that organization allows—even encourages—laziness. The fallacy here is the assumption that the relationship between behavior and attitude is so close that opinions can be inferred from actions. But the truth is that people who attempt to make sense of an organization do so by observing narrative enactments.

To change an organization might require new stories, new interpretations of existing stories, or new principles to guide the enactment and interpretation of narratives. But organizational change requires that the company become, in terms of actions taken and rewarded, what it wants to be perceived to be and how it wants employees to behave.

This line of analysis helps us reconcile two orientations to organizational communication and employee performance. One paradigm operates out of a positivistic and mechanistic model that postulates that behavior results from incentives that can be translated and manipulated by those who control rewards and punishments. According to this top-down, managerial model, managers manipulate the reward environment—the thoughts and actions of employees. This model assumes that behavior flows from opinions, which flow from jargon and thought of the company—which is governed by management. Behavioralist and interpretativist approaches to organizational communication acknowledge different degrees of mechanism. Another paradigm of organizational communication assumes that individuals make various idiosyncratic interpretations of their circumstances based on the meaning—culture—that exists in the organization. In this case, culture is more of a perspective and frame of references that can be used to calculate and negotiate rewards.

If culture is thought to consist of beliefs and values that make sense in a company—to help employees serve the organization—that alone does not give a sense of the structure and principles of the organization, or the activities that are performed by each employee. Narrative provides form that makes sense of culture.

Form is longitudinal; activities transpire over time in a coherent and meaningful way as the principles of the organization. The narrative of each employee's activities transpires as a repeated story. It demonstrates the principles that are embedded in the activities.

Through enactments, employees play out the undirected play. By knowing the principles of the narrative, they enact the play. They perform roles appropriate to their interpretations of the context, which is defined by principles embedded in the narrative. Two sets of principles interact in the experience of each person: (a) those that run throughout the culture of a company and allow people in different departments to enact roles that are compatible and complementary, and (b) those that individuals use to interpret how each person's narrative fits the culture of the company.

Organizational change is based on enacted changes of meaning. These changes may be overt, with key people making strategic attempts to change what and how employees perform by giving a new sense of company vision, mission, and tactic. This kind of change may occur through the strategic alteration of the culture, myths, histories (interpretations of the corporate history), metaphors, symbols, images, persona, and narratives that make up the corporate culture. As well as being changed strategically, the meaning of the organization may change accidentally— nonstrategically. Slowly, people may come to talk about the company as obsolete and an unpleasant place to work. Narratives, images, symbols, persona, and so on; all of the parts of culture may slowly come to reflect this meaning. Once they do, the company, because it is nothing but the enactment of tasks and relationships, becomes what the employees think it is. Changing employees—firing many and hiring others—is unlikely to change the company unless the culture also changes. The employees who remain keep stories alive and pass them along to new employees who may enact the culture that existed before the turnover. The "massive turnover of 1985" merely becomes part of the narrative of the culture and adds evidence for a negative view of the company.

Rather than using stories to guide behavior, managers are advised to enact a coherent, coordinated, and goal-oriented Narrative in conjunction *with* employees.

CONCLUSION

Narrative, as enacted, is a basic unit of analysis because it shows how principles become translated into steps (moments, interaction, relationships, and tasks) that become the company. Meaning can never be perfectly understood across the layers and groups of people that make up each company. Nevertheless, communication becomes meaningful across many experiences because of strategic ambiguity (Eisenberg, 1984, 1986), unobtrusive control (Tompkins & Cheney, 1985), and politically motivated meanings (Mumby, 1987). Narratives give a sense of how experience is structured, how reality is ordered, and how people should act and react. Instead of the specific accounting for the general, the general accounts for the specific (wearing of company logos, logos on goods produced, services expressed with logos, images of company—with logos). Enactments occur in the name of creation and order, because corporate culture is a theology.

4

Information: Uncertainty Reduction, System, and Satisfaction

An organization is an information obtaining and processing system. Members create, sort, interpret, select, transmit, store, trade, negotiate, and retrieve information. Members' effectiveness depends on their ability to obtain, create, interpret, and convey information regarding their company's environment and performance, as well as their own. Information has commodity value because people want it and use it, even as a power resource. They manufacture, destroy, trade, buy, and sell it. On the downside of this equation, we have misinformation and disinformation. Addressing those concerns, this chapter features information as a variable in organizational communication. If we describe communication as the effect persons have on one another, then it is synonymous with information: What people do on behalf of a company is interpreted by others as information; people—as the voices of their company—communicate by affecting one another.

The approach presented here contrasts markedly with the narrow view that information is something conveyed or transferred from one person to another. That view would assume, for instance, that a memo contains X amount of information, which a sender placed there to transfer it to a receiver. In such a model, the receiver should recognize the amount (X) of information that the sender placed there. A preferable view of information is that people discover it through their contact with persons inside and outside the company. In this sense, interpretations produce information (even the lack of it) that increases or decreases the amount of uncertainty an interpreter experiences. Thus, in the case of the memo mentioned previously, the sender provides X amount of information but the receiver obtains Y amount of information. This information obtained even includes interpretation of why that memo was received from that writer under the circumstances at that time. Emphasizing this point, Deetz and Mumby (1985) observed, "All information is perceived information" (p. 370).

Over the past two decades, organizational communication researchers have developed models to explain how organizations operate—by giving attention to communication and information both as independent and dependent variables. Organizations exist because their members enact the personae of roles and premises needed to produce collective, focused behavior. Collective or individual behavior is useful only to the extent that it achieves rewarding outcomes. To determine whether outcomes are rewarding and whether strategies are successful in achieving them, members of organizations acquire and interpret information regarding activities and outcomes. Through enactments, and interpretations of those enactments, company members make themselves meaningful to one another (and to themselves) so that work efforts can be coordinated to achieve goals.

From a systems perspective, information can be used to explain how organizational members learn what they need to know to be able to coordinate their activities with one another. A crucial part of the lives of organizational members is the definition and negotiation of interpretations of information—what information is and what it means for them as members of a company and for the company itself. Shared information and its accompanying interpretations establish *zones of meaning* throughout each organization. Zones of meaning result from experiences and jargons unique to each group, particularly work disciplines, departments, and divisions; zones reflect differences in education and training of members of the group. As these interpretations reflect shared meaning, they are translated into coordinated efforts so company members can achieve collective results.

Attention to information and its interpretation assumes that each company consists of thinking people, a position that leads researchers to be interested in the cognitive processes people employ as they enact organizational relationships with one another (Jablin, 1982a, 1982b; Weick, 1979a, 1979b; Weick & Browning, 1986). This approach allows researchers to use information as a variable to explain how communication directs behavior and regulates relationships. This view also assumes that randomness is the inverse of organization. People in organizations seek to impose meaning, and reduce or eliminate randomness.

Any system needs to develop interpretative frameworks for making sense and using information to make decisions. For this reason, supervisors generate procedures that tell members how to interpret and distribute information. Nevertheless, interpretation of information is subject to individual differences. One of the most important differences is the need to reduce uncertainty that exists because people are self-interested in the actions of one another and their own ability to achieve self-efficacy (Berger, 1987; Berger & Calabrese, 1975; Rogers & Kincaid, 1981).

How do people reduce uncertainty? Is an uncertainty paradigm applicable to all aspects of organization members' personal need to know and the relationships they must develop to function properly? To what extent are their efforts to obtain and process information motivated by a need to cooperate and coordinate activities? In what ways does persuasion shape the interpretative frameworks they employ to make sense (collectively and individually) of information and thereby to reduce uncertainty? How important is information to employee satisfaction? How do the form and content of narratives provide interpretative frameworks? To answer these questions requires attention to intra-individual, interpersonal, group, and macrosocietal levels of analysis.

These questions assume that differences between amounts of information people have and what they need are a crucial factor in assessing the health and productivity of organizations, as well as their ability to achieve the level of quality expected by persons who purchase their goods and services. This line of analysis suggests that company members use information to assess the quality of their interpersonal relationships and that without shared interpretative schemata, members of a company cannot coordinate efforts because they would have no means for interpreting what information is relevant and meaningful to themselves and others. They do not know what others expect of them and cannot convey what they expect of others. Schemata are interpretative mechanisms needed to define information, determine the boundaries of a relationship, know which actions are needed to define and maintain a relationship, and understand which rewards and constraints maintain or terminate relationships.

Information about goals and mission becomes important to the standards of quality employees seek and affects their efforts to achieve those standards. In this regard, tests of relevance and meaningfulness are subject to individual as well as group interpretations. Organizational members use persuasion to get one another to utilize specific interpretative schemata. Without a shared interpretative system, and the information needed to operationalize it, members cannot coordinate their activities. Information and interpretative schemata unique to each organization and its subunits generate meaning by which members enact their organization.

AN INFORMATION/SYSTEMS PARADIGM OF ORGANIZATIONS

To understand information in organizations requires attention to assumptions of an information/systems paradigm that treats companies as systems. Each system exhibits various degrees of openness to its environment (to other systems), and information is the means by which each system is able to adapt to its environment. Whereas biological systems, such as a human body or a tree, take energy from their environments, companies take information from other systems. Some of this information is used as feedback to steer the organization by determining whether actions produce desired results.

The process goes like this: Systems (whether organizations, groups, or individuals) have goals. They act to achieve those goals. During this process, information is taken in as input; after it is processed it becomes output, which in turn can become input for another system. As feedback, information is received and used by members to assess how well their activities and those of their company are achieving the goals (B. A. Fisher, 1978, 1982).

What is a system? B. A. Fisher (1982) argued that it is "the 'all' of a thing" (p. 199). This "all" can be an entire company, a division, department, work group, interpersonal relationship, or individual. All of what can be thought of as systems can refer to individuals as well. Individuals are part of many systems: departments, policy systems, information systems, and work systems, for instance. Thus, a system is any entity that can be viewed as a whole even though it is also a part of some larger system. Each system interacts with various degrees of openness with all other systems with which it has contact. What one system observes another system doing and saying can be information.

As a whole, each system consists of subsystems (subunits), sub-subsystems, and so forth. Subunits of an organization are arranged in levels. This hierarchy can be captured in an organizational chart, for instance, consisting of a president over five vice presidents. Each division under each vice president is a subsystem of the total organization. Each division is divided into subsystems—each having a manager. Each manager is the boss of a department. The work in the department could be divided between various units (subsystems). This view of hierarchy depends on levels of specialization, whereby each level consists of subordinate levels.

An organization can be divided into many kinds of systems based on unique functions. If management draws together people from several departments, the group (such as a quality circle or focus group) that results is a system, even though it does not correspond to a level in the organizational chart. In addition to levels, organizational systems can be defined in terms of function, such as the marketing system, production system, human resource development system, or transportation system. One functional system can cut through other systems; for instance, a company may have a budget system that is shared by many departments. What the company does is a work system; each department contributes to that system in its unique way. The profit center of an organization earns revenue; all other systems cost money rather than make it.

Often when people discuss systems, they think only of the people on the inside of an organization. But a system can include people who are outside of an organization. Is it unreasonable to consider customers as part of the organization's marketing system? Vendors, who are outside of an organization, actually are part of its production system. Systems interlock; once they do, they become a larger system. For instance, marketing interlocks with the manufacturing system, which joins the people within the organization who create a product along with vendors who supply raw materials and persons who supply and service manufacturing equipment. The systems of an organization can be cut in many ways. For this reason, a system is any configuration of people that enacts a similar role. Marketing personnel enact a different role than do people in production, for instance.

A system exhibits many characteristics, one of which is degrees of openness, the extent to which information can flow into or out of it. This concept implies its counterpart, closedness. According to B. A. Fisher (1982), "The most popular definition of openness is the free exchange of energy between the system and its environment" (p. 199). Openness is the extent to which enactments by one system can be known and interpreted by members of another system. People inside one system may have to work hard—as in sales—to get information into another system, such as customers. People outside, such as journalists, may have to work hard to obtain information from a company.

The flow or exchange metaphor is helpful *and* misleading in the discussion of systems. It can lead to the belief that information flows as electricity moves through a wiring network or water flows through a plumbing system. By extension one might think that information flows normally in an organization unless something interferes with it. Likewise, water flows in the pipes in a house in well-regulated ways until a pipe bursts. If an appliance needs electricity or a faucet demands water, it is made available by the system that contains it. By this analysis, we might assume that as people need information all they have to do is ask for it or seek it.

Looking at the organization in the broadest sense, Farace et al. (1977) distinguished between absolute and distributed information and suggested that a major issue in regard to the quality of each organization is how well information is distributed—in the right amounts, to the right people, and at the right times—as it is needed. An important correction to this view is that people feed information into a system strategically; they control what flows and how it flows by gatekeeping. People often have no actual way of knowing whether they have too much or too little information to make decisions. Estimates of sufficiency of information assume that people know the total amount of information that is available (total information) and compare that to what they need and have. This model assumes that people in an organization have roughly the same opinions as to what any piece of information means and how important it is. Such assumptions may be faulty.

One view of systems theory—relying on cybernation—suggests that if a system is in equilibrium with its environment all is well. If the information obtained and interpreted by a system leads its members to believe that their activities are achieving their collective goals, those activities—enactments—are likely to be continued. Likewise, according to cybernation, if feedback indicates that activities are not producing desired goals, those activities are likely to be abandoned, modified, or replaced. Goals may be altered to reflect what members of the system are capable of achieving. Systems desire equilibrium with other systems.

Caution must be exerted to keep in mind that information becomes meaningful only in terms of the evaluative schemata that are used to evaluate and process it. If information is used as feedback to determine how well tactics that were selected are operating to achieve goals for which they were selected, then attention must be given to the schemata that are used to receive, process, and utilize the information. A standard use of the cybernetic model is to think of companies as capable of self-regulation or self-correction. Self-regulation occurs when individuals obtain information about their performance; this information comes in the form of negative or positive feedback that results when an action is taken to achieve some goal. If the goal is achieved (such as throwing a basketball through a hoop), the individual thinks this action can be repeated in the same way to accomplish the same end. If the person fails to make the basket because the ball is thrown so that it falls short, this feedback can lead to self-correction that indicates to throw the ball harder. If the ball is thrown so hard that it bounces off of the backboard and does not go through the hoop, the self-correction is to throw it easier.

At each step in the process, efforts taken are based on the individual's ability—not only athletic ability, but also the ability to conceptualize the goal and activities needed to achieve it. Beyond this, the individual must either intuit how to correct the behavior needed to make the ball go through the net, or someone must instruct the person. In this way, the person—and by implication, companies—must *learn to learn*. This task is made more difficult because "the problem of change hinges on the way systems deal with variations that influence their current mode of operation" (Morgan, 1986, p. 239).

In passing, it is worth noting that this paradigm is helpful in discussions of quality and productivity. Feedback about the extent to which the quality of a product or a service compares to those by competitors or meets consumer expectations can be used to reinforce or change performance standards. Likewise, productivity is a result of constant attempts to maximize the ratio between input and output.

Although provocative, this equilibrium view of systems is deceiving. Just because all appears to be going well does not mean that changes have not occurred or are not occurring in the environment that will make old activities no longer appropriate or useful; these changes may require new goals or new activities. For instance, corporations in the 1950s were lulled into complacency that left them unprepared for protest outbursts by civil rights groups, environmentalists, feminists, and other activists who created a totally different operating and public policy environment for businesses through increased legislation and regulation.

A sense of closedness can occur at the individual, department, corporate, or environmental level. To support this position, one might turn to Weaver's (1988) analysis of the problems U.S. corporations are having in adapting to the international marketplace. Over the years, despite their claims to the contrary, U.S. corporations gained a lot of favorable regulation and legislation that defined the operations of the economy and domestic marketplace. By gaining this kind of control, companies created their operating environment and adapted to it—and it to them. By doing so, however, they became static and lacked the creativity and foresight needed to adapt to the international marketplace. Tariffs, subsidies, official monopolies, tax breaks, wage controls, defense spending, and government-sponsored research—these kinds of policies led U.S. corporations to create an operating environment that lulled executives into lethargy and weakened their ability to adapt to the robust international marketplace.

Believing they have achieved a state of equilibrium can mislead members of a company into assuming that all is going well, when in fact changes are occurring to which the company must respond but cannot because it does not know what signs suggest need for change. Also, an equilibrium model does not explain how systems exert themselves into their environment and shape that environment. This latter theme, developed in chapters 9 and 10, is important because through product or service advertising and public policy statements, as well as activities related to them, organizations shape (at least attempt to shape) their environment. For instance, it was not public demand for athletic shoes that led to their manufacture and sale. That demand was created through marketing and advertising.

Systems can affect their environment as well as respond to them. B. A. Fisher (1982; Krippendorff, 1977) emphasized this view as he noted that an open system can generate its own information and thereby define its environment and establish its boundaries. An open system is not merely a pawn caught in the dynamics of its environment. Had people read incorrectly the information about human ability to fly, the airplane would never have been invented. In this sense, an airplane was imposed on the environment because some people were open to quite different interpretations of what the information meant in regard to people lacking natural ability to fly. In a similar vein, people have taken useless substances, such as crude oil, and developed entire industries rethinking the human ability to transport themselves and goods. A key to the degree of openness is the extent to which people can discover *what information is* and to know what it means for the organization. Doing this is not as easy as it might seem.

A system can generate information that it can feed into other systems, thereby changing them. This model helps explain a company's marketing efforts that require that a product be developed, but also indicates why information must be fed to other systems—buyers—to tell them about the product's characteristics and availability. Also, companies make information available to other systems, such as regulators, legislators, journalists, the general public, and activists. This information may explain the company's policies or operations and affect how its activities are perceived (favorably or unfavorably) and regulated.

Feedback should not be thought of as something that is single faceted, that which a sender gets back from a receiver in response to a message, for instance. Feedback, in business contexts, is often multifaceted. If a member of a customer relations department has an exchange with an irate customer, the goal of the customer relations person may be to achieve understanding and agreement on the part of the customer. All that is said by the customer can serve as feedback that the customer relations person can use to determine whether the message design logic used during the exchange and its implementation are successful. To the extent that feedback suggests that they are successful, they will be continued, on this customer—and probably will be used when dealing with other irate customers. In contrast, one would assume that if feedback suggests that the message design logic and its execution are unsuccessful, they are likely to be refined, modified, or abandoned.

Having said this, analysis might stop by looking only at the feedback in the relationship between the customer relations person and the irate customer. But after the exchange with this irate customer, the customer relations person is also likely to receive feedback from other people. For this reason, feedback is multifaceted. Peers make comments that can be used as feedback by the customer relations person to refine the communication tactics to be employed under similar instances. Each peer might provide different kinds and amounts of feedback. Likewise, the boss may provide feedback. This latter source of feedback could be intangible (praise) or tangible (a raise and promotion). Feedback can be negative as well as positive. It can be inconsistent and conflicting. What one peer thought to be a wise tactic, another might advise against. The boss' advice may add to the confusion and uncertainty felt by the customer service employee.

The assumption is that people take feedback from multiple sources and amalgamate it to develop a coherent and competent communication style. People read feedback selectively. Because of the ways people attribute causes to their own behavior, when information confirms self-judgment, persons making the judgments are likely to attribute it to their personal characteristics. When it is negative, the circumstances of the job are likely to be blamed for the outcome (Kelley, 1972, 1973).

Interpersonal relationships—positive or negative—affect the feedback used. Feedback is obtained through communication, what others do and say and what that means for the person receiving it. Individuals interpret what they perceive others as doing or saying in ways that can serve as feedback. Based on this enactment paradigm, what is interpreted as feedback is learned as part of the culture and climate of each organization. It is quite possible that members of companies misread the feedback. A classic performance/interpretation "rule" found in the cultures of many organizations is that "everything is okay until someone tells you differently." As was evidenced by the asbestos industry, issue monitors for companies can become so persuaded by their own rhetoric that they become insensitive to changes in their environment that they should interpret as vital information (Heath, 1991).

Misinterpretation is quite possible. People read feedback with a bias that may lead them to confirm what they want to believe and disconfirm what they do not want to believe. The "absence of communication" actually is communication. If the boss or a respected peer in a company does not tell another member that some part of his or her behavior is incorrect, the message probably is that it is correct. By not communicating, members of organizations do communicate. This situation is easy to see in terms of feedback that members seek to confirm or disconfirm opinions and behavior. What others do and do not do can serve as information. The crucial question, not only facing members of a company but also persons who attempt to study them, is how do people come to know what they should (and do) treat as information. The key is the sense people make of the enactments other people perform.

If people are uncertain about their circumstances, they are likely to employ a variety of tactics to reduce that uncertainty. They prefer to seek information through established channels and from appropriate sources. If that effort is too costly in proportion to its rewards or is perceived unlikely to reduce uncertainty, rumor and a contrived sense of the company will suffice for members to believe they know what is going on. How people communicate about information gives a sense of what it means. For instance, some information is so secretive that bosses cannot talk about it. This communication indicates that divisions exist between those who do have access to information and those who do not; this access communicates status distinctions. It also says that information that is readily available is not as important as information that is difficult to obtain.

These observations demonstrate how the information/systems paradigm is an interesting starting point for understanding organizations. Brief reflection, however, suggests that the model can be simplified so much that it is misleading. Refinements are needed to make the model useful. In that regard, our understanding of information must rest on concepts of interpretation, sufficiency, and reduction of uncertainty. Each of these terms focuses on the information seeking and processing efforts of individuals who obtain and interpret information. This approach does not treat information as a fixed entity that flows throughout a system, but rather as the product of individual interpretations.

INFORMATION: A SUBJECTIVE PROBABILITY MODEL

What is information? Some observers, particularly Shannon and Weaver (1949), viewed it as data; any bit of data that allows a person to reduce by half the total amount of uncertainty in a decision. For instance, a person might wonder whether a jacket is in the closet. By looking in the closet, the person could determine whether the jacket is there or elsewhere. It either is or is not—a binary decision; if it is not there, it is somewhere else.

Applied to an organizational context, a person might wonder whether a shipment has arrived at the warehouse. The answer, "yes" or "no," reduces the uncertainty. Other answers, such as "I don't know" or "John says it has not" may not reduce uncertainty, but increase it. For this reason, Shannon and Weaver's (1949) view of information works within situations where a fixed decision is possible, but does not answer crucial questions, such as "Does my boss like me?" or "Am I doing a good job?" Many questions do not lend themselves to fixed answers.

These illustrations distinguish between what information is and the kinds of concerns it allows people to address, and they emphasize that information is needed because uncertainty exists and is uncomfortable. If people did not experience uncertainty, they would not need information. In this vein, Krippendorff (1977) reasoned that "*information* is equated with making choices" (p. 157). The amount of information conveyed by a message is the difference between the amount of uncertainty *before* the message was received and the uncertainty *after* the message was received (Krippendorff, 1975). Each piece of information may have more or less effect on the uncertainty experienced by the person making the decision. Information may increase as well as decrease uncertainty.

The extent to which information has impact on uncertainty is an estimation of its subjective probability—the extent to which people interpret the information as believable and useful. This is a measure of the extent to which concepts are associated with one another (Fishbein & Ajzen, 1975). The amount of uncertainty that exists at a given moment and the degree to which any piece of information affects that uncertainty is a function of interpretations people place on the information. In this regard, Farace et al. (1977) contended, "Uncertainty is the term used to express how confident or sure you are about something. Uncertainty refers to the predictability or structure of some set of events, such as the presence of one or more patterns: the less predictable, the less structured, the more uncertainty is present" (p. 23).

Viewed as subjective probabilities, instead of binary units, the range of judgments regarding information falls on a scale of 0 to 1. Any bit of information, for instance, might increase the degree of uncertainty from .3 (30%) to .6 (60%). Or it may lower certainty from .88 (88%) to .73 (73%). Information moves degrees of certainty in a range from 0 (uncertainty) to 1 (certainty). Developing this line of analysis, Conant (1979) reasoned that information is "that which changes what we know" (p. 177). He emphasized that "the receipt and interpretation of a message always entitles the receiver to adjust its knowledge about its environment in some fashion." For that reason, "Information is that which changes knowledge, and a message can be said to convey information to a receiver if and only if the receiver's knowledge is changed as a result" (p. 177).

Any message contains information only to the extent that it affects what the receiver is willing to believe. Thus, it is subject to interpretative frames applied by the people who attempt to make sense of and use it. For example, Jones, a salesperson, hoped to land an important contract after having lunch with a buyer, Johnson, who demonstrated interest in the product. Verbal and nonverbal cues indicated interest. Johnson told Jones that no moves could be made until approval was received, and expressed assurance: "That should be no problem." Jones reported this exciting news to his superior, who said, "So you got taken in by Johnson—all lunch and no order." What seemed to be good news, information that suggested a potential sale, was merely lunch conversation by a person who had the reputation of promising big orders to get a free lunch. Once lunch was over and paid for, the interest went away.

This line of analysis confirms three important points. First, information is necessary because people experience uncertainty, which, because it is unpleasant, motivates them to seek information. Second, information affects judgments based on subjective probabilities, a scale from 0 to 1. Third, interpretative perspectives analyze information in different ways and generate different conclusions. Coordination in an organization assumes that people develop, share, and utilize reasonably similar interpretative systems. As Farace et al. (1977) concluded:

> The more uncertainty present in a given situation, then the more "information value" a pattern has when it appears. Given all the possible outcomes in a particular situation, when you learn which specific pattern occurs, your uncertainty is reduced; you have gained information. Thus, the more predictable a situation, the more information we have about it—and thus the lower its uncertainty. Conversely, the less structured a situation, the higher its uncertainty—so when a particular pattern does appear, uncertainty decreases and hence more information is obtained. Information can be viewed, then, as the use of pattern to reduce uncertainty. (p. 24)

The process of acquiring and using information is often characterized as being easy, but that may not be the case. Information must be acquired and then interpreted. It may be difficult to obtain, and its interpretation may be subject to dispute. These conditions are likely to increase during periods of turbulence.

INTERPRETATION: TOWARD AN UNDERSTANDING OF ORGANIZATIONAL MEANING

Based on how it is interpreted, information may increase or decrease uncertainty. Interpretation depends on the narratives used by the person or group that is making sense. Themes and values that operate during this process affect how the information is interpreted and whether other individuals and groups make similar or perhaps markedly different interpretations. For this reason, narratives, themes, and values—the extent to which they are shared by individuals and groups who encounter information—are vital to the voices expressed in the interpretation. If many voices are reflected in the interpretation of the information, that may lead to a jangle of conflicting interpretations; however, if only one Voice is reflected in the interpretations, that may suggest that although the organization gives the appearance of unity, it may suffer narrowness and an absence of wholesome conflict. The voice of each individual mingles with voices of all other individuals to create a collective dialogue. What each says is meaningful in the context of what others say (Burke, 1973).

Circumstances under which information is encountered influence its effect on uncertainty. Information results not only from what occurs, but also what is expected to occur (Berlo, 1977). If you expect someone to be hostile and the person is nice, does that increase or decrease the uncertainty about your relationship with the person? If checks from one company are routinely on time and one is slow, does that create uncertainty about the company's solvency or change in policy? Or, if a company is typically slow in paying, does getting a check early create uncertainty? If a company that is routinely thought to violate community standards of environmental responsibility announces an environmental program, does that proclamation affect uncertainty?

Enactment becomes meaningful because interpretations are assigned to the behavior of others. The act of giving out information becomes part of its informational value. For instance, when information is passed out in a meeting, people ask what it means. When a boss gives it attention (or treats it with indifference), that action contributes to its informational value. If a boss does not talk about a problem or ignores an issue, those actions have informational value.

An enactment model of organizational communication assumes that information relies on meaning derived from interpretations of behavior. This view is supported by Farace et al. (1977) who concluded that people create information by their patterns of behavior. Thus, *one of the primary ingredients in the concept of information is the discernment of pattern in the matter/energy flows that reach an individual* (p. 22). For instance, a member of an organization can make sense of some situation by recognizing a pattern. To the extent this pattern has meaning as part of a narrative, it constitutes information. If the boss talks with one member of a group more than other members and does so in what seems to be a more cordial manner, this pattern can be interpreted as indicating that the boss likes the person, perhaps more than the other employees. This information might lead one fellow employee to associate with that person, in the hope the fondness will rub off. Another fellow employee might avoid contact with the favored employee because of an aversion to people who use ingratiation to gain favors from the boss.

Each of these actions can constitute patterns that may serve as information that members of the work group use to interpret friendship and reward patterns. Each pattern can serve as a bit of information. The boss does or does not associate warmly with X employee. Awareness of these patterns may have varying degrees of impact (0,1) on each employee's attempts to reduce uncertainty regarding the relationship and reward patterns of the work group. Because people enact an organization by what they do and say, their actions become meaningful to others with whom they enact the organization.

Patterns only have the meaning people assign to them; information is not self-defining. Weick (1979b) stressed that point as he observed, "The basic raw materials on which organizations operate are informational inputs that are ambiguous, uncertain, equivocal" (p. 6). Agreeing with this position, Farace et al. (1977) concluded that "there are no 'objective' patterns that exist apart from the ability of at least one individual to recognize them" (p. 23).

This principle is easy to intuit; recall how the activities of fellow employees make less sense at the outset of a job (perhaps when a person is new to a company, department, or task). After some instruction and observation, occurrences become meaningful. People learn how to act (communication planning and message design logic) so that they increase the likelihood that what they do will be interpreted in a way they prefer. Employees learn the ropes of a job by knowing which performance and interpretation rules to follow to demonstrate their competence. They learn what to do to enact a desired meaning in others. An experienced employee might instruct a new one, "Always look busy even though you don't have anything to do." Contrary advice might be, "When you run out of work see the bosses; don't fake your work! They can spot an employee who is pretending to be busy." Farace et al. (1977) reasoned that "recognition of patterns is a basic fact of our growth and maturation as individuals" (p. 23).

Interpretation can occur, as can enactment, at the points when systems come into contact with one another whether they are individuals, groups, or organizations. Analysis throughout this book focuses on interpretative efforts and processes appropriate to each level within organizations. At the interpersonal level, personal cognitive schemata operate. At the department level, as well as the macro-organizational level, processes of obtaining, interpreting, and making sense of data are a matter of group *and* individual effort and entail collective interpretative schemata.

An increasingly popular explanation for how this interpretation occurs and persists relies on the concept of corporate culture (Smircich & Calas, 1987). As members of an organization tell stories about other members (former and present), they impart bits of information about the corporate culture. Stories, for instance, are replete with statements about organizational norms. Members learn what the acceptable workday is, how hard members of the department work, and what quality of work is expected, to mention a few of the pieces of information and evaluation acquired through stories. The company newsletter is likely to contain articles about employees whose work is exceptional; the expectation is that other employees will be inspired to imitate or exceed those standards. One member might have been formally or informally punished for violating company or work group norms.

The meaning of any occurrence depends on interpretative schemata used by individuals who encounter it. What is said and done in an organization is different if the interpretative schemata of its members are more similar than different and vice versa. If interpretative schemata differ, they need to be compatible. If they are not, what each person does and says may fail to be meaningful enough for members to coordinate their activities. Interpretative schemata result from the shared reality and sense making provided by organizational culture.

Explaining this process in terms of enactment, Weick (1979b) proposed this model: "Enactment is action that produces the raw materials which can then be made sensible. Recall that sense-making is commonly retrospective. Sense is made of previous actions, ones that have already occurred. Enactment produces the occurrence that can then be made sensible by the selection process" (p. 133). According to Mitroff (1983), culture consists of written and unwritten rules, language (jargon), jokes, history, myths, rituals, awards (rewards), and symbols. The kind of personnel a company selects also becomes part of its culture, as do its clients and vendors. An organization that buys subpar materials from disreputable vendors creates a different culture than does one that buys the best materials from reputable vendors. Culture is conveyed by the relationships the organization has with its stakeholders.

Enactment produces data that serve as information. In this sense, enactments define the circumstances in which they occur. Such is the case because people act based on their definition of each situation. Acts agree with definitions of situations in which they occur. Employees who are busy are enacting work that implies that the environment calls for being busy. Employees lounging at rest enact the definition of coffee break. Part of the problem of achieving mutuality of under-standing comes about when parties involved do not interpret enactments in similar, or at least compatible ways. The converse of that statement is also true.

MONITORING EXTERNAL ENVIRONMENTS

Organizations are interpretative systems (Daft & Weick, 1984). For this reason, we should understand the structure, personnel, and interpretative systems involved in information processing. People who manage companies must obtain and interpret information about external environments that affect their organizations (Dutton & Duncan, 1987; Dutton & Ottensmeyer, 1987). Such information is vital to planning and adaptation. It requires monitoring that, depending on the size of the company, can entail sophisticated surveys and issue-monitoring tactics by public affairs and marketing units, or it may entail asking customers in small family-owned compa-nies if they enjoyed their meal or know of items that should be stocked. Sensitive to this need, Daft and Weick (1984) observed, "Organizations must develop information processing mechanisms capable of detecting trends, events, competi-tors, markets, and technological developments relevant to their survival" (p. 285). The same is true for departments, groups, and individuals.

The way an organization goes about obtaining, processing, using, storing, and retrieving information is a focal aspect of its structure (Stinchcombe, 1990). Indeed, the structure of an organization comes into being through these information processes.

Part of the problem individuals have in serving companies is knowing when information should trigger changes in plans and activities. Key triggering factors include the level of activity needed to obtain and use information, assessment of the urgency of obtaining and processing it, and knowledge of responses that are feasible in light of it (Dutton & Duncan, 1987).

This discussion demonstrates one weakness of applying traditional informational and cybernetic models to explain how organizations operate and the ways they can be improved. Such efforts fail if they do not explain how people come to know what information is and how feedback can be interpreted; this problem is amplified if different, even conflicting, interpretations exist in the company, or between it and persons outside of it. Scholars (such as Dutton & Duncan, 1987; Dutton & Ottensmeyer, 1987; Huber & Daft, 1987) search to uncover the variables that affect how people recognize, obtain, and process information on behalf of organizations. These variables include those unique to each environment, amount and kind of information, and analytic and cognitive skills of persons who are expected to process the information.

This analysis considers the degree to which key persons in a company are able to discern whether the information they obtain is valuable or irrelevant. Efforts are made to determine whether the amount of uncertainty people experience when they encounter information is influenced by the degree to which problems are poorly defined and understood. The amount of activity committed to obtain and process information is influenced by the degree of uncertainty, the extent to which people are accountable for activities that depend on the information, and the variety of internal interpretations that are possible (Dutton & Ottensmeyer, 1987).

To describe the process by which people obtain and interpret information regarding external environments, Daft and Weick (1984) proposed a three-part model: scanning (data collection), interpretation (data given meaning), and learning (action taken). Assuming that a company needs to find the best ways to know its environment, this model rests on the premise that "information about the external world must be obtained, filtered, and processed into a central nervous system of sorts, in which choices are made" (p. 285). Although individuals must obtain and interpret information for an organization, the process entails sharing. "Individuals come and go, but organizations preserve knowledge, behaviors, mental maps, norms, and values over time. The distinctive feature of organization level information activity is sharing. A piece of data, a perception, a cognitive map is shared among managers who constitute the interpretation system" (Daft & Weick, 1984, p. 285).

The processes of obtaining, interpreting, and sharing information usually involve a small number of people. Often this group reports to the people at the top of the organizational hierarchy, but that is not always the case. All persons in a company are in a position to obtain information regarding conditions external to it. For this reason, "Organizations can be conceptualized as a series of nested systems, and each subsystem may deal with a different external sector" (Daft &

Weick, 1984, p. 285). One difficulty that occurs, particularly in large companies, is gathering and processing a lot of information in a coordinated and coherent manner; some information may be meaningful to people at some levels of the company but not to people at other levels. Getting the information to the people who need it and who can use it requires sophisticated intelligence systems.

Interpretative processes are not random. They correspond to the nature of each company, whether its culture prompts sensitivity to external environments. Organizations accustomed to marketing are likely to be much more sensitive to their external environments than are other companies, particularly those with relatively little competition. Managers often are key interpreters, and interpretation is a key managerial function. How information is gathered and interpreted depends on (a) the extent to which management believes the environment to be interpretable, and (b) the degree to which a company actively penetrates its environment looking for information (Daft & Weick, 1984).

Based on this analysis, Daft and Weick (1984) used a model that features four interpretative modes: enacting, discovering, undirected viewing, and conditioned viewing. *Enacting* occurs when an organization intrudes into its environment because it is believed to be unanalyzable. In this way, organizations create environments. New behaviors create reactions that constitute information by which key personnel in the company determine how well it is doing. Personnel experiment, test, and stimulate. The *discovering* mode also involves intrusion. The difference is that the company believes that it has a correct understanding of the environment and merely tests that hypothesis. This mode uses measurement probes to generate information about the environment. *Conditioned viewing* assumes that the environment is analyzable. This mode relies on established data collection procedures and traditional interpretations. *Undirected viewing* is also nonintrusive. It does not entail objective data because the environment is assumed to be unanalyzable. Managers rely on their own perceptions of the environment and do not employ formal management systems within the organization.

Efforts to obtain and interpret information from external environments are difficult in "quiet" times because information seems not to exist. But as has repeatedly been demonstrated in this century, the calm precedes the storm. The quiet period of the 1950s preceded the turbulent 1960s and 1970s, which witnessed more protests by a wider array of groups and passage of more regulation than at any period in the history of business in this country.

In contrast to quiet times are turbulent periods that are unstable and generate information that is difficult to characterize, particularly if new interpretative frames are required. Huber and Daft (1987) argued that during turbulence, information increases in *quantity*, the number of messages received per unit of time. Because new interpretative frames are needed, information in turbulent times becomes more *ambiguous*, subject to competing interpretations. During turbulence, companies often commit additional resources to receiving and interpreting information.

Companies that deal with new regulatory agencies or with old ones that are promulgating new regulatory standards experience more uncertainty than do companies that are regulated by established regulatory agencies with a history of promulgating regulations. The degree of uncertainty correlates to the clarity and sufficiency of information the agencies provide about their policies (Ungson, James, & Spicer, 1985).

How people within systems read information from their environment is crucial to the kinds of changes made and their magnitude, as well as the structure of the company. A cybernetic model suggests two options. The first is the realization that "systems can maintain stable identities by sustaining processes of negative feedback that allow them to detect and correct deviations from operating norms, and can evolve by developing capacities for double-loop learning that allow them to modify these norms to take account of new circumstances" (Morgan, 1986, p. 239). This latter effort, Morgan noted, can occur because of random changes within the total system, not just interaction between the system and its environment. How does an individual system change itself vis-à-vis its environment? This structural arrangement is reactionary, taking the definition of the relationship from the feedback from the activities on its behalf.

By adopting a new identity a company can assume a new relationship with its environment. This enactment is not just a mode of perception whereby we see or emphasize certain things while ignoring or downplaying others, but is a much more active process. By projecting itself into its environment and thereby organizing it, a company produces itself as it acts in relation to that environment (Morgan, 1986). Thus, a company can conceive of itself as merely adapting to its environment— reading feedback to determine whether it is reaching its goals. Its efforts are designed to be stable, merely adjusting to feedback from the environment. In this case, information is interpreted on the basis of the established relationship between the environment and the company. If the environment changes, turbulence is likely to occur. Not only is there a lot of information, but the ways in which that information is interpreted are likely to be highly uncertain.

In this case, uncertainty is high until the situation begins to stabilize. Once that occurs, efforts are made to impose certainty on the company and its means for adapting to its environment. This adjustment can happen within a company, as well as between it and its environment. Persons within a company may be happy to operate out of a stable cybernetic model using negative feedback; as long as they do not do something wrong, they believe nothing bad will happen. By the same token, they are not geared for change, but for bureaucratic routine. If the environment begins to change, the question is whether they will be able to change and survive. In contrast to the bureaucratic and adaptation model is the option that occurs when individuals or groups (departments or divisions) within the company attempt to change it.

Three options apply: the bureaucratic model, change model, and exertion model. Because it relies on negative feedback, the *bureaucratic model* stresses stability. Information is used to determine whether mistakes are being made and then to avoid them. This model tends to be a closed loop whereby the company merely uses information to determine whether it is making mistakes. According to this model, if no mistakes are being made, the company and its members are doing well. The *change model* places a premium on adaptation. It exists in any system that demands that its parts (subsystems) change or become useless to the company; in view of this mode, information is received and processed with the intent of dynamically adapting to its system. The last model, *exertion*, results when individuals (subsystems) proactively seek to influence or change the system. Innovation of a new product line is an example of this latter case, such as the creation of the computer industry or the oil industry. "As organizations assert their identities they can initiate major transformation in the social ecology to which they belong. They can set the basis for their own destruction. Or they can create the conditions that will allow them to evolve along with the environment" (Morgan, 1986, p. 245).

STRUCTURAL–FUNCTIONAL APPROACHES TO ORGANIZATIONS

Based on the belief that information and meaning are essential factors in organizational performance, researchers are confronted with determining which approach to use in their analysis. The structural-functional model of organizational communication features networks—patterns by which members of the organization communicate with one another and the extent to which they believe they have too little or too much information (Farace et al., 1977). The assumption is that how information is distributed within and among systems is vital to understanding organizational communication. Information in one system (such as the marketing department's awareness of customer preferences) needs to flow into another (management, for instance, which needs it to create or refine its strategic plan).

This approach to organizations assumes that they (as well as the members that make them up) are information processing organisms that can be studied and improved by learning whether they communicate and process information effectively. The analysis involved in structural-functionalism features three broad concepts: organizing, information, and communication. Organizing refers to "the processes of function and structure in an organization, to the uncertainties that accompany the day-to-day life in an organization, and to the fundamental points that organizations are not fixed, unchanging entities" (Farace et al., 1977, p. 19). Any company, in this view, is the product of functions and structures that are the result of organizing. Structural-functionalism treats information as a commodity that is stored, sent, created, retrieved, and utilized throughout and among organizations. These activities can be analyzed according to level, function, and structure through the company. Levels include the intra-individual, dyadic, group, and total system. Communication is an important organizational variable, because the behavior of members demands "control, coordination, and interdependence" (p. 51). The primary functions for which communication is used are "production, innovation, and maintenance" (p. 58). Farace et al. (1977) observed that it is inappropriate to say that all of what happens in an organization is communication and "that all organizational problems are therefore communication problems" (p. 7). Such a stance "eliminates the concept of communication from further use as an explanatory or analytic device" (p. 7). According to this view, "*communication refers to the exchange of symbols that are commonly shared by the individuals involved, and which evoke quite similar symbol-referent relationships in each individual"* (p. 26).

According to this view, communication and information can be defined by the functions to which they relate. For instance, "Production messages are those that direct, coordinate, and regulate the activities of the organizations' members in such a way as to bring about the desired end results" (Farace et al., 1977, p. 58). Innovation involves "eliciting or generating proposals, suggestions, and/or new ideas for changing organizational practices in such a way as to increase efficiency, morale, or other important goals of the organization....The second aspect of the innovation function is often included with the first, although it actually deals with a considerably different type of problem. Here we refer to messages which deal with the issue of *implementation* of new ideas and practices" (pp. 58–59). Communication is used to promote new ideas and accomplish change. "Maintenance communication, on the other hand, serves a purpose which is quite distinct from either production or innovation communication" (p. 59). It maintains individual self-concepts, relationships, and production and innovation functions. Discussions of functions focus on the content of messages, whereas analysis of communication structure considers patterns by which messages move throughout the company. Function and structure are linked in such ways that a breakdown in either can harm the communication system.

A linear model underpins the theory of structural-functionalism—who says what to whom and with what effect. It assumes that people learn to apply the rules of who to talk to, in what way, to what end, and in what context. This analysis combines information theory, systems theory, and rules theory to explain how and why people do what they do in organizations. It assumes that communication can break down when one person does not understand the message or does not get the message or information as intended by the person who sent it, perhaps because one or both persons do not follow the appropriate rules. Thus, this model relies on a sender–receiver linear paradigm instead of an enactment paradigm.

Although structural-functionalism makes important contributions, it fails to address some essential points to understanding organizational behavior. One key concern is its failure to explain how rules and interpretations occur that give members of an organization an understanding of what information is, what it means, who to send information to and receive it from, and whether they have the information they want and need. Part of the failure of structural-functionalism arises from the tendency of subscribers to information theory to think of information in neutral terms, an approach derived from Shannon and Weaver (1949) who observed, "information must not be confused with meaning" (p. 8).

INFORMATION PROCESSES AND ORGANIZATIONAL STRUCTURE AS ZONES OF MEANNING

In contrast to the structural-functional approach, enactment theory views organizational structure as consisting of zones of meaning. The focal point is the meaning that exists in one network or subunit; this theory asks whether people in another system or network know or share that meaning. For instance, customers of a particular soft drink company may be lured away by a competitor. This change in preference may result because they conclude that one product is better than the other. One way of diagnosing this situation is to ask whether information flows from one system—segment of customers—to another—the company, particularly the marketing department. But what does this information constitute? Meaning! Social reality! What meaning or social reality does the segment of customers have that the marketing department needs? Flow is the process of transmitting information. Information is the vehicle by which it flows, but the need is for the company to obtain insights into the customers' *zone of meaning*, or what they think of the competing soft drinks.

To refine the concept of network, we should treat systems as zones of meaning. The issue is the interpretations an individual, department, or company employs to know which actions are expected, needed, or meaningful to achieve the goals the company or department is expected to accomplish or for which the individual is rewarded. Having information does not mean that it will be interpreted in ways that lead to coordinated efforts. Each person, each dyad, and each department may possess unique meanings—social realities. The meaning shared by people in one zone must relate to meanings in other zones with which they interact. Each zone speaks with a unique voice. How well the voice of one zone is known to and shared by people in other zones will influence the exchange of information, compatibility of interpretations, and persuasive influence between them and determine whether the collective Voice is coordinated and coherent, or a jangle.

An enactment view of organizations argues that communication results when what one person does and says is meaningful to another. Therefore, information does not flow, it occurs through enactment. Rather than looking for the flow of information to correspond with an organizational chart, an enactment model instructs us to look for how the structure of an organization is created by what people do that is meaningful to one another. Communication occurs, and the perception of what happens is interpreted and translated into information. Once enactments are interpreted and given meaning, they constitute information that can be used to make decisions relative to the uncertainty that exists in a given situation. Idioms that are used to interpret these enactments reflect zones of meaning unique to each organizational unit. Such zones are characterized by unique, specialized jargon and their accompanying interpretative perspectives. An entire company is a zone of meaning related to its unique product or service. It is divided into different zones that exhibit various degrees of compatibility.

An engineering department, for instance, constitutes a different zone of meaning than does a personnel department, an accounting department, or a marketing department. Marketing personnel may have different views of what the company is than do people in manufacturing or procurement. A different zone of meaning exists in accounting than in field operations. The ability of different zones to communicate is a matter of terminology or jargon. It may also be a matter of the persona of the members of groups, as well as their views of where they fit into the company.

Culture determines what is information. Such interpretations occur on at least two levels. One is scripted. In every organization, certain routines dominate the thinking of members. One factor related to the degree of routine or scriptedness is the tenure of the people in the discipline or in the particular organization. After years of exposure to a set of terms, individuals become scripted in their definition and the resultant interpretation of information. Unique jargon constitutes scripts. For instance, the electric generating industry uses the term *bus* in quite a different way than a transportation company does. Persons who work in nuclear generating plants think of them in quite different ways than do people who are unfamiliar with nuclear energy. *Bonds* and *debentures* are technical terms used in brokerage houses and by investor relations experts. For persons in the discipline, key terms and concepts and the data that relate to them become routine, but to the new person (one who is in various stages of assimilation) the terms are new. And the way in which definitional and evaluative terms are used to make interpretations can be a problem.

Scripts and schemata relate to uncertainty reduction. Schemata tell us when we are uncertain, how uncertain we are, and how we should reduce uncertainty—how we should reduce the uncertainty we see others experiencing. The culture of each company is full of statements (scripts) that help members determine what meaning is. A list of statements illustrates that point: "Discriminating customers with discriminating tastes," "State of the art engineering," "A leader of the pack," "Quality is job one," "The customer knows best," and "It's a job."

A crucial analytical measure according to this model is the extent to which people within a zone share sufficient meaning to coordinate their efforts with those of persons in interdependent zones. If engineering develops an innovation but marketing does not know what it means, then an improper relationship exists between these zones. In that case, the zones are probably so loosely coupled that they lack requisite coordination to achieve coordinated outcomes.

The degree of scriptedness can relate to the amount of belief consensus and perception of turbulence—internal turbulence and external turbulence. This can also be a factor of information overload and underload. Without proper scripts, an individual does not know what information is, which information is valuable, which information is missing, and which is available. Structural-functionalism assumes that cognitive complexity is a key variable in information processing, but factors modifying complexity are the degree to which information is scripted, the extent to which an individual knows what the script is, and the extent to which the individual can use the script.

Interaction between information and interpretation provides a structure that reflects individual interpretative frames, interpretations by groups, and organizational culture. Analysis of information at system and subsystem levels should be compatible and integrated in a way that gives coherence to this structure. According to this model, management has a sense of meaning—expressed as themes, narratives, and metaphors. It obtains and pools information that is subjected to analysis according to its frames of reference. The management system obtains information from other systems in the organization, but management needs to employ meaning that is compatible with that residing in other zones of the company.

Issues of interpretation begin at the individual level. One way to address this issue is to think of information as being integrated into composite packages, each of which has different weights and evaluative valences. This point of view is supported by Azjen and Fishbein (1980), who argued that people integrate a lot of information (in the form of beliefs) into their opinions. This information contains positive and negative elements. Action is the result of the belief that performing the behavior or holding the opinion will produce negative or positive outcomes. The likelihood of behavior based on attitudes is influenced by each individual's estimates of what persons who are important to the individual think about the action. The attempt to understand judgment and behavior entails "consideration of the beliefs individuals hold about themselves and their environment, that is, to the information they have about themselves and the world in which they live. We assume that human beings use or process this information in a reasonable fashion in their attempts to cope with their environment" (p. 62). Individuals want to hold useful attitudes (opinions, judgments, or beliefs). To do so, they seek information and attempt to make sense of it in terms of what it does for their need to understand and adapt to their environment.

This model assumes that individuals, groups, and systems experience different degrees of uncertainty and have varying levels of desire to reduce it. Bits of information are not isolated, but fit into matrices of levels of complexity. These matrices contain positive and negative pieces of information that are used to achieve rewards and avoid losses. This decision matrix is influenced by the social reality that operates in each zone. How do individuals know what is information and what it means without evaluative schemata that are communicated and shared with others inside and outside of the organization?

People in one department cannot and need not know all of what people in other departments know—what meaning they have. The crucial measure is the extent to which vital meanings are shared. Lack of coordination among organizational units can occur if they operate out of uncomplementary meanings. One measure of sharing is to determine—in a coorientation model—whether members of one department understand key issues as do members of a department with which they are interdependent. In addition to understanding, another coorientational dimension is satisfaction. In what ways and to what extent are personnel in one department satisfied by what they know about members, operations, or policies of another department? This question is aimed at disclosing how well units in an organization are able to coordinate their efforts. For instance, what the company means to management is likely to be different from what it means to employees, but if the gulf between these meanings is too great, the Voice is likely to be discordant.

Everyone who shares meaning constitutes membership in a particular zone of meaning; in this way an organization exhibits structure. For instance, on a university campus, several large zones of meaning can be identified. The entire university should constitute one macrocosmic zone. It should have the same meaning for people inside the organization as it does for its external stakeholders. Administration is a zone, as are faculty and students. Meaning, in the form of information and interpretative schemata, flows from faculty to students and from students to faculty. As students acquire meaning from faculty they become more and more part of the faculty's zone. Among the faculty, different disciplines exist. People in the communication department may share meaning with people in engineering, for instance, but each department has meaning unique to its academic discipline. All faculty members need not have the same meaning for the campus to operate effectively. The crucial point is that meaning be shared sufficiently so that on organizational issues more similarity than dissimilarity exists. Otherwise, the organization will be poorly coordinated.

In recent years, computerized management information systems have been developed to cut through the normal channels—formal and informal—via which information travels from people who generate it to people who utilize it. Management information systems eliminate some problems typically associated with *gatekeepers*—people who are in positions to determine which information gets into a system and which does not. If an organization utilizes a management information system, management tells people which information to provide for that system. In this operation, issues of coordination and compatibility of interpretation are paramount.

Having this kind of arrangement does not minimize the need to interpret the information. Interpretation is basic to the meaning unique to each zone. For instance, people who work in the construction site of an organization might pour 50,000 yds of concrete. What meaning surrounds this activity? Through the information system (whether an information management system or not) this amount of concrete can be broken down into several numbers, for instance: amount of concrete, labor cost associated with handling it, and cost of transportation and storage. The meaning associated with concrete from a management perspective may not be much more than a few figures. At the workers' level, concrete—its handling—constitutes different meaning. It is part of their identity. It constitutes a heritage of workers who have raised families by handling and pouring concrete. What are costs of insurance and workmen's compensation to management are stories about injured employees captured in the culture of the laborers. Efforts to reduce costs of labor, handling, storage and such can be translated by laborers into jobs, livelihoods, and families. This illustration indicates that information flow between the two systems—zones of meaning—is not just data. What is crucial is the interpretation of those data, the meaning. This meaning may be unique to participants in one or more zones of meaning. Ultimately, how the efforts of those people become coordinated depends on how unique *and* similar interpretations of that meaning are.

When we think of the persons who link systems to one another, we consider people who bridge the boundaries of one zone of meaning and get people in another zone to understand the meaning contained in the first zone. This model helps us understand why people communicate within and between zones. It is not merely to exchange information, but rather it is to obtain and share meaning so that the social reality of one zone can be understood and made compatible with that of the other zone. People in an organization can operate in a zone of meaning without having much contact with people in other zones. This is another way of describing people in one system or network not linking networks or spanning boundaries of systems. Even if information flows between the two units, if meaning does not also flow so that one social reality affects another social reality, the zones may be incompatible.

Each zone of meaning, and each person in that zone, interprets the informational value of what happens by examining it through frames of references embedded in the terms unique to the zone. These interpretative filters correspond to what Burke (1966b) called terministic screens. Burke (1969a) advised us to concern ourselves with "the analysis of *language* rather than with the analysis of 'reality.' Language being essentially human, we would view human relations in terms of the linguistic instrument" (p. 317). Part of the unity and cohesiveness that exists within a work unit in an organization is due to the fact that its members share similar social realities. Their communication is the basis of identification (Burke, 1969b) because they share interpretations of the enactments they and others perform. Organizational structure exists as zones of meanings.

As people communicate with one another, they convey interpretations. What they communicate and how they do so reflects their interpretations of each situation. Through this communication—verbal and nonverbal actions—participants in one zone become known to others in different zones. In this way, membership in zones changes. New members enter a zone by learning its meaning; members leave a zone once they no longer share its meaning. Activities depend on the extent to which interpretations of the people who receive information compare with the interpretations of the people who enact that communication.

To understand companies requires insights into relationships between actions (individual and collective behavior), thoughts (interpretation), and words (narratives and metaphors). Through talk, images of organization are disseminated throughout a company and are acquired by members in their efforts to assimilate into and function in it. Through talk (including action and the interpretations others make of it), a company fosters an image of itself to its members and to stakeholders who interact with it. The mind contains images of how the company is operated. These images become important through communication.

Even if it is the head of the organization (CEO, president, vice president, manager, supervisor, or foreman) who has the image, that image has no reality or importance until it is interpreted by stakeholders. It is likely to be communicated directly through statements about the image ("In this company employees are our most important resource.") and indirectly through actions ("If people cannot get on the team and play ball then let them go to some other ball park—send them packing.").

What people in the company say becomes meaningful for other members (as well as external stakeholders) in two ways. Statements reflect criteria by which the company is operated and therefore tell people in contact with it what it is and what it is striving to be. Sometimes these statements correspond and the company speaks with one coherent Voice. Sometimes they produce discord that harms trust and increases uncertainty. As Morgan (1986) concluded, "Modern organizations are sustained by belief systems that emphasize the importance of rationality. Their legitimacy in the public eye often depends on their ability to demonstrate rationality and objectivity in action" (p. 134).

UNCERTAINTY IN INTERPERSONAL RELATIONSHIPS

Many factors influence information exchange and interpretation. How information is given and sought is likely to be governed by factors of social exchange (Miller & Jablin, 1991b). In that sense, it is a commodity to be traded, according to exchange rules fraught with rewards and costs. It is influenced by the culture and climate that impinge on relationships. How it is exchanged reflects employees' efforts to save or challenge the face of the parties involved; it defines relationships. Throughout the development and deterioration of relationships, uncertainty reduction motivates people to exchange and interpret information.

Culture and climate of each company influence how its members share and interpret information. Culture and climate are affected by managerial styles as, Morgan (1986) observed, "Bureaucrats make decisions by processing information with reference to predetermined rules. Strategic managers make decisions through formalized or ad hoc processes, producing policies and plans that then provide a point of reference or framework for the information processing and decision making of others" (p. 81). Members of an organization view information in different ways, depending on their experience, perceptual schemata, roles, needs, and managerial philosophies. Managers' styles affect the scripts their employees use to interpret information.

Communication goals of relational partners not only predict how they interpret information, but also how they share it strategically. Studying information seeking and sharing during negotiations, Donohue and Diez (1985) treated information "as any statement or set of materials that may provide knowledge of the opponent's expected outcomes" (p. 309). They found that during negotiation, information is given or withheld strategically as it helps negotiators achieve their goals. During negotiation, information is likely to be used on a win–lose basis, and participants are likely to impose rigid obligations on one another to respond. (Recall the times you have said during negotiation, "If you will give me this fact, I will give you the one you want": "Tell me when you can deliver the goods and I will offer you my best price.") Directives, such as "Tell me about your product" or "what is the earliest time you can provide shipment," are used to encourage the negotiation partner to reveal key information. Negotiators use face-threatening strategies to get their partners to comply with requests and to reveal information. A face-threatening statement challenges the negotiation partner, such as "Are you authorized to set a shipment date or do you have to check that with your boss before you can set a date?" More face-threatening statements are likely to occur when negotiators are highly competitive and have divergent goals. Participants are unwilling to cooperate when no rigid guidelines prevail for how the negotiation will be conducted, when they have a substantial relational history, and when they are personally involved in the negotiation outcomes. When an open, integrative tone permeates negotiation, participants become more willing to share information based on the assumption that they will get the information they need in exchange. Social exchange theory reasons that people constrain and reward one another during negotiation based on how they perceive each other to enact the negotiation.

Relationships develop and deteriorate through information exchanges about how satisfying the relationship is for each person. Fairhurst, Rogers, and Sarr (1987) reasoned that through "verbal interaction, definitions of the relationship are offered, accepted, rejected, or modified. With each interchange, patterns of relational constraint emerge" (p. 396). Dominance is communicated in interpersonal communication by the extent to which a partner controls the floor (amount of time spent talking) and the ability to control topic shifts (Palmer, 1989).

Salem and Williams (1984) found that uncertainty and satisfaction are inversely related: Increased uncertainty decreases satisfaction. They did not find that co-workers are the primary source of information or that high uncertainty has a detrimental effect on relationships with co-workers. One assumption of information seeking, on the part of employees, is that information can increase job satisfaction, in large part by lessening role conflict and role ambiguity. If that is the case, management is remiss if it does not try to provide information that improves job satisfaction. Even if such information is not provided, it will be sought to reduce uncertainty. Involvement—perception of self-interest—is associated with willingness to seek information (Heath & Douglas, 1991). Individuals are more positive about organizational change when they obtain information from formal rather than informal sources and when the information is ample and accurate (Vielhaber, 1983).

Information is vital to individuals' attempts to assimilate into new positions or companies (Miller & Jablin, 1991a, 1991b). As they enter a company, people need information about how it functions so they can predict reward–cost ratios. They need to know the intricacies of the zone of meaning they are entering and how it relates to their expectations and prior experiences. Assimilation is fraught with uncertainty. If new members lack access to information, their socialization efforts—the assimilation process—are likely to be hampered (Feldman, 1981). Informal networks are particularly important to acquiring information needed for assimilation (Lincoln & Miller, 1979).

Members who are assimilating into a company are willing to participate in social exchange to obtain information. This effort reflects their need to become self-efficacious (Jones, 1986). Newcomers use formal sources of information, such as newsletters, policy manuals, and training programs. They gather a great deal of information from interpersonal contact and personal experience, such as performing tasks and monitoring self-performance. Miller and Jablin (1991b) believed that newcomers prefer to use official company sources, especially supervisors, and turn to other employees as secondary sources of information. Co-workers are important if supervisors are inaccessible. Information seeking is subject to personal factors such as self-esteem, cognitive complexity, and socialization style. Many information seeking tactics are employed; each tactic is employed at a given moment based on the social exchange cost–reward ratio. In this sense, employees estimate what they have to exchange for the information they want and consider its cost. Some information seeking is overt, such as asking questions. Some is covert, entailing indirect means such as use of third parties, testing limits, disguising conversations, observing, and surveilling.

In their efforts to obtain information, individuals employ tactics that conform with predictions of contingency theory. Information is sought based on its likely effect on uncertainty. Sources of the information, as well as the tactics to obtain it, are selected based on the likely outcome set against the cost. Efforts to obtain information are sensitive to climate and culture.

FOCAL POINTS OF ANALYSIS

As we examine the processes by which information is obtained, shared, and interpreted in companies, our attention is directed to intra-individual factors, as well as those of groups and the entire company. Underpinning this process are factors such as amount of uncertainty, need to reduce uncertainty, and sufficiency of information. Also involved are the costs and rewards of the process of seeking and interpreting the information. This effort focuses on individual needs to become part of zones and to change zones in strategic and goal-directed ways.

- How is information shared and interpreted collectively in the company and by individual members? What influence do different zones of meaning have on the information that is used, and how it is shared? Are collective efforts fostered or frustrated?
- Which information seeking/giving strategies are employed and which cost–reward ratios do people see attached to giving and receiving information?
- How successfully does information cross organizational boundaries between the company and the systems that need and use the information? Do appropriate, constructive zones of meaning bridge these boundaries?
- Are managers and their personnel satisfied by the amount and quality of the information they have?

CONCLUSION

Information is a key variable in the way companies operate, but rather than focusing on whether people have sufficient information, a more constructive approach to assessing the quality of a company is to identify zones of meaning and determine whether they overlap and interlock sufficiently to sustain the efforts of the employees among themselves and in coordination with stakeholders outside of the organization. Analysis that focuses on zones of meaning is offered as a refinement of the traditional information network analysis that looks at how information flows between individuals and the units in which they operate.

People seek information and apply schemata to interpret the behavior of one another and to know which behavior they should enact to be perceived as competent in support of their company. One problem people face in this regard is knowing which information is useful. This question is vital to those who are responsible for guiding the destinies of organizations, divisions, and departments. It is vital to employees throughout a company who want to know how well they do their job and how they relate to the company, to one another, and to people who are outside of it.

Writing about information exchange in an organization is easy. Establishing the processes required to obtain and interpret it—vital to the success of a company—is difficult. Information must be packaged; it does not always come complete with instructions regarding how it is to be interpreted and used. From the point of view of stakeholders, this means that if organizations do not provide information and explain what it means so they can understand what is going on, they are likely to turn elsewhere for information, opinion, and interpretation. They are likely to give their stakes to the people and organizations that do the best job of creating reliable and useful interpretations, a challenge to companies seeking to achieve productivity and quality.

5

Managing as Symbolic Action: Enacting Interpretations in Organizational Settings

For many years, interest in perceptual processes, employee attitudes, managerial styles, tangible reward systems, and role performance carried the most weight in studies of organizations. In the past decade, however, meaning has come to play a central role in these studies. Recent interest in interpretative approaches has focused attention on symbols utilized by organization members to regulate their activities and to build harmony with external stakeholders. Part of the impetus for this trend, as stated in chapter 4, is individuals' need to obtain and interpret information in order to eliminate or lessen uncertainty. In their personal and organizational lives, people strive for meaningfulness, predictability, and permanence. For this reason, they adopt the grammar of symbol systems unique to the companies and their subunits to which they belong and with which they interact.

So powerful is the impact of language on perception and thought that Burke (1934) reasoned, "If language is the fundamental instrument of human cooperation, if there is an 'organic flaw' in the nature of language, we may well expect to find this organic flaw revealing itself through the texture of society" (p. 330). Words, especially those central to each corporate culture, serve as terministic screens that filter perceptions of reality concerning each organization's marketing, operating, personnel, and public policy environments.

Investigators have drawn attention to verbal and nonverbal sources of meaning such as narratives, stories, myths, premises, metaphors, and artifacts. In this analysis, narratives, themes, and metaphors have been featured as unobtrusive means for control (Tompkins & Cheney, 1985), tactics by which members exercise power politics (Mumby, 1987), and images of organization (Morgan, 1986). Smircich (1983b) set the tone for this analysis as she concluded, "The stability, or organization, of any group activity depends upon the existence of common modes of interpretation and shared understanding" (p. 55). Shared meaning allows organization members to engage in routine, coordinated activities and gives them focal points for handling turbulence. Taking issue with the notion that management's view of culture dominates subordinates' thinking, *BusinessWeek* ("Corporate culture," 1980) concluded: "Employees cannot be fooled. They understand the real priorities in the corporation. At the first inconsistency they will become confused, then reluctant to change, and finally intransigent" (p. 151).

To coordinate their employees' efforts, managers should empower them by enacting an appropriate narrative with them. Stressing this point, Koch and Deetz (1981) concluded, "Message construction cannot only or even primarily be concerned with the effective presentation of information but fundamentally involves an enactment of the consensual reality which allows the information to be understood in one way or another" (p. 4). This consensual reality defines, predicts, and coordinates activities, and is conveyed through narratives unique to each company and industry. Stressing the importance of culture as consensual meaning, Bantz (1983) defined organizational communication as collective efforts to create, maintain, and transform meanings and expectations. Thus, companies create and process culture as shared meaning.

Meaning is captured in many vehicles. One such vehicle, metaphor, contains dominant themes and shapes thoughts and actions of people in organizations (Deetz & Mumby, 1985). So do image (Morgan, 1986), archetype (Mitroff, 1983), and paradigm (Pfeffer, 1981). Interest in such vehicles has shifted research and managerial perspectives from a mechanistic functionalism to interpretivism (Putnam, 1983).

This chapter examines the vehicles by which meaning is employed in organizations. It builds on the foundation laid in chapter 3 that narrative form and content give coherence and provide order for enacting companies. Chapter 4 focused on how interpretations reduce uncertainty. This discussion argues that despite all other measures of what a company is or should be, what really counts is the meaning internal and external people enact on behalf of or in response to it. Meaning of relationships, work performance expectations, and goal achievement guide activities of managers and employees and affect how the company is regarded by external stakeholders. The theme of this chapter is that meaning defines the contingencies organizational members enact as they adapt their efforts to the performance guidelines, constraints, and rewards voiced in organizational culture.

Culture consists of jargon unique to each company, and its subunits. It contains the knowledge of the company (expressed as beliefs and attitudes) as well as its values and rules, those relating to communication behavior, work performance, and interpretative frameworks. Although no company has a single culture, its variations (subcultures) define which behavior and judgments are appropriate and allowable. To the extent that it focuses on some alternatives to the exclusion of others, culture influences the actions of company members.

Meaning does more than define reality. It prescribes how people should act. Because of their shared interpretations of this meaning, members of companies know what is expected of them. Enacting interpretations entails negotiating stakes with other members of the company and with people who interact with it. The combination of knowing what is expected and knowing the reward–cost benefits of performing enactments is a crucial aspect in explaining how people coordinate organizational behavior. Words vital to individual and collective performance constitute propositions that prescribe preferred actions. In this sense, we think of these key terms as propositions.

MANAGEMENT AS SYMBOLIC ACTION

Management is symbolic action (Pfeffer, 1981). But so is the activity of employees and stakeholders of each company. Arguments that management is symbolic action are instructive in what they accomplish as well as what they fail to do. Pfeffer's (1981) view of this issue, for instance, featured managers' persuasive use of language and other symbols, such as ceremonies and settings, to create shared meaning among employees about the reality relevant to the organization and its members. This view assumes that managers write the scripts that employees enact.

Pfeffer's commitment to this managerial view of organizational communication reflected his desire to reconcile two competing positions, one that external forces shape organizational behavior and the second that interpretations of organizational meaning shape employees' perceptions and behavior. If management is to guide an organization, he reasoned, it must "provide explanations, rationalizations, and legitimation for the activities undertaken in the organization" (p. 4). Managers have even more power when people do not have information about the organization and lack well-formed opinions. Under such circumstances, management can create "symbolic" versions of the organization. When employees have data about an organization, Pfeffer advised managers to establish "paradigms or systems of shared meaning" that are stable and resist change (p. 21).

Discussing this line of analysis, Eisenberg (1986) concluded, "Through communication individuals over time create, maintain, and transform the social realities they inhabit. Organizations are richly textured 'symbolic fields' in which root-metaphors, stories, and myths continually generate interpretations for ongoing events" (p. 89). This preferred view of symbolic action goes beyond the notion that symbols are vehicles by which information is conveyed between people and across time (Eoyang, 1983). A more accurate view is that symbolic action "is not merely a literal indication of specific objects or events, but a metaphorical process through which one object or event is understood in relation to another" (Boland & Hoffman, 1983, p. 187). Symbolic action occurs, not because symbols refer to things, but because people enact the meaning, especially the attitudes, that are embedded in words. To act is to attitudinize, to "dance an attitude" (Burke, 1973, p. 9).

Sensitivity to the impact meaning has on organizational behavior distinguishes interpretivism from the functional, mechanistic approach. Contrasting these views, Putnam (1983) pointed to the mechanistic assumption that "an organization portrays a sense of uniformity in philosophy, goals, and procedures. Action is purposefully and rationally consistent with this uniform mission." This managerial bias is "governed by a concern for technical efficiency and organizational effectiveness" (p. 45). A functional view of organizational communication treats messages as "tangible substances that travel across physical boundaries. Meanings reside in the sender's view of the message content. Transmission problems block information flow and lead to bureaucratic ineffectiveness" (p. 45).

As Putnam (1983) continued, "Interpretivists adopt a meaning-centered view of organizational communication. Social reality is constituted through the words, symbols, and actions that members invoke." For this reason, messages can be treated "as the symptoms of and means for developing social meanings" (p. 40). Interpretivism prefers an enactment view of organizational communication that features meanings. These "meanings are enacted from verbal and nonverbal messages. They evolve from interaction processes and from the ways that individuals make sense of their talk. Process refers to interaction that evolves over time through ongoing sets of interlocked behaviors" (Putnam, 1983, p. 45). Interpretivism postulates that people seek to formulate useful attitudes that lead to rewards and avoid punishments.

Factions are important focal points, especially for *critical interpretivists* who examine these issues with the purpose of "uncovering communication distortion and to free individuals from exploitation, alienation, and arbitrary forms of authority" (Putnam, 1983, p. 48). The purpose of critical interpretivism is "to remove blockages and contradictions that prevent individuals from developing their own potential and from constructing their own activities" (p. 48). The key issue is whether the amount of agreement needed to enact a company comes from management or results from interaction between employees who also engage in decision making with managers (Putnam, 1983). This point of view extends also to external stakeholders who challenge or affirm the meaning companies use as rationale for their decisions and operations. Critical interpretivism examines which organizational practices and meanings are undesirable because they are counter to the human spirit. It seeks to differentiate between value orientations that achieve happiness and those that produce unhappiness.

This analysis can extend to activities that occur beyond the boundaries of organizations. Giving breadth to interpretivism, Eisenberg (1986) concluded: "Some writers have gone so far as to argue that symbolic domination is *the* critical process to study in organizations. But while most current research focuses on the impact of domination *within* organization, the trend seems to be toward examining how communication and power in organizations affects and reflects inequities in society as a whole" (p. 94). This theme is discussed in chapters 9 and 10. The objective is to think of organizations' symbolic action through culture. Such discussions consider whether managers lead or follow the development of culture and how organizational behaviors flow from it and contribute to it. In both senses, members of organizations must manage the meaning needed to coordinate their efforts—systematically and knowledgeably, rather than randomly.

This brief review of organizational meaning requires that we consider the relationship between words and actions as a foundation for examining management and employee performance as symbolic action. An important theme in this analysis is the image or persona of management that can influence employees quite independently from the acts of individual managers. Management, especially in large companies, is meaning, as symbolic action. Employees often make statements that reflect the view that management speaks with a singular, univocal persona. Evidence of this phenomena is found in statements such as "management wants," "management says," "management goals," or "He/She is management." The image of management, as a set of performance expectations, may be more potent than the actuality of management. Acts by individual managers are the voices of the management Voice. If employees challenge decisions made by individual managers, they refute such statements by generalizing "that is a management decision."

Culture, subculture, and other focal points for investigating organizational meaning provide what Shrivastava and Schneider (1984) called *organizational frames of reference*. These consist of the *categories* organizational members use to make data meaningful; one dominant means for categorization is archetypal business metaphors. These frames are brought to life in an organizational sense once they are translated into *methods* for ordering, storing, and making sense of information as is done, for instance, through accounting practices or strategic planning. Organizational interpretative frames and management systems are contrasted to other systems, personal experience, organizational rules, and decision rules to determine whether they match what organizational members think to be reality (*reality tests*). These frames become useful for understanding companies when they are translated into organizational systems and used to plan, evaluate, and guide the company.

WORDS AND ACTIONS

How does meaning lead to action? The traditional word–idea–action relationship draws on mechanistic assumptions that behavior results from incentives that bosses manipulate through rewards and punishments. This model assumes that they control employees by manipulating rewards and the thoughts employees have about them. This model assumes that behavior flows from opinions, which flow from language and thought of about the company, which managers shape.

Taking a contrary view, Bem (1972) argued that attitudes follow behavior; when people act, they form attitudes. When they think about their behavior they rationalize why they act as they do and conjure up attitudes that are congruent with the behavior. In organizational terms, employees' attitudes toward their jobs may follow, rather than lead the performance of those jobs. According to this theory, to change employees' attitudes toward their jobs requires that the job be changed. For instance, a manager might design a job to make it more important to the organization rather than attempt to persuade the employee that it is vital. This change should work, the argument goes, because people infer opinions from their behavior and attempt to manage impressions so that actions and opinions are consistent. If employees move slowly and seem unmotivated, those employees are likely to think of themselves as lazy or the jobs as not worth doing. People who work long and hard hours may infer that the jobs are quite important otherwise they have no reason to work so hard. Based on this logic, managers may learn that they empower

employees by enacting work in ways that constructively conform to employees'
attitudes, those needed for appropriate performance.

A meaning-centered paradigm of organizational communication assumes that
individuals make idiosyncratic analyses of their circumstances based on interpretations that make sense because of organizational culture. This meaning influences
job expectations and self-concept. Employees' response to this meaning is their
enactment of what they believe the culture and reward–punishment ratios are. In
this sense, culture is a perspective or frame of reference employees use to calculate
and negotiate rewards. Expanding this view, Deetz (1982) reasoned that culture
consists of words; for that reason, "every perception comes from an orientation and
is meaningful in the first sense in and through that orientation" (p. 134). Because
meaning is shared through words, "all knowledge is relational or positional rather
than personal" (p. 134). Even so, individuals are prone to idiosyncratic interpretations based on their cognitive schemata and decision heuristics.

Emphasizing the collective nature of this process, which combines meaning and
action, Bantz (1983) concluded that "if individuals communicate and organize
solely within the confines of their shared reality, consensus can constrain the
expectations, messages, and meanings that members enact. Thus individuals create
their organizational practices; these social arrangements, in turn, can restrict
options for their behavior" (p. 56). Culture results from collective efforts and entails
powerful group pressure for each person to enact the shared culture. This approach
to explaining the relationship between actions and words emphasizes its collective
and normative nature.

Thus, managers have influence over culture, which in turn is interpreted and
influenced by groups and individuals. Group interpretations, however, have a
powerful modifying effect on those of individuals. Job performance is an enactment
of behavior individuals think is rewardable and appropriate, intending to obtain
rewards and minimize costs, given the constraints of management and other group
members. Shared reality can be used to make these calculations and consequently
shape individual cognitive schemata and decision heuristics.

To understand the collective impact on the word–action relationship requires
interpretation of the connection between meaning and enactment. Meaning grows
out of enactment. Enactment is raw material that is interpretable by fellow enactors.
Individuals interpret their own enactment in terms of the organizational culture and
the feedback others make in response to that enactment. What each person does
has meaning for others; through enactment people make themselves known to one
another. Interpretation of that impact is meaning. These interpretations are persuasive because of the social exchange that operates in each relationship, group, and
organization. Thoughts and actions are subject to advocacy; they are negotiable.
People create and revise meanings to the extent that they reduce uncertainty and
bring rewards and help avoid punishments.

Rather than featuring management as the focal point for the creation of organizational meaning, Weick (1983) proposed a model consisting of: (a) personally
constructed reality (what each person thinks), (b) generalized constructed reality
(meaning shared by the group), and (c) objective reality (events in the environ-

ment). He postulated that the reality of organizational events "consists of small grains of truth that are enlarged into constructions by interdependent actions" (p. 18). Emphasizing the impact language has on shared organizational reality, he reasoned: "As language becomes more varied, rationality becomes less bounded. Furthermore, low variety in language may produce poor problem solving in complex environments because most of the environment is not sensed. In complex environments, however, this same low variety language may be sufficient for sensing most of what is crucial" (p. 27).

This "meaning" orientation assumes the presence of the company, its operations, its personnel, its products, and its relationships with other entities. All relationships are meaning driven. What the company does—as well as what individuals do—is important for others only to the extent and in the ways that the activity can be interpreted by private and shared meanings. What individuals perceive situations, relationships, tasks, themselves, others, and rewards to be goes a long way toward accounting for how they act. Stressing the connection between language and perception, Deetz and Mumby (1985) concluded, "No matter how mediated, all human knowledge is ultimately grounded in perceptual experience. All knowledge verification and change ultimately rest in further perceptions" (p. 369). Individual perception, in an organization, is modified by collective perception. "Information is not objective and value-neutral. It only exists in the perceptual and expressive activities of cultural members" (p. 370).

The relationship between words and actions is subject to interpretations that company members make of one another and events that occur. Consonant with assumptions of attribution theory, people are hypothesis testers, albeit "unscientific" and "naive" (Sillars, 1982), and they are not very accurate in making judgments requiring subjective estimations of probabilities (Fischoff, 1976). They hold hypotheses about organizations, employees, rewards, work, and customers that they test against information that comes to them through the actions of others. Organizational analysis can look for the hypotheses employees use and the evidence they rely on to affirm or disconfirm them. Hypotheses follow heuristics such as: "Around here you can't trust other employees to do their work."; "Management doesn't know what it is doing."; "Everything works smoothly in this place because each person knows what to do and does it." These examples suggest the information that would confirm or disconfirm them—and imply the kinds of perceptual biases that accompany the data analysis. This analysis is sensitive to the terminology that is used to frame judgments and inferences.

In attempting to understand the word–action relationship, we should remember that individual judgments and actions reflect the presence of the company, the members of it. Stressing the impact organizational setting has on interpretations and actions, Conrad (1983) concluded:

> A person chooses to act in particular ways in certain situations. Although his or her choices may be highly individualized, they are not random. They are guided and constrained by a person's perceptions of what actions are appropriate in a particular situation, perceptions influenced by an individual's memories and interpretations of

present and anticipated actions. People constantly monitor the actions of other organizational members to construct meaningful explanations for those actions. Through a complicated sense-making process, they gain an understanding of how and why people act as they do and a conception of how they should and should not act. Their frameworks for interpreting human action constrain their own behavior by defining some responses as nonsensical and others as sensible and appropriate to the situation. Of course, most people are not aware of their interpretive frameworks nor of the processes through which they choose among alternative actions. (p. 183)

Group constraints take many forms, one of which is creation of names for members who are team players and for those who violate group norms. To be labeled favorably and avoid unfavorable monikers is an incentive to go along with group norms. Symbolic punishments and rewards are particularly powerful in situations where group or occupation identification is more powerful than organizational identification.

As individuals learn their company's culture, they become aware of group interpretations and expectations that may be at odds with their own interpretations. Pilotta et al. (1988) reasoned that organizing "is a process presupposing that individuals step beyond their individuality, that is, get beyond immediate and idiosyncratic sensory experience" (p. 323). This dialectic between individual interpretations and those of organizational culture gives a focal point for analysis. Members take on the interpretation and expectations embedded in their organizational culture as a means for becoming effective in the company. "The mere fact that the cultural text is written by no one does not change the fact that it must be written nonetheless, nor does it make any less valuable the understanding of the means, orientations, and processes through which communication processes effect its authorship. From this standpoint, organizations represent communication systems symbolically interlocking sense and situation, meaning and action" (Pilotta et al., 1988, p. 333).

Meaning develops through a dialectic between individuals, actions, and the company as organization. Each individual idea or person is interpreted in terms of the meaning of the whole organization. Likewise, the meaning of the whole results from the meaning of its parts. "Understanding is not a cumulative process but a transactive one. It is not the sum of test scores or indicators which aid understanding but the relations that exist between them in the individual cases which make the array of activities make sense together" (Deetz, 1982, p. 145). Trying to balance individual and collective views, Deetz (1982) reasoned, "Commonality is necessary for understanding to take place, but difference is necessary for it to be productive" (p. 145).

Culture is a framework members of a company have available to themselves as they define and negotiate the judgment–action–reward–punishment equations unique to their company and its subunits (Roloff, 1981, 1987). People acquire behavior and opinions by taking on the language—jargon—of their company. Individuals idiosyncratically apply those terms to themselves to obtain rewards and avoid punishments, and they estimate their competence to use the persona other members use to achieve rewards and avoid punishments (Bandura, 1977). The culture of a company results from dialectical tensions when participants attempt to achieve a reasonable and predictable shared reality—sense of meaning and thought embedded in language—that can lead to collective, coordinated, and predictable behavior that is useful for them and their company. The relationship between words, thoughts, and actions is not linear. What mediates the influence of other people is each person's desire to hold useful attitudes (Petty & Cacioppo, 1981, 1986).

Meaning has a life of its own. It results from what management says and does, and how those statements and actions are interpreted by employees. Enactment theory assumes that narratives encompass individual actions by this organization, its management and members. Managers and other employees add to and shape this dialogue and influence its interpretation, but even in small companies, managers do not singularly create the meaning that employees enact. Enactment is a dialectical process from which meaning emerges.

Repetitious, integrated, and consistent presentation of message increases the likelihood a company and its employees speak with a coherent and coordinated Voice. If these tactics result from enactments where actions and statements reinforce one another, they announce that key themes should guide statements, actions, and judgments of employees. If employees deviate from these themes they know that they are not in tune. New employees learn the themes as they assimilate into the company. Themes are part of conversations and guide appraisal of employees and allotment of reward or punishment. Employees use these principles to learn both what is expected of them and constraints for failing to adhere to the themes. Through consistent enactment, those narratives become basic to the interpretations company members use to guide their behavior. Behavior that is repeated confirms the attitudes related to it. In that way, action forms and reforms attitudes.

Enactments by managers must correspond to the meaning they intend to establish. Employees interpret meaning of mission statements, policies, procedures, and slogans by seeing how they are enacted. For instance, if a company that espouses a commitment to high quality encourages employees to have low product-quality standards (low in the mind of the employees), that action defines quality. Another example results from companies' struggle to combat absenteeism. Focus groups made up of hardworking, low-absenteeism employees may recommend that workers who are always at work should be rewarded for their loyalty. On issues such as this, management is caught in a dilemma. They do not deny that those focus groups have valid desires to be rewarded for their effort (especially because those who come to work do the work of those who are absent), but management assumes attendance as a minimum performance standard and does not want to give special reward for what it assumes is a minimum expectation.

People's interpretations tend to be egocentric; Sullivan (1988) postulated that "workers who see themselves as well-rewarded, high performers tend to develop job satisfaction schemas. Managers who employ meaning-making communication that stresses a view of the organization as one in which all employees are hard workers and good performers could facilitate worker construction of a satisfaction schema" (p. 107).

Management defines corporate culture by what it says and does. Individual voices of managers are interpreted metaphorically as enacting the Voice of management. What is done and what is said define one another. These statements and their accompanying actions are interpreted by employees who compare them against their expectations of what the relevant meaning should be. If management says that it expects quality, but fails to enact quality in the way expected by employees, the prevailing interpretation (Voice) is that quality is a slogan, not a commitment.

A key question facing persons who use meaning and culture to analyze companies is how meaning and culture change or persist over time. At the outset we are interested in these questions because we look to culture and meaning as the basis for explaining how people come to share the products of sense making. People in a company have to see the world in serviceably similar ways and share principles and themes. Culture is conveyed in artifacts, such as stories, that may have archetypal and totemic qualities. Mission statements, regardless of the level of the unit, are fraught with ambiguity, but set themes that focus activities. Change occurs when meaning is thought to be unable to produce individual and collective rewards.

The dynamics of organizational culture as meaning can be demonstrated by the example of an electric utility company. As it adapts to its environment, it changes or maintains the meaning that is embedded in its culture. Some of culture does not change because certain core units of thought do not change: (a) the company is mandated by law to supply electricity to customers who pay for service, (b) electricity is generated in ways that remain standard over time, and the utility transmits electricity in ways that change very little, and (c) worker performance—shaped by themes such as "work safely"—remain the same, even though techniques and materials change.

A company needs stability, but it also must be capable of strategic, thoughtful, and planned change. This may require changing the definitions of work norms and rewards, which is likely to affect the way people do their jobs. Through systematic efforts management can influence the culture of a company by altering how it is enacted; likewise, by pressing for changes, workers can change the culture of the company. Culture creates views that are usable by organizational members at all organizational levels. It describes appropriate and inappropriate options that members enact given their definitions of goals, means, and constraints of each situation.

IDENTIFICATION: ORGANIZATION, WORK, AND GROUPS

How members enact their jobs in a company is related to their identifications with the company, their job, profession, and other members of the company. A dialectic exists between each individual and the company, between each person and other persons whose efforts impinge on one another. Actions are defined by the political conditions under which members obtain rewards and avoid costs, by which they constrain and are constrained. In the process of achieving proper identifications, people—as well as companies—struggle to manage multiple identities (Cheney, 1991).

Describing the dialectic between individual and organization, Backman (1988) reasoned that efforts to achieve congruency motivate individuals to accommodate themselves to one another. Each person's identity is "the product of both persons' attempts to employ these processes to achieve states of congruency as they both attempt to maintain and at times change themselves, their behavior, and the behavior, characteristics, and views of their partners" (p. 240). Backman identified four processes central to the development of this social self: (a) cognitive restructuring—use of actions and reactions to create a sense of self, (b) selective interaction and evaluation of actions and reactions which have meaning for the self, (c) impression management, and (d) role and identity negotiation. The dialectic that organizational members employ when creating meaning involves efforts to identify with the company, other members of it, their work, and members of the community external to the company.

Meaning is the foundation of identification—the bonding that occurs as people see themselves as members of an operating unit that experiences degrees of cohesiveness and coordination. Identification affects how they respond to the meaning contained in the culture of the company in which they operate. As Cheney (1983a) observed, identification occurs this way: "*A person identifies with a unit when, in making a decision, the person in one or more of his/her organizational roles perceives that unit's interests—as that unit's interests—to be relevant in evaluating the alternatives of choice*" (p. 353). Identification and organizational involvement increase when personnel believe their company provides opportunities for achievement and permits personal access to meaningful membership, and when no competing sources of involvement and identification exist (M. E. Brown, 1969).

Identifications affect cognitive schemata and decision heuristics. For instance, Rotondi (1975) found that managers do not identify more with their companies than nonmanagers do. Both groups identify with their occupations, community groups, and work groups. They identify with their occupation and one another more than with their company. For this reason, they interpret the meaning of their company in terms of their occupation and work group more than the organization per se. The focal point of identification that is strongest for each individual determines loyalty. When people identify more strongly with their profession than their company, they tend to experience role conflict and alienation (Greene, 1978).

As Cheney (1983a) noted, "Identifications are important for what they do for us: they aid us in making sense of our experience, in organizing our thoughts, in achieving decisions, and in anchoring the self. Perhaps most important for students of communication, identifying allows people to persuade and to be persuaded" (p. 342). Identification is linked with motivation, job satisfaction, job performance, individual decision making, role orientation and conflict, interaction patterns, and length of service.

The identifications people make can motivate their judgments and actions. For instance, during a Desert Storm interview telecast in 1991, as U.S. troops were preparing to engage Iraqi forces in the ground war phase of the action, one Marine said that his greatest fear was not being killed but in not being true to the Marine Corps. He acknowledged the mystique of the Marines as an excellent fighting force. Persons who have been with organizations for a long time become strongly identified with them, in part at least as a means for justifying their involvement with them. "I must believe in this organization and what it stands for because I have been here a long time" is a version of Bem's (1972) proposition that people monitor their behavior to determine their attitudes.

Another example: Filling out an instrument that asked employees to indicate their value priorities and those of the company for which they worked, one longtime employee was slow to fill out the form; he worked meticulously to rank-order what he thought was the value priority of the company and then quickly filled out the form for his own value priority by using exactly the same list. When he noticed the person conducting the training session was watching him, he said, without any sense of apology, hesitation, or embarrassment, "When a company has fed you and your family for a long time you belong to that company."

Presocialization and assimilation processes involve taking on identity and becoming identified with occupations, work groups, and organizations. Identification involves learning idioms and meanings of the group so that the individual can communicate with other organization members, identify with them, think as they think, and act as they act. Identifications occur through narratives. They convey scripts that are unique to their company (Cheney, 1983a; Tompkins & Cheney, 1985) and the industry. Part of the unobtrusive control exerted by the company results from identifications that convey perspectives and premises that distinguish between legitimate and illegitimate behaviors, as well as rewardable and punishable behaviors. Persons who demonstrate strong identification with an organization are prone to use premises important to it as they make decisions, especially when they consider the consequences of their decisions on behalf of it (Bullis & Tompkins, 1989). To act contrary to the group is to be divided from it—to lose identification with it; to act in concert is to merge (identify) with it.

Identification exists insofar as members think that they support the company's goals and help it achieve those goals. Members identify with a company to the extent that it can help them achieve individual, personal goals; those individual, personal goals could be either directly related to the company, such as achieving skills and training that advance a career or lead to upward mobility, or indirectly related, such as making a living and paying bills. In such cases, the focus of identification leads to unique sets of meaning. For instance, working overtime to one employee means doing more to help the company, whereas another employee can interpret that effort as a means for earning more income.

The power of identification can quickly be captured in an example. Let's assume that management has decided to change operations and opinions to increase the quality of the products manufactured by the company. What a difference this change process would entail if employees held a skeptical hypothesis ("Here we go again with another experiment that will not last") as opposed to a supportive hypothesis ("Management has been successful in discovering and implementing the kinds of change that make a difference to the success of the company and pass the rewards of the effort on to employees"). In the first case, employees have a weak identification with the company, whereas the identification is strong in the second example.

Time is a factor in this analysis because meaning is time specific. "Interpretations are cyclical, both because they cannot be understood outside of their historical context, and because they exist as part of a mutually causal relationship with communication and action" (Eisenberg, 1986, p. 90). They result from routine activities as well as "through the emergence of root-metaphors that provide frameworks for making sense of the organizational world" (p. 90). As interpretations change, so does enactment; as enactment changes, so does interpretations and identifications.

According to Pilotta et al. (1988), employees constantly re-create the rules of organizational life, the meaning that influences actions and orients collective choices. "Moreover, these ground rules informing the selection and the interpretation of organizational activity function the most efficiently when they are both invisible and condensed, therefore obviating the need for deliberate reenactment of some original circumstance" (p. 326).

Connecting thought, words, and actions, Morgan (1986) concluded: "Images and metaphors are not only interpretive constructs or ways of seeing; they also provide frameworks for action. Their use creates insights that often allow us to act in ways that we may not have thought possible before." This connection is important because a company is the result of underlying images and ideas. People organize as they *imaginize*; "It is always possible to imaginize in many different ways" (p. 343).

In complex ways, words and actions come together to coordinate efforts through shared constructions of reality, identifications (with organization, occupation, work group, and community groups), interpretations of rewards and costs, knowledge of organizational themes, and terministic screens that make some actions appear productive and appropriate, whereas others are not. Considering this point, Morgan (1986) contended that "there is a close relationship between the way we think and the way we act." Thus, he concluded, "many organizational problems are embedded in our thinking" (p. 335). The good news, however, is that "an appreciation of the close relationship between thoughts and actions can help to create new ways of organizing" (p. 335).

MANAGEMENT OF SYMBOLS: MEANING AS POWER

Managers often think they are expected to create the meaning that their subordinates enact. Within limits, managers can influence workers' performance by how and what is communicated, especially through themes, premises, metaphors, narratives, and nonverbal symbols (Pfeffer, 1981; Pondy, 1978, 1983; Smircich, 1983a; Smith & Eisenberg, 1987). If people enact the views they hold, then whoever defines those views exerts influence. As Eisenberg (1986) argued, "power inheres in language-in-use—in the metaphors, myths, stories, and rituals through which members of dominant coalitions control the issues that those with less power feel they may address" (p. 93). Power is exerted through premises and assumptions. Because interpretations of reality lead to actions consonant with those views, Deetz (1982) concluded, "Meaning structures are filled with privileged interests" (p. 139). Power meaning structures often are binary, specifying that employees should do one thing and not do another. "Power can be said to be greater if it can exert influence in the face of attractive alternatives, and it increases proportionately as there is an increase in freedom for the power receiver" (Pilotta et al., 1988, p. 329).

Pilotta et al. (1988) reasoned that "power within an organizational (action) system exhibits the capacity to influence individual choices among available selections simply by translating preferred selections into expectations" (p. 329). To be part of the power system, individuals "learn to access the power code" (p. 329). This view of power suggests that people can exert power unintentionally by influencing the basis of others' decisions. Enactment leads people to do X as opposed to Y. In this sense, doing includes saying; the interaction between doing and saying becomes the basis for transmitting information and exerting social influence.

According to Sullivan (1988), managers exert influence through three kinds of speech acts: "(a) those that reduce employee uncertainty and increase his or her knowledge; (b) those that implicitly reaffirm the employee's sense of self-worth as a human being; and (c) those that facilitate the employee's construction of cognitive schemas and scripts, which will be used to guide the employee in his or her work" (p. 104). The first kind of statement is needed because employees are uncertain about how to perform to achieve rewards. People work with greater motivation if they share one another's views of reality regarding the efficacy of their jobs. This sharing involves using the same schemata and scripts. Schemata are ways of thinking, whereas scripts are ways of acting. Both reflect organizational culture. Each can be shaped through formal training and performance counseling. However, despite these formal means for establishing scripts and schemata, supervisors often do not consciously realize the influence they are having. As Sullivan observed, "They foster schema construction unintentionally through countless informal interactions in which they simply play the role the organization has asked them to adopt, as upholders of the values embodied in the organizational culture" (p. 107). And "dominant schemas, the ones that guide role formation, and in turn much of work behavior, are constructed in association with the informal meaning-making talk of supervisors rather than their uncertainty-reducing communication" (Sullivan, 1988, p. 108).

Nonverbal symbols used by managers influence organizational climate. Observing the communicative power of nonverbal artifacts, Ornstein (1986) discovered three kinds of symbols: *authority* (logos, seals, or photographs of leaders), *empathic* (plants or artwork), and *reward* (trophies, badges, or plaques). She found that "authority symbols connote meanings of legitimacy, empathic symbols connote meanings of warmth, and reward symbols connote meanings of recognition" (p. 218). Authority symbols convey a sense of company structure but limit individual autonomy. The effect of authority symbols is lessened when empathic and reward symbols are present. Empathic symbols connote that individuals have autonomy. Similarly, high levels of reward symbols give the impression that individual effort is rewarded.

Diagnosing the management of power begins by considering what power means for organizational members. For this reason, Conrad (1983) postulated that power is multidimensional. One dimension guides practical decisions and actions. Another dimension has political orientations that guide the choices regarding "which battles to fight, which adversaries to oppose, and which issues to raise." The third dimension of power, "structures of interpretation," consists of deeply held assumptions about appropriate and inappropriate actions in an organization (p. 186).

Although managers influence organizational meaning, they are not the sole force shaping what people believe. In each organization, a diagnostic focal point is to identify "which individuals and groups control the interpretations and worldviews of others" (Eisenberg, 1986, p. 94). Some of the most important and powerful meanings in any organization exist independent of any single source of influence and exhibit a life of their own. In that way, "power is exercised throughout the organizational life cycle and is manifested in stories, myths, and metaphors" (p. 94). Extending this view, Deetz and Mumby (1985) concluded: "Power is not fundamentally a property of individuals or groups, but of systems of meaning which constitute information favoring certain individual and group interests" (p. 369).

Some metaphors dominate the thinking and actions of the members of companies. Any word, theme, narrative, or metaphor is powerful when it "positions cultural actors to make certain distinctions, to highlight certain aspects, and make other parts of the world into background. Idiosyncratic, personal, and sectional positions intersect and compete with general social institutions to provide a relatively stable but incompletely shared cultural perception" (Deetz & Mumby, 1985, p. 370). Subunits give unique and idiosyncratic interpretations to dominant words, narratives, and metaphors. For this reason, they exist as zones of meaning that are coupled (loosely or tightly) with other units depending on the extent to which the meanings are shared, understood, and enacted.

This analysis demonstrates the crucial point that perceptions are not neutral; they exhibit persuasive and political influence. To act one way reflects different political alliances and reward expectations than do other acts. Observing how perceptions become political, Deetz and Mumby (1985) concluded, "What arises initially as interactively formed perception in a practical context can become reified, reproduced, and protected from examination in further experience and expression" (p. 371). Each zone of meaning exerts force on other meanings, some of which are external to the organization, whereas others are internal. For this reason, the "origin of power is not with the individuals who possess information, but in the system of meaning which constitutes information" (Deetz & Mumby, 1985, p. 372). Data are merely data until they are interpreted and their implications are understood. How they are interpreted has a lot to do with the power exerted through zones of meaning.

Ideology is embedded in dominant metaphors that make "sense only because we are able to overlay one aspect of our experience on another" (Deetz & Mumby, 1985, p. 377). Metaphors contain ideology, the product of political interests within the company. Perceptions are restricted by metaphors and perspectives—orientations by which individuals view reality. This analysis applies not only to interpretations of physical reality, such as the ethics involved in strip mining and clear cutting as ways of doing business, but it also gives insight into management styles, interaction rituals, and scripts that constitute what is said and how it is interpreted.

Power is neither a universal concept running throughout all companies, nor merely the opinions of managers. It takes several forms: power as good, resource control, instinctive drive, political influence, charisma, and controlling others while maintaining personal autonomy (Goldberg, Cavanaugh, & Larson, 1983). These versions of power exist not only in the thoughts of managers, but also for subordinates. They become enacted. Exhibits of power grow from the personae of role performance.

Dominant Narrative sets a context for the meaning of terms and symbols that permeate a company. Terms take on meaning in context, one of which is the language society or culture into which each employee is assimilated. Each language society has unique idioms and meanings for more broadly held idioms—idioms that are known and used by other subgroups or subcultures. In this way, meanings, subject to influence by managers and employees, have a life of their own. Dominant Narratives of organizational life resist change. For this reason, the greatest influence organizational actors have is not over dominant meanings, but in their application and interpretation of which enactments are appropriate to achieving meaningful ends.

CONVERGENCE OF GROUP MEANING

Shared meaning, shared reality—these concepts dominate interpretivist approaches to organizational communication as a rationale for how people in companies know how to coordinate their activities. Consequently, they raise an important question: How do members of an organization come to share meanings? Shared reality exists within zones of meaning and results from terministic screens unique to the group. Jargon and idioms constitute terministic screens that give specific views of reality. By sharing jargons and having similar experiences, persons in each zone of meaning come to have frames of reference or perspectives that lead to or allow them to coordinate efforts.

The process by which individuals come to have a shared meaning is called *convergence*. One explanation of this phenomenon is that people have experiences about which they talk. As they talk they realize that others have had similar experiences. Once they share terms for that experience, meaning converges (becomes shared; Rogers & Kincaid, 1981). This convergence model "stresses the mutual exchange of information in order to reach common meanings" (Rogers &

Kincaid, 1981, p. xiii). People give meaning to information that is exchanged until convergence occurs.

Koch and Deetz (1981) are among those who have criticized this view of convergence by arguing that the sharing of reality comes from not having similar experiences or coorienting to things in reality. Rather, they argued, "perception is of an already (interpreted) meaningful world" (p. 2). By taking on language and the perceptions that accompany them, people come to share views of reality that may differ from views shared by members of other subunits. This model features language; once terms are imposed on experience, they give peculiar interpretations of those experiences. Language—unique jargon—is the key to convergence, not shared experience. People learn those jargons during assimilation. Knowledge of each jargon and the unique perspective it contains is basic to employees' identification. People like to be like those "who speak their language."

Providing an important explanation of convergence, Bormann (1983) sought to learn how people create, raise, and sustain group consciousness. How does that "sum total" occur? He answered that convergence results when organizational members share fantasies, not of experiences, but of the talking about those experiences.

Fantasies result when a member of a group comments on experiences other members talk about and know in common. In this way people make public what was internal to them; they also take into themselves what others think. The fantasy takes a narrative form. "When members of the organization share a fantasy, they have jointly experienced the same emotions; they have developed the same attitudes and emotional responses to the personae of the drama; and they have interpreted some aspect of their experience in the same way. They have thus achieved symbolic convergence about their common experiences" (Bormann, 1983, p. 104). The power of symbolic convergence, Bormann believed, is due to "the human tendency to want to understand events in terms of people enacting purposive scenarios" (p. 104). This analysis consists for four key concepts. The dramatic message that enlivens shared experience is a *fantasy theme*. When people share fantasies and fantasy types, they join in a *rhetorical vision*. This vision unifies the fantasies and gives the persons who hold them a view of the company and its relationship to its subunits and its environment. All of the people who share the vision constitute a *rhetorical community*.

Reacting to any view of convergence that requires group discussion as the basis of its explanation, Eisenberg (1986) argued that too much discussion can actually be harmful in a company because it allows people to discover where they disagree rather than necessarily producing agreement. Eisenberg continued, "Strong bonds can be created in organizations without shared interpretations, and efforts to promote sharing may in fact inhibit the formation of such bonds. Through the limitation of communication or use of ambiguous or metaphorical language, groups can focus on a sense of community, while at the same time preserving unique beliefs and interpretations" (p. 92). For this reason, he suggested that organizational communication research "can benefit from the emphasis on commonality and complementarity" (p. 92). Persons who enact companies and study them should not be so enamored of group processes as the basis for achieving consensus. Uniformity is not necessary or inherently fruitful in a company. In addition, "the presumption that shared understandings are necessary for smooth coordination should be questioned. It appears that smooth coordination can occur even under conditions of minimal sharing" (Eisenberg, 1986, p. 92). Arguing for ambiguity, Eisenberg reasoned that each person is privileged to have idiosyncratic interpretations. The power of requisite variety may actually come closer to assuring that a best interpretation exists and more realistically acknowledging the impossibility of achieving consensus.

From this review of different versions of convergence, a theme emerges that regardless of shared experiences or shared talk, a key aspect of convergence is the shared vocabulary that gives people similar perspectives, unique to each zone of meaning. Central to each vocabulary is a complex of metaphors, themes, and principles that guide coordinated behavior. According to Deetz and Mumby (1985), "Information as structured by particular metaphors serves hidden power interests and ultimately certain groups and individuals by presenting a social reality which preserves the prevailing system of domination which arose at particular times reflecting certain historical conditions" (p. 384). Bits of information cannot stand as a message separate from the experience, language, and context that give them definition. For instance, an experienced worker may interpret information differently than a less experienced worker might. Part of this can be understanding and increased acuity created by experience, and it can be a "trained incapacity" that results because people have grown accustomed to one set of interpretations beyond which they cannot see (Burke, 1965).

Organizational change is based on enacted changes of meaning that may or may not be fostered by management. These changes may be overt with key people attempting strategically to change what and how employees perform by giving a new sense of company vision, mission, and tactic. For example, managers of a division of Southwestern Bell Telephone decided to implement a program to improve the quality of employee performance. They promulgated the slogan, "Even though we are the only phone company in town, don't act as though we are." Customers were encouraged to call and complain about their service. They did. Employees were upset by the campaign, because it implied they were arrogant and indifferent. It caused them additional effort to lessen customer complaints. The bottom line was good, however, because after the program was implemented, surveys of customer service showed increasing levels of customer satisfaction.

This kind of change may occur through strategic alteration of culture, myths, histories (interpretations of the corporate history), metaphors, symbols, images, persona, and narratives that make up the fabric—enact—of the corporate culture. As well as being changed strategically, the meaning of an organization may change accidentally—nonstrategically. Slowly, people may come to talk about the company as obsolete and an unpleasant place in which to work, or external occurrences may cause jolts that require new interpretations. Narratives, images, symbols, persona—all parts of culture may slowly come to reflect this new meaning. Once change occurs, the company is likely to become what employees think it is.

Interpretations may converge. Employees come to understand and share compatible views.

ORGANIZATIONAL CULTURE AS METAPHOR

More than ways of embellishing discourse, metaphors are means for thinking about and seeing our world (Morgan, 1986). They express culture. Some metaphors are totemic, explaining origins of companies, departments, or processes, whereas other metaphors are archetypal—universal to many companies and occupations. As examples of managerial archetypes, Mitroff (1983) pointed to drill sergeants, wet blankets, land mines, and mortars; each company has archetypal managers. Other archetypal metaphors include a school's mascot or its mission (turning out "rocket scientists" or "underwater basket weavers"). Being universal, metaphors supply unity and predictability.

Metaphoric language is understandable and memorable, especially when it is part of routine conversations (McCabe, 1988). Metaphors produce frames for understanding. How individuals comprehend one another depends on their ability to share existing frames of understanding and create new ones by using old frames, a unique quality of metaphors (Engel, 1988). Frequent use of metaphors in company communication is associated with traits such as openness, flexibility, and responsiveness (Fine & Lockwood, 1986). They are more likely to be used to express feelings than to explain what people did (Fainsilber & Ortony, 1987).

Metaphors compare two concepts, based on A-is-B relationships. People coordinate their efforts in companies by using metaphors as units of analysis that rest on commonplace A-is-B expressions such as, "This company is: a machine, ...a mad-house, ...a zoo, or...one big happy family." Viewed as A-is-B relationships, metaphors are voiced as "X employee is a ..."; "This department is a ..."; or "This company is like a ...." The focal point of this analysis is to isolate recurring and predominant metaphors that constitute clusters. Employees use clusters as a way of seeing the company or anything else. Each term in the cluster modifies other terms making the entire cluster a meaningful statement. Such analysis reveals "current reality and conceptions of the members of the organization" (Koch & Deetz, 1981, p. 13).

Examining symbolic clusters, Pondy (1983) found military myths and metaphors embedded in language used in Chinese communes. Hirsch and Andrews (1983) isolated the unique jargon and image clusters that are employed during rough and tumble corporate takeovers: courtship, warfare, western, chivalry, macho, nautical, games, "Jaws," and sport. Key personae in takeovers are head hunters, cupids, black knights, white knights, sharks, and hired guns. Jargon unique to the Navy, Evered (1983) found, includes abbreviations, acronyms, and vocabulary of seafaring, including nautical slang. These terms express a Navy culture and lead to enactments that are typical of it.

Cluster analysis of metaphors begins with an identification of the few dominant metaphors that exist in a zone of meaning. These metaphors do not stand alone but modify one another. Therefore, cluster analysis explores interconnections between metaphors. For instance, in an organization, commitment to quality and productivity may be two dominant metaphors that are championed at the management level. One department understands these metaphors and sees them as complementing one another, to believe that quality of effort will increase productivity. Another department, because of the nature of its operations, believes that an increase in quality will harm productivity; taking more time to do a job well can lower productivity because more input is required to achieve less output (although of a higher quality).

Individual metaphors become meaningful as they are associated with global (archetypic, totemic, or root) ones, especially those that characterize and differentiate kinds of structure. Individuals use metaphors to describe key aspects of each company. They are used in regard to self, colleagues, customers/clients, company, management, subordinates, industry, products, service, planning, policies, and operations. Each group that uses the same metaphor in the same way is a *metaphoric subculture*, which thereby shares views of reality. We look for agreement (the same metaphors are used for the same objects or activities) and understanding (extent to which the meaning of the metaphors is shared by individuals at different levels of the organization). For these reasons, metaphor is a viable candidate for explaining how loosely coupled organizations can operate.

Morgan (1986) reasoned that metaphors are powerful because they allow people to see something in terms of something else. "By using different metaphors to understand the complex and paradoxical character of organizational life, we are able to manage and design organizations in ways that we may not have thought possible before" (p. 13). For instance, he continued, organizations can be thought of "as machines made up of interlocking parts that each play a clearly defined role in the functioning of the whole," as "organisms" with particular needs, or "brains" capable of innovation and thought, as "cultures" each of which has unique "ideas, values, norms, rituals, and beliefs that sustain organizations as socially constructed realities" (pp. 13–14). They are "political entities" or "psychic prisons." As brains, "organizations are information-processing systems capable of learning to learn" (p. 80). Each metaphor conveys its unique set of schemata, scripts, and enactments.

By examining the images of organization, Morgan (1986) sought "to understand and grasp the multiple meanings of situations and to confront and manage contradiction and paradox, rather than to pretend that they do not exist." He chose "to do this through metaphor, which ... is central to the way we organize and understand our world" (p. 339). He reasoned that with metaphors "we can frame and reframe our understanding of the same situation, in the belief that new kinds of understanding can emerge from the process" (p. 340). His system of analysis allows for descriptive statements that can compare organizations to one another—as well as comparing departments, relationships, and the orientations of individuals. Some organizations (or departments) are more machine-like and bureaucratic than others. Some are more creative and innovative—as a brain.

Demonstrating why organizations can be treated as metaphors, Morgan (1986) reasoned that they can be used diagnostically and analytically to determine what is going on. They can be used to manage and design organizations, what he calls *"the injunction of metaphor"* (p. 331). Each dominant metaphor "has its own injunction or directive: a mode of understanding suggests a mode of action" (p. 334). The potency of each dominant metaphor is its teleological quality from which "we can follow the implications of a powerful image to its logical conclusion" (p. 336).

Each dominant metaphor gives voice to a central idea (*O*). Individuals can vary from the central idea in how they enact the idea, but the idea is a stabilizing and directive force by which individuals coordinate and focus their behavior. For this reason, metaphors are appropriately suited for discussions of companies. For Morgan (1986), one objective of metaphoric analysis is "to develop a way of thinking that can cope with ambiguity and paradox" (p. 342). For this reason, he claimed, "Images and metaphors are not only interpretive constructs or ways of seeing; they also provide frameworks for action. Their use creates insights that often allow us to act in ways that we may not have thought possible before" (p. 343). He believed that "the use of metaphor implies *a way of thinking* and *a way of seeing* that pervade how we understand our world generally" (p. 12). Diagnostic metaphors emerge from conversations by employees: "This place is a zoo"; "This department is a think tank"; "We are successful because we do a great job of staying on top of the competition by knowing more about products and markets than our bozo competitors do"; "John is a land mine waiting to getchya"; "Joan is the departmental life preserver."

Metaphors are a major feature of zones of meaning. The real action in metaphoric analysis of companies depends on the proposition that people conceive of reality through a system of interlocking metaphors (Lakoff & Johnson, 1980). Metaphors give members the opportunity to bring together zones of meaning because they allow them to discuss one "thing" in terms of some other "thing." If metaphors are to allow employees to coordinate their efforts, "the more heterogeneous the subcultures, the more complex the metaphor needs to be" (Krefting & Frost, 1985, p. 161). The task is to reveal how metaphors operate in organizational settings. Examining how groups and individuals converge in meaning, Srivastva and Barrett (1988) discovered that, at least under experimental conditions, group members generate and modify root metaphors during stages of group discussion, giving it a sense of idea development, social construction of reality (*O*). "The group's metaphorical constructions act as paradigms, a set of explicit and implicit theories: the basic assumptions, beliefs, and philosophies which the group is continually constructing for itself and which underlie the logic, the perceptions, the judgments, and the selection and sorting of data" (p. 62).

Metaphors stabilize organizational behavior by suggesting which acts are appropriate or inappropriate. Metaphors have this power because they offer a specific view of reality. People act based on the view of reality that they hold. They act as though their view is correct until they learn otherwise. In this way, words influence actions because they define the acts that are appropriate to an interpretation of each situation. Different groups—subcultures—in a company may feature different metaphors. Different metaphors reveal different perceptions of the world and may lead to different enactments because people enact the view of the world that they hold.

They are a comfortable companion with narrative analysis, which is inherently metaphoric. The essence of each narrative is its unifying metaphor. Shared reality breaks into meaningful units in the following way. Narratives give the context that makes metaphors and stories meaningful. A dialectic exists between narratives, metaphors, and stories. Analysis can focus on narratives: extent to which company members are familiar with them, the meaning members associate with them, and interpretations and enactments that arise from them. Each narrative consists of stories and metaphors; subculture membership requires familiarity and use of its unique set of metaphors.

Organizational meaning can be reduced to premises that are embedded in metaphors. For instance, Eisenberg (1984) noted the dramatic change that occurred when an organization shifted from a military to a family metaphor. The metaphor of corporations as manufacturers might be used to look at companies to see which measures can be applied to increase productivity and innovativeness so that products can be made and sold more efficiently. Metaphors of companies as marketers, managers, or financial entities give us pause to think about assumptions and focal points of analysis that might be used to know how a company could be made more effective.

Once employees sense change in an organization, they determine whether it is rewarding or too costly; they interpret new enactments by setting them against dominant narratives and metaphors. This comparison gives them a sense of whether their personal interests are being fostered or harmed. They interpret enactments of management by comparing what they expect and prefer against what they find. They look to see whether enactments confirm or disconfirm previous narratives that had been established and enacted companywide. The metaphor that defines the enactment is used, in conjunction with appropriate schemata and narratives, to interpret the company.

Using this line of analysis, Smith and Eisenberg (1987) determined that conflict between managers and hourly employees can arise because each group keys off of different root metaphors. Each focuses actions (enactments) on different themes; if the themes are incompatible, conflict is likely to occur. Smith and Eisenberg (1987) observed how conflict arose when employees believed that the family metaphor that an organization's management had created was being threatened by new employee hiring and retention policies. Instead of using relational variables as important focal points for the study of organizational communication, Eisenberg (1986) directed attention to the importance of understanding what is going on; he has paid attention to the meaning individuals have in an organization and the ability of some to control this meaning.

Using Disneyland as a case study, Smith and Eisenberg (1987) concluded that the apparent cause for a strike by employees was "fundamental differences in world-view between management and employees" (p. 368). Analysis shed insight into the change of emphasis from "drama" to "family" as root metaphors—those central to clusters. Managers and employees developed incompatible interpretative frameworks. Analysis of meaning gives insights into the operations of a company, in this case, the bases for conflict between management and employees. Analysis assumes that the interpretations that exist in an organization "are not monolithic, but rather multiple world-views [that] can and do coexist within a single organization" (p. 368). Different world-views can lead to "second-order differences" that become subgroup ideologies, or subcultures. "Second-order differences can remain latent for long periods of time, and if and when they finally surface as conflict, their depth and nature are often misunderstood, and mistaken for first-order conflict. Such misunderstandings are important since one result of unrecognized second-order conflict is a lingering inability to manage differences effectively" (p. 368). Because metaphors capture the essence of interpretative frameworks, once they are identified they offer data to shed light on the reasons for conflict. As key metaphors change, so does the company. "Changes in and competition among root-metaphors can illuminate organizational members' struggles over appropriate definitions of reality, over conceptions of what work life should be like" (p. 368).

Smith and Eisenberg (1987) agreed with Deetz and Mumby (1985) that metaphors are not neutral, but contain ideologies, shape information, and direct attention to preferred interpretations of events. "Organizational metaphors are useful for understanding how two central dialectics of organizing—stability–change, and autonomy–coordination—are managed. For each of these tensions, emphasis on one pole to the neglect of the other is risky; the challenge is in maintaining an effective balance" (Smith & Eisenberg, 1987, p. 369). This balance occurs because managers and subordinates use metaphors to give continuity to activities and thoughts by explaining the unfamiliar in terms of the familiar, thereby creating cohesiveness by directing attention to activities and organizational expectations, allowing some freedom in the interpretation.

The key is the ability to maintain a central idea (O) that can organize activities and promote cohesiveness and coordination without expecting identical thoughts and behaviors. Instead of "idea" or "theme," Smith and Eisenberg (1987) used the concept of root metaphors to locate the meanings that "guide the symbolic development of an organization" (p. 369). Because they are symbolic frames, root metaphors undergird a broad range of meaning and unobtrusively "capture a fundamental, underlying world-view" (p. 369). They are part of the meaning of an organization insofar as they allow employees to complete statements such as, "This company is like...," "Working here is like...," or "My fellow employees are like...." Metaphors cluster meaning.

Instructing us to look for metaphors that dominate the frames employees use to describe their activities, Koch and Deetz (1981) suggested that we need not look for the frequency with which a metaphor is used, but its centrality to the clusters. In diagnosing Disneyland, Smith and Eisenberg (1987) discovered two root metaphors: drama and family. The conflict between management and employees at Disneyland occurred because the employees believed they were the caretakers of the Walt Disney dream of a playground utopia, a drama. Drama is the central theme in the metaphoric cluster. Based on that theme as a focal point, Disneyland employees modified the theme to feature a related metaphor, family: "The employees' impulse to preserve Disney's founding vision resulted in a revised interpretation that even Disney may not have fully endorsed. Their interpretation placed primary emphasis on Disney employees as 'family,' and it was the protection and preservation of that interpretation that led ultimately to conflict with management" (p. 373).

This version of the metaphor arose from Disney's enacted concern for his employees and for the park as a clean, safe place for families to enjoy themselves. Employees came to see the park as a haven and think of themselves as family, an attitude management fostered because it sparked cohesiveness. Financial problems led executives to introduce measures that appeared to threaten the sense of family that had grown among employees over the years. Executives proposed a wage freeze and eliminated benefits for future employees. Employees perceived these changes as a threat to family. Management waged a communication campaign utilizing the family metaphor claiming that families change and have to adapt to hard times. The strike further divided the factions because management enacted threats, ultimatums, terminations, and hiring of nonstriking employees. Management attempted to create a drama that prescribed how employees were expected to work. What was needed was a joint enactment of a narrative appropriate to change.

In the Disneyland controversy, management tried to alter the culture by changing the symbols and how those symbols were enacted. Employees resisted, the dialectic of the act and the counteract. This analysis demonstrates how culture is difficult to create and easy to destroy: "Once there was trouble in paradise, employees had in mind the culturally shared interpretation of 'management as adversary' to fall back on" (Smith & Eisenberg, 1987, p. 377). The archetypal metaphor, "management is our adversary," was available and powerful; it is one of the overarching narratives in which American business is cast. To resolve the Disneyland controversy, a new metaphor was needed to get employees and managers focused on mutual goals, or the company needed to return to operations that were consonant with the old root metaphor.

This analysis demonstrates how metaphoric analysis allows several points of view: the *personal*—what one person thinks his or her situation is; the *organizational*—what that person thinks about some phenomena because of his or her role in a company; the *role*—what the individual thinks based on how his or her role suggests the phenomena should be interpreted; *relational*—what that person thinks another person thinks of the situation and how that influences their perception; and the *situational*—which interpretative criteria the situation makes salient.

Observing the insights culture studies have made to the understanding of how members of companies participate in the creation of shared reality, Mumby (1987) cautioned that this view "articulates a rather limited and theoretically naive view of the relationship between organizational symbolism and organizational reality. While such research adequately describes organizational sense making at the surface level, it does little to explicate the *deep structure* process through which certain organizational realities come to hold sway over competing world-views" (p. 113). As a corrective, metaphoric analysis has supplied focal points needed to find key elements of culture. Prevailing metaphors in an organization or department shape each person's perceptions of what constitutes information and how it is to be used and processed. The Voice of each company and its members reflects an enactment of the images held in members' minds regarding the kind of organization it is (and the kinds of persons in it).

ZONES OF MEANING AS SYMBOLIC ACTION

Meaning is essential to the discussion of climate, culture, and structuration. DeWine (1988) reasoned that culture is the product of individual thoughts that not only are meaningful but also reflect organizational climate. Climate can be defined as positive and negative attributes that employees use to describe a company, as well as their relationships with it and other people in it. Culture consists of units of meaning that are transmitted from one employee to another in the form of stories, myths, images, and metaphors; this meaning is embedded in the narratives employees share with one another and persons outside of the organization.

Management may attempt to set the tone for operations and policy by featuring abstract terms and phrases: "At Ford, quality is job one"; or a utility company logo, "Service, Safety, and Community Spirit." Annual management meetings often feature terms high in abstraction such as *productivity*, *revenue enhancement*, or *quality*. University administrations are prone to advance terms such as *excellence*, *leadership*, *community partnership*, *outreach*, *caring*, and *uplift*. How these terms are interpreted results in the formation of zones of meaning that constitute the symbolic action appropriate to each zone.

Left at a high level of generality, terms may have some use in creating culture, forming climate, and fostering performance. However, the dialectic between managers and subordinates results in employees seeking specific meanings. "What does 'productivity improvement' (or any other term) mean and what does it have to do with me?" an employee is likely to ask. Without further definition, the term remains unmeaningful or different definitions abound. Some subunits and some individuals are likely to ignore the term and others may, to varying degrees, define and implement it into individual or departmental thinking.

Abstract terms achieve more precise meaning by being associated with specific activities or operations, management procedures, and the reward system. After years of dealing with vague terms and not bringing performance closer to expectation, the management of a major company realized that it had no specific definitions and measures of its key terms. Eventually, that mistake was corrected when executives in the annual management meeting announced specific safety guidelines (*x* "reportable accidents" per *y* hours of work), productivity measures (*x%* reduction in costs while maintaining *y* levels of performance), and quality of service (*x%* complaints per *y* customers). These standards were translated into department and individual performance standards; reward incentives were formed in conjunction with individuals, departments, and focus groups. Deciding together, managers and employees generated usable strategies for improving performance on these terms and produced performance measures for them. Meaning became usable. Morale improved. Work and planning became focused. The Voice of the organization was more coherent because the voices of managers and subordinates were similar, creating well-functioning zones of meaning.

Organizational structure is based on the meaning people assign to the relationships they have with one another, on an individual basis, and collectively—the entire organization. Because the concept of structuration assumes that people in the company enact its structure and then enact their relationships with one another, key parts of the residue of those enactments constitute the company picture that they carry in their minds and convey to one another.

Compare the structuration and the meaning in two scenarios. Scenario one: "Well I did not know who to call, so I started telephone roulette. I called X department and posed my question to the person who answered. He had no idea what I was talking about and said that I needed to talk to Joan in purchasing. She never got back to me. So I started over. I called the Y department. The young woman who answered was very pleasant and said that she had had a similar problem. She suggested that I call Frank in purchasing. When I called Frank, he said that Joan was the only person who could help but she was very busy. I gave up and said...." Scenario two: "I wasn't sure of myself on this project so I started telephone roulette by calling X department. The person there put me in touch with Maxine in purchasing who I found to be the most competent person I have encountered in this company." Both scenarios contain meaning about the company, its personnel, structure, and relationships.

Companies never achieve consensus; individuals and subunits always exhibit different meanings. Subunits have their own cultures, however similar they are to that of the entire company. As Smiricich (1983a) said, "Organizational life is characterized by multiple or counter realities that could become a source of tension, provoking innovation and creativity, or engendering disintegration and disorganization" (p. 224). Groups are definable by meanings unique to them. Not only do groups inside a company exhibit meanings different from one another, but so do stakeholder groups outside of the company.

Management is expected to understand the internal and external meaning environments and foster appropriate enactments. Smircich (1983a) challenged management to create and maintain "an organizational world view, a system of shared meanings or collective ways of thinking that actualize the continued sense of organization" (pp. 234–235). To do so requires that information be interpreted and premises be established to foster enactment. People follow them because they define which enactments are preferred. Meanings cannot be prescribed, but must be the product of narratives enacted by managers with employees.

Deetz (1988) observed that studies of culture can help researchers and organizational diagnosticians locate "*distorted interest representation*" and "*enhancing fulfillment of openly selected goals*" (p. 339). Such a position is justified because studies of culture "may tell us something about the nature and production of meaning in life and may help managers make 'better' decisions, but most important, they help reveal the forces and means by which certain interests hold sway over others and human need fulfillment is distorted" (p. 338). This kind of analysis works because any "organization is composed of a number of 'stakeholders,' such as workers, stockholders, suppliers, and consumers." In this context, "the study of culture is the study of how these interests get articulated and represented in decisions that are made" (p. 338).

Employees need operating guidelines to assure a level of performance that keeps activities in line with management expectations. Some operations are extremely precise, and penalties for failure to comply can be severe. A list of the kinds of operating procedures illustrates that point: maintenance and operating standards in a nuclear generating plant, in a chemical plant, in a tax office, in a bank teller's booth, in surgery, in arrest procedures for police officers, in procedures for confronting suspected shoplifters, in the handling of the corporate books. Without doubt, individual organizations have unique standards, and the ways in which these standards are interpreted, implemented, and rewarded constitute essential aspects of each organization's culture.

Requisite variety is the other side of the coin. Throughout an organization, key concepts such as the mission statement are rarely translated into specific actions and themes by management. Employees must make some of those judgments. How those judgments are made in one subunit may differ from other subunits. Requisite variety is a concept that assumes that enough meanings can exist so that all people can have unique but interrelated meanings—and perform unique but interrelated actions. In this sense, the sum of all meanings is more than a whole.

Companies are interlocking zones of meaning; a culture is shared sense making that reveals levels of knowledge: (a) expert knowledge (training and development, formal education), (b) experience knowledge—what people learn on the job from doing it, (c) formal policy command knowledge—the "party line," including internal formal communication such as company newsletters and employee publications, and (d) formal policy knowledge—the interpretation of the party line— how things really are. This kind of knowledge often exists only in verbal communication, and it leads people to know when to "throw away the policy book and do things right." Most people's experience—organization and social—is limited to a narrow field of experience—their department, their discipline, or their work group. Managers have to work to give employees a sense of the company as a company to enlarge the culture—making people aware of the big picture—the Voice. But those managers also have to listen to and appreciate the interpretations subordinates make of the big picture.

Meaning ranges from issues of the person as self, to the self as an employee— including roles and responsibilities associated with the job. Meaning exists in regard to persons internal and external to the organization. People have meaning about customers—are they valuable human beings who are to be treated with respect or are they cattle to be herded from one place to another? Anyone who has flown several airlines probably has an impression—meaning—of what the company and its employees mean when they use the word "passengers."

On the information side of the equation, uncertainty motivates individuals to seek and interpret information in ways that enable them to reduce uncertainty. On the persuasion side of the equation, compatibility and positive relationships result from the desire to be competent and have positive relationships. This incentive provides the motives needed to negotiate and define the obligations required to create and maintain relationships. Through this dialectic, meaning forms the premises for enactment of those relationships.

The notion of an organization—the people who make up the company—making decisions is commonplace. We imagine that each day various people and various levels make many decisions. The boss (perhaps president or CEO) makes decisions that affect the value of the stock of a publicly traded company. The personnel manager makes a decision to create an innovative human resource development program or to create an innovative employee retirement program. The folks in research and development decide to continue work on what appears to be a major breakthrough in the design of a new product. An individual decides to go to lunch. That person decides to go to lunch with one person as opposed to another. An employee decides to repair a weld after lunch; during lunch that seam gives way and the plant explodes killing 18 co-workers. All of these are decisions reflect some degree of consciousness. Each has implications for others. Each is more or less public in process as well as the outcome. All of this brings us to consider how people in organizations know how to make decisions. What premises and assumptions guide individual and collective decisions?

Pilotta et al. (1988) defined culture as consisting *"primarily of an open-ended context framed by significant symbols and modes of legitimated social action that enables selective responses to changes in the communication environment"* (p. 317). Cultures make sense of time and space. They define responses people make to their circumstance. They reduce internal and external environments to manageable principles, concepts, norms, and behaviors. "The role of meaning in linking organizational membership independently of individual personalities and attitudinal preferences should not be ignored in any analysis that wishes to understand organizational behavior from the standpoint of an interpretive system" (Pilotta et al., 1988, p. 325).

How does management communicate culture to its employees? In answer, Pilotta et al. (1988) thought a company needs meanings that define and order the options available to managers and employees. Language is vital to this process. It differentiates compliance from rejection. "The more complex the action system, the greater the need for a functional differentiation between the language code in general and special, symbolically generalized communication media like power, trust, truth, or money" (pp. 326–327). "Media" include day-to-day activities, what is done and said. This approach to organizational communication should not be limited by viewing words as vehicles for conveying knowledge rather than as symbolic action. Culture is not conveyed, but enacted. Collective enactment is meaningful when patterns become understandable and repetitive. What is said—in terms of language—is reinforced, contradicted, and clarified by what is done.

At the organizational level, culture is contained in documents—such as policy manuals and annual reports—that widely proclaim dominant thoughts of the company. What is said at the management level takes on Voice. It should embrace what going on in the company—all of the individual statements—voices. The relationship between the individual voices and the company Voice is a dialectic. How this dialectic works itself out results in an organizational grammar members use to understand the key relationships between metaphors that constitute their culture.

ORGANIZATIONAL GRAMMAR

The language of a company, or a subunit, exhibits a grammar that is crucial to understanding the organization. This grammar exists because when people talk, think, and write in a company they employ different parts of speech to feature dominant functions. The important parts of speech are nouns, verbs, and modifiers (adjectives and adverbs). This grammar consists of the relationship between terms unique to the company or one of its subunits. These grammars dominate thoughts, judgments, and actions. They are embedded in metaphors and narratives. Applying this view, Weick (1979b) reasoned:

> Organizing is like a grammar in the sense that it is a systematic account of some rules and conventions by which sets of interlocked behaviors are assembled to form social processes that are intelligible to actors. It is also a grammar in the sense that it consists of rules for forming variables and causal linkages into meaningful structures...that summarize the recent experience of the people who are organized. The grammar consists of recipes for getting things done when one person alone can't do them and recipes for interpreting what has been done. (pp. 3–4)

Organizational goals and missions are expressed as nouns. Profit is a powerful noun. Products and services are nouns. Automobile companies sell cars. Airlines sell transportation. Hotels sell accommodation and luxury. Performance goals set the number of cars to be sold. Goals include number of houses or computers sold.

Goals and missions stated as nouns:

Profits	Service	Dividends	Innovation

Activities (as in procedures and policies) stated as verbs:

Issue	Tabulate	Operate	Calculate
Innovate	Research	Reconcile	Produce
Manage	Supervise	Coordinate	Open
Close	Write	Interview	Listen
Speak	Communicate	Understand	Motivate
Evaluate	Defend	Solve	Engineer
Finance	Liquidate	Paint	Coat
Salvage	Protect	Standardize	Propose

Performance criteria stated as adjectives and adverbs:

Excellent	Fast	Quick	Cautious
Deliberate	Educated	Trained	Skilled
Managed	Supervised	Coordinated	Open
Closed	Warm	Unique	Late

Unique arrangement of nouns, verbs, and modifiers reveal the culture of each unit of analysis: society, organization, groups as zones of meanings, culture, work unit, group, and individual. As these grammars exist in the culture of individuals, we can predict that they have an instrumental role in judgment, thought, interpretation, and action.

FOCAL POINTS OF ANALYSIS

- What expectations of individual and collective performance are embedded in themes, narratives, metaphors, enactment–statement ratios, and grammars?
- To what extent are organizational members and external audiences aware of narratives, metaphors, and themes?
- Do these groups understand and agree on narratives, metaphors, and themes?
- How are narratives, metaphors, and themes created in the company or a unit of it?
- Which narratives, metaphors, and themes recur?
- Are they present in communication plans, premises, cognitive schemata, and decision heuristics?
- Which terms constitute the grammars of members of a company, the voice of management, and key stakeholders? What is the grammar of each zone of meaning?

CONCLUSION

Some companies groom their images so carefully that they are nothing but image (Cheney, 1992). A similar observation can be made about the people who work in companies. All of these entities can exhibit a persona that lacks substance. Statements and the meaning they achieve through the actions of members of a company are the reality of the company, the essence of its symbolic action. Sensitive to these meanings, Putnam (1983) claimed that "interpretive approaches aim to explicate and, in some cases, to critique the subjective and consensual meanings that constitute social reality" (p. 32). People behave as they do based on their perceptions of the world—including their organizational world—and act in ways that are appropriate to that scene.

6

Companies as Negotiated Enactment of Stakeholder Interests

Companies are a collective means by which people assert their self-interests. To achieve their personal and organizational goals, owners and managers need employees and customers. Employees become involved with companies to assert their self-interest and to satisfy personal, economic, and social goals. Customers assert their self-interests as they select among products and services. In this sense, companies can be discussed "in terms of a set of organizational problems of different meaning and consequences for different organizational stakeholders. Problems are solved by sets of strategies and activities proceeding from different rationalities proposed by different stakeholder groups" (Shrivastava et al., 1987, pp. 90–91). This approach is compatible with Putnam's (1989) view of "organizing as negotiation" (p. 251).

Because persons and companies act in ways that affect each other's interests, we can define organizations as negotiated enactments of stakeholder interests. Stressing this point, Mumby (1988) concluded, "Organizations are not stable, fully integrated structures. Rather, they are the product of various groups with competing goals and interests. An organization services a group's interests to the extent that it is able to produce, maintain, and reproduce those organizational practices that sustain that group's needs" (p. 166). Essential to this enactment are individual decisions to seek, give, and hold stakes in the form of rewards or costs. Stakes are negotiable and affect the creation, maintenance, and dissolution of relationships. Stakeholder analysis allows us to see how organizational and individual behaviors enact self-interests and affect relationships.

Each company communicates with many stakeholders. How well it communicates is crucial. In this era of increasing regulatory constraint, managers need to understand how to position their company to take advantage of or remediate the constraints imposed by various stakeholders, whether internal or external. Some companies have become increasingly sensitive to the stakes their workers hold. Workers are able to assert their interests through legal and regulatory actions. They can sue if they believe they have been discriminated against or treated badly. They can "blow the whistle" if the company is violating laws, regulations, or contracts. They can leave and join another company.

Persons outside of organizations assert their self-interests by seeking and granting stakes. Neighbors in the locale of a company's plant may assert their self-interest by complaining about the health hazards it creates. How this self-interest is defined and asserted can impinge on the company's goals and operations. If the plant puts out pollutants that neighbors believe are harmful, they can exercise regulatory and legislative control of those emissions. In this regard, self-interests of neighbors are not simple—not merely a matter of health, for instance. A plant in a community is a source of jobs—a way its neighbors assert their self-interest. It can affect the tax base of the community and can be a matter of civic pride.

When regulation and legislation are used to negotiate stakes, other self-interests become involved. Self-interested parties include legislators, regulators (local, state, and federal), judges, and other members of the judicial system including lawyers, and activist groups such as those concerned about environmental or consumer issues. When many interests are involved, people are likely to experience conflict. Because of their various identifications, people may experience conflict regarding their self-interests, for instance as neighbor to a plant, an employee, and a parent of students in public schools funded by tax revenue from a chemical plant. Neighbors who are worried about pollution created by the plant may be concerned about losing their job, as well as not receiving taxes from the company if it is forced or decides to relocate. Loss of taxes could affect the quality of public education. Legislators do not want to lose a plant, but also do not want to lose elections by being soft on issues related to the health of their constituents.

Internally, relationships between employees as well as those between employees and their bosses are fraught with efforts to obtain and grant stakes. One obvious stake is the salaries and wages a company pays. Employees assert their interest by trying to obtain as many rewards (tangible and intangible) as possible. The company asserts its interest by obtaining stakes held by employees. One stake is willingness to work for company X as opposed to company Y. The amount and quality of work can be stakes that employees hold, which they choose to give. Companies have stakes other than wages and salaries. They can give promotions, titles, projects, reassignments, relocations, and many other stakes that employees can achieve by asserting their self-interest.

This analysis demonstrates that people, who are involved with companies, assert their self-interest by seeking and granting stakes. How they do so affects relationships and is a vital aspect of communication. Relationships affect how stakes are given and withheld. How they are given and withheld affects relationships. Negotiation of stakes is basic to communication in companies.

The processes of negotiation correspond to predictions of social exchange theory. Laying a foundation for understanding how relationships are enacted, Roloff (1981) observed that "*social exchange is the voluntary transference of some object or activity from one person to another in return for other objects or activities*" (p. 21). He continued, "*Self-interest is defined as the tendency to seek preferred resources from others*" (p. 25). These stakes may be exchanged between people (boss and subordinate, co-workers, employee and customer), between units (two departments), between organizations (a company and a trade association or an environmental group), or between a company and external entities such as another company, customers, regulators, or legislators.

Of substantial consequence is the negotiation of meaning, as is the negotiation of actions based on that meaning. Willingness to comply with frames of reference depends on the dynamics of social exchange. Employees and management negotiate these frames of meaning. Employees decide with varying degrees of rationality and intentionality to comply with or flout these expectations.

Even when openness is valued in a company, employees are willing to reciprocate openness only when managers are open. Before they disclose, people determine whether they can do so safely. Women, more than men, seek to determine whether their partners can keep a confidence and deserve to be trusted as well as whether they are sincere, likeable, respected, a good listener, warm, and open (Petronio, Martin, & Littlefield, 1984). One person can lead another to disclose by demonstrating these traits. If empowerment is a value embedded in the culture, employees enact it to the extent that they are rewarded for doing so and based on their perception that managers are serious in achieving empowerment. In this way, agreement, understanding, and compliance with cultural perspectives are stakes to be negotiated.

This chapter examines the negotiation of stakeholder relationships by featuring principles of social exchange. This analysis demonstrates that enactment of resources is a vital aspect of organizational communication and shows how information and meaning affect the exchange of stakes. The chapter is mindful that stakeholder exchanges are guided by encompassing narratives.

STAKES AND STAKEHOLDERS

Organizational enactments result when internal members, as well as people outside of organizations, exercise their self-interests. Self-interests are stake dependent. They interlock. Persons are interdependent for receiving rewards and minimizing costs.

A stake is something that a party desires. It can be symbolic. It can be tangible (a decision to buy one product rather than another or to give one salary level rather than another) or intangible (positive or negative regard). It must be transferable, something that can be given or withheld.

A stakeholder is a person (or group) who can exercise (give or withhold) stakes (rewards and costs) in another person's or group's interest. Stakeholders hold stakes that are valued and sought by others. According to Freeman (1984), stakeholders are "groups and individuals who can affect, or are affected by, the achievement of an organization's mission" (p. 52).

Although it is easy to think of one party as stakeholder and the other as stakeseeker, each party is likely to hold stakes sought by the other. As both parties may be stakeholders, they also may be stake dependent, meaning that each party relies on the other to grant a stake. A boss holds stakes such as promotions, salary level, wages, amount of overtime, work assignments, praise, or recognition. One view of subordinates is that they are only stake dependent and stakeseekers. But that analysis is incorrect. An employee can decide to work for one company or boss, or another company or another boss. Quality of work performance, such as accuracy, safety, or productivity, constitutes stakes that each employee holds that the supervisor wants. Likewise, regard, recognition, cooperation, or loyalty are stakes that subordinates can grant.

Setting the tenor for discussing stakeholder relationships, Roloff (1981) concluded, "*Interpersonal communication is a symbolic process by which two people bound together in a relationship, provide each other with resources or negotiate the exchange of resources*" (p. 30). Believing that stakes are a rational part of company life, Freeman (1984) observed that stakeholder analysis must consider: (a) who holds stakes and how they are perceived, (b) how organizational processes are used to manage stakeholder relations and the extent that these relations "'fit' with the rational 'stakeholder map' of the organization," and (c) whether transactions of stakeholder exchange correspond to "the stakeholder map and the organizational processes for stakeholders" (p. 53). This framework makes explicit that stakeholders and stakeseekers negotiate their exchanges based on their interpretative schemata, cognitive abilities, and message design logics, as well as communication plans and skills. These factors are sensitive to prevailing circumstances.

Looking at stakes from the perspective of company interests, Mitroff (1983) concluded, "Stakeholders are all those interest groups, parties, actors, claimants, and institutions—both internal and external to the corporation—that exert a hold on to it. That is, stakeholders are all those parties who either affect or who are affected by a corporation's actions, behavior, and policies" (p. 4). Viewed from outside companies, stakeholders are "those individual actors and parties, organized groups and professions, and institutions that have a bearing on the behavior of the organization as revealed in its policies and actions on the environment" (p. 22). Although stakes and stakeholder analysis are vital to organizational strategic planning, they occur at all levels of organization: company, department, work group, and interpersonal.

The assumption of stakeholder analysis is that if one party does not receive a stake then another party will, or the stakeholder will keep the stake until an appropriate recipient comes along. What are stakes, who holds them, why are they stakes, how important are they, how can they be used, how willing is a stakeholder to use them, what will happen if they are used, and what can be done to get the stakes played in the right way? These questions need to be asked as part of the analysis and management of stakeholder relations.

Social exchange operates out of rules such as, "If my relational partner does X, then doing Y constitutes a sufficient (or insufficient) exchange." If a co-worker does employee X a favor, what does X have to do (stake) to repay that favor? Perhaps one person will exchange shifts with another. What is the exchange for this gesture? Does the person have to exchange shifts in return, is it sufficient to merely offer to exchange shifts, or is some other exchange required—such as performing a task the person does not like: "If you take my shift on Thursday, I will do inventory for you, because I know you don't like to do inventory." Fair exchange may be interpersonal liking. People might do a favor for one another merely because they like one another and want to be liked.

A *direct stakeholder* relationship is one in which stakeholders can exercise stakes directly on one another. An *indirect* relationship results when one or both stakeholders must rely on the other to represent the case for the distribution of stakes; stakes may have to be obtained from or passed to someone who is not directly involved. Some examples:

1. Two employees who compete for the same promotion have to rely on the boss to distribute the stake—the promotion. The relationship is indirect because how well the employees negotiate their stakes with the boss determines what their relationship will be after the promotion is announced.
2. Employee A may be in a position to get a vendor or a customer to exercise the stake needed by employee B.
3. A boss may need his or her boss' approval before granting a promotion; this permission is a stake.
4. A customer needs a banker's approval before making a purchase; a person seeking a sale relies on the customer's ability and willingness to go to a banker and obtain a loan.
5. A vendor may need the boss' approval before a product can be sold at a particular cost or delivered at a particular time.

Stakeholder relationships may be symmetrical or asymmetrical. A *symmetrical* relationship exists between stakeseeker and stakeholder when stakes are perceived to be equal in worth and both parties are willing and able to exercise them. For example, two associates in a department of a company would have a symmetrical relationship when each is willing and able to "cover" for the other by performing work activities for one another. Person A in this relationship might handle the work overload of person B one day knowing that person B will return the favor. Enactment of the relationship can transpire compatibly because both parties know the other will reciprocate—social exchange—in the proper amount, with the proper ability and willingness, and at the appropriate time. In this case, reciprocation of the favor is a stake; each party is a stakeholder to the extent each can choose to grant and reciprocate.

An *asymmetrical* relationship exists when stakeholders hold stakes of different value or participants are unequally able or willing to grant stakes. For example, a boss may have money for raises for six employees, each of whom could receive different amounts. What stakes do the employees hold that the boss values? Loyalty, performance, personal fondness, appreciation, and trust are obvious ones. Are they equal to the money involved in the raise? If not, the relationship is asymmetrical. This analysis becomes even more complicated when it is recognized that the worth of any dollar in each raise can have unequal meaning for each employee; some may need or want the money more than others. Some may be satisfied by receiving any raise; for instance, a raise has symbolic value indicating that the boss recognizes the employee's contribution to the department. Those who get the biggest raises may nevertheless be unhappy because they believe their contributions deserve even more reward.

An asymmetrical relationship can exist between departments. One boss may be more willing than a counterpart in another department to give raises to employees rather than spend the money on something else. An experienced boss may be able (empowered) to give raises without guidance from a superior, whereas a more junior boss may not enjoy that freedom. In that example, the experienced boss is more able to give the raise than is the less experienced colleague. The dynamics of these relationships follow those predicted in social exchange theory. The worth, ability, and willingness of parties depend on prevailing meanings that surround these activities (attribution) as defined by the culture of the company.

How stakes are negotiated relates to managerial and subordinate style. If a boss attempts to deny stakes to subordinates, the managerial style is autocratic. A managerial style that allows for open negotiation of stakes is democratic, participative, and empowering. A subordinate who plays out stakes secretly, selfishly, and distrustingly is a saboteur, perhaps leading to lose–lose relationships. One who gives and seeks stakes openly and fairly is a team player, probably leading to win–win relationships and empowerment.

Power and stakeholder analysis are intimately entwined. Stakes may be unequal in value. They may be negotiated with different amounts of skill and as a result of superior message design logics and communication plans. Knowing that their lives are important (stake) to their parents, children might say, "I will hold my breath until I get my way." If a child could actually force suffocation, the strategy would have more value in negotiations with parents. Because involuntary responses will make the child breathe again, the parent need only wait. Nevertheless, some parents are persuaded by this enactment and give in rather than wait for nature to come to their aid.

Interest in communication aspects of stakeholder analysis leads us to ask whether each enactment is strategically appropriate and is handled skillfully. Perception of the reasons why stakeholders or stakeseekers act as they do is sensitive to assumptions of attribution theory because people make attributions about whether the persons involved deserve the rewards or constraints received. Such attributions may be based on situational or dispositional explanations.

MULTIPLE STAKEHOLDERS AND SOCIAL EXCHANGE

Stakeholder analysis entails the ability to identify stakes, isolate the attribution processes, and discover the communication plans and skills used to negotiate them. This analysis may focus on many stakeholders at the same time. For instance, if a boss gives a raise to one person and not to others who believe themselves to be equally deserving, several stakeholders are involved, including friends and enemies of the persons involved. Multiple stakeholder analysis extends to organizational settings. A company is a stakeholder for employees because it can give or withhold employment, salary, promotions, and benefits, but how stakeseekers perceive the negotiation of stakes is likely to affect their exercise of stakes in the company's interest. Employees hope the organization thrives and are prone to act in ways that help it obtain the desired level of stakes if those stakes are equitably exchanged. Angry employees can sabotage a company by delivering products or services of inferior quality or by working in ways that harm productivity and threaten its survival.

Stake dependents in a company may require someone else, perhaps their supervisor or a person in another department (such as a contract negotiator/administrator or expediter), to represent their interest. A boss of one department may have a stake in the outcome of how well a contract is negotiated by a person who is several organizational steps away. For this reason, stakeholder analysis is part of network analysis that gives attention to the flow of stakes, information about them, coordination of their exchange, and perception of stakes across networks.

An empowering view of employees realizes that they hold and seek multiple stakes. Employees can reward or punish one another in a network. They gang up on one another, and on the boss or company. As well as functioning inside of a company, employees may also be external stakeholders. They may grant stakes by buying or deciding not to buy products made by the company. The list of possibilities could also include employees being neighbors to their company (environmental issues) or a political ally (member of company political action committee) or enemy. By this analysis, a company is expected to communicate with—send messages to and receive them from—a long list of stakeholders: competitors, suppliers, buyers, employees, customers, regulators, neighbors, and legislators.

Social exchange theory predicts that persons negotiate the giving and withholding of rewards and punishments as part of the enhancement or deterioration of a relationship. Stakeholder exchange is not merely withholding and granting of rewards and constraints. Exchanges are purposeful, strategic, and self-interested. To interlock in stakeholder negotiations, participants need similar definitions of what constitutes rewards and constraints and how important they are. Participants in a relationship have to be able to assess the informational value of what each other does during the enactment, addressing the question of what rewards and constraints are involved in this relationship.

Stakeholders negotiate exchanges based on their ability and willingness to give and receive material (economic) or social rewards or impose sanctions. Social exchange theory postulates that stakeholders grant rewards or withhold costs to obtain stakes in exchange. Other parties may enter the equation by giving and receiving stakes in competition. A boss, for instance, can give stakes, such as a promotion, to only one member of a department. Several members may compete for that stake. Or a bad job assignment may be in the offing, and members of a department compete to avoid that job. To compete for this promotion or to avoid the undesirable assignment, employees may play various stakes to win the favor of the boss. These stakes could include doing certain tasks especially well or without supervision. Stakes may be social such as inviting the boss to lunch, dinner, or a ball game, being especially nice, or remembering a special event (the boss' birthday).

At face value, this set of equations seems to be relatively straightforward, but it is not. Even a moment's reflection indicates that parties may differ in regard to their perception of the magnitude of a reward, fairness of exchange, and effect of an exchange on a relationship (not only with the target of the exchange but with other players such as co-workers). In this exchange, stakes can be social or economic, tangible or symbolic. They can be given willingly or obtained with difficulty. Fairness of an exchange may depend on interpretations participants acquire as members of the same zone of meaning. Fairness results from the selection of rules by which parties engage in exchange.

Perception of fairness may correspond or differ, as may the perception of which rules of exchange are appropriate and inappropriate. Perceptions of fairness and appropriateness of the rules of exchange are subject to interpretation and, therefore, can be influenced by rhetorical appeals. Players often try to influence the perceived value of stakes and the rules for their exchange.

Social exchange theory focuses on a few variables that seem essential to understanding how effective an exchange is. Exchanges depend on perceptions of *equity*. Stakeholder relationships depend on equitable exchange or granting of stakes. For example, employees might say or think, "The boss always lets Jones have the best jobs—and get away with lots of absenteeism. How come the boss never lets me do that?" An employee who needs a favor might work 3 hours of overtime in exchange with a co-worker who will work 1 hour of overtime. In that example the amount of time may be inequitable, but fair. Stakeholder relations depend on perceptions of *fairness*. Equity assumes that the people in a stakeholder relationship treat one another the same. In a company, some people, because of training, seniority, or position, get stakes that other people do not. Thus, the issue of fairness arises when people talk or think about disparity. If perceptions of fairness do not match between the stakeholder and the recipient, one or the other is likely to feel slighted or taken advantage of.

Timeliness is an important variable in stakeholder relationships. It refers to the length of time stakeholders have to grant stakes or repay them. Sometimes, for instance, time limits of exchange are specified, such as delivery or payment conditions stated in a contract, or the period of probation before a person is granted a permanent position in a company or department. Stakeholder relationships can be affected by perceptions of *willingness* to represent a recipient's case in order to obtain stakes. People within a department expect their boss to be willing to advance their cause—obtain stakes—from other departments or upper management. If a boss is unwilling to seek stakes, employees may be less willing to grant them. In addition to willingness are perceptions of *ability* to represent the interests of a stakeseeker, such as a boss's ability to obtain stakes for someone else. This ability may affect relations with employees. *Intimacy* is a factor in stakeholder relationships because one person might expect the other to have an exclusive exchange relationship, such as a customer and vendor who have been doing business with one another for a long time.

In an organization, economic and social stakeholder exchanges differ in terms of conditions for exchange. Economic exchanges typically involve specified obligations in regard to amounts and time frames of exchange. For example, contracts, policy statements, or specifications may state the conditions of the exchange—cost, quality, and time. Economic exchanges are often subject to constraints by institutions such as the legal system. They are more impersonal and more easily detached from persons involved. To demonstrate this last point, realize that money can actually change hands, whereas trust cannot. Although person B can pass money from person A to person C, no similar exchange of trust is as likely. If person A tells person B to trust person C, person B is likely to make the final assessment of whether the trust is justified. Although people may bargain in regard to the amount of the economic reward, once that sum is fixed that is the amount expected to be exchanged. No similar precision can be enacted for trust or other intangible rewards.

Equity of exchange is a factor to the extent that perceptions of participants make it so. Ability to control the granting of stakes is basic to definitions of power and dependence. Inequity does not explain the relational adjustments as well as does indebtedness. One person may give a lot to one person—inequity—but the second does not give anything in return because the person does not feel indebted. The rewards were not wanted—or their effect on the relationship, if reciprocated, is not desired. Social exchange acknowledges that participants' perception of short- and long-term consequences of exchange affects these ratios.

In these ways, multiple stakeholder analysis notes all of the stakeholders and stakeseekers that are involved in an exchange. It focuses on these interlocking relationships and on the similarities and differences of perceptions of the value of stakes and the importance of their exchange. Multiple stakeholder analysis also consists of observing the exchange rules and their use by the persons who enact the exchange. To be unaware of the need for multiple stakeholder analysis is to miss the dynamism of organizational communication.

MEANING AND STAKEHOLDER RELATIONS

Through negotiation of stakes, employees enact organizations as undirected plays. By knowing narratives of exchange, they enact the play. They perform roles appropriate to their interpretations of the scene of the drama. Two sets of principles interact in the experience of each person: (a) those that run throughout the culture of the company and allow different people in different departments to enact roles that are compatible and complementary to one another, and (b) those that exist as individual interpretations of how each person's narrative fits the culture of the company. Shared fantasies give members of negotiating teams the ability to center on common enemies and past negotiations (Putnam, Van Hoeven, & Bullis, 1991).

What a stake means to one person may differ from what it means to someone else. Is a promotion good or bad? Most people jump to the conclusion that a promotion is good and therefore serves as a stake all employees seek. Not everyone wants the responsibilities and difficulties that come with promotion. It could mean that former friends and colleagues—including interpersonal relationships outside of the company—would change. Issues such as value, willingness, ability, timeliness, equity, and fairness are subject to interpretations by the persons involved.

Stakeholder relationships are fraught with meaning. Meaning governs the interpretation of the value of stakes, relationships between stakeholders, and negotiation and exchange processes. Stakeholder relations involve rhetoric, or persuasive influence.

What each person does to exert self-interest and obtain stakes has informational value. Performance of person A becomes information, for instance, that the boss can use to calculate (reduce uncertainty) the value of that performance to the organization. The perceived value of this performance depends on the interpretative schemata the boss applies. Under such circumstance, a boss may apply different schemata than the employee. The boss could think the quality of performance is lower than the employee does. The employee may rhetorically seek to influence the interpretative schemata the boss uses during the appraisal process. The boss may rhetorically seek to shape the subordinate's perception of the appropriate schemata. In this way, superiors and subordinates insert meaning into the evaluative process.

From an enactment point of view, what one participant does during an exchange can become information that may be interpreted as deserving an exchange from the recipient of the enactment. The ease by which stakes from one system flow to another is a measure of the openness of the two systems. If an exchange does not appear equitable to one or both parties, the degree of openness of either system is likely to change in proportion to the perception that closedness or openness is most likely to result in the desired degree of exchange, or the ability of the parties to enact the desired and expected exchange.

Meaning affects how each stakeholder or a group of stakeholders relates to one another. As Befu (1980) concluded, "The norm of reciprocity, rules and strategy of exchange, and cultural frame of reference are all intricately interrelated and organized into a system" (p. 213). The basic part of this system is universal norms of reciprocity, which assume that people are obliged to reciprocate exchanges with one another. Rules of exchange are affected by culture. "To the extent that these rules allow certain latitudes of interpretation by individual actors, actors are free to apply them in ways which they consider most advantageous. These rules and strategies, however, do not make much sense unless they are seen against the background of the cultural frame of reference" (pp. 213–214).

To demonstrate the narrative elements of the negotiation of stakeholder relationships, we return to the principle, established in chapter 3, that enactment occurs over time, through a series of encounters, all of which adhere to knowable themes that give order to the exchange. We are reminded by Burke (1969b) that enactment "is developed through a succession of encounters, each of these encounters may represent a different 'principle,' and each of these principles or stages may so lead into the next that the culmination of one lays the ground for the next" (p. 197).

Organizational culture is narrative. Activities transpire over time, through interaction between characters, and according to principles that guide individual enactments. People who are familiar with those plots exchange stakes accordingly. Interpersonal attribution depends on characterizations participants in an episode place on one another given the narrative that is relevant to that episode. The persona one person enacts defines the narrative of that enactment and sets the stage for corresponding enactments by other characters. If one person wants to negotiate stakes in a distrustful way, for instance, relational partners are prone to reciprocate distrust.

This narrative model captures the longitudinal nature of corporate culture and enactment of stakeholder relations. Culture consists of narratives replete with characters, plots, and themes. Employees come to understand the processes required of them, as the performance of activities (steps in a narrative) that are guided by principles embedded in culture. Enactment of each person's and each partner's dramas is set in the Narrative of the organization. Principles that guide individuals' enactments have to be negotiated in light of their interpretation of the larger narrative. Appeals individuals make to one another as they negotiate their relationships become meaningful and persuasive in the context of the narrative roles, plots, and themes.

Organizational rhetoric influences how persons involved in episodes vie to see which narrative interpretation will be given to the processes of stakeholder negotiation. A narrative may justify some actions and deny others—feature some principles and make others irrelevant. If one person gets the other to accept a particular narrative interpretation of a situation, that person has exerted power by determining which facts, principles, roles, and exchanges are appropriate. The other person in the episode enacts responses based on that scenic definition.

If culture consists of beliefs and values that help employees make sense of a company, that alone does not give a sense of the structure and principles of the organization, or the negotiation of stakes that is performed by each employee. Narrative provides form that makes sense of culture; form is longitudinal. Activities transpire over time and do so in a coherent and meaningful way as the principles of the company—enacted through the principles of each member. The individual narrative of each employee's activities transpires as a repeated story. As well as giving form to activities, narrative demonstrates how encompassing principles become embedded into each stakeholder exchange. The narrative of each exchange follows a form that is sensible because it allows participants to know how each step reflects (or does not reflect) principles embedded in the culture.

Consistent with this point of view, Wilkins and Dyer (1988) defined organizational culture as "socially acquired and shared knowledge that is embodied in specific and general organizational frames of reference" (p. 523). Culture is the product of symbolic action through which people create shared frames of reference and make sense. For members of a company to negotiate stakeholder relationships requires that "they develop general and specific frames of reference—culture maps—that enable them to define a situation they encounter and develop an appropriate response" (p. 523).

Not only does culture guide the enactment of stakeholder negotiations, but it also is a product of those negotiations, as is organizational climate. If stakeholders negotiate in a deceitful and distrusting way, that becomes part of the company culture and climate. Through enactments, four kinds of organizational change can occur: "(a) one general frame is replaced by another, (b) an existing specific frame becomes the pattern for a new general frame, (c) old specific frames are replaced with new ones, and (d) new specific frames are learned without replacing old ones. Frame switching, the movement in and out of different specific frames which are an expected part of the culture, is not culture change." Rather, changes in specific frames affect "the general frame" (Wilkins & Dyer, 1988, p. 524).

Many different frames exist in a company. Some of them guide negotiations of stakes. Frames correspond to zones of meanings. Each zone has its own set of assumptions and definitions regarding the value of stakes, processes by which they are exchanged, and effects on relationships if they are played one way as opposed to another.

Frame change will be influenced by the amount of contact people have with alternative frames, as well as the success and stability of the prevailing narratives. Stability is more likely "if the history has been codified in organizational stories through which members are told how the organization has survived past challenges by using the general frame, even when it seemed difficult to do so" (Wilkins & Dyer, 1988, pp. 525–526).

Frames can be changed by management, circumstances, or subordinates. When alternative frames exist, the current frame is likely to be fluid. The degree of fluidity is likely to reflect the extent to which stakeholder exchanges produce satisfying outcomes for both parties. For this reason, the longevity of negotiation frames in a company or a relationship is determined by the self-monitoring of the parties involved and their belief that their interests are served by the protocols of exchange. Some individuals are more adaptive than others and can switch frames that guide negotiations of stakes within a relationship or across relationships. For this reason, "participants who are comfortable with switching specific frames may learn to value adaptation, and this may increase their willingness to adapt the general frame in new situations. Moreover, this also may indirectly lead to lower commitment to the general frame" (Wilkins & Dyer, 1988, p. 528).

Cultures are control systems that provide norms for stakeholder negotiation. For this reason, "culture in the form of shared expectations may be thought of as a social control system" (O'Reilly, 1989, p. 12). Culture consists of norms of appropriate attitudes and behaviors. In this way, culture consists of "socially created standards that help us interpret and evaluate events" (p. 12).

Friction and misunderstanding in a company, between companies, and between individuals may result when different frames define norms of exchange. In this way, "there is an important difference between the guiding beliefs or vision held by top management and the daily beliefs or norms held by those at lower levels in the unit or organization. The former reflect top managements' beliefs about how things ought to be. The latter define how things actually are" (O'Reilly, 1989, p. 13). It is no surprise that "failure to share the central norms or to consistently reinforce them may lead to vacuous norms, conflicting interpretations, or to micro-cultures that exist only within subunits" (p. 13). When all parties share frames that guide the exchange of stakes, a strong culture exists. "Organizational members must come to know and share a common set of expectations. These must, in turn, be consistently valued and reinforced across divisions and management levels" (O'Reilly, 1989, p. 13).

People expect narratives to be accurate (or at least credible) in their details regarding the negotiation and value of stakes. An explanation of an exchange might lack credibility because the facts presented do not support that particular story. People expect narratives to be coherent and sequential over time as well as factual.

Organizational rhetoric creates and applies principles that are embedded in narrative and enacted by actors who negotiate relationships. These relationships confirmed or disconfirmed in light of principles unique to each culture. Individual narratives are compared against the company narrative. This comparison reveals which principles of social exchange are appropriate. Narrative form and substance describe the negotiation of stakes. Rhetoric is essential to the formation and sharing of meaning that defines roles and obligations each person expects and is expected to enact as means for obtaining rewards and avoiding undesirable constraints through the enactment of stakeholder relations.

MANAGEMENT ARCHETYPES AND STAKEHOLDER EXCHANGES

As well as tangible resources such as money, stakes can be purely symbolic. Among the most important of these symbolic stakes are archetypal images of organizations and managers that people believe in and use to enact organizations. As long as archetypes are accepted, they allow organizations, departments, and individual personae to be enacted in particular ways. If an archetype changes, then so must the personae of the persons who are enacting it. For this reason, people who believe in archetypes are their stakeholders. Those who wish to enact the archetypes seek the support of those who believe in the archetypes. Expression of this belief occurs through actions that affirm or disaffirm the archetypes. This expression of belief is a stake.

In recent years, new images of management have accounted for much of the change in how companies are operated. For instance, environmentalists and consumer activists have altered the public definition and standards of corporate social responsibility associated with being an ethical company. Through negotiations, managers and employees have reevaluated reward systems and means for sharing decision making. Such redefinitions have changed the nature of archetypes, stakes, relationships, and processes of negotiation.

These changes occur because people who manage companies have archetypes in mind that shape their views of what their company should be and how they should manage it. Companies are managed according to archetypes that express values and assumptions regarding which operations are appropriate. Definitions people enact on behalf of companies are reflected in the words and nonverbal actions they use to refer to stakes, stakeholders, and actions needed to obtain those stakes.

Managers portray one or more archetypes, as interpreted by their employees (Mitroff, 1983). Recurring images of managers can be reduced to metaphors that result from what they do and say as they enact specific narratives. Some managers are drill sergeants, wet blankets, innovators, superheroes, saints, Dr. Jekyll/Mr. Hydes, friends, buck passers, exploders, saboteurs, can'ts, don'ts, we'll-sees, or get-back-to-yous. The list of possible managerial archetypes is too long to complete here, but many archetypes probably come to mind as you think about people you have worked for. As you read these archetypes, you are likely to recall people who have portrayed them. Sometimes archetypes are maintained simply because they exist, guide, and stabilize individuals' views of what they should be doing and saying in their role in the company. In this way, archetypes are like dramatic roles played by actors.

Members of each department are stakeseekers in the efforts the supervisor exerts in their behalf. How the supervisor perceives them influences how the stakes will be distributed. For instance, supervisors who are dominant assume that their subordinates want to be less involved in decisions. This conclusion is likely to be reinforced if subordinates perform poorly; then, supervisors are likely to become even more dominant. If they are dominant, supervisors are likely to prescribe rather than negotiate work; this situation leads employees to feel less involved, which can lead to more dominance on the part of supervisors who are prone to give employees lower performance ratings (Fairhurst et al., 1987). In a similar vein, subordinates express more job satisfaction when they have bosses who are argumentative, but not verbally aggressive. Subordinates see this kind of boss as being effective in terms of representing the department to higher levels of management. This boss is likely to increase subordinates' sense of career satisfaction and belief that their rights are being protected (Infante & Gorden, 1985).

Operations and policies by companies exhibit many archetypes: "Employees are not to be taken seriously and allowed to participate in decisions."; "Customers are important to this company."; Quality can be a stakeholder according to this analysis—"Quality is not as important as is getting the job done quickly; only a few customers will complain and we'll deal with them later."; "Most employees are sheep that will follow management's lead. If they don't want to follow, then they are a problem and should be gotten rid of." Statements such as these are archetypes that affect perceptions of who key stakeholders are and what their relationship is to the company, as well as the company's relationship to them.

The concept of stakeholder helps focus properly on the balance between the company and those who depend on it or are affected by it. It emphasizes the sense making and shared reality that people participate in and enact with a company because they have a stake in doing so. According to Mitroff (1983), this relationship can be modeled as "a double line of influence," one that "extends from each stakeholder to the organization and back again." For this reason, "an organization may be thought of as the entire set of relationships it has with itself and its stakeholders." A company is not an entity, "a thing per se but a series of relationships between a wide series of parties. As these relationships change over time, the organization itself may be thought of as changing, as becoming a different organization" (p. 22). Companies and stakeholders relate to one another through many actions, all of which communicate a variety of messages that create and affect their relationships.

Relationships can be expressed as archetypes. It is obvious, in this regard, that no company could exist without customers; thus, buying is an archetypal relationship. Likewise, customers could not buy products if there were no manufacturer or seller. People in various departments and at different levels in a company have a stake in what others do in the company. To define their stake with a company and with others in the company and outside, people learn to rely on the social reality that defines that relationship and characterizes their self-interest. Managers who build and steer organizations operate out of self-imposed archetypes that define their relationships with their stakeholders. Conceptions managers have of themselves, their employees, their customers, organization (company, department, or staff), and others are cast in definitions imposed on them.

Standards are communicated from management to employees as archetypes. Employees accept or reject the standards prescribed by management and communicate their reaction through their verbal and nonverbal behavior as they create goods and perform services.

How the stakeholders are defined—how the relationships between them are characterized—is crucial to the ways that stakeholders find or do not find that their interests are served by the company. How the company (and members of it) acts in regard to its many stakes and stakeholders is predicated on the archetypes. Conceived in this manner, organizational communication is all that is said and done that helps stakeholders enact their relationships with the company (and other members of it) as well as the ways the company communicates its relationship with its stakeholders.

Embedded in organizational archetypes are rules and personae that are assumed for the performance and maintenance of stakeholder relationships. The archetype of the customer is played out as having to pay a price for goods or services that is at least enough to keep a company in business. Likewise, the archetype of the employee consists of performing tasks that support the company and help it achieve its goals. If the company goes out of business, so does the employee. Similarly, if people in one department do not execute their stake in other departments correctly, the relationship between the departments deteriorates, as it does between people.

From this point of view, it can be argued that structural relationships among members of a company carry stakes defined by archetypes. If one department (manufacturing, for instance) requires materials supplied by another department (such as procurement), then they share a stakeholder relationship. That stake is a major part of the structure and relationship between the departments. Supervisors of departments have a stake in the performance of their subordinates. If the performance is inadequate, someone else may be selected to be supervisor.

Effort expended by stakeholders and stakeseekers to define and adhere to archetypes is not trivial. Actions are performed in regard to self-interests that can be achieved only through relationships with others. If that is the case, then acquiring information about those others and the expectations that go along with relationships becomes a major, not trivial cognitive activity. Central to this effort is the belief that *people seek useful information and opinions* (Petty & Cacioppo, 1986) whether serving as members of a company or interacting with it (buying, selling, managing, engineering, accounting, marketing, and such). To have useful information and opinions requires the learning of or creation of a useful social reality that contains several powerful archetypes.

Theories related to social reality assume that reality cannot ever be known with certainty. What makes a difference to people is what they think reality is. The search for useful opinion and information is an attempt to obtain a social reality that can define the archetypes and stakes that are required to associate with a company. For this reason, people who enact companies and the relationships with them have a stake in the archetypes that govern those enactments. People seek to protect such archetypes by what they say and do. They see their stake in the maintenance of those archetypes and seek the concurrence of stakeholders to believe in those archetypes.

PERSONA AND RELATIONSHIPS IN STAKEHOLDER NEGOTIATIONS

During negotiation of stakes, parties enact specific orientations and personae. They may define the stakes they hold in a favorable way and downplay the value of the stakes others hold. This use of the rhetoric of definition extends to how the parties involved define one another. Individuals not only present a persona but they also try to get the person they negotiate with to enact a particular persona—which is called "second persona"—during the communication episode and vis-à-vis the relationship (Black, 1970).

One party tries to get the other negotiation party to adopt an appropriate second persona, by statements such as "Be reasonable," or "You know how valuable I am to this organization." In this way, relationships become defined and rules are established by which negotiations transpire. Vital to the development of relationships, this tactic assumes that people learn communication plans (including scripts) and message design logics needed to negotiate stakes. The personae adopted define which scripts are appropriate and inappropriate. How these stakes are enacted affects relationship development and organizational structure.

Some personae are carefully groomed. For example, Mobil Oil Corporation has enacted a persona of an aggressive defender of its industry and freedom, especially free enterprise and freedom of speech. Mobil has spent millions of dollars to place opinion editorials in major newspapers to address key issues, such as how the oil industry does business, how specific federal government policies are unwise, and how irresponsible journalists unfairly attack businesses. In addition to this persona of aggressiveness, Mobil enacts a persona of commitment to the fine arts through its financial sponsorship of "Masterpiece Theatre." These personae are designed to support Mobil's marketing efforts. This aggressive advocate and fine arts patron persona assumes a second persona that says, "I like an aggressive company, especially one that favors the fine arts." Audiences that respond favorably to the issues that Mobil discusses and its aggressive stance also buy its products, thereby giving their purchasing stakes to Mobil (Schmertz, 1986).

In similar fashion, IBM's corporate persona was designed to foster an image of competence and technical precision. The persona of IBM was "Big Blue," a corporate leader in computer design and a market leader on the New York Stock Exchange. In the face of a general public that was slow to adopt and use personal computers, IBM softened its image and had former cast members of the popular television series "M*A*S*H" speak for them. Gone was the IBM persona of three-piece suits and button-down collars. In their place were sweaters—a cozy persona of a company seeking to assist the average person in learning to use *friendly* computers. The personal computer division of IBM had taken on a new, softer, and friendlier persona and assumed that it could identify with persons whose "second persona" was to respond to computers in a cozy, rather than button-down fashion. The assumption is that stakes (whether purchases or support for public policy positions) are granted more willingly if the two personae complement one another.

This review of two companies' personae establishes what a persona is at the corporate level. Similar personae are created by what people do at departmental and interpersonal levels. Departments in companies have a persona. The persona of the manufacturing division of a company is going to be different than those of marketing, legal, or accounting. The persona of accounts payable is "45 days net for payment after invoice has been received," whereas the persona of accounts receivable is "prompt payment leads to good long-term relations." As well as departmental personae, people in an organization exhibit personae as they communicate. Some people are friendly and warm, whereas others are devious and unworthy of trust. These personae translate into metaphorical narrative characters, and they influence the negotiation of stakes.

For example, a manager may enact a set of policies on the assumption that subordinates will enact the second persona of accepting and enacting them. In a job interview, the person with the job enacts a persona that relates to the availability of work, in part conditioned by the availability of the labor pool. In a buyers' market, a prospective boss may take a persona that says, "We are special because we have a job." In a sellers' market, the boss may take the opposite stance, "You are special because you are considering us as an employer." Each of these has a corresponding second persona.

Because second persona is a relationship factor, it is also a structural factor whereby people persuade one another to assume a particular role and its accompanying point of view from which to receive and interpret information, as well as seek and grant stakes. Some information found in messages indicates what the first persona thinks the relationship with the second persona should be. How people coordinate efforts and strive toward (or thwart) cooperation rests on their willingness and ability to accept the second persona offered by others.

The second persona relationship provides interpretative frameworks for making sense of the information enacted in communication. How that information is interpreted and acted on is likely to be the result of what receivers see as the intended second persona and whether they are willing or able to accept that persona and act from that point of view.

One way that superior–subordinate relations can be diagnosed is by looking at the stakes that are exercised and the personae that are exhibited during these transactions. These relationships have a symbolic quality, constituting symbolic action. This point of view is brought to life by Mitroff (1983), who noted that some bosses are drill sergeants, whereas others are wet blankets. Some are innovators who encourage their subordinates to exercise their imaginations in thinking of new ways to perform their tasks; others are bureaucrats who stifle creativity. Persons who enact organizational personae have a stake in whether those personae are accepted. If they are not accepted, then different personae are required. For instance, a teacher must have students to teach. Likewise, a supervisor must have subordinates to supervise. If students are unwilling to enact the stakes of being studious or subordinates will not enact the stakes of accepting leadership and instruction, then the relationships break down.

If the relationships break down and the personae are not accepted, then organizational actors have no means by which to predict how they should act and how others will act toward their enactments. Such anarchy leads to randomness, which is anthithetical to organization. For this reason, company members have a stake in how they and others enact compatible and complementary personae. For these reasons, personae are negotiable. They become communication styles and are essential to how members of a company present their persona through participation in interpersonal or group communication or through internal and external correspondence.

Implicit in the statements in regard to second persona is a variety of relationships that are possible. Rewards and constraints are stakes relational partners give and withhold based on how each party enacts his or her persona. Viewed from the point of view of the superior (boss), a managerial style is conveyed in the presentation of persona. The persona portrayed by the superior assumes a second persona on the part of the subordinate; whether the subordinate wishes to reciprocate in that matter is crucial. Key statements in the communication by the superiors establish the kind of persona they expect subordinates to enact.

Think, for instance, of the second personae conveyed in these statements that may be used to end memos: "Your usual cooperation will be appreciated," or "Failure to comply may lead to termination." Each of these closing lines for a memo conveys a different persona, and assumes a different second persona, than does a close such as "If you have questions or comments, please call me at extension 1234."; "I trust this report will help you."; "Please keep me in mind as you ...."; "If I can be of service, ..."; or "We'll get back to you by Friday." Each of these statements illustrates message design logics a sender may use to offer the receiver a role, a second persona. Acceptance or rejection of that second persona has implications for the negotiation of stakes in superior–subordinate relationships.

How participants in a company assert a persona and its corresponding second persona influences the relationship that develops. If the second person accepts that persona, the relationship progresses according to the norms implicit in it. Acceptance does not preclude that the relationship does not change over time. Even that kind of metamorphosis is negotiated by what one person does that implies the response on the part of the second, and the consequent giving and receiving of stakes. Imagine that after several weeks or years of working for the same boss an employee offers suggestions to the boss with the intention of changing the work design in the department—as it affects the activities of the subordinate. Such recommendation is likely to be accompanied by a statement such as, "I've been thinking of some ways that we could improve our work in this department. I would be pleased to discuss these with you at your convenience."

Such a statement (first persona of a helpful and competent employee) initiates a relationship that gives the boss the option of accepting advice from the subordinate. In the persona of a bureaucratic, autocratic management organization, the boss is likely to respond in one way; a different persona is likely in an organization that practices participative management. The parties in this drama negotiate their relationship by what is offered as a second persona and what is accepted, and the stakes that are exchanged through those enactments.

Organizational members, as well as external constituents, have a stake in themselves. It is natural to interpret events and enactments in terms of the self-interests associated with their reward–cost ratios. Narrative is one way people grasp the sense of themselves and others in the enactment of the company—the undirected play. Evidence of this narrative form can quickly be obtained by noting how its events are recalled and reported in stories. "I went into the boss today to get that raise I deserve. I said.... The boss replied...." So goes a story of a raise that begins "once upon a time," and may end with "lived happily ever after."

Discussing the narrative form of enactment, Gergen and Gergen (1988) observed that:

> The self-narrative is a linguistic implement constructed by people in relationships and employed in relationships to sustain, enhance, or impede various actions. It may be used to indicate future actions but it is not in itself the basis for such action. In this sense, self-narratives function much as histories within society do more generally. They are symbolic systems used for such social purposes as justification, criticism, and social solidification. (pp. 19–20)

Typical elements of a stakeholder narrative are valued end points, events related to the goal state, order or sequence of events, causal linkages between events, and demarcation signs: "Once upon a time"; "and then I responded." Narratives define characters, make explicit the relationships that are appropriate, and the exchange of stakes that is likely to keep them going. To violate the dictates of the narrative is to strain the relationship requiring that individuals correct it, abandon it, or sanction one another. In these ways, personae are central to the negotiation of stakes and the consequent development of relationships.

Goals are important in stake negotiation. They relate to the message design logics bargaining members employ. When negotiation team members perceive that members of another team share their goals, they are likely to employ *support team proposal* and *raise aspiration* as themes in message design logics. When these persons perceive a high level of trust in their negotiations, they tend to use *defend/clarify own proposal* and *raise aspiration* strategies (Turner, 1990).

Relational variables such as openness, control, trust, and dominance become intimately associated with the ways stakeholders negotiate their relationships. Control and trust are factors related to stakeseekers' ability to get stakes executed in their favor. Control is directly proportional to stakeseekers' ability to get a stake executed in their behalf. If the stakeseekers can assure that the stake will be given, they have a high degree of control; if people cannot assure themselves of this outcome, then the stakeholder has control.

Trust is a measure of the predictability of a stakeholder's execution of stakes in one's favor. If one person can trust the other to deliver stakes as promised (reward dependability) then trust exists in the relationship. Trust is fostered by a stakeholder's willingness and ability to execute stakes and should have a positive effect on the openness of the relationship.

In the dialectic of relationship enactments, one person may seek to dominate. This can be explained in terms of stakeholder relationships by noting one person's superior ability to control the stakes—their worth and granting—in regard to another. Inequity of stakeholder distribution, lack of trust that stakes will be delivered, unwillingness to seek stakes on behalf of the other—all of these factors can keep one person dominant over the other in terms of granting stakes. Dominance can occur when one person has a disparate number or value of stakes sought by the other.

Discussions of control and trust feature stakeholder relationships based on the predictions of social exchange. For instance, increased positive execution of stakes leads to relationships dominated by positive rather than negative variables. Decreased positive execution decreases the presence of positive relational variables. Increased negative execution decreases the presence of positive relational variables. Decreased negative execution of stakes increases the presence of positive relational variables.

These relationships come to life, Tompkins and Cheney (1983) concluded, through account analysis. As employees give accounts of behavior (describe behavior and reactions to it), they enact what they think is a rationale that justifies their actions—especially those that are deviant. Such accounts, Tompkins and Cheney argued, can be examined as the "sources of decision premises and organizational identification" (p. 123). These accounts "allude to the rules that they employ when making decisions to deviate or to conform with the established structure" and functions of an organization (p. 123). Persons who deviate from norms of a company are confronted with wanting to behave in one fashion—which is deviant—while maintaining identification with it. They realize that stakes can be given or withheld based on compliance or deviance. This mode of analysis is also instructive for learning about the meaning held and enacted regarding companies by outsiders, such as customers, vendors, or critics such as consumer or environmental groups.

Employees' views can be brought to life by examining the premises that are revealed as they talk about their activities in a company, on behalf of it, and in response to it. Tompkins and Cheney (1983) concluded, "As an organizational actor explains particular decisions, he or she may reveal the means by which alternatives are found and choices made" (p. 127). An account is "the actor's statement about why he or she performed certain acts and what social meaning he or she gave to the actions of himself or herself and others" (p. 129). These accounts become important focal points of analysis whether used by members of a company, relational partners, or consultants who are diagnosing relationships.

Such accounts reveal meanings or interpretations the persons employ when thinking about and acting toward others and their environment. Some key points in these accounts are perceptions of the rules and premises that seem to be operating. Accounts are disclosed in the context of episodes. The key, Tompkins and Cheney (1983) argued, is that accounts reveal decisional premises that constitute propositions that guide or influence behavior. These accounts also reveal the person's relationship with self and others, particularly in the case where the account is used to justify deviant behavior. The kinds of identifications people use to describe why they deviated from a standard are instructive of their sense of the dominant premises that define relationships and identifications.

In these ways, persona and relationships are vital aspects of stakeholder negotiations. What people think of others, themselves, stakes, and relationships is vital to understanding how and why they exchange stakes as they do. Personal characterizations are crucial to identifying the relationships between stakeseekers and stakegivers. How this negotiation is enacted is influenced by narratives organizational members believe to be appropriate to the communication episodes, their willingness and ability to use those narratives, and the premises they employ.

ORGANIZATIONAL STRUCTURE AS STAKEHOLDER EXCHANGES

Organizational structure is enacted through relationships that result as persons inside and outside of an organization seek and grant stakes. For this reason, members of organizations have a stake in the structure of the organizations to which they belong and with which they interact. This structure, especially as it reflects archetypes, helps them predict exchange processes, interpretative frames, personae, and distribution of power. If the structure enacted in an organization fails to deliver stakes to the persons using it, they will change the structure. For this reason, organizational members and external publics have a stake in maintaining or changing organizational structure.

Companies cannot exist without individuals seeking and granting stakes in structural patterns. These negotiations result from interpretations members place on themselves in regard to their place in the structure, other members of the company, its subunits, and its structural relationships with persons outside of it. For instance, the idioms unique to relationships between departments or between boss and employee guide the interactions that transpire. The processes by which stakeholders negotiate their interests is a valuable means for discussing the regulation of performance that occurs in and is imposed on subunits. It describes the organizational patterns individuals follow as they give and receive rewards.

As means for understanding this aspect of organizational communication, structural-functionalism and interpretivism give contrasting perspectives of the structure that occurs within a company. The basic question is how people who make up a company regulate themselves and others (coordinate, maintain, integrate, and innovate) well enough so they can work toward compatible goals. Structural-functionalism approaches the issues related to negotiation and regulation as though a company were an object (Burrell & Morgan, 1979; Daniels & Spiker, 1987; Farace et al., 1977). In contrast, interpretivism treats companies as cultures that structure themselves through interaction and negotiation patterns (Pacanowsky & O'Donnell-Trujillo, 1982, 1983; Putnam, 1982).

Stressing the virtues of interpretivism, Pacanowsky and O'Donnell-Trujillo (1982) observed that it liberates "our conceptions of what counts as an organization and what counts as organizational behavior. These conceptual shifts allow us to recoup our notions of the role of communication in organizations" (p. 117). Interpretivism argues that views of reality are embedded in idioms by which people create a company. Because key terms provide filters, the people of a company have a stake in the idioms that guide their behavior, and with which they negotiate the exchange of stakes. If an idiom changes, the structural relationships it implies change. When that occurs, individuals adjust themselves to new rationale for giving and seeking stakes. Knowing the idioms and structures associated with them gives individuals a sense of certainty that they know how to exchange stakes.

In one culture, stakes will be defined and negotiated differently than if they are set in an alternative culture. If a culture defines bosses as superior and workers as subordinate, for instance, the definition and exchange of stakes will be different than if a team spirit is built on effective efforts to empower employees. A highly autocratic culture provides a different structure than does one that features openness and distribution of power. In an empowered environment, employees will have stakes, know what they are, and be willing to negotiate them for the mutual benefit of the company. Within the structure of a company, premier departments assume that they have a disproportionate amount of stakes and have the privilege of determining how they will be negotiated.

Viewed as negotiated stakeholder relations with persons external to organizations, the definition of companies and their relationships changed dramatically after the 1960s when consumerism, civil rights, and environmental groups redefined the relational structures between companies and external audiences. Persons outside of companies learned more about the stakes they had and how to play them. They gained more access to the decision structures of companies. In this way, structure reflects meaning that translates into the ways stakes are sought and granted. As the meaning of companies changed, so did the structures that related to the negotiation of stakes.

One of the most important changes in this regard was the advent of consumer relations departments, many of which knew that good customer relations was a competitive advantage. Now, for instance, many companies have opened their structure to outsiders who have complaints and comments. Dealership recalls are routine. Toll-free 1-800 lines abound and are even available for routine matters such as advice on how to cook turkeys or use products. This view of boundary spanning as the negotiation of stakes suggests important improvements in the conception of systems and their relationship with their environments. Such boundary spanning is enhanced by employing the conception of structure as processes of stakeholder exchange rather than merely thinking about the flow of information through networks.

Stressing interpretivism, Pacanowsky and O'Donnell-Trujillo (1983) defined organizational communication as "cultural performance" (p. 126). This analysis assumes that "Each organization has its own way of doing what it does and its own way of talking about what it is doing" (p. 128). As Pacanowsky and O'Donnell-Trujillo (1982) concluded, "Each organizational culture has its system of facts which members use to explain how and why the organization operates the way it does" (p. 124). These interpretations affect stakeholder relationships between people, between people and units, between units, and between persons inside and outside of companies. For instance, people in communities where chemical companies operate may employ different assessments of the risk of living near or working in the company than the companies' managements do. Such differences influence the processes of stakeseeking and stakegiving.

Meanings play a key role in the kinds of stakes people believe they have and the structures they use as they seek or give them. As Morgan (1986) suggested, "An organization's self-image is critical in shaping almost every aspect of its functioning and in particular its impact on the context of which it is part, and thus organizations should give considerable attention to discovering and developing an appropriate sense of identity" (p. 246). An image of openness is enacted through different structures than is closedness.

Do people inside of a company participate in the same or different zones of meaning that people outside do? If not, misunderstanding and false impressions can occur, and lead to difficulties in the exchange of stakes. For instance, a large facility, perhaps an electric generating facility or a refinery, might periodically emit a plume of white vapor. To a plant chemist, that plume is harmless water vapor that occurs because ambient temperature is such that the water vapor turns to a cloud—a natural and harmless occurrence. Seeing the event, a neighbor near the plant might think the cloud is full of harmful chemicals and alert (a stake) the local Environmental Protection Agency representative. Did both parties "see" the same phenomenon? Yes and no. Do the zones of meaning of the parties affect those interpretations? Yes. Does easy access to the informational structure of the company give the stakeholder a means for obtaining the information needed to reduce uncertainty? Could be. In this case, misunderstanding can occur when an event has two separate, perhaps conflicting interpretations, and when structure frustrates efforts to reduce uncertainty and allay apprehensions. In such occurrences, the structure between the entities should lend itself to a positive exchange of stakes.

In making such interpretations, it is sufficient to think of individual words and entire idioms as perceptual screens that affect action and judgment. Each organizational discipline or departmental unit has its own idiom. The same is true of industries. Automobile manufacturers who have to consider marketing limitations on pricing and selling automobiles see the issue of safety features differently than do members of the insurance industry who have to bear the costs of automobile repairs and medical treatment for accident victims. Costs of safety equipment become part of the task of marketing automobiles (cars may be considered too expensive relative to the ability or willingness of customers to pay). Likewise, costs of car repairs and medical treatment affect the price of insurance and become a factor in customers' ability or willingness to pay for cars. When interpretations are at odds and each side is jockeying for advantage in the negotiation of stakes, the structure between auto insurance companies and automobile manufacturers is likely to be adversarial.

Adherence to the vocabulary that is unique to each zone of meaning has structural implications as stakes that can be negotiated. Zones have vocabulary, some of which is unknown to members of other zones. Knowledge of the vocabulary of powerful zones increases a person's power. Assimilation into a zone or denial of access to it is a stake. People who aspire, for instance, to enter management (a structural position) are required to learn its language. Sensitive to this issue, Morgan (1986) offered the following insight: "The characteristics of the culture being observed will gradually become evident as one becomes aware of the patterns of interaction between individual, the language that is used, the images and themes explored in conversation, and the various rituals of daily routine" (p. 121). Does a culture that prefers teamwork correspond with actions that are taken, such as rewarding individuals who disrupt team efforts?

As Morgan (1986) reasoned, "In talking about culture we are really talking about a process of reality construction that allows people to see and understand particular events, actions, objects, utterances, or situations in distinctive ways. These patterns of understanding also provide a basis for making one's own behavior sensible and meaningful" (p. 128). For this reason, Morgan (1986) continued, "When we observe a culture, whether in an organization or in society at large, we are observing an evolved form of social practice that has been influenced by many complex interactions between people, events, situations, actions, and general circumstance" (p. 139). Enactment of a culture expresses the social practice members of the company think is most appropriate. If a company espouses devotion to service, enactments must communicate "service" to persons who seek that stake from the company. The structure must be service oriented, as opposed to one prepared to deny service or rationalize why it cannot be performed to the customer' satisfaction.

Employees struggle to acquire the interpretative systems, schemata, by which to understand their company's structure. Who are the important people? Who can help you get your work done? Who should you not rely on? What is unimportant to one person may be quite important to another. Knowing what is important to important people is a stake people seek and give. It is a ticket needed for entry to power structures.

Power is an important stake sought and given in any company. Tompkins and Cheney (1985) argued that it accounts for regularities—structures—in organizations. Power and control can be distinguished: *Power* is "an ability or capacity to achieve some goal even against the resistance of others"; and *control* is "the exercise or act of achieving a goal." In this sense, especially reflecting stakeholder analysis, control belongs to "those members who can provide services essential to organizational goal attainment. Organizational power then is the ability or capacity of a person or persons to control the contributions of others toward a goal" (p. 180).

By extension, power resides in meaning rather than people or position, and arises out of the ability and willingness to grant stakes needed to achieve goals. This interpretation is important for the following reason: "We live in an age in which power is separated from its source. Natural persons, including owners and agents, are now men and women marginal to the corporation and are easily replaced. The sum total of power held by natural persons has decreased while the sum total of power held by juristic persons has increased" (Tompkins & Cheney, 1985, p. 181). Power and structure are translated into being through "three (inescapably communicative) processes: (1) the direction of work tasks; (2) the evaluation of the work done; and (3) the rewarding and disciplining of the workers" (p. 181). Structure results as work is enacted and as people are rewarded for it.

For that reason, tightly coupled organizations make the source of power apparent to workers. For instance, an assembly line is an apparent source of power that directs activities; the presence and operation of the assembly line defines the stakes that must be exchanged. In that sense, an assembly line directs work tasks and requires little explicit supervisory communication. Similarly, bureaucratic companies direct work tasks merely through routines that leave little discretion to supervisors or workers. A "concertive" organization simultaneously displays "'loose' and 'tight' properties" (Tompkins & Cheney, 1985, p. 184). Tight coupling results from definition of tasks—what is to be done—whereas loose coupling results from the latitude of acceptable means by which tasks can be done. Thus, "employees, particularly managers, are allowed a great deal of decision-making freedom while they adhere tenaciously to a set of core values; they communicate directly with one another in order to handle novel cases or the challenges of innovation" (p. 184). Control of individuals determines how tasks will be performed and what the outcome of effort will be. How this control is exercised through stakeholder negotiations defines each company's structure.

Structure results from identifications shared by members and by companies and persons outside of them. How this structure is enacted results from premises and assumptions both parties hold based on their identification. Managers are assumed to take on the burden of creating identifications that shape the exchange of stakes. Noting this process, Tompkins and Cheney (1985) concluded, "Upper management may view part of its job as the 'managing' of identification" (p. 192). Simply stated, "*A decision maker identifies with an organization when he or she desires to choose the alternative that best promotes the perceived interests of that organization*" (p. 194). The kinds of identifications individuals enact result from adopting situationally relevant premises that influence their participation in a company or in regard to it.

To the extent that A identifies with B, they enact a structure different than would be the case where identification did not exist. In this way, each "organization member is limited at the outset to alternatives tied to his/her identifications; other options will simply not come into view, and therefore will not be considered. Thus identification can be used to explain how alternatives are recognized as such by the organization member" (Tompkins & Cheney, 1985, p. 194).

The double interact is a focal point of organizational control. Illustrating the double interact, Tompkins and Cheney (1985) concluded:

> Supervisor A gives *directions* to subordinate B; subordinate B complies (or fails to comply) and the "messages" concerning compliance and goal attainment are monitored through feedback loops leading back to A; supervisor A assesses the results of B's performance and accordingly dispenses *rewards* or *punishments* to B. This double interact of control—directing, monitoring, and rewarding/punishing—simultaneously provides us with the basic act of organizing and demonstrates why communicating and organizing are nearly synonymous. (p. 195)

Technical control results from physical controls, such as assembly line operations. Bureaucratic control arises from rules. Concertive control is enacted through themes and premises. Emphasizing the interaction between thought and action, this analysis specifies how relationships become structured through the exchange of stakes, related to members' identification.

This enactment view of structure contrasts with traditional approaches that see power as resulting from the interaction between structure and function—or merely as organizational charts. Making that point, Conrad and Ryan (1985) argued that "members develop a language of power that both articulates the dimensions of the construct that actors have developed and validated intersubjectively." This validation provides "the construct of a concrete linguistic reference. Persons are defined as powerful or powerless, actions are viewed as power plays, and domination or submission; inaction is defined as acquiescence" (p. 242). Language invests power through metaphors that become central to the thoughts of individuals who exchange stakes. Viewed this way, "deep structures of power" result from recurring patterns of action, what people adopt as routines and express as myth and metaphor (p. 243).

Power is enacted through at least four symbolic forms: justifying, rationalizing, threatening, and promising. Company members engage in these communication processes and thereby enact them. By enacting recurring communicative displays, members "produce deep structures of power. Through guiding and constraining actors' choices, these preconscious patterns of action influence what is communicated overtly and how it is communicated, thereby perpetuating the deep structure" (Conrad & Ryan, 1985, p. 243). The voice each member enacts becomes the company Voice.

Managers play an instrumental, but not exclusive, role in the creation of structure and proportioning of power and control. Managers do this because "(1) their formal organizational roles provide them with superior access to information and almost complete control of the dissemination of decision-relevant information, (2) their training and experience provide them with superior verbal skills, and (3) their ability to control workers' access to information that would undermine the myths of rational decision making and thus perpetuate the image that their analytical and verbal skills legitimize their superior organizational roles" (Conrad & Ryan, 1985, pp. 251–252).

What managers do in this regard is modified by what others do in response. This dialectic is a company's structure. It defines and reflects how stakes are negotiated and what personae are appropriate to the process. Structure comes to life through stakeholder negotiations. People have a stake in maintaining or changing structure as it is needed to seek their rewards and avoid unnecessary costs of participating in or interaction with a company.

FOCAL POINTS OF STAKEHOLDER ANALYSIS

- How does culture define stakes, stakeseekers, and stakeholders? What are the stakes, who is seeking them, and who holds them? Under what conditions are they given and held?
- What premises of stake exchange operate in terms of the following variables: equity, timeliness, fairness, willingness, ability, and intimacy?
- How does the exchange of stakes affect and reflect organizational climate, especially control and trust?
- Are exchanges symmetrical or asymmetrical?
- What attributional processes and schemata accompany the negotiation of stakes? How do these processes and schemata affect enactment and the resultant relationship?
- What persona and second persona are involved in the seeking and giving of stakes?
- How is structure enacted by the negotiation of stakes? What structure results from this exchange?

CONCLUSION

Companies are enactments of individual self-interests. Self-interests are enacted through the negotiation of stakes. People seek and give stakes through processes that reflect principles of social exchange and result in structure. Efforts to define and exchange stakes are heavily influenced by the meanings that shape interpretative and relational schemata. This analysis emphasizes the importance of interpretivist insight into the meaning people enact. This meaning comes to life through the exchange of stakes that constitute rewards and costs regarding self-interests.

These self-interests interlock as people seek and give stakes. How that exchange is accomplished reflects the culture and climate of companies as well as the personae of the members involved.

Pacanowsky and O'Donnell-Trujillo (1982) reasoned that research is designed to help managers know what to do to make organizations run effectively. They stressed the need to look for instrumental variables—those that account for why one organization works, whereas another is ineffective. This effort has led to important conclusions, such as "Whereas the underlying motive of traditional research is coming to an understanding of how to make organizations work better, the underlying motive of the organizational culture approach is coming to understand how organizational life is accomplished communicatively" (p. 121). Culture should be studied "as sense-making, as a reality constructed and displayed by those whose existence is embedded in a particular set of webs. But the web not only exists, it is spun. It is spun when people go about the business of construing their world as sensible—that is, when they communicate" (p. 123).

This sense is not trivial. It is vital if people are to know how to enact a company by negotiating stakes. Stakes are essential to the definition of the relationship between persons internal and external to companies. Subject to persuasive influence and vital to the enactment of relationships, stakes offer a focal point for understanding organizational processes and effectiveness.

7

Interpersonal Contacts: Enacting with Boss and Others

When we consider interpersonal communication in an organization, we may focus narrowly by thinking only of co-workers talking to one another or supervisors interacting with subordinates. We should also realize that interpersonal communication transpires when people inside a company interact with those outside of it, as occurs when sales personnel represent products and services to customers or clients. We may err by thinking that interpersonal communication occurs face to face. In large companies, employees routinely communicate interpersonally with one another, for instance by phone or writing, without ever meeting face to face. A variety of new electronic innovations offer many possibilities for interpersonal contact through mediated channels. With these cautions in mind, this chapter discusses one-to-one communication in companies.

"Interpersonal communication," Weick (1987) observed, "is the essence of organization because it creates structures that then affect what else gets said and done and by whom" (p. 97). Organizational performances are interactional, contextual, episodic, and improvisational (Pacanowsky & O'Donnell-Trujillo, 1982). Interpersonal communication is important for the exchange of information and coordination of activities. Employees' perception of the quality of communication in their organization depends on their interaction with their supervisors, the climate in the company, and appraisal others make of their work performance (Pincus, 1986).

Superior–subordinate communication refers to contact between boss and employee. From their immediate bosses, employees want job-related information that may affect their performance, satisfaction, teamwork, and turnover. From higher levels of management, they seek information that gives scope to their efforts and can affect unit outcomes such as productivity, commitment, morale, loyalty, and trust. Especially in the last sense, the chief operating officer is supposed to (and may by accident) set the relational tone for the rest of the company. CEOs often pride themselves with this responsibility even though they tend to communicate downwardly, getting little upward communication from employees. Most of each CEO's day is devoted to interpersonal contact, but the direct effect of those episodes does not extend very far downward even in small companies, except as it is translated by each manager to people below (Pincus, Rayfield, & Cozzens, 1991).

To lessen the effects of this asymmetric communication, one large company in Houston held an annual meeting during which senior executives answered employees' questions in open session. That company used its public relations staff to increase employee contact with management, albeit largely asymmetrical. It used videos that were updated monthly, each of which included "candid" comments from management, as well as segments on policies and operations. It published six employee newsletters, each of which contained material designed to answer questions asked by different audiences. Each newsletter contained management comments on a unique theme. In these ways, that company tried to bring an "interpersonal climate" to the communication of executives.

Research continues to shed light on processes and functions of interpersonal communication in companies. This research focuses on variables that affect the quality, creation, continuation, and termination of interpersonal relationships in companies, but much of that work has failed to give attention to culture and meaning, which affect those enactments. It is important to consider whether interpersonal episodes are influenced by interaction processes and cultural interpretations unique to each company.

Cultures contain different shared realities that suggest why some communication behaviors, communication plans, and message design logics work for people in some but not other organizational settings. Interpersonal enactment is affected by employees' sense of the personae that are appropriate to organizations, their identification with and commitment to them. Behavioral responses presume interpretative schemata. Because they share meaning that includes expectations regarding other members' behavior, people enact interpersonal episodes through the exchange of stakes; they negotiate rewards and costs of relationships vital to work performance.

All factors are not equal in the communication acts that lead to the creation, continuation, and termination of interpersonal relationships. Key factors are shared interpretations and expectations of which actions are necessary for coordinated effort. The stories people tell about their organizations contain action markers (comments about persons acting) and constraint markers (statements about limits on individual freedoms) (Holt, 1989). Vaill (1978) found that expectations held by supervisors and employees are important to the cooriented efforts to exert leadership. People involved in an interpersonal relationship use what they believe is supposed to be happening as the standard to determine whether they are satisfied with the relationship. Such expectations seem to be predicated on an archetype each person has regarding what is expected of an *average* communicator (Pavitt & Haight, 1986). Such expectations of communicator competence are framed by definitions of organizational scenes, acts, and actors as standards for determining who is competent and which behaviors are appropriate under which circumstances.

Communication competence is a central factor in organizational success. When individuals perceive themselves and their interpersonal partners to be competent communicators they predict that they will be satisfied by the communication, perceive one another to be able to provide confirmation, and recognize each others' ability to communicate appropriately (Spitzberg, 1991). Additional evidence of the importance of interpersonal competence is the finding that (computer) professionals who use client-oriented interaction behaviors are perceived more favorably and thought to be more competent in their work than are their counterparts (Guinan & Scudder, 1989). Liking increases between people when they think their communication partners are supportive and similar (Berger, Weber, Munley, & Dixon, 1977).

Interpretative frames express expectations people have of what each should do during interpersonal episodes. Cappella and Greene (1982) argued that when these expectations are not met people are negatively aroused and relationships may deteriorate. However, if the people making the violations can reward their interpersonal partners, the violation may be ignored, and can even enhance relationships (Burgoon & Hale, 1988). Such judgments about expectations and violations are context and culture sensitive (Burgoon, 1985).

With these overview principles in mind, this chapter discusses interpersonal processes by which individuals negotiate stakes, seek and give information, influence opinions and behavior, coordinate activities, and compete for resources. Relevant contexts include interviews, negotiations, superior–subordinate contact, conflict resolution, compliance-gaining efforts, and expressions of friendship. Communication styles of interpersonal partners manifest themselves through personae that enact archetypal metaphors such as drill sergeants, whiners, underexplainers (who assume others can read their minds) and overexplainers (who assume others are stupid or untrained). Enactments entail communication skills such as those related to telephone manners, business correspondence, interviewing technique, coordination of work activities, and negotiation. Interpersonal communication is affected by the ways people attribute the causes of others' and their own behavior as they give their world a sense of causal meaning and control.

In keeping with previous chapters, a central theme in this chapter is that narratives guide interpersonal enactments through the development and execution of communication plans; they give continuity to interactions. Meaning contained in company culture guides decision heuristics, which in turn influence which enactments form interpersonal relationships. These enactments affect and are affected by the climate that comes to life through relational variables, especially control, trust, and intimacy. As people prepare themselves to enter and become functional members of a company and its subunits, they learn which actions are needed for success and satisfaction as company members. Such processes must be manageable and knowable; they need coherence, control, and valence. Conversations and other interactions exhibit *coherence* when comments flow from one to another in sensible ways. Persons have *control* if they can influence the direction of conversations and relationships. *Valence* refers to how participants evaluate the process of conversation and interpersonal exchange (Rose, 1988).

COMMUNICATION SCRIPTS, PLANS, AND MESSAGE
DESIGN LOGICS

Some interpersonal communication is highly routine and scripted. At times, it requires execution of complex communication plans that employ message design logics, some of which can be quite elaborate. Contingency theory holds that people are prone to prepare communication plans (Hewes & Planalp, 1987) and select message design logics based on their interpretation of each situation (O'Keefe & McCornack, 1987). For example, what an employee decides to say to be courteous to the boss depends on the situation, desired outcome, and skill at using the relevant interaction plans. Narratives and the personae implied in them are important to individuals' selection and development of communication plans. People learn through narratives the outcomes to which actions lead and the interaction routines that are appropriate to the people involved under the circumstances. Depending on each individual's skills and insights, as well as time constraints and uniqueness of situations, communication plans and design logics vary in complexity. Evidence of the intricacy of this process can be found in the fact that some employees in some circumstances can make what would be thought to be insulting comments to their bosses and find that those statements are not only appropriate but thought to demonstrate skill and closeness. In other companies or under less skillful use of the statements, sanctions could be quite severe. An insult is situational.

Such plans, especially in instances where superiors appraise subordinates' activities, are likely to be frustrated by mystery, a recurring human problem (Burke, 1969b). Rather than getting to know one another, participants in such situations are prone to select plans that consist of "prepackaged scripts for the situation that derive rules from commonly understood cultural values and standards" (Goodall, Wilson, & Waagen, 1986, p. 75). Interviews, as a type of interpersonal enactment, are likely to be best when participants lessen the mystery between themselves. Such mystery can result when interviewees do not know what the appraisal means for their future or whether it places them in the favor of superiors. Similarly, the interviewee can withhold information in an appraisal interview and thereby prevent the boss from knowing what is going on in the department, such as who works hard or who are slackers. In the worst sense, mystery becomes a ritualized enactment of the order of the company; in the best sense, order is a constructive result of acts by which both parties lessen mystery.

How each relationship develops or seems to develop to the persons involved is expressed in terms of metaphors that capture the stages and expectations of the relationship, such as those typical of a sales presentation or negotiation. Examples of metaphors include relationship as machine ("our relationship is running smoothly" or "the wheels just came off") or relationship as power politics ("we are allies" or "I will blind side and ambush the boss at Thursday's meeting"). A main metaphor may come to life as the essence of a unique cluster of metaphors that is used to describe the relationship; the main metaphor is a key term that encompasses the cluster of related metaphors. How well a relationship develops depends on the compatibility of the metaphors the partners employ to guide their enactments (Owen, 1990).

Communication strategies vary in terms of the degree to which they are planned and strategic. On one end of the continuum is mindless use of scripts that have been learned through socialization, awareness of symbols provided by management, and work experience. Scripts control and legitimate activity, give meaning to events and actions, organize activities, predict and guide behavior, buffer role conflict, provide schemata for evaluating behavior, and conserve cognitive capacity—keep people from dwelling on what to say (Ashforth & Fried, 1988).

Highly scripted enactments require little communication planning. Some highly scripted behaviors include the greeting and customer service enactments of telephone receptionists, conversations customer relations personnel use with customers, and sales presentations. Such enactments may be carefully groomed by managers who attempt to have employees speak with a coherent Voice. Employees often obtain scripts as a result of training provided by human resource personnel within companies and by consultants. Typical of this training is that provided to convenience store personnel who are even scripted for the eventuality that robbers will hold up the store where they work.

Companies even create scripts that are used repeatedly in written and oral communication. Some of these scripts are developed in random ways and are employed simply "because that is the way we do things here." For instance, in scripted, mindless ways, personnel may end memos with phrases such as "Your usual cooperation will be appreciated," or "Failure to comply may lead to termination." They may have no idea what degree of cooperation they expect, but they know that ending is standard in their company. Or they may stress the doom of not complying with orders without much thought to the effect that statement has on the company climate. Or they may begin memos and letters by writing, "Please find attached...," even though no one is pleased to find anything. Although the degree of scriptedness may seem to be more prevalent for employees at lower levels, it is also characteristic of communicative actions by higher level employees. Public relations experts give executives scripts, including the training they need to meet the press, in the event they are interviewed by skilled and assertive reporters.

Even when interpersonal communication does not seem to be scripted, it nevertheless exhibits patterns. For instance, managers exhibit patterns when they engage in fact-finding and appraisal interviews with their employees. About 20% of the time they avoid investigative or fault-finding statements. They start such conversations with investigative comments about 33% of the time and make fault-finding statements about one half of the time. But even then, managers avoid extreme fault finding and reserve formal procedures for the most severe and intransigent violators (Morris, Gaveras, Baker, & Coursey, 1990).

In contrast to the times when people have and use scripts, however, is the wide range of comments that are relatively loosely scripted. Pacanowsky and O'Donnell-Trujillo (1982) cautioned "that even similar performances will be different in terms of content or in terms of the actual order in which the performance unfolds. Thus, loosely scripted performances, even those that can be classified together, have a uniqueness that ought not to be ignored. The analytical directive, then, is to explore the uniqueness and variability of these performances" (p. 134).

In loosely scripted conversations, individuals negotiate the continuation or change of topics in strategic ways. Persons engaged in conversation tend to extend the conversational topic of their partner when it is comprehensible and when they are attentive to their partner. When conversational partners are interested in introducing a conversation topic and being attentive, they are careful to make a link between what was being said and the topic to which they want to shift (Tracy, 1984). In this sense, conversational flow is negotiated; interactants exchange stakes as they demonstrate attentiveness and respond to the others' selection of conversational topics.

A substantial amount of organizational behavior is acquired by observing tactics bosses and other successful persons use. Using their bosses as models, employees tend to use communication tactics that they believe are successful, produce rewards, and avoid punishments. How extensively bosses' behavior is used as a model depends on the degree to which subordinates perceive the behavior to be successful and the extent to which the employees believe they can use the behavior to achieve the same results (Weiss, 1977).

Focusing on these issues in a health care context, Morse and Piland (1981) found that nurses select communication strategies based on the target of that communication. Specific to their professional persona they believe that the following communication strategies are preferred in descending order: listening, routine information exchange, management of conflict, small-group communication, and instructing. Differences occur in communication tactic selection based on whether the nurses are talking to one another, to a patient, or a doctor. For instance, they would seldom give advice, orders, or instructions to doctors; nor would they persuade doctors. They feel more comfortable exchanging information with other nurses than with doctors.

One of the important communication and cognitive processes that occurs as individuals enter a new organization or subunit is learning its unique scripts. Pacanowsky and O'Donnell-Trujillo (1982) reasoned that scripts are an important part of organization assimilation. Each new member needs to learn scripts and know when each is appropriate to perform. "Organizational culture is, in large part, constituted in the various rituals which members regularly or occasionally perform. These rituals orient members temporally, synchronizing their focus and introducing a sense of regularity into the culture. By participating in these rituals, members not only punctuate their experiences but are provided access to a particular sense of shared reality" (p. 135). In addition to ritual, company communication takes the forms of passion, sociality, politics, and enculturation. Enculturation entails members' acquiring social knowledge, understanding how tasks are performed, and learning communication skills necessary to behave competently.

Assimilation into organizations seems to entail a progression of stages. Presocialization requires information seeking, modeling, and role playing, which lead to estimates of self-efficacy and impressions of the company and job position to be entered. How each individual progresses through these stages is likely to be affected by the uncertainty the person experiences, as well as the degree to which the person is self-interested in successfully assimilating into a worthwhile and meaningful job. Presocialization entails learning the social reality related to the job, its expectations vis-à-vis the individual, and the company (and industry). This phase may also entail the adoption of narratives and metaphors regarding the self, job, expectations, company, division, discipline, and industry. Part of the effort at this stage is the formulation of attitudes toward work, company, co-workers, customers or clients, industry, and self in those circumstances. It entails translating these attitudes into probabilities of reward outcomes, norms of expectation, and costs (Ajzen & Fishbein, 1980) and into the dynamics of social exchange (Roloff, 1981, 1987). Based on these factors, people negotiate relationships to become more comfortable with what each expects of the other and delivers in terms of rewards and punishments.

Communication plans reflect the message design logics of the person who is developing them. Such design logics correspond to the principles of contingency theory. The available array of message design options includes *expressive logics* designed to disclose personal information, *conventional logics* used to enact communication through rules, and *rhetorical logics,* which are appropriate for affecting judgments and behaviors. Design logics are selected to accomplish goals given the nature of the persons involved and the situation (O'Keefe & McCornack, 1987; O'Keefe & Shepherd, 1987).

Message design logics are goal oriented. That is, different goals require their own strategies or design logics, whether the event is expressive, conventional, or rhetorical. In the first case, language is selected to express feelings. In the second case, communication occurs through the enactment of cooperative social rules. And the last entails strategies that relate to the creation and negotiation of personae and situational definitions. What kinds of message design logics would people select if a subordinate did not complete an assigned task? Whereas men and women might prefer equally expressive or conventional approaches to such situations, women more than men select rhetorical message design logics (O'Keefe, 1988).

An important component of superior–subordinate communication is the message design logic a superior uses to persuade subordinates to do the "right" thing or to behave in the way the superior thinks is appropriate. A strategy used by one type of manager may have favorable results, whereas this may not be the case for a manager operating under different conditions. Some of the factors that help to explain the variance regarding the best strategies to use are gender, age, ethnicity, length of tenure in the organization, and perceptions of credibility. Thus, compiling a coherent and comprehensive list of the most appropriate and effective compliance-gaining strategies across individuals and situations is problematic. When subordinates believe they agree with their supervisors on rules, they evaluate their supervisors higher. In this relationship, factual accuracy or actual agreement is not as important as perceived agreement (Eisenberg, Monge, & Farace, 1984).

Managers appear to perform a few identifiable and archetypic personae. Mintzberg (1973) discovered three managerial archetypes: interpersonal (figurehead, leader, and liaison), informational (monitor, disseminator, and spokesman), and decisional (entrepreneur, disturbance handler, resource allocator, and negotiator). Perhaps the best question to ask is whether, according to contingency theory, the persona exhibited by a specific manager at a particular time in a company is the one that produces optimal results.

Approaching this issue from a dramaturgic orientation, Trujillo (1983) identified several additional interpersonal roles managers perform: figurehead (performing symbolic acts such as signing checks or similar documents and representing the department at functions), leader (creating the department climate and motivating as well as guiding subordinates), liaison (performing a linking function with other departments), monitor (gathering data—surveillance—on internal and external events), disseminator (influencing flows of information within the company and between it and outsiders by performing gatekeeping activities), spokesperson (communicating to external audiences in terms of needs and requests of internal persons and groups), entrepreneur (initiating change), disturbance handler (intervening to produce harmony), resource allocator (dividing resources, rewards, and punishments in the group), and negotiator (advancing the interests of one group by giving and receiving stakes).

Because sexual harassment is a serious interpersonal and policy issue in companies today—especially coming to a head when it occurs between superior and subordinate, it offers an excellent example of the negotiated enactment of cultural narratives. Sexual harassment can result because individuals enact different narratives of sexual contact in company contexts. What is a meaningfully legitimate enactment for one person may differ from the performance expectation held by the person who perceives harassment. Responses to undesirable sexual overtures result in message design logics, the outcome of which can have serious reward–cost consequences. Bingham and Burleson (1989) reasoned that in such situations, the person suffering the harassment is likely to want to achieve instrumental, relational, and identity goals. For this reason, victims' message design logics are selected to maintain a positive relationship and identity while arresting the offensive behavior. In such situations, rhetorical design logics are most effective, with conventional and expressive logics being less effective, in that order. Rhetorical strategies include redefinition of the situation along with appeals for the harasser to retract any threats that are made. Conventional strategies include deflection, whereas expressive responses voice strong negative feelings. Use of all three message logics in conjunction is perceived to be more effective that use of any one by itself in terms of achieving goals.

As we explore the plans and scripts characteristic of interpersonal communication, we seek to know which factors affect efficiency, satisfaction, influence, distortion, conflict, and compliance in superior–subordinate relationships. This relationship suffers the potential for struggle and conflict due to the formal authority embedded in the superior's position and because managers often try to dominate the construction of social reality in a company. In their role, managers attempt to have subordinates understand the world as they do. Such efforts manifest themselves during the stages by which new employees enter a work unit, when new bosses negotiate their relationship with members of an established work unit, and as part of the appraisal and job definition process. Superiors and subordinates attempt to balance personal and organizational interests. In these ways, the negotiation of the relationship between superior and subordinate is perplexing and often full of undefined tension, mystery, and ambiguity. Similar analysis can be applied to understand how work colleagues negotiate interpersonal relationships, as employees do with persons external to companies.

NEGOTIATING ORGANIZATIONAL RELATIONSHIPS

A concern in organizational communication is the manner in which people negotiate the ways in which they enact company relationships. In the most encompassing sense, relationships are affected by narratives that members use to make sense of themselves and others in their company, the company itself, its industry, and the political economy that surrounds it. These narratives define reality and suggest which personae are appropriate to the circumstances at hand. People use stories they encounter on a day-to-day basis in companies to define themselves, define each other, enact relationships, learn the meaning of relationships, learn how they are enacted, and learn which variables are vital to them.

For each company and its members, many narratives exist that could be selected to guide interpretation and interaction. Individuals select narratives based on their awareness of those that are relevant and the extent to which they seem appropriate to produce desired rewards and minimize costs. Bosses often attempt to influence employees' behavior by framing narratives and limiting the number of narratives that employees believe are appropriate to the circumstances at hand. In response to these constraining efforts by bosses, employees attempt to influence their working environment by interpreting and introducing narratives in their own interest.

Some events occur that seem to violate the narratives that are relevant to account for the enactments expected in that situation. In such events, one correction would be to change the acts so that they correspond to the event. Another approach, especially important for managers, is to repair the theme or account for the deviant actions, especially in cases where interpretations of events and actions could undermine the integrity of the narrative. One tactic in this regard is to account for the plot error by blaming the persona of the person who violated the plot (e.g., the person is "unstable" or "irresponsible"). Another is to portray the person as being a violator of the ideology of the narrative (e.g., the person has failed to be a "company player.") The violation could be explained because the person was duped, for instance, or that the violator is one of a kind and not to be treated as typical (Guerro & Dionisopoulos, 1990).

These enactments correspond to the tenets of social exchange theory, which postulates that people influence one another by selecting and defining the constraints and rewards by which they enact their relationships. They reward and constrain one another based on their interpretations of the rights, responsibilities, and rules they hold regarding the development of interpersonal relationships.

Because of the interlocking nature of relationships in a company, these negotiations are a central feature in how people enact interpersonal relationships.

In this way, each person's enactment is a dialectic with the scene and other actor(s) in it. Narratives guide interaction and self-presentation; these actions are dialectical (Gergen & Gergen, 1988). This dialectic consists of the act, response to the act, and what the persons involved in the relationships learn from the response to the act. What is learned from the response to the act becomes important to the continuing interaction and developing relationship.

Detection of deception is an instance that supports this thesis. For example, McCornack and Parks (1986) found that as relationships develop, participants become more able to detect their partner's deception, although other researchers are less confident that familiarity improves the detection of deception (Buller, Strzyewski, & Comstock, 1991). When people believe they are being deceived, they tend to use probes to reveal the deception as well as become suspicious. When deceivers perceive their partners to be using probes or to exhibit suspicion, they work hard to mask their deception by attempting to avoid giving signs of nervousness or arousal in their gestures and body movement. They speak more deliberately, fluently, and assertively (Buller et al., 1991).

What one participant does in a relationship affects what the other does and how it is done. In this way, subordinates observe superiors' behavior and estimate that behavior is similar to their own when they think that the superior is successful by using that behavior. Willingness to use their supervisor's actions as a model for their own behavior is unrelated to perceived reward power—the ability of the superior to reward subordinates for adopting the behavior. What determines whether subordinates use their superiors' actions as models of preferred behavior is the extent to which they believe that behavior can be performed to achieve desired outcomes (Weiss, 1977). For this reason, the behavior of managers may also be influenced by the extent to which they feel rewarded by their subordinates' willingness to model that enactment.

This influence may affect the extent to which relationships exhibit openness, trust, and intimacy (Millar & Rogers, 1976). Interpersonal relationships exhibit dialectical polarities, such as openness–closedness, or stability–change, that people use to negotiate the limits of their relationships. Relationships fluctuate so that at one moment they are closer to one polar extreme (openness) and then move toward the opposite polarity (closedness) (Altman, Vinsel, & Brown, 1981). Openness is an especially important factor in the development of relationships, in particular because factors that impede the flow or exchange of information in companies can be detrimental. Openness is measured by the frequency of exchanges between organizational members. For instance, the amount of openness in an employment screening interview correlates positively with the duration of responses by interviewees (Tengler & Jablin, 1983).

Openness by one person tends to motivate the other person to respond in kind. Even if it does not lead to reciprocated openness, communication acts that are interpreted as open indicate that openness is appropriate and encouraged in the communication situation. This kind of response can be explained by speech accommodation theory, which postulates that people demonstrate similar communication patterns when they want to be liked by the other person (Street & Giles, 1982).

Speech accommodation theory postulates that participants in interpersonal communication tend to match responses with one another if they like each other and if they want to be liked by the other. Also, if one person in a relationship respects the other, the patterns of communication are likely to converge toward those of the respected partner. For example, if one person speaks quickly, the other is likely to do so also if the person respects the other. Looked at from the vantage point of enactment theory, participants in interpersonal communication negotiate how the interaction will be enacted. One person initiates a conversational pattern—a set of verbal or nonverbal cues. Once this happens, the communication partner elects to match the pattern or not. Matching is thought to be a sign that a relationship is developing in a positive manner; it is a stake. When responses are matched, participants indicate to one another that they are willing to foster a relationship and want to be liked. If they refuse or are unable to match the response, the relationship may deteriorate. Note the presence of identification in this analysis; the more people identify with one another, the more their enactments are likely to be similar.

Focusing on the employment interview, Anderson (1960) found that if an interviewer sees an interviewee as a desirable candidate for the job, that fact will be signaled by increasing the amount of time spent talking to the candidate. Put in enactment terms, the interviewer enacts liking by increasing the amount of time spent talking to the interviewee. Conversely, if the interviewer is uninterested in the candidate, that fact is likely to be enacted by less talking, which demonstrates that the interviewer does not want to spend time with the interviewee. Problems of attribution enter this situation because the amount of time as an enactment of liking or disliking is measured from each participant's point of view. Those estimations may not agree. The enactment may not lead to the proper signal—"I think you are a good candidate"—if the interviewee does not see this "amount" in the same way that the interviewer does. For this reason, to offset problems of mistaken interpretation of the information in amount of time spent talking, the candidate and the potential boss may have to resort to other communication strategies, such as explicit statements that clarify their attributions.

How comfortable persons are with such statements can be influenced by their degree of intimacy. The amount of intimacy between superiors and subordinates and between co-workers is negotiated. Personal details are exchanged as stakes; people decide to grant stakes or seek them in exchange by creating liking and exclusive relationships with one another. Such cases are easy to note when, for instance, customers create intimate, exclusive relationships with certain vendors ("I will only buy from you.") or when a employee will confide in one co-worker, but no one else.

To some extent, these exchanges result in congruent beliefs about the exchange as each person experiences it. How partners interpret this exchange is influenced by the extent to which they have had other shared experiences. Beyond congruency, an even better explanation for how people converge and diverge in their relationships features dialectic. Their identities and thoughts are the products of both persons' attempts to achieve congruency while maintaining some aspects of the relationship and changing others. Backman (1988) reasoned that four factors are central to this process: (a) cognitive structuring—use of actions and reactions to create a sense of self, (b) selective interaction and evaluation of the actions and reactions that occur that have meaning for the self, (c) self-presentation (impression management) and altercasting that result from efforts to present a consistent sense of self and to have that sense validated by interactional partners, and (d) role and identity negotiation that begins with idealized or imagined views of how participants like to see themselves in each relationship.

Enactments are predicated on the negotiation of relationships that feature efforts to be efficacious, to be perceived to be efficacious, and to receive feedback regarding the extent to which others believe the behavior is efficacious. The motive to change is a reward or cost incentive; part of the success of change is based on whether the other person buys in and counterenacts in ways that affirm that change. If a boss wants an employee to change (or if the employee wants to change), the relational partner must affirm those actions.

Getting information from others is an important part of company performance. Employees tend to feel that they have an adequate amount of information about the work that is expected of them. But they are uncertain whether they have the information they need regarding their performance, pay, promotional criteria and qualifications, and goals of the organization. Whether employees believe they have sufficient information is important because their feeling that they know what is going on relates to the degree to which they identify with the company and are committed to it (Penley, 1982).

Interviewees and interviewers use cues during in an interview (employment, counseling, and appraisal) to monitor their relationship. For instance, amount of time each person talks, length of each conversational unit, amount of speech latency, amount of criticism or praise (in an appraisal interview), duration of eye gaze, and use of nonverbal cues that indicate relational elements (such as friendliness, warmth, openness)—all of these affect the flow of the interview. These cues are used to interpret the success or failure of each interaction as well as the attractiveness of the interpersonal partner as a communicator. Specific actions are selected based on an assessment of which ones are appropriate as well as which feelings and attributions are relevant to the situation. Behavioral patterns used to enact each interaction are intended to achieve various functions: coherence, task, information exchange, persuasion, intimacy, impression management, dominance, control, or reinforcement. The choices made are likely to produce amounts of positive or negative arousal—feeling states associated with or produced by various acts during the interaction (Street, 1986).

What one person does may lead to confrontation with another. Confrontation can be an effective communication strategy for resolving conflict. Enactment of confrontation episodes occurs in stages starting with initiation and progressing through development to closure. Because of the stigmas associated with confrontation, it is often difficult to enact. Factors affecting the decision to be confrontational include the degree of urgency, nature of the relationship, responsibility to confront, appropriateness of time and place, and perceived outcomes (Newell & Stutman, 1991).

All of this discussion about the negotiations that transpire during interaction indicate that people cannot truly be themselves unless others in the immediate environment allow them to do so. Burke (1966b) contended that "the very essence of a character's nature is in a large measure defined, or determined, by the other characters who variously assist or oppose him" (p. 84). For instance, individuals may have pictures of themselves as open communicators. They may take pride in having an "open door policy" with subordinates, encouraging self-disclosure and open discussion regarding task or emotional issues at work or at home. They would likely value relationships in which openness is encouraged and thereby reciprocated. Actualizing this type of persona would, in part, depend on the personae of individuals in the environment who negotiate the amount of openness desired in each relationship.

In these ways, people negotiate their relationships. They do not just happen. Some enactments are more appropriate than others in light of the narrative participants use to guide their interactional episodes. Relationships develop and are accompanied with a history idiosyncratically recalled by both partners. They reveal patterns that are used, as they are recalled, to conduct subsequent interpersonal episodes. Conversations and contacts that people have affect their abilities to enact relationships. The negotiation of these relationships is governed by patterns that relate to efforts to achieve self-efficacy—to feel empowered.

EMPOWERMENT THROUGH INTERPERSONAL RELATIONSHIPS

Relationships between people constitute the structure and power distribution in a company. Much of what makes them feel empowered begins with their interpretations and reactions to the relationships they develop. These relationships are not only vital in and of themselves, but also because they lead to and result from efforts to achieve goals through coordinated, interlocking activities. In this dialectic of activities, the extent to which one person feels empowered results not only from an individual sense of accomplishment, but more importantly from a sense of achievement that results from collective acts. Persons can only achieve what they accomplish together.

Companies across the country are engaged in substantial efforts to increase the quality and productivity of their operations. One major part of that effort is to empower employees. For a complete understanding of the enactment of empowerment, it is important to realize that power is not only given by those who have it, but it is also negotiated by employees based on the amount of power they have due to the stakes they hold, the organization's need for those stakes, and the employees' willingness and ability to negotiate them. Culture and climate are an essential part of this equation.

The advantage of having empowered employees is obvious. "When people make what they perceive to be free and irrevocable public decisions, they are likely to be committed to both those choices and their implications" (Wilkins & Dyer, 1988, p. 526). When individuals hold opinions, make decisions, or undertake actions that they attribute to be caused by their own predispositions, they are more likely to believe in and adhere to those actions, opinions, and judgments than if they attribute them to be the result of external causes, such as "I'm doing this because I need the job," or "I'm doing this because my boss wants me to."

Viewing empowerment as the enactment of power, Conger and Kanungo (1988) reasoned that "organizational actors who have power are more likely to achieve their desired outcomes and actors who lack power are more likely to have their desired outcomes thwarted or redirected by those with power. This orientation has led theorists to focus on the source or basis of actor power and on the conditions that promote such dependence" (p. 472). Managers can share power by giving subordinates "formal authority or control over organizational resources" (p. 473). Empowerment can result from a variety of "participative management techniques such as management by objectives, quality circles, and goal setting by subordinates as the means of sharing power or delegating authority" (p. 473).

People have a need for power and desire to influence and control their own destiny. Those who are unable to do so feel a lack of self-efficacy. "Power in this motivational sense refers to an intrinsic need for self-determination or a belief in personal self-efficacy" (Conger & Kanungo, 1988, p. 473). The key: "Any managerial strategy or technique that strengthens this self-determination need or self-efficacy belief of employees will make them feel more powerful" (p. 473). In this way, Conger and Kanungo (1988) defined empowerment "as *a process of enhancing feelings of self-efficacy among organizational members through the identification of conditions that foster powerlessness and through their removal by both formal organizational practices and informal techniques of providing efficacy information*" (p. 474).

People monitor their interactions to determine whether they have control. Any sense of control is retrospective. People process information about their actions and infer the degree to which they believe they *had* control and thereby determine how much control they think they have (Albrecht, 1988). If people do not believe they *had* control, they will not feel empowered. In such assessments, behavioral, cognitive, and personal factors play important roles. When managers believe they have self-efficacy, their performance increases and becomes more goal oriented. Such positive outcomes increase as they refine their self-schema, which helps them regulate their goal-directed behavior (Wood & Bandura, 1989). Do similar outcomes result for nonmanagers?

Climate and culture only come to life through enactment. Despite what people are told, they only know culture and experience climate by what is done and said. Therefore, enactments do a great deal to inform and influence employees about the degree of power they enjoy in a company. An empowering climate is one in which mangers share control and increase the extent to which employees learn to trust both managers and themselves. For this reason, the first step toward empowering employees is to allow them to participate in meaningful decisions. Properly designed decision systems "encourage people to be involved and send signals to the individual that he or she is valued. These may range from formal efforts such as quality circles and advisory boards to less formal efforts such as suggestion systems and opportunities to meet with top managers in informal social gatherings" (O'Reilly, 1989, p. 20). Managers enact an empowering narrative with their employees.

In addition to involving employees in decisions, feelings of empowerment rise when managers' enactments correspond to the company's espoused values. Employees want to know what is important. To gain such information, they watch and listen to others, especially persons above them. They look for patterns. When top managers not only say that something is important but act in ways consistent with that message, employees begin to believe them (O'Reilly, 1989). These enactments lead to shared meanings; even more important is the realization by employees and managers that they share meaning because the Voice that results from actions is consistent with shared values.

Workers are empowered by receiving consistent messages from co-workers. Favorable responses provide employees information that they interpret to mean that important people are paying attention to them and favorably regard their effort. This enactment consists of a stakeholder exchange of positive regard. In addition to regard of co-workers is the Voice of the organizational reward system. Management enacts the operant reward system by what it does; for instance, managers might indicate that they prize innovation and quality, but if they reward one and not the other, the rewarded criterion will dominate the control system (O'Reilly, 1989).

Demoralization occurs when employees are disillusioned that what they find in their jobs differs from their idealization of those jobs. In such situations, Switzer and Switzer (1989) concluded, a cycle occurs that begins with idealization, moves through frustration, and results in demoralization if uncorrected. This cycle can be broken. Employees have an idealized view of their jobs, but can become demoralized when barriers prevent them from achieving those ideals. Demoralization harms work productivity because attention is given to the source of discontentment rather than the accomplishment of tasks. This frustration leads to a sense of powerlessness. For this reason, managers need to provide resources for employees to use to break the cycle. This remedy would include attributional processes needed to locate the causes of demoralization and communication resources employees can use to eliminate frustration. These measures are particularly important when employees are attempting to enter the company. The problem may occur if recruiters and interviewers portray the company in a way that is too rosy. This problem continues into the new employee orientation phase if new hires are given an unrealistic view of the company and of the tasks that they will be expected to perform. Presentations need to be realistic and employees need to be given resources to prevent a distorted view. Openness is an important managerial trait because it allows employees to have contact with a resource for preventing and eliminating frustration.

Feedback from the boss and co-workers provides important insights into how to enact the persona of a company. Cusella (1982) discovered that feedback from high-expertise sources has more impact whether it is positive or negative, and motivation to comply with feedback is greatest when employees receive positive feedback from high-expertise sources. Stone and Stone (1985) found that feedback is perceived to be more accurate when several sources give the same feedback. Feedback that is favorable (positive) is perceived to be more accurate than unfavorable feedback. Feedback has more impact on self-perceived ability to complete tasks when it indicates that the tasks have been successfully completed. Individuals' level of self-esteem has more impact on self-perceived task competence than does feedback. When information is received as feedback from several sources, it is discounted if it is less favorable than the feedback received from another source.

The climate that permeates interpersonal relations affects the communication between superiors and subordinates and their sense of empowerment. The content of interpersonal communication reveals information about relationships. For this reason, dominant managers decrease the extent to which their subordinates feel involved in decisions and decision processes. When managers are not dominant, their subordinates are more willing to communicate, to seek and share information, and to be involved in the making of decisions. In such cases, managers perceive their employees as wanting to be more involved. Managers who dominate their subordinates decrease the amount of negotiation that transpires with them. Dominant mangers tend to misunderstand their subordinates, assume that they do not want to be involved in decisions, and assign lower performance assessments to them. The dominant manager communicates an "or else" definition of the relationship. The amount of dominance in a relationship depends on the perception of the participants, but is also defined by responses they make to one another. Managers are more responsive to subordinates when they perceive that subordinates seek to be part of the decisional process (Fairhurst et al., 1987).

The relationship between superiors and subordinates affects the flow of information between them, as a power move, or stake exchange. Messages are more likely to be distorted between superiors and subordinates if the subordinate does not trust the superior's use of power. Distortion is also dependent on the subordinate's perception of the boss' influence on persons above in the organization, the subordinate's aspirations for upward mobility, and the subordinate's trust of the superior. Supervisors are prone to withhold information when they experience role conflict with subordinates. In contrast, when supervisors communicate openly and frequently with their subordinates, the subordinates reciprocate in kind. When superiors are friendly, approachable, and considerate of their subordinates, information flow increases and is less distorted (Fulk & Mani, 1986).

Empowerment is related to willingness and ability to make needed changes in company operations. Because of the difficulty in breaking existing enactments, people have analyzed the tactics required to effect organizational change. Examining how relationships affect change, Vielhaber (1983) found that positive interpersonal relationships lead to positive attitudes toward change. Employees who rely on informal channels are not as positive about change as are people who rely on formal channels, especially when those channels provide ample, accurate information. Positive attitudes toward organizational change promote job satisfaction and job involvement. A social exchange explanation of this phenomenon is that if people enjoy positive and equitable outcomes from relationships they will foresee those same outcomes as circumstances change.

Empowerment is the result of enactments that affect individuals' perceptions of the amount of control they have had and are therefore likely to have in subsequent situations. For this reason, empowerment is a vital part of the relationships that develop between people in companies, and results from feelings they have about themselves in relationship to others.

ORGANIZATIONAL ASSIMILATION: BECOMING PART OF A COMPANY OR DEPARTMENT

People spend much of their life preparing to enter organizations, and do so by receiving information through interpersonal contact and well as through mediated channels, such as employee relations material and orientation programs. People witness assimilation processes as they watch television and entertainment films. They read about those processes in fiction and news accounts. Such information is important because the average person's lifetime involves assimilation into many organizations. People change careers an average of three times and jobs even more frequently, which entails becoming part of new organizations or departments. Many people recognize that employees are more productive if they assimilate into their company and department satisfactorily.

Because socialization is a routine part of people's lives, managers may overlook that phase of organizational communication. All too often, when people enter a company or department, they have to fend for themselves. Nevertheless, some organizations and some departments have effective programs to help new employees enter and become meaningful participants. Some of these programs involve extensive corporate orientations that overload new employees with information they will never need or may not remember when they do need it. Other assimilation programs are gradual and use mentors to answer questions and assist assimilation efforts. Some departments merely rely on open door policies.

Through communication activities with other members, new members learn which activities are important and which ones are trivial. They learn social information, such as how members occupy their time during lunch, how they celebrate holidays, and how they handle interpersonal conflict. Some information comes to them by observing what goes on in the department. Many employees learn the ropes by listening to stories about the company and department. The efforts members make to become assimilated into a company are influenced by their life perceptions, role expectations, and self-assessments (Jablin, 1985)

Jablin (1982b) defined organizational assimilation as "the process by which an individual becomes integrated into the 'reality' or culture of an organization" (p. 256). He contended that this process involves two interrelated components. First are the strategic as well as unconscious attempts of the organization to socialize employees. Second, employees go through a process of accepting or rejecting organizational norms as they form an organizational reality. This process entails modification of members' roles to accommodate their needs, goals, and values. These roles and norms are negotiated as members socially construct a reality of the company.

Assimilation entails three stages: presocialization, encounter, and metamorphosis (Jablin, 1984). During the *presocialization* phase, the individual attempts to achieve information and skills needed for successful entry. *Encounter* occurs when individuals experience the organization and match what they find against what they expected. *Metamorphosis* results when they become functioning members of the organization.

Presocialization results in the development of expectations that are tested during encounter and metamorphosis. An important question regarding new employees' socialization involves the issues surrounding where their expectations regarding the activities at work originate. Preparation to occupy certain employment positions begins early in life. Using a developmental framework, Jablin (1985) traced an individual's background from childhood through the chosen vocation in adulthood. Prior to encountering a particular organization, people formulate expectations and beliefs concerning how people communicate in particular occupations and work settings. Anticipatory socialization includes anticipation of vocational aspirations or motives and the organizational contexts in which to actualize such goals.

Anticipatory socialization involves the anticipation of vocational and organizational choices (Jablin, 1985). During the process of vocational choice, individuals gather information about a variety of occupations, as they progress from childhood to adulthood. This information is communicated by many sources and is evaluated in light of the individual's self-concept. The primary sources for this occupational information are the family, educational institutions, job experiences, peers, and media. From these sources, the individual obtains information regarding styles of communicating in certain occupations. For example, an individual who is interested in becoming a lawyer may perceive lawyers to be dominant in their communication styles, whereas social workers may be perceived to be quite open.

Products of presocialization are refined and checked against what is encountered during later assimilation phases. Encounter entails what actually happens regarding a job, company, industry, discipline, and occupation. At this stage, individuals match their expectations against the reality provided by the company and other members. The degree to which an employee experiences satisfaction is based, at least in part, on expectancy value theory. How well did the individual predict the reward–cost ratios that were encountered? Satisfaction at this stage is likely to result from the ability and willingness of participants to accommodate to one another through processes of social exchange. If the gap between expectation and encounter is too great, it must be narrowed; otherwise unhappiness and dysfunction are likely. The gap can be narrowed by altering expectations or by changes made by the individual or other members of the company. If the individuals are able to accommodate to the company or vice versa, they likely become metamorphized into it; if satisfaction is not possible and exit is, then the latter is likely to occur. Metamorphosis entails learning and utilizing the shared reality, accommodating to the reward–cost ratios peculiar to the organization and the particular department in which the individual works. During this stage, individuals refine their attitudes toward the organization in terms of expectancy values and learn what is necessary for the satisfactory negotiation of social exchange (Jablin, 1985).

Acquisition of communication skills, or their improvement, is part of the presocialization and encounter phases. These skills are role related, what is expected for the individual to perform as expected. The effort depends largely on the development of appropriate interpretative schemata and behavioral scripts (Cude, 1991). Acquisition of skills is important because new organizational members are motivated to demonstrate their competence. As they make their way into group membership, new employees observe and test tactics. They are keenly interested in the processes and requirements for developing relationships (Miller & Jablin, 1991a).

Assimilation requires that new hires learn group norms and expectations. According to Bormann's (1983) symbolic convergence explanation of this process, organizational members attempt to understand their reality by sharing group fantasies that "provide key communication episodes that create a common social reality and accomplish sense making for the participants" (p. 100). The term *fantasy* refers to participants' use of narrative, dramatic imagery, and wordplay to enact and to later reenact an event. A fantasy is a creative and imaginative interpretation of events. By sharing these fantasies, participants make the events known and thereby form a bond of shared experience. Members have their own interpretations of an event, and once the fantasy is made public, the members can begin to converge in their interpretations of events. The public overlapping of interpretations produces symbolic convergence.

No matter what the individual's experiences, an important part of assimilation results from the adoption of the unique jargon and culture in the company and department. With the idioms vital to the company, individuals are able to enact their interpretations of work expectations in ways that coordinate with others' expectations and enactments.

Through myths, rites, and rituals, as well as the specific language used to describe these activities, people share meanings of organizational life. For example, employees of the Disney Corporation are referred to as "cast members." Their organizational roles are "parts" that they play, and the administrative offices are known as "backstage." This important cultural information is shared with each new employee early during orientation. In fact, part of the new employee training includes a quiz that expects members to recite the names of Disney's Seven Dwarves (Smith & Eisenberg, 1987).

In this way, Disney Corporation provides an excellent example of the impact organizational culture can have on employees during assimilation. New employee socialization plays a critical role in maintaining cultural intensity. Many organizations strategically indoctrinate their new members in a way designed to carry on the traditions captured in organizational culture. The ways in which members interpret and communicate these interpretations to other members influences the quality of work relationships and of work life.

Prior to employment, individuals seek information about organizational positions by using organizational literature and interpersonal interactions. The employment interview plays a critical role in communicating cultural attributes to the potential employee. During the interview, the interviewer may convey positive attributes regarding the company through reenactment of certain fantasy themes. When attempting to recruit a new member, the interviewer may strategically design messages to direct positive attention to the company and encourage the recruit to become a member, thus closing the gap between *we* and *they*. During evaluation of the potential new employee, an assessment is made regarding whether the person has the ability, knowledge, skill, and desire to become a member of the group. This decision depends on a variety of factors including competence, gender, attraction, ethnicity, and the persona of the individual. Final assessment includes an evaluation of whether the person possesses similar perceptions of the world of work. Often organizational members seek members who complement the team.

Following the presocialization phase, the new hire enters a period of being "broken in." This encounter stage is rich with information about the specific company and department into which the individual is attempting to assimilate. Success or failure for new employees during the encounter phase depends substantially on the accuracy of their perceptions of the new environment prior to entering the company. Employees may develop unrealistic expectations of their job or career (or the company) during anticipatory socialization. If expectations are unrealistic, employees may experience disillusionment and disappointment. Printed material about the organization and statements made during the interview can foster unrealistic expectations, due to the positive way in which the organization is described. Due to persuasive communication in either printed materials or in recruiting new hires, an individual may attribute only positive characteristics to the organization, without acknowledging negative ones. If the new employee anticipates in a fairly accurate way the organizational environment eventually experienced, the encounter phase will be less destructive or disillusioning (Switzer & Switzer, 1989).

More often than not, expectations of the newcomer will either be reinforced through daily interactions with organizational members, or these interactions will serve to stimulate a reorganization and reinterpretation of roles and responsibilities. The new organizational member will learn on a daily basis what is considered routine behavior. For instance, during a planning session to improve the employee induction program of a company, a woman told the story of arriving early at her new job in the company. She had not been warned that she would have to clear security before passing through the lobby and gaining entry to her office area. On her first day, clearance was particularly time consuming. Having worked her way through security, she rushed out of the elevator hoping to make a good impression in the new department. On the way to her new office, following directions from the area receptionist, she encountered her new boss at 8:05. He greeted her by saying, "Around here, we go to work at 8:00."

During the encounter phase of organizational assimilation a wide array of behaviors may be acceptable on the part of the newcomer, because established members will attribute nonnormative behaviors to newness. Much of the communication activities may center around setting the newcomer straight regarding what constitutes acceptable and normal behavior. These interactions may occur in implicit or explicit ways. For example, if a new employee begins to refer to her boss as "Mary," when it is common knowledge that she prefers to be called "Ms. Jacobson" there are a number of ways that this important cultural information can be shared. A peer may pull the new hire aside and explain the nuances and preferences of the boss. Such interactions help achieve a coherent Voice for the department. One difficulty is the variety of sources that supply information to newcomers, some of which is likely to be contradictory. Newcomers are called on to interpret and decide which information fits with their self-interests and is accurate.

Stressing this point, Bormann (1983) suggested that much of what happens in organizations is disorganized and chaotic. Through symbolic convergence, order can arise out of chaos. Effectiveness occurs to the extent that members converge symbolically by agreeing and coordinating one organizational Voice. Managers are advised to realize the need new employees have to learn the narrative of the department. Savvy managers realize that they need to enact the narrative with their employees.

During the metamorphosis stage, newcomers become active in organizational decisions and participate in their roles in a more appropriate manner. Decisions about how to develop autonomy and individualize roles in personalized ways are an integral part of this process. If an employee has experienced conflicting messages regarding norms and expectations during the encounter stage, the metamorphosis stage provides an opportunity to attempt to resolve this conflict. The conflict may be confronted on an intrapersonal, interpersonal, or intergroup basis.

During metamorphosis, an individual's organizational identification and commitment are reinforced (Jablin, 1985). Often at this point any initial disillusionment or disappointment has either dissipated or been accommodated to by the newcomer. If the necessary adaptations are not made, the employee is faced with the choice of leaving the company or staying in what is perceived to be an unsatisfactory environment. Some individuals attempt to change the climate and culture of the company rather than leaving or accommodating to it. Such efforts may result in disappointment and frustration on the part of the unhappy member, as well as the boss and co-workers.

An employee's assimilation into a new organization involves the negotiation of interpersonal relationships, often with the goal of achieving similarity, coordination, and understanding regarding company goals and policies. During negotiation, a struggle is likely to occur when members encourage the newcomer to "think like a member of the team," as the newcomer struggles to balance the desire to be a member of the team and to make unique and innovative contributions. Through communication, the *we* of the company or of a specific group within it is distinguished from the *they* of the outsiders.

During assimilation, newcomers obtain information from several sources in the company. Cultural stories, rites, rituals, and fantasies are shared between peers, as well as within the superior–subordinate relationship. Communication between subordinate and superior may have substantial impact on the subordinate's perceptions of the effectiveness of the company, commitment to it, and identification with it.

People also experience assimilation when they transfer from one subunit to another. The communication activities that characterize these moments in organizational experience are important. Investigating the activities people employ as they transfer from one organization to another and as they stay behind accommodating to the transfer, Kramer (1989) proposed a model that consists of three stages: loosening, transition, and tightening.

During the *loosening* phase, the person being transferred typically tells the people who are staying what they need to know to perform the person's job. During this phase, persons who are staying anticipate the loss of a work group member and communicate social support. After the transferee has left, the persons who stayed enter the *transition* phase, during which much of the communication is designed to cope with the loss of the member. At this time, the person who is transferring starts the process of being assimilated into a new work group, which entails developing new work group relationships. During the *tightening* phase, the transferee uses communication to strengthen normal work relationships and establish network links beyond the immediate work group. As the person who transfers becomes more involved with the new work group, contact with the members of the old group lessens.

Communication that transpires during assimilation, by both the person who is leaving and those who are staying, tends to be designed to reduce uncertainty. Social exchange occurs as people trade work information and social, relational comments as part of paying regard to one another and obtaining needed information. Transferees often experience substantial uncertainty about the new job, new fellow employees, and new work and living locations. Persons who stay behind are uncertain about the abilities of the replacement, the implications of transfer for their own careers, and how the job change will affect them (Kramer, 1989).

People come and go in companies and departments. Such transactions, although routine, entail uncertainty that must be reduced through communication that is enacted in accord with principles of social exchange. Such transitions can be eased by the availability of organizational information and supportive communication. Lacking this support, assimilation and transfer can be an organizational jolt. A vital part of this transition is the assimilation into a new zone of meaning.

COMPLIANCE GAINING AND INTERPERSONAL CONTROL

Organizational enactment involves getting others to comply with requests. That principle has been the focal part of substantial research and discussion. In chapters 5 and 6, this process was discussed in terms of norms, meaning, and stakeholder exchange. Here the issue is addressed specifically in an interpersonal context. For example, employee A asks employee B to trade shifts or to cover during lunch; or a boss seeks to increase subordinates' willingness to complete tasks at a specified level of quality or productivity. Granting compliance is the equivalent of granting a stake. Seeking compliance can involve requesting or exchanging stakes.

Compliance gaining involves social exchange. During compliance-gaining efforts, people employ messages designed to accomplish their goals without incurring costs and sanctions that result if they violate constraints implicit in the situation. During communication planning and selection of message design logics, people select messages based on their analysis of the situation. For instance, when people seeking compliance perceive that the person of whom the request is to be made is likely to resist, they are likely to use facts and arguments to support their request if consequences related to the request are short term, intimacy is low, and perceived rights to persuade are high (Cody et al., 1986). Facts and arguments are used when individuals have not established sufficient intimacy and awareness of one another to employ other tactics, such as threats, rewards, or expert advice.

Directness increases the force of requests, especially when higher levels of intimacy exist between relational partners (Jordan & Roloff, 1990). This suggests that people who do not know one another well or have not established an intimate relationship may prefer indirect, low-risk requests. By the time people have developed intimate relationships they know the costs of asking for a specific compliance and know how to enact the proper exchange.

Gender and organizational level differences are related to the kinds of strategies managers use when influencing subordinates. Female managers are more likely to use influence strategies involving altruism, disguised requests, or explanations than male managers. Upper level females tend to use more threats and promises than do their male counterparts. At lower levels, female managers rely more on rewards, ingratiation, or altruism than do their male counterparts. Lower level managers rely more on punishment-based strategies than do upper level managers (Schlueter, Barge, & Blankenship, 1990). These findings suggest the operation of archetypal managerial metaphors.

Gender differences affect how people respond to refusals to comply with requests. If compliance-gaining tactics are met with refusal to comply, superiors are likely to resort to rewards or punishments as strategies to achieve compliance. Women are more likely to use that tactic than are men (deTurk, 1985).

The higher managers are in an organization (the archetypal metaphor of the powerful boss) the more power they feel they have over subordinates. Male managers believe they have more power over their subordinates than do female managers. Higher level managers assume that they are more influential in the organization than do lower level managers. Male managers think they have more power in the organization than do female managers (Schlueter et al., 1990). Because they are based on self-report data, findings such as these reflect perceptions of power embedded in the managerial bias derived from the archetypal metaphor of the powerful male boss.

Refining analysis of the process of compliance gaining, Dillard et al. (1989) postulated that people's actions are shaped by two kinds of goals, "(1) primary or influence goals which instigate the influence process, and (2) secondary goals which shape it" (p. 19). Primary goals arise from one person's desire to change the behavior of another person. They are used to gain compliance and to activate secondary goals. Five kinds of secondary goals are typical in compliance situations: identity goals, interaction goals, personal resource goals, relational resource goals, and arousal management goals. *Identity goals* are the result of the self-concept. *Interaction goals* relate to estimations of social appropriateness and self-presenta- tion. *Personal resource goals* are aimed at obtaining or maintaining valued assets— relational, material, physical; decisions involved with the selection of this category of goals center on a rewards–cost matrix with which the person selecting the goal decides whether it would produce rewards or incur costs, assuming the target could retaliate following the request. *Interpersonal relationship resource goals* reflect the source's estimations of the extent to which their use might help or harm the relationship. *Arousal maintenance goals* are designed to keep interactants' level of arousal within tolerable limits given their idiosyncrasies. People select goals based on whether their use would make them or the target apprehensive, uncomfortable, or nervous. Secondary goals influence the strategies that are selected to achieve compliance. The study of goals supplies insight into why some strategies are used, whereas others are not, in efforts to persuade some people in some situations, but not in other situations.

Utilizing a motivational goal model, influenced by Petty and Cacioppo's (1981, 1986) theory of involvement, Dillard et al. (1989) postulated that as the desire to achieve an influence or primary goal increases so does the thoughtfulness (time and effort) of the selection of the secondary goals. People are prone to take more time to select tactics when the desire to achieve the goals is high. This message planning has several dimensions: planning, effort, directness (extent to which the message makes clear the intended behavior outcome the source desires of the target), positivity (use of positive and negative constraints, consequences, and incentives), and logic (use of logic and evidence). Setting each of these dimensions against the goals, the researchers discovered that influence (primary) goals corre- late with planning, effort, and logic. Identity goals correlate positively with planning and logic, but negatively with directness. Interaction goals correlated with planning and positivity. Relational goals correlated with positivity, whereas arousal negatively correlated with positivity, directness, and logic. Influence goals associ- ate with cognitive effort and behavioral goals, whereas secondary goals are associated with communication variables. These results are compatible with enact- ment theory, which assumes that people present impressions and enact persona fitting with their estimations of the circumstances as defined by the climate and culture of the company.

Compliance and control are vital parts of interaction. For instance, Palmer (1989) found that individuals control access to conversations and determine how long others can talk. Such nonverbal strategies are used to exert control. Interper- sonal partners who talk more are usually considered more dominant. Managing floor time and choosing which topics to discuss and for how long are important nonverbal behaviors in the development of interpersonal relationships. In companies, we would expect bosses to exert influence by determining which topics are covered, who talks, and for how long. The power to gain a floor in conversations relates to the ability to share ideas with others and to influence them and gain compliance. People who are denied access to the conversational field may have to yield to others' interpretations of the situation. Dominance is associated with the length of time people keep the conversational floor. Amount of talk and willingness to yield the floor, change topics, or accept topics are stakes that can be used to negotiate relationships. Willingness to accept others' control of the conversational floor and topic selection is a giving of stakes.

In organizational settings, members have expectations of the kind of behaviors they believe are appropriate to the negotiation of relationships. These expectations are defined by relevant narratives in the culture of each company. Snavely and Walters (1983) examined the relationship between social style and perceptions of communication competence. Administrators who are highly responsive are perceived to be more competent than are those who are perceived to be low in responsiveness. Responsiveness, in this sense, consists of versatility, social anxiety, self-disclosure, empathy, and listening. Enactment of management personae is best (thought to be more competent) when managers are perceived to be responsive to subordinates.

An important episode entailing compliance gaining and control occurs during appraisal interviews, especially those in which superiors attempt to reinforce or change subordinates' behavior. Whether through formal or informal procedures, superiors evaluate subordinates. Examining employee reaction to appraisal interviews, Downs (1990) discovered that they were more satisfied by the appraisal interviewing processes when they perceived that their bosses understood them and the quality of communication was high.

Another important instance of compliance gaining occurs as organizational members try to exert leadership. Whether superiors attempt to exert leadership with subordinates, or whether the effort transpires between co-workers, organizational members seek to have others comply with their efforts. Pfeffer (1978) reasoned that leadership is inseparable from the attributional schemata that operate in an organization. Leaders take credit for what goes well and attribute failures to environmental factors. "Occupants of a leadership position come to assume symbolic value, and the attribution of causality to those positions serves to reinforce the organizational construction of meaning that provides the appearance of simplicity and controllability" (p. 29). Through actions, each "leader attempts to reinforce the operation of the attribution process that tends to attribute causality to that position in the social structure" (p. 29). People seem more successful when they separate themselves from failure and claim success.

Leaders who are best at adapting to environmental constraints and opportunities are most successful. Often leadership needs to be diffused among many people for the entire group to be successful and for employees to be empowered. This conclusion is reinforced by the concept of requisite variety that assumes that if enough people feel the need to exert leadership functions then the functions needed to guarantee success are more likely to be exerted than if only one person shoulders the responsibility to be leader. What determines the necessary functions? Meaning. What functions are needed in this regard? Lundberg (1978) proposed the following functions in answer: having self-expectations of leadership, achieving the needed level of activity, avoiding being distracted, being open, having useful "shadows" (confidants, mirrors, and consultants), being appropriately open, and building useful coalitions.

In these ways, enactments occur through expressions of performance expectations. One version of this expectation is requests for compliance. Such efforts are influenced by the personae, climate, culture, and narratives that operate in each department and organization.

FOCAL POINTS OF INTERPERSONAL
COMMUNICATION ANALYSIS

• How scripted are interpersonal communication episodes? How successful are those scripts? How comfortable are the scripts for employees and those with whom they interact?

• Are models employees emulate to learn which scripts to use ones that lead to outcomes compatible with company and department mission and goals and do they create the climate and culture that is preferred in the company?

• Do employees create and employ communication plans using appropriate message design logics?

• Do interpersonal enactments reveal speech accommodation to converge or diverge?

• Is each employee's need for empowerment met by giving the person control over work through meaningful participation in its design? Does the organizational reward system correspond to what management says is rewardable behavior? Does the information, as feedback, employees receive from bosses and co-workers confirm which actions are valuable to the company and satisfying to the employee?

• How well are employees assimilated into organizations? How effectively do they transfer from one department to another in those organizations? Are communication processes needed for successful assimilation fostered by culture and climate?

• How well do individuals exert and yield to one another's efforts to achieve compliance and control, especially in terms of diffused leadership and empowerment?

CONCLUSION

The way in which a superior communicates with subordinates can influence the climate within a subunit of a company. At the same time, the communication style exhibited by subordinates to their superior has impact on climate, culture, and the perceived effectiveness of boss and subordinate. Information flowing from subordinate to superior has been referred to as upward communication from a structural–functional frame of reference. On the other hand, downward communication refers to those messages moving down the organizational chart, from superior to subordinate. Often, the organizational chart is ineffective in predicting the flow of communication in an organization. A better means for understanding why people communicate as they do with one another is to examine the narratives that guide the interactions in each company.

Given this perspective, we might wonder how far most managers deviate from what seem to be the preferred characteristics of managerial communication: coaching and encouraging employees, encouraging employees to be involved, motivating self, solving problems, using direct and adaptive interpersonal style, and being an effective listener (Glaser & Eblen, 1986).

8

Networks: Many People Speaking with a Single Voice

A number of years ago, network analysis was the heart and soul of organizational communication theory and analysis. A general systems orientation led researchers to conceptualize organizations as networks, and networks of networks. The concept of network has been particularly useful to proponents of structural-functional analysis who are keen to explain how information flows in an organization and evaluate whether people have too much, too little, or the correct amount of it to do their work, coordinate their efforts, and feel integrated into the organization (Farace et al., 1977). Through evolution the term *network*, a noun, became a verb; now people network to gain personal advantage through personal contacts.

Although that shift in idiom leads to a narrow view of networks, it reminds us that when we conceptualize them we should keep in mind the degree to which they are enacted interpersonally. People in a network obtain and give information interpersonally, but also in one-to-many contexts, many-to-one contexts, and group contexts. For instance, groups, such as business meetings or even morning bull sessions people engage in as they prepare for work, bring several people together in a network to share information, solve problems, create climate, develop culture, and make decisions. Examining departmental meetings, Mumby (1988) noted, they are "a necessary and pervasive characteristic of organizational life" by which coordinated work occurs; moreover, they are "one of the most visible and important sites of organizational power" (p. 68). This analysis focuses on structure as power enactment, such as the person who calls meetings and sets agenda, the persons who are invited to attend (versus those who are excluded), and symbolism of enactment as enactment (meeting in a boardroom—with or without catered lunch—versus a tailgate meeting of a repair crew of an electric utility).

As a complement to the structural-functional approach to network analysis, structure can be viewed as a cognitive picture of how people interact as they enact an organization; structure comes to life because of the enactment of those pictures (McPhee, 1989). We strengthen the concept of network by noting that each one constitutes a zone of meaning. On this issue, Weick (1987) concluded, "Structures form when communication uncovers shared occupational specialities, shared social characteristics, or shared values that people want to preserve and expand. The structures themselves create additional resources for communication such as hierarchical levels, common tasks, exchangeable commodities, and negotiable dependencies. The additional resources constrain subsequent contacts and define more precisely the legitimate topics for further communication" (pp. 97–98). These structures become embedded in organizational and societal narratives. If networks exist because of the flow of information, that information helps create, and is interpreted by applying, the meaning unique to each zone.

The content of each zone results as people within each network have unique experiences and create or learn the jargon of the culture that defines the tasks they perform as well as specify who are appropriate sources of information and influence. When companies are small, their networks are intimate and intra-organization interpretations are similar. As a company grows, people within it tend to think of themselves as members of networks and subnetworks, more than of the entire organization (e.g., members of an academic department first, a college second, and the university last). When that occurs, those people are likely to find that information flow across one or more networks becomes more difficult because more people can interrupt it and alter its meaning. For this reason, zones of meaning become differentiated and idiosyncratic. The meaning of each zone is fundamental to interpretations of what constitutes information. When members become segmented into networks, management needs to foster the flow of vital information and to generate a sense of shared meaning that brings cohesion between persons within networks and between networks.

Many people characterize the organizational structure of a company with a combination of lines and boxes that contain names and titles. The lines place boxes beneath boxes. All of the boxes are beneath the top box—the one that contains the top boss. Even though a company can be depicted this way, that does not mean those boxes and the lines actually constitute its structure. Enactment of the company depends on what people think are their place and role in it, as well as the interpersonal and intra-organizational relationships those people have with others. All of the action is between people, even though they may use mediated communication such as memos (paper or electronic), employee newsletters, or employment bulletins. People interacting constitute the "structure" of each organization.

Upper management, along with staff functions such as public relations/employee relations, may communicate broadly with employees. In many large companies, a portion of corporate culture is created or reaffirmed by messages from centralized offices that use electronic and print media to disseminate information and policy. One major function of formal internal communication originated by management is to build employees' commitment to corporate goals and performance standards. Through this communication, employees obtain a sense of management's view of corporate culture, that they reflect on, add to, and adopt in varying degrees.

This chapter discusses networks as enactments. As useful units of analysis, networks are identifiable patterns of information flow, each one of which has unique meaning that comes to life through enactments. Information flow through networks is a focal point in organizational analysis. Such analysis focuses on units that are larger than interpersonal dyads, acknowledging that they are a vital means by which networks operate internally and by which they become linked. As units of analysis, networks provide means to identify and analyze structure. Levels move upward from individuals, to interpersonal dyads, to networks, and ultimately the Network of all networks ostensibly blended into one organization. Networks span the boundaries of each company, the points at which it contacts external networks. The marketing network, for instance, links a company with its network of customers. Marketing personnel attempt to intersect and foster a zone of meaning shared by persons outside of the company. If their attempts succeed, persons become bound into a coherent enactment of selling and buying goods and services.

NETWORK ANALYSIS

As focal points of organizational analysis, networks are both very easy and quite difficult to conceptualize and study. It is easy to treat them as a means for describing who communicates with whom and in what frequency; that analysis looks for patterns, like the nerve structure of a human body or its cardiovascular system. Nerves branch out from the brain. For the left hand to coordinate with the right hand requires that linkages occur through the brain. In a similar way, if people in a marketing department want to communicate with their counterparts in the new product development department, they need links. That link could be a vice president over both departments; it could be a meeting of managers of the two departments, or it could result from formally established groups that bring key people together from the two departments. They could be linked by two neighbors, each of whom works in one of the departments, or the links could be golf buddies, shopping friends, or members of a tennis or garden club. Each of these patterns and its accompanying links is of interest and suggests something different about the structure of the company—the flow of information and influence inside of it. The tough version of network analysis results from the difficulty of knowing the meaning that is created based on these interactions.

Network analysis rests on the principle that organizing is a process, something that is ongoing, not static. Making that point, Weick (1979b) concluded:

> The word *organization* is a noun, and it is also a myth. If you look for an organization you won't find it. What you will find is that there are events, linked together, that transpire within concrete walls and these sequences, their pathways, and their timing are the forms we erroneously make into substances when we talk about an organization. Just as the skin is a misleading boundary for making off where a person ends and the environment starts, so are the walls of an organization. Events inside organizations and organisms are locked into causal circuits that extend beyond these artificial boundaries. (p. 88)

The process of organizing is partially accomplished through person-to-person interaction. Reflecting assumptions basic to enactment, Weick featured the importance of the interact, a process by which two people are interlocked. What one person does affects another who responds. Thus occurs an interact. "The unit of analysis in organizing is contingent response patterns, patterns in which an action by actor A evokes a specific response in actor B (so far this is an interact), which is then responded to by actor A (the complete sequence is a *double interact*" (p. 89).

Networks are enacted through interpersonal relationships between people who interlock to form a web. As Monge (1987) reasoned, "At the network level of analysis, communication processes involve relationships rather than attributes. A relationship is not the property of an individual; it is a characteristic that is defined in reference to two or more people taken together" (p. 241). The result is a network, "a structure that is built on the basis of communication relationships" (Monge, 1987, p. 241; see also Monge & Miller, 1985). How network relationships are enacted affects (and results from) understanding, political arrangements, and joint enactments, whether person to person, group members, groups, or intra-organization.

To conduct network analysis, a researcher might ask members of a company to log into a diary the names of co-workers with whom they communicate each day. They might record what they communicate about and how often. This analysis views networks as being "regular patterns of person-to-person contacts that can be identified as people exchange information in a human social system" (Monge, 1987, p. 243; see also Farace et al., 1977). The basic units of network analysis are the persons involved and their relationships, operationalized by comments such as "shares information with," "talks to," "receives reports from," or "discusses ideas with" (Monge, 1987, p. 243).

Based on these data, a chart can describe who communicates with whom. That analysis reveals patterns, which can be described as stars, wheels, lines, isolates, and boundary spanners, for instance. Such analysis is problematic because to say that two people have communicative contact does not describe the content of their interaction, or the meaning shared by the groups they link. To indicate that bosses link their departments to upper management is not to say much about the quality of the relationship between the departments and management or the content shared by the two zones. To define the meaning contained in networks requires disclosure of metaphors and stories that abound in companies. It may even require a reading of memos, procedures, and policy statements, but no document is likely to reveal the information that elites, often associating with one another in informal settings, run departments: "You have to go to lunch with the boss to know what's going on."; "That group of buddies runs the department."

Exploring this phenomenon in regard to how companies achieve innovation, Albrecht and Hall (1991) discovered that core individuals play a central role in innovation networks. Through multiple interactions, insiders have disproportionate influence over innovation. They exhibit dense linkages and high volumes of social (personal) and work communication. Insiders believe that they are superior to outsiders in terms of trustworthiness, supportiveness, credibility, influence, and receptiveness to innovation. Outsiders have a similar impression of insiders. This research highlights the importance of personal relationships in organizations, especially in terms of impact on innovation and the enactment of networks. It also indicates that influence is not enacted by one person, but through elite groups.

Companies consist of formal and emergent networks. Formal networks are those that have been designated by someone in authority to prescribe who should communicate with whom; in one sense, the organization chart is a formal network, as is the authorized means by which department A makes contact with department B. In contrast, emergent networks (also called informal networks) evolve from day-to-day enactments, regardless of whether someone specified that the people involved should have formal communication (Monge, 1987).

Analysis of networks can focus on four levels. *Personal* networks consist of linkages members have with one another. *Group* networks constitute a larger view of the interaction by determining how personal linkages define groups of individuals as communication participants. At the *organizational* level, groups (such as departments) connect with one another based on the kinds and degrees of interaction. The final level of network, *interorganizational*, involves communication patterns and relationships that exist between organizations (Burt, 1980; Monge, 1987). At each level, important characteristics for analysis include concerns such as how enactments foster or hamper relationships between units—individuals, group members, groups, or companies. Network analysis can disclose how interactions at all levels enact relationships (whatever their function) between the units. Analysis also focuses on these networks as zones of meaning, each of which has its unique sense of shared reality and communication rules.

As well as analysis of organizational levels, network investigations focus on other key organizational units. Setting the stage for such efforts, Monge (1987) listed the key elements of a network: number of people who constitute it, strength or intensity of relationships between those people, symmetry (whether the flow of information and exertion of influence is symmetrical or asymmetrical), transitivity (flow patterns, such as how A communicates with B; B communicates with C; in this way, A communicates with C.), reciprocity, and multiplexity. Reciprocity is revealed by the extent to which respondents agree "about the existence or strength of their relations with each other" (Monge, 1987, p. 244). Multiplexity is revealed by examining the kinds of relationships between each set of people. Networks are characterized by degrees of connectedness and reachability. "For personal networks, reachability is the number of linkages it takes to connect one individual to another in the network. At the organizational level, reachability is the average number of links separating individuals" (Monge, 1987, p. 245).

Such analysis focuses on incentives people have to create and maintain networks by using one another as sources of information and advice to reduce uncertainty. In this way, cohesiveness results from reliance on one another. The degree of cohesiveness is reflected in the extent that information obtained from many sources is more similar than dissimilar. As suggested by uncertainty reduction theory, cohesiveness relates to commitment to the organization (Hartman & Johnson, 1989).

Reliance on others can result in multiplexity. Multiplexity refers to the extent to which network relationships overlap, whereby individuals have more than one kind of relationship with one another. Persons who exhibit extensive multiplexity have many kinds of relationships with many people, thereby enjoying the opportunity to acquire a rich amount of information, to reduce uncertainty, and to serve as sources of information for others. Persons who have multiplex relationships identify more strongly with their organizations. The kinds of topics these people discuss correlate with their identification with the organization, a reflection of shared meaning. Because relationships are defined by the people who make them up, they change over time as people assimilate into or leave the organization (Bullis & Bach, 1991).

As multiplexers, links are a vital point in network analysis because their increased levels of communication activity allow information to flow between networks. Operating at system boundaries, they are a conduit for information exchange between systems. Supervisors are important links. How they perform this function is crucial. When they experience role conflict, they are likely to withhold information. Role conflict occurs when they experience pressure to comply with one role that will prevent compliance with another. Positive aspirations for upward mobility tend to encourage subordinates to distort the information they provide through summaries to their supervisors. Gatekeeping appears, at least in part, to be a power game. As gatekeepers, superiors are likely to withhold information when they believe their subordinates withhold it. In contrast, openness leads to reciprocated openness, as supportiveness increases sharing or decreases withholding (Fulk & Mani, 1986).

In addition to being useful for identifying links that enhance or impede the flow and interpretation of information, networks are focal points in the analysis of employees' sense of belonging and organizational identification. Eisenberg, Monge, and Miller (1984) found that employees tend to be committed to a company if they recognize that they are a part of communication networks, even though they are not highly involved in their jobs. The extent to which people perceive themselves to be assimilated into an organization predicts whether they are likely to function as links (Jablin, 1985).

Location in a network can take its toll on organizational members. Isolates, persons who have few connections with other members of a network, experience less stress and burnout than do other members. Members who belong to groups but are not links experience less stress and burnout than do links (E. B. Ray, 1991). Results such as these, when coupled with the findings of S. C. Thompson (1981), suggest that the personae enacted by organizational members, as well as their perceptions of control and interpretations of stress, contribute to their sense of organizational and personal well-being.

Where people are located in organizational networks affects their perception of the extent to which those networks are open or closed, especially in superior–subordinate relationships. The lower people are in an organization the less they believe such relationships are open. The size of the organization is also a factor. People in small organizations believe that more openness exists than do members of large organizations (Jablin, 1982a).

Links enjoy a privileged position to exert power. They establish political relationships between those networks. People who link systems are in a position to exert organizational power and use information to negotiate stakes. Whether they exercise power through the politics of upward influence in organizations, according to Porter, Allen, and Angle (1981), depends on motivators (scarcity of resources and personal stakes), personality factors (willingness to take risks and desire for power), and power strategies (overt and covert).

Albrecht (1984) found that people who link networks use information to achieve control and exert power; they identify more closely with their jobs than do persons who do not serve a linking function. Their roles and position in networks lead them to gatekeep a lot of information, which gives them the feeling that they are a knowledgeable part of a team. The good news is that they tend to use this power to foster teamwork and group effectiveness. Hickson, Astley, Butler, and Wilson (1981) concluded, "Boundary spanners in direct contact with environmental uncertainty have more opportunity to cope with uncertainty, and hence exert more power" (p. 172). Organizations, and the networks that compose them, are systems of power because they provide opportunities for resource control due to the fact that all members in an organization, to varying degrees, are resource dependent.

Monge (1987) discovered three domains of study relevant to boundary spanning: (a) *process* variables, such as filtering, distortion, searching (scanning and monitoring) for information, representing organizations externally, and representing external stakeholders to the dominant coalition, the organizational elite; (b) *personal* variables, such as self-monitoring skills of gatekeepers or boundary spanners, interpersonal communication skills, and power variables; and (c) *structural* variables, such as flexibility or rigidity of the organization leading to different degrees of openness/closedness and relationships between the people in the different organizations between which the boundary spanners operate. Examining how structure, culture, and communication adeptness of personnel affect dealings with media reporters, Theus (1991) found that structure is not as important as culture and adeptness. In dealing with external persons, such as reporters, organizational ideology influences the flow of information between companies and them.

Such analysis can mislead researchers into believing that boundary spanners are easy to identity. Nevertheless, Monge (1987) observed, "Organizations must identify their boundaries and distinguish their environments from what they consider to be themselves. The flow of information through internal networks is essential to organizational functioning; but organizations must also establish linkages with relevant parts of their environment. Without the ability to gather and distribute information with the environment, most organizations would languish in isolation" (p. 254). Huber and Daft (1987) emphasized the importance of each company's information environment. The need is to identify and diagnose the flow of information from the company and from key publics to it. Members of the company need to monitor the extent to which these networks contain similar or compatible zones of meaning.

This analysis stresses the importance of meaning that is assigned to the information that flows in networks. If care is not taken, that realization can be omitted during structural-functional interpretations of networks. Culture defines who are important sources of information, which information is important, and whether it is reportable. Reportability results from interpretations as to the importance of the information within the interpretative system and the political costs and rewards of sharing or withholding it—stake exchange. At each decision point, the key is interpretation, which is shaped by organizational culture. Cognitive skills of the persons who serve as boundary spanners and the interpretative frameworks they employ influence which information flows between companies and their environments and how it is interpreted. Filtering is a product of interpretation, whether intentional or unintentional.

For example, myopia that resulted from the corporate culture of the asbestos industry led its leaders to misread the salience and consequences of data that linked asbestos to health problems and to fail to appreciate subtle shifts in values of corporate social responsibility held by internal and external stakeholders. Over a 50-year period, these shifts came to invalidate conclusions and assumptions managers of the asbestos industry were taking for granted as they monitored employee and public reaction to the health hazards associated with their product. Thus, the industry continued to produce and sell its product long after it should have had ample evidence that asbestos was producing severe health problems and that those problems would lead to liability claims sufficient to harm its financial viability. Asbestos industry managements received information from dozens of studies and many independent sources that argued that asbestos was linked to health problems, but this information was suppressed or ignored rather than used to correct operations (Brodeur, 1985).

Myopia at play in the industry resulted from interpretations of data regarding health hazards of asbestos and legal interpretations of product liability. This rhetoric became internalized as culture that guided perceptions and judgments of asbestos industry leaders and employees. This culture was the product of the rhetoric of industry management; employees had no information about the health hazards of asbestos until independent medical studies revealed the link. Until that revelation, key premises exerted unobtrusive control over the actions and thoughts of managers as well as employees (Tompkins & Cheney, 1985). The rhetoric of management establishes and confirms principles and premises that give coherence to the interpretative culture of each company ("Corporate culture," 1980; Gorden & Nevins, 1987). As well as being a product of this rhetoric, culture determines which principles and premises guide the thoughts, judgments, and statements of management. In this dialectic, management becomes an audience for its own rhetoric leading to innovation or limiting adaptability. To the extent that they lack information and opinions different from those of management, employees tend to adopt the culture of management.

What can be missed in network analysis is the likelihood that members of networks do not perceive the networks in the same way. People persuade one another to adopt one view of the dynamics of a network as opposed to another.

Each individual's perceptions of the communication in a network tend to be influenced by the dynamics of the formal structure, as well as individual and collective interests. Individuals' perceptions of their communication relationships with other people in the network are influenced by their unique interests, sense of structure, and opinions about the interests of the members of the network (Corman, 1990).

Narratives shape the opinions about organizational structure and enactment. Through interaction, individuals obtain perspectives of each network and its members, as well as acquire a sense of the members' collective expectations. This meaning-laden approach to organizational existence assumes that people calculate how their interests can be maximized in concert with others. Narrative form and content, role persona, and metaphors are means by which individuals attempt to understand the fit between their interests and those of others in the network as means for estimating its dynamics. How networks come to life results in large part from the organization's efforts to obtain, process, utilize, store, and retrieve information (Stinchcombe, 1990).

This review of network characteristics and their effect on their members suggests that they are more than means by which information flows from one person to another, and through that person to yet another. Networks may serve multiple functions, such as sharing information to reduce uncertainty, sharing ideas to innovate, assimilating and integrating members (while excluding others), socializing, and exerting political influence. Each network may serve all of these functions or some of them. For instance, an individual may turn to one colleague to obtain information and to a different person to socialize or politicize. Individuals not only take their identity from organizations, but also from the networks to which they belong. The meaning they have regarding the structure of a company and its network dynamics is likely to be a major part of their awareness of how that organization operates and how they are expected to function in it.

NETWORK STRUCTURE AS ARGUMENT AND POWER

As well as being vehicles of information flow, networks are systems of interpretation that result from argumentation and establish power relationships. Fundamental to the dynamics of each network, culture contains narrative content and form that, once they are adopted, become themes that are enacted through interpersonal and intra-organizational relationships.

This approach to networks extends the analysis relevant to them far beyond what would be the case if they were only viewed as patterns of information flow among organizational members. An interpretivist view of networks acknowledges that culture prescribes how individuals can and should use networks. For instance, culture establishes guidelines for how much company time employees should use to socialize. It limits which information can be shared between which individuals. Culture unique to each company and each subunit indicates who is privileged to have certain kinds of information, and it provides interpretative frameworks for making sense of that information. One way that power has been expressed in recent years has been the privilege of having access codes to computerized company databases. Power people have access to files that are not made available to others, thereby making an information network a power network.

Culture outside of organizations affects which information is made available to which individuals. For instance, it suggests which information a vendor should, must, or never provide a customer. It prescribes which information a company makes available to activist groups and regulators. At a personal level, culture influences which information company members share with outsiders, such as members of their families ("You never tell me anything about your work").

Members of networks not only share information, but they also interpret it and use it to argue for and against competing points of view. Those conclusions become integrated into policies, procedures, and traditions, and therefore constitute the basis of power insofar as they influence behavior and judgments.

Making this point, Weick and Browning (1986) described how the structuration of an organization comes alive through arguments that its personnel create and assert. This view assumes that companies are rational entities (in varying degrees) where organizational features (goal clarity, means–ends consistency, and hierarchical integration) parallel elements typical of arguments: a priori assumptions, consistency, and reason giving.

Argument is used to interpret network interaction as narrative. Storytelling is not mere diversion. "Stories connect facts, store complex summaries in retrievable form, and help people comprehend complex environments. All stories are not created equal. Stories with higher narrative rationality should be more effective when used to socialize newcomers, process data, convey values, and change corporate culture" (Weick & Browning, 1986, p. 255). Narratives affect decision making. The structural-functional assumption that people make bad decisions because they have bad or inadequate information may ignore the fact that the information is good, but the interpretations are faulty. Networks are enacted zones of meaning in which people wrestle to interpret and characterize the information they acquire and share. When one set of arguments and interpretations prevails over others, it establishes operating rationale for the members of a network.

This line of analysis has substantial implication for views of organizational communication that suffer from a managerial bias. "The implied advice for managers who try to solve problems is that when they try to be rational, they may overemphasize logic and forget that there are multiple logics and multiple rationalities and that stories incorporate much of what arguments leave out. If a manger can argue logically with facts and then cover the same points with stories that ring true and hold together, then he or she has understood the issue more thoroughly" (Weick & Browning, 1986, p. 255). This position demonstrates the potency of story as organizational rhetoric and continues the theme that managers are advised to enact appropriate narratives with subordinates and fellow employees. It reflects commonplace assumptions that material is persuasive when it contains fact that is enlivened, through story for instance. Treating stories as rhetorical devices, however, can obscure the importance of treating network structure as narrative.

Narratives reflect archetypal network structures. On the one hand are the archetypes that reflect network structures, such as "Never go around the boss," "Most business is done at the water fountain," "Know the secretary (or clerk) who knows what's going on," or "If you want to get a job done find the person who knows how to do it." More narrowly, each company has its unique narratives of network structures, which are specific applications of archetypal structures that are unique to it.

Looking beyond the mere informational value of narratives, Mumby (1987) used them to explain how ideology, story, and power interrelate. Stories provide members with a sense of structure and offer closure whereby some views of organizational reality dominate competing views. This interpretative approach questions whether narratives merely convey information or whether they are used to create and implement organizational structure by imposing interpretations that privilege some members and marginalize others. Taking the latter view, Mumby (1987) argued that political themes in stories are used to show what each company expects of its members. Thus, "narratives not only evolve as a product of certain power structures, but also function ideologically to produce, maintain, and repro- duce those power structures" (p. 113). Narratives are "an ideological force that articulates a system of meaning which privileges certain interests over others" (p. 114). Culture is a control variable exerted throughout networks (C. A. Ray, 1986).

Mumby's (1987) analysis suggests that dominant individuals in a company are privileged to interpret events as they chose. Despite such privilege, less dominant individuals also provide their interpretations, although their meanings are likely to gain less adherence. Therefore, it is not simply individuals who are dominant, but dominance also resides in themes and meaning portrayed in narratives. As such, when less dominant individuals articulate dominant themes, they are more likely to move toward an increasingly dominant position within the structure of the company. As Mumby reasoned, "political reading of narrative draws attention to the relationship between narrative structure and the process of interpretation, and, as such, focuses on the process by which dominant meaning systems arise" (p. 113). For these reasons, narratives can legitimate or delegitimate political structures and meanings. These structures are translated into relationships that constitute networks and the ways to interpret information that exists in them.

Examining the weakness of an information approach to narratives, Mumby (1987) concluded that "power is exercised when ambiguous or equivocal informa- tion is interpreted in a way that favors the interests of a particular organized group; or, alternatively, when organizational ambiguity is utilized and amplified to dis- guise the exercise of power" (p. 116). For this reason, narratives interpret which activities are preferred in a company and express the expectations of some individ- uals over those of others. More than informing, narratives "help to *constitute* the organizational consciousness of social actors by articulating and embodying a particular reality, and subordinating or devaluing other modes of 'organizational rationality'" (p. 125).

Narratives are political because they result from and prescribe relationships between actors and between actors and the company. They "position subjects within the historical and institutional context of the material conditions of existence. A politically informed interpretation of institutional narrative must therefore explicitly take up this duality of structure, and uncover its 'strategies of containment'" (Mumby, 1987, pp. 125–126). Reflecting on a distinctly managerial view, C. A. Ray (1986) observed that "the top management teams aim to have individuals possess direct ties to the values and goals of the dominant *elites* in order to activate the emotion and sentiment which might lead to devotion, loyalty and commitment" (p. 294). This view holds that people are "emotional, symbol-loving, and needing to belong to a superior entity or collectivity," a view which may reflect the hopes of management more than the reality of common practice (p. 295).

Because of interpretations that exist, as well as varying amounts of contact and political influence networks have with one another, they exhibit degrees of connectedness and certainty. To deal with such issues, the concept of loose coupling has proven to be useful "precisely because it allows organizational analysts to explain the simultaneous existence of rationality and indeterminacy without specializing these two logics in distinct locations" (Orton & Weick, 1990). Being able to explain the degrees to which networks interlock has challenged researchers. This analysis is important because some organizations, for instance the operations of a police SWAT unit or a team of fire fighters, are markedly different from members of a research and development center. Nevertheless, each functions. Each achieves goals in ways that are productive and of different levels of quality. The concept of loose coupling "allows theorists to posit that any system, in any organizational location, can act on both a technical level, which is closed to outside forces (coupling produces stability), and an institutional level, which is open to outside forces (looseness produces flexibility)" (Orton & Weick, 1990, p. 205).

Culture is useful for explaining the ability of loosely *and* tightly coupled organizations to function. Discussing loosely coupled systems, Orton and Weick (1990) insisted on treating them as a dialectical rather than unidimensional concept. The underlying puzzle Orton and Weick identified is this: "Organizations appear to be both determinate, closed systems searching for certainty and indeterminate, open systems expecting uncertainty" (p. 204).

Argumentation and power, exerted through culture, are important means for accounting for the ability of networks to balance rationality and indeterminacy. How they operate in conjunction with one another results from the meanings that they enact. Organizational units, regardless of the hierarchical level, are interdependent. These networks "vary in the number and strength of their interdependencies" (Orton & Weick, 1990, p. 204). Although they are coupled, they may be loosely coupled. "The fact that these elements are also subject to spontaneous changes and preserve some degree of independence and indeterminacy is captured by the modifying word *loosely*. The resulting image is a system that is simultaneously open and closed, indeterminate and rational, spontaneous and deliberate" (Orton & Weick, 1990, pp. 204–205). Based on this analysis, Orton and Weick recommended the following categories of networks: "If there is neither responsiveness nor distinctiveness, the system is not really a system, and it can be defined as a *noncoupled system*. If there is responsiveness without distinctiveness, the system is tightly coupled. If there is distinctiveness without responsiveness, the system is decoupled. If there is both distinctiveness and responsiveness, the system is loosely coupled" (p. 205). The concept of coupling can be viewed as unidimensional or multidimensional. The unidimensional approach views tightly coupled systems "as having responsive components that do not act independently, whereas loosely coupled systems are portrayed as having independent components that do not act responsively" (Orton & Weick, 1990, p. 205).

Orton and Weick (1990) recommended a dialectical definition of loose coupling. Viewed this way, loose coupling occurs when unclear connections are made between means and ends that often result because "people have bounded rationality due to limited information processing capability, low and inaccurate memories that obscure, emphasize, or forget details, and short attention spans" (p. 211). Loose coupling seems preferable to tight coupling, because the former is both distinctive and responsive. Loosely coupled systems are good because they are capable of requisite variety. Loosely coupled systems are more adaptable.

As composites of the efforts of many people in concert with one another, networks offer requisite variety. If one relationship is likely to produce the information, advice, or socialization that a network member desires, more relationships increase the chances of the person achieving those goals. Therein lies the importance of multiplexity.

How can loosely coupled networks function properly? Enhanced leadership is one means for holding a unit together. By getting out of their office and finding out what is going on, managers get involved, offer interpretations, and focus attention on vital activities. To enact that strategy helps managers to influence the behavior of subordinates by getting them to focus on controllable and essential behaviors and by empowering them with the freedom to adapt and experience control that results when their behavior achieves local needs. Enhanced leadership entails the dialectic of getting personnel to share values expressed as metaphors, the glue that holds the network together.

Argument and analysis that lead to collective decisions agreeable to organizational members are vital to the operation of loosely coupled units. Used in this sense, argument is the process of collective analysis. Members assert opinions and react to those expressed by others. "If organizations are determined to be means–ends structures for attaining preferred outcomes, and if loose coupling is produced by uncertainties about these means–ends structures, then agreement about preferences is the only source of order that is left" (Orton & Weick, 1990, p. 212). Interpretative frameworks give networks the ability to interact internally and externally.

This view of loosely coupled systems preserves "a dialectical interpretation when it builds on the premise that looseness on some dimensions should be complemented by coupling on other dimensions" (Orton & Weick, 1990, p. 213). Five dependent variables are used to determine the success of loose coupling: *persistence* (the kind of stability that resists change and continues operation), *buffering* (activities that lessen the turbulence that results from loose coupling), *adaptability* (the ability to accommodate and change), *satisfaction* (the feeling that arises from self-determination, empowerment, and a sense of efficacy), and *effectiveness*. Loose coupling is a means by which to deal with the inherent dialectic of organization: "(a) a source of order which consolidates, unifies, or coalesces diverse elements or fragments and (b) elements or fragments, which are consolidated, unified, or coalesced by a source of order" (p. 216). According to Eisenberg (1984), unified diversity is a way to achieve coordination through shared meaning.

Viewed in these terms, networks are the enactment of systems of meaning through which organizational members make sense of and coordinate activities. How each network operates, obtains and processes information, and negotiates political relationships reflects its unique culture. Employing Weick's (1979b) approach to network analysis, Bantz (1990) used the routines entailed in news gathering and news production to demonstrate how network members enact meaning by interpreting information they obtain. In this process, the interpretative framework results from people in the network talking to one another. Through interaction, news production workers attempt to impose meaning on their environment. Networks are influenced by opinions of key players who interpret news events in ways others confirm by echoing. These interpretations are based on what Weick (1979b) called causal maps, which foretell how news events will be interpreted. In this way, networks are enacted as zones of meaning, frameworks for interpretation.

This interpretation of organizational influence is a version of the rhetoric of definition—the suasive creation of perspectives that others live. In that sense, the jargon that is unique to each network provides terministic screens for its members. Those who occupy key points in a company may create or embrace narratives that others adopt. Those key points need not correspond to the formal organization chart. In this sense, narratives create and disseminate corporate ideology that defines the personae of the players, their relationships, and assumptions they are encouraged to apply. In this way, narratives create structure because they establish interpretative and political relationships. Stories create, reproduce, disseminate, and maintain power relationships because they give a view of the world that members accept. Narratives are rhetorical devices that are used to negotiate the stake exchanges involved in power relations.

Is the corporate culture that emerges the mechanism that influences organizational behavior? Or do organizational members interpret the information obtained from stories idiosyncratically? It appears that members of organizations make varying degrees of calculated decisions regarding how and when to enact their roles on behalf of and in the context of the company. Therefore, employees do not always enact the prescribed roles in the manner that management expects. Reinterpretation of management narratives is part of organizational power struggles. For this reason, culture results from enactments of employees. Stories do not grow out of culture; culture is the product of stories (Smircich & Morgan, 1982; Weick & Browning, 1986). Network structure, whether analyzed in terms of perceptions of which information sources are best or what the power relationships are, consists of narrative form and content.

GROUP COMMUNICATION

Excellent organizational structure entails speaking with a single, coordinated Voice, one that is coherent and focused on company goals. We might imagine that outcome could occur because management promulgates the preferred Voice that employees adopt. Perhaps this could be accomplished through "strong culture," which has been alleged to account for the success of "excellent" organizations. That, however, is an ideal held by naive managers and cynical employees. One way to increase the coherence and singularity of Voice is to maximize employee involvement, to give them a sense of power by allowing their input and judgments on organizational matters that involve their interests and draw on their expertise. In this way, management and employee networks come together constructively (Bormann, 1983; Rogers & Kincaid, 1981).

Similar results occur when people from different departments or other networks come together to share information and make decisions. Information and premises that are important to one department and could be important for another department may not cross the boundaries of the two. Thus, when we think of the distribution of information throughout a company, we need to consider why, for instance, information held in the engineering department is unavailable to persons in other departments who could use it. Some people may have information that others can use, but those who have it may not know that others want it or can use it.

Contact through groups—attending meetings for instance—increases requisite variety, one of the positive features of networks. Increased opportunity to share information enhances the likelihood that people who want and need it will receive it. Requisite variety also operates to the extent that people are encouraged to comment on decisions suggested by others. Such comments increase the likelihood that judgments and advice, which can enhance the quality of decisions, reach the people who can wisely use them.

Group processes influence how people make decisions and implement policy. Groups constitute a network in and of themselves and they often link two or more networks. They span boundaries and bring people together from different networks. They are not only a factor in the climate in the organization, but they also are important to decision-making processes and information sharing. If it is necessary for people to share information and compare judgments, then groups offer an important means to achieve those ends.

Processes by which group members achieve outcomes should be more productive if they employ the same decision rules. Rules are used to decide which information is relevant to the decision the group is trying to make and how it should be weighted and combined in the decision. When groups are similar in their decision rules and are allowed to interact, they perform better than their counterparts (Beatty, 1989). Groups employ metaphors as they discuss information and share ideas, especially topics and ideas that are difficult to articulate, unpleasant, or controversial (Srivastva & Barrett, 1988). Metaphors help people find common ground between zones of meaning. For this reason, culture is vital to group efforts. Interpretative frames that are part of each culture suggest why specific bits of information receive more or less importance in some groups. For instance, in lean times, management might give substantial weight to layoffs to reduce company costs, whereas employees might focus their thoughts and recommendations for cost containment on lowering management salaries and cutting their perks.

Group activities and outcomes are enhanced or impeded by the task functions performed and socioemotional climate of the group. Members of groups, whether designated leaders or not, perform functions the group needs to achieve its goals, such as gathering and analyzing information and making insightful decisions. Socioemotional or climate-making functions are needed if group members are to operate properly, enjoying the supportiveness needed to share opinions and argue openly and constructively. When group members emphasize task strategies, the quality of the outcome is higher, and when they focus on the process used to make the decision, climate or socioemotional feelings are more positive (Jarboe, 1988).

Although meetings (a typical form of small group) often get a bad rap for being too long and allowing too many people to talk too much, when discussion is open and ideas are exchanged the conclusions that result are better than those that receive less exchange of ideas and opinions. Moreover, people are more satisfied when they believe they have been given ample opportunity to share information and voice opinions (Burleson, Levine, & Samter, 1984). The quality of group interaction depends on whether members consider positive *and* negative features of alternative decisions. People need to understand the problem they are attempting to solve and agree on requirements that must be met for an acceptable choice (Hirokawa, 1985, 1988).

Arguments in decision groups can devolve into heated and counterproductive wrangles, but they also can clarify points and sharpen decisions. Arguments are an important part of group decision making, especially when they take the form of *assertions* that express facts or opinions. Arguments result in *elaboration*, during which group members add support for their assertions, and *agreement*, during which they voice support for each others' assertions (Meyers, Seibold, & Brashers, 1991).

For many years, researchers believed that group decisions were best when they resulted from systematic group decision-making processes; advocates of that point of view sought to learn which patterns were optimal. In contrast to those efforts, other researchers believed that group decision-making processes were largely unstructured and for that reason doubted that any definitive pattern predicted or enhanced the stages through which group decision making progresses. Although groups suffer periods of disorganization, decision making follows a unitary sequence that consists of periods of critical analysis and integration, decision stages that involve problem solution and conflict resolution, and periods during which discussion is solution centered (Poole & Roth, 1989a). Group activities conform to the tenets of contingency theory because they seek the best means to solve problems under the circumstances.

The decision-making route group members take to solve problems and make decisions results from group structure characteristics, specifically power concentration, size or number of members of the group, and its cohesiveness. Size and cohesiveness interact markedly; the bigger the group the more difficult it is to achieve cohesiveness. Task characteristics, specifically value orientation, goal clarity, and openness, also predict the route group members will take during their efforts. The extent to which groups have to recycle through discussions they conducted previously depends on goal clarity and value orientation. The extent to which the decision topic is novel to the group and requires innovativeness are factors that predict how often a group must go back over discussion territory already covered. In this way, much of the discussion that occurs among group members is devoted to examining which strategies are likely to help them achieve their outcomes (Poole & Roth, 1989b).

In an effort to increase productivity and quality of service or products, employee task forces and quality circles have been used. Sometimes these two kinds of groups are thought of as being the same, although one version of task force is a group is employed to elicit opinions—perhaps of customers in a test market—through the use of questions asked by skilled moderators. Quality circles and focus groups were popularized in the past decade as U.S. companies sought to achieve the level of productivity and product quality that was becoming increasingly typical of Japanese companies. Quality circles were implemented to empower employees by involving them in decision processes and by enhancing their feelings of organizational identification. This strategy holds promise for increasing the amount and quality of information that is shared and judgment that is brought to bear on issues critical to productivity and quality.

Managers create a quality circle (or an employee task force) by selecting key employees from different departments or divisions and challenging them to recommend ways the company can improve itself. An assumption that is critical to the positioning of quality circles and of the selection of the personnel to participate in them is that employees often have information and suggestions related to how work could be done at a higher quality or more productively. Without some mechanism that circumvents the normal flow of information and advice in the administrative hierarchy of the company, members of management are likely to never have the information and suggestions they need to make changes. Therefore, needed changes might not be made.

Although quality circles have the mandate to concentrate on work design and morale issues, they also have been given the chance to suggest ways for improving climate. Here the equation is assumed to be that improved climate leads to increased productivity. Creation of a quality circle (one or several) itself is a statement that managers entrust and empower subordinates to recommend changes regarding work design and climate. How management responds to suggestions made by quality circles affects their efforts and morale. If management is unresponsive, circles fizzle; if a circle's suggestions are responded to thoughtfully and seriously by management, it becomes more fruitful in its suggestions and activities. Quality circles cannot correct a company that does not believe in employee empowerment. They become part of the statement a company makes about itself in terms of participative management and employee involvement (Smeltzer & Kedia, 1985).

If managers respond to group recommendations promptly and wisely, they avoid exemplifying the archetypal metaphor that as long as company members are talking about something they are not doing anything about it. For this reason, researchers have investigated whether quality circles add value to an organization, and if so, how they can be used effectively. Stohl (1987) examined whether circles can be positioned to usefully connect two or more networks. Are quality circles merely an artificial device added to normal efforts of networks or can they be effectively integrated into regular organizational routines? Addressing this concern, Stohl (1987) observed, "The general argument set forth is that quality circles that have developed linkages with organizational members/groups outside their own work area and level in the hierarchy will be more effective relative to other quality circles in the same organization lacking such linkages" (p. 418).

Measures of success of a quality circle depend on its productivity: number of problems raised and percentage of them solved, perceptions of group's effectiveness by group members, and perception of its effectiveness by supervisors and managers. Properly designed and integrated into a company, quality circles create a framework to generate and analyze information, to bring expert resources to bear on problems and innovations, and to increase social support for employees who are trying to improve the organization from the bottom up.

They provide a mechanism that links many organizational groups. For this reason, if a quality circle can get more information from a number of diverse groups it will be more influential "in (1) convincing management that its proposal is sound and worthwhile, (2) gaining commitment of resources to carry out the solution, and (3) assuring implementation of the solution by those members of the organization who must carry out the new plan" (Stohl, 1987, p. 420). If quality circle members think they are being effective, they are likely to be successful and managers are likely to perceive them as being effective. The more broadly a quality circle reaches out for information and suggestions the more likely managers are to perceive it to be effective and the more likely it is to have its proposals accepted and implemented. Quality circles that enjoy a high degree of cohesiveness are perceived by their members to be effective. They help employees meet social needs as well as increase the chance that innovative suggestions will be generated and implemented. Groups that have the most tenure in a company and have the most linkages with other networks are perceived to be most effective (Stohl, 1987).

One advantage of quality circles is their ability to change the dynamics of a company by lessening the constraints people experience in the form and content of their communication because of the position they hold in a network. Once people become members of quality circles, they feel less isolated and are more involved. Members of quality circles provide links. They interact more with other members of the company and with members at more levels of it. For that reason, quality circles lessen restrictions created by hierarchical barriers. Membership in quality circles gives employees a more positive attitude toward their company and increases their knowledge of it. Increased access to people within the organization's hierarchy, more information about it, and greater participation in its activities strengthen employees' sense of job satisfaction (Stohl, 1986).

An important rationale for the proper use of groups is that open, interactive discussion increases the accuracy of group decisions, thereby resulting in an *assembly effect* (Burleson et al., 1984). Though group participation, individuals come to share similar views of reality and know the views of the members of the group. This contact gives them the opportunity to know where agreement and disagreement exist. Such efforts and perceptions can lead to increasingly coherent and coordinated enactments.

STRUCTURATION: ENACTMENT OF STRUCTURE

Members need to know how to use company structure to obtain the information they need and exert influence on decisions that affect them. That realization challenges managers to think of structure as a mechanism that can hamper or enhance the flow of information and influence. An organization can be so chaotic, exhibiting high uncertainty, that people inside *and* outside of it have a hard time finding the information they need. If people seek information, they ought to be able to know which department (or other structural unit) can supply it and how to get it from the unit. If a person needs details on how to fill out a medical insurance form, a call might be placed to the benefits department—assuming that a company has one. Material inventory data would be sought by contacting key personnel in the warehouse. Training schedules could be obtained from the human resource department. Structure and ability to obtain information are important to the functioning of a company as well as to its climate. Employees feel more satisfied in an organization and believe they are more involved when they have the information they need (Penley, 1982).

The structure of an organization is a means by which chaos is lessened, the environment is made less random, and information acquisition becomes more predictable. In a small company, "Bertha" or "John"—those key employees typical of every small company and some large ones, might be the person to see about all three matters: health benefits, warehouse inventory, and training. That structure, however, can be bureaucratic (and powerful) because if few people have all the information they can hold the rest of the company hostage. If a key person is absent for a day, other employees may be rendered helpless. We have all encountered the problem of trying to do business with a person who says, "Bertha/John is gone today. You'll have to come back when she/he is here. She/he is the only one who can help you."

That brief illustration demonstrates the point that structure is not static; it is not fixed. That realization is the crucial aspect of *structuration*. Structure (organization) is enacted by what people do, not merely by management's promulgation of a chart that creates organizational subunits, such as departments and divisions. The concept of structuration captures the essence of enactment.

Structural-functionalism assumes that information flow is the essence of organizational structure. Networks are focal points of analysis, and key concerns revolve around information overload or underload, asking whether people have enough or too much information to meet their needs and match their ability to process it. By extrapolating that approach, structures and functions unique to each company can be thought to consist of the formal organizational chart as compared to how information actually flows between individuals and groups.

Viewed that way, communication structure is "repetitive patterns or networks of communication exchange" (Farace et al., 1977, p. 207). Communication load refers to "the amount of time and effort (resources) members of the organization spend in communicating and/or processing information" (p. 207). Analytical concepts typical of this line of analysis include rate (speed at which messages flow throughout an organization), redundancy (number of times a person receives similar messages), efficiency (ease with which information flows), and distortion (changes that occur during input, processing, and transmission of messages). These factors can be cast in terms of functions (production, innovation, and maintenance) that are supported by information that exists in an organization. *Production* refers to which information is needed and used to get jobs done. *Innovation* requires messages and information needed to explore alternatives. *Maintenance* is used to keep the system operating.

A problem results when information is distorted as it is shared within a company. Simply put, distortion exists when meaning of data at one level is not the same as it is at another level. Distortion can result when information moves upward from subordinate to superior, downward from superior to subordinate, or between employees at the same level. Distortion can result because people add or remove information from a message they pass along. It exists when information is altered through interpretation. It can result from gatekeeping, when one party does not allow (does not send) all of the information (received or available) to reach the person above or below. Summarization occurs when the person transmitting information gives some or all of it a particular emphasis. Withholding results in some information not being sent (Roberts & O'Reilly, 1974).

Capturing the essence of structuration, Monge and Eisenberg (1987) argued that networks should be thought of as dynamic and emerging, rather than static and fixed. Indeed, a correlation may exist between the health of the organization and the extent to which its networks are dynamic and emerging. One of the tough balances in the operation of a company is to achieve the proper balance between orderliness and flexibility. One extreme of orderliness is a bureaucracy; structure is routine and static. That kind of organization typically lacks flexibility. Under some conditions, as argued by contingency theory, such an organization might be best; it certainly could satisfy the requirement of providing information predictably. At the other end of the continuum, chaos should not be mistaken for structure that is dynamic and emerging. Each of us probably has experienced a company that is so lacking in a coherent Voice that nothing seems to be routine, systematic, or predictable. The challenge is to achieve a proper balance (Morgan, 1986).

One solution to that problem places less emphasis on the flow of information in a network and gives more attention to the structure of the organization as the product of what people believe it to be, the meaning of structure and interaction in and between each network. As conceived by Poole and McPhee (1983), structuration depends on organizational climate, interaction rules, and meaning. As they concluded, "Climate arises from concrete practices and understandings that necessitate tracing the specific relations of meaning to action" (p. 209).

In accord with that approach, members of a company match or compare their sense of its structure through what they say and do. If some members, for instance, believe that its has open structures, whereas other members believe the opposite, then the structure is not open, or at least it is not open for all members. Some members of a company, for instance, might believe that they are privileged to complain about what is going on; in addition to their complaints they may even offer solutions. Those members would be enacting an open structure. If a boss constantly calls such people whiners and cautions that the company does not like whiners, then the enactment of that climate is not open even though the boss professes to have an open door policy.

Each company's climate (and that of its subunits) is likely to result from and predict which communication rules are enacted. "Coorientation of communication rules is a necessary condition for successful coorientation. Communication rules form the basis for intersubjectivity in organizations; they are the point of contact of individual members' perspectives" (Poole & McPhee, 1983, p. 206). This interaction between climate and communication rules assumes that structuration results from interaction, based on this equation: Interaction depends on enactment of communication rules—who says what to whom with what goal under which circumstances.

Vital to how company members enact structure are their knowledge, communication skills, and resources. These are acquired as each person interacts with others in a system. The knowledge organizational members have, for instance, depends on what others allow them to have, especially in situations where power is a key factor. Knowledge is power. The giving or withholding of it is the exertion of power. "Organizations are structured to the extent that there is a definite pattern of influence among levels" (Poole & McPhee, 1983, p. 212). Knowledge, in this sense, also results from the culture that pervades a network—a zone of meaning.

Featuring power to explain structuration, Mumby (1987) reasoned that "production of organizational reality can be explained in terms of its structuration through ideological meaning formations; such meaning formations simultaneously produce and are created by the structure of power interests in organizations" (p. 113). As a device for helping to produce structure, culture expressed through narratives fosters sense making, Mumby believed, but argued that it does not explain "deep structure, the process through which certain organizational realities come to hold sway over competing world-views" (p. 113).

To correct that shortcoming, Mumby (1987) reasoned that "narratives provide members with accounts of the process of organizing. Such accounts potentially legitimate dominant forms of organizational reality, and lead to discursive closure in the sense of restricting the interpretations and meanings that can be attached to organizational activity" (p. 113). Ideology, power, and narrative are interrelated because "narratives not only evolve as a product of certain power structures, but also function ideologically to produce, maintain, and reproduce those power structures" (p. 113). This synergism between narrative, ideology, and power demonstrates how each affects the other; the three interact so that each supports the other.

Ideology is particularly important in this case because it gives an encompassing perspective that people use to understand power relationships and sense the orderliness that is interpreted to be the structure of each company. Some individuals, groups, and structural processes are privileged by narratives and ideology that portray the structure of the company. Groups are not merely privileged by some mechanism, such as an organizational chart; their presence and influence in the company results from what they do and say to assert their influence. The dialectic of each assertion is the ways in which other organizational members interpret, modify, or accept it. "In this sense, power and ideology are not purely structural phenomena, separate from the interaction of social actors; they are both the medium and outcome of that interaction, embodied in the 'systems of signification' of the organization" (Mumby, 1987, p. 119).

An example can demonstrate how structure is enacted. The production department sends material to another department. Members of the company believe the following statement about the production department is true: "The material it provides is usually 2 days late and lower in quality than what is needed." If no one does anything to correct that situation, the production department has exercised its power to set its own performance standards. People who enact the structure of the company have several political options: (a) they may seek the influence of some authority in the company to pressure for better performance, or they may assume that management does not care about meeting schedules or maintaining production quality; (b) they may make their plans accordingly and be ready to explain that the quality of material and the delivery delays are out of their control; or (c) they may set schedules early and specifications high to compensate for the lack of diligence on the part of the production department. In this way, operating premises become vital to organizational climate, interaction rules, persona, knowledge, communication, and supervisory skills. These factors influence the enactment of structure.

In that sense, Poole and McPhee (1983), concluded, "Climate is an *outcome* of day-to-day practices in structured organizations. Members' experiences generalize to reinforce or challenge the prevailing climate" (p. 215). Enactment of climate results from and generates specific rhetorical processes that are used to reproduce and maintain it. "An authoritarian climate that is both consensual and structured implies different degrees of power, rights, and rewards for members high and low in the organizational hierarchy" (p. 216).

One of the factors affecting structure is the relationship between superiors and subordinates or leaders and followers. Social exchange theory reasons that perceived equity and effectiveness of efforts to reciprocate exchange of resources will affect the relationships that result between participants. This becomes a very real factor when subordinates evaluate the quality of the exchange (rewards) their superiors have been able to obtain for them in light of the performance efforts given by the subordinate. "I really work hard and produce, but my boss is unable to X for me in return." This typical "fill in the blank" script of organizational life indicates the social exchange required to maintain or abandon certain structural relationships. If a superior cannot satisfy the expectations of workers who believe themselves to be deserving, then some structuration outcomes are likely. The subordinates might flaunt the lack of effectiveness, the relationship may deteriorate, or the subordinate may leave the unit or organization seeking reward elsewhere. Thus, structuration is defined by self-interests of the participants, stakes they and the other stakeholders have, each party's willingness and ability to exercise their stakes, and prevailing interpretations of equity.

Summarizing this relationship, Hollander (1980) observed that superior–subordinate transactions are influenced by *system progress* and *equity*. The first concerns how and whether group goals are attained. Equity refers to subordinates' perception of whether they were treated fairly. Subordinates believe they have a right to be fairly rewarded if they are expected to remain inside the group and be dedicated to its efforts. Estimates of equity draw on comparisons of what others of comparable characteristics and responsibility do and receive for their effort. Hollander cautioned that "the leader especially needs to be alert to perceived inequities, and will likely be blamed for them as a determiner of rewards. These perceptions are subjective judgments, since rewards and costs are always relative to the people involved and their particular needs" (p. 118). Subordinates exert counterinfluences that reinforce or challenge interpretations or actions of their superiors.

This view of structure depends on the meaning that arises through enactments by individuals who make up organizational units. It stresses the importance of goals. One question, however, concerning goals, is whether they actually are important to shared enactment. Addressing that point, Weick (1979b) asserted that people need to agree on means, even if not on ends:

> Individuals come together because each wants to perform *some* act and needs the other person to do certain things in order to make performance possible. People don't have to agree on goals to act collectively. They can pursue quite different ends for quite different reasons. All they ask of one another at these initial stages is the contribution of their action. Why that person consents to make the contribution or why that contribution is needed is secondary to the fact that the contribution is made. Partners in a collective structure share space, time, and energy, but they need not share visions, aspirations, or intentions. That sharing comes much later, if it ever comes at all. (p. 91)

The process of structuring begins when individuals come together, even though they have diverse ends—what they want from the company and what they need to feel satisfied. As they come together, they focus on means, not goals. After the organization has functioned for some time, a shift may occur. People still have diverse ends or goals, but those become subsumed under goals that are shared and encompass individual differences of the people. These are needed to coordinate the efforts of the individuals involved. They assist individuals in knowing what rules to follow and what cost–reward ratios are involved in social exchange.

Weick (1979b) reasoned that people can organize without having shared goals or without even knowing the individual goals of one another. He contended that "it is not even necessary that people see the entire structure or know who their partners are. What is crucial in a mutual equivalence structure is mutual prediction, not mutual sharing" (p. 100). That analysis is basic to enactment theory, which postulates that the basic unit of structure and coordination in a company is a predictable set of actions among it members. Thus, "all you need to know is (1) that a person's behavior in some circumstances is predictable, and (2) that other behaviors can be predictably related to one's own activities" (Weick, 1979b, p. 100).

Weick (1979b) reasoned that structure requires two factors: assembly rules and interlocked behavior cycles. "Assembly rules are inferred recipes that influential organizational members appear to be using when they create a process. Assembly rules can be viewed as procedures, instructions, or guides that members use to mobilize several double interacts into larger processes that are directed as inputs" (p. 113). Relationships are negotiated by how each party acts and reacts—adjusts— to the actions of the other party as both attempt to achieve interlocked behavior cycles. When a company exhibits high equivocality of rules, it experiences turbulence because all interaction choices are equal. Low equivocality of rules means that choices are less random and therefore more predictable.

How do people know what is needed to negotiate and coordinate these interlocking activities? Interlocking relationships take on meaning through culture. Although different means can be obtained from the same goals, if people only do *something*, that behavior can become random and pointless. It can suffer entropy and become unproductive because people cannot estimate the extent to which their efforts are obtaining goals if they do not know what those goals are, how others interpret and share those goals, and whether others' efforts are focused on comparable if not the same goals. The key to interlocking effort is the recognition of a theme (O) by which participants define each situation to give themselves the sense of which activities and meanings are relevant to their coordinated activities.

Management faces the task of getting people to focus on the same unit goals as means for coordinating interlocking behaviors. Although personal goals may differ, structuration assumes that people enact organization by knowing which actions are appropriate to achieve specific goals. Even if members do not know each others' motives, they attribute them out of the need to believe the world is predictable. People enact in one way as opposed to another because they think that act will produce the right outcome and satisfy what they believe others expect of them.

What they enact and how they interpret that action and perform corresponding counteraction is influenced by interpretative frames. Culture is a means by which individual perceptions and judgments become generalized so that people can predict each others' behavior and their response to it. If behavior does not grow from interlocked perspectives, it may become random—tending toward entropy. When behavior is similar and predictable leading to goals commonly believed to be appropriate, it speaks with a nearly singular voice. Viewed this way, structure arises from the sense people make of the actions of others and their own reactions. Narratives give these actions perspective and let people know what is expected of them as they enact structure with others.

Structuration requires reasonably predictable patterns of information sharing. It entails ideology and power structures. Climate results from and contributes to perceptions of structure. All of this is important for individuals who look for meaning in the joint enactment of their interlocking relationships with other people who, at least to a sufficient extent, share a vision.

FOCAL POINTS OF NETWORK ANALYSIS

- What patterns characterize information flow in an organization? How do they correspond to the zones of meaning that subunits use in their enactments?
- Do management-level efforts foster boundary spanning to facilitate flow of vital information and foster a sense of meaning that fosters cohesiveness?
- Are groups an effective part of the company's efforts to set and meet quality improvement and productivity goals?
- Do employees feel that they can use networks to obtain information they need and share information they believe is important to other members of the company?
- Are employees integrated into networks in ways that enhance their identification with the company and increase their sense of empowerment?
- Are the interpretative systems used by members of interlocking networks compatible and complementary or contradictory?
- Do the communication processes and interpretations help or hinder identification with network membership?
- What metaphors characterize the information, decision premises, and stages of analysis that recur in group decisions?
- Do the political dynamics of network structure work for or against employee involvement?
- Do people understand and effectively perform their roles as links?

CONCLUSION

Many strategies have been employed to blend formal organizational systems—those that transpire through the established organizational chart of each company with informal structures that bring people together by cutting across departmental and organizational lines. That effort has renewed the belief that groups are useful.

Networks are a useful focal point of analysis because they combine the structural and functional relationships that people enact as they coordinate their efforts with many people who are scattered throughout a company or are arrayed in its external environment. Networks are a web of interlocking interaction in complex, system-wide structures. Along with structural-functional interpretations of networks, interpretivism gives insight into the workings of networks, particularly when they are conceptualized as zones of meaning.

That theme is extended in the next two chapters, which analyze how companies interact with their external audiences. External publics exist as zones of meaning with which information is shared and judgments are enacted on behalf of, or contrary to the interests of each company.

9

Markets, Images, Issues, and External Stakeholders

Companies try to impose themselves on their environments, rather than merely adapt to them. They attempt to shape their environment by their presence in it, by what they do and say. For example, Ford Motor Company gave us the mass-produced automobile industry. Now cars are central to our culture; our lives are symbolized—and threatened environmentally—by them. IBM and its competitors gave us a world of mainframe computers, and Apple started a successful personal computer market. Steel companies shaped our ideas about buildings, tools, and bridges. The garment industry influences our taste in clothing. The entertainment (print, video, TV, radio, and film) industry lures us from our homes or keeps us there to gratify our needs for information and entertainment. Each of these examples and dozens more hint at the meaning each organization uses in its effort to obtain public acceptance as well as define our national culture. These enactments can lead key audiences to identify with organizations, a central goal of external communication efforts.

From an enactment perspective, this discourse is ontological, rather than purely informative or persuasive. Its meaning results from acts of saying and doing. For instance, the purchase of a Ford Motor car is an enactment of narratives of power, independence, and self-efficacy that join customer and manufacturer. Likewise, environmental protest and recycling activities enact the narrative of a world of beauty as opposed to a "trampled garden." As Campbell and Jamieson (1978) reasoned, this enactment is "a recurrent rhetorical form, a reflexive form ... in which the speaker incarnates the argument, is the proof of the truth of what is said" (p. 9).

To assert themselves onto their environments, companies spend billions of dollars on product and service advertising, corporate identity campaigns, glossy annual reports, lobbying, and issue advertising. They incur these expenditures to attract attention, gain acceptance, and assert opinions. Employing one-to-many formats that rely on print, radio, video, and television media, much of this communication is designed and executed by public relations, advertising, and marketing professionals. To understand how businesses assert their presence, this chapter and chapter 10 consider how communication affects zones of meaning that support marketplace activities, such as buying and selling, and takes stands on issues that affect policy relationships between company managements and their external stakeholders. Of particular importance is the way this communication increases or decreases the identification key publics have with those companies.

This line of analysis is crucial because if we stop after discussing communication that transpires inside companies we ignore the fundamental reason why they are formed. They occur because people collectively can have more impact on external stakeholders than they can individually; people need to work together to obtain rewards from external stakeholders. In that pursuit, meanings are used to define and join interests of organizations to those of external audiences as they negotiate the exchange of stakes. This last point is vital because it emphasizes the fact that audiences are not passive vessels into which companies inject messages and thereby exert unconditional control. It acknowledges the powerful impact the messages of outsiders have on companies. Indeed, companies often try to enact control by indicating that they agree with the statements of their critics; they in fact hold those opinions more dearly than their critics do.

Typical stakes held by outside audiences include decisions to buy and sell products or services. Customers who hold buying dollars decide to allot them to company X instead of company Y; the assumption is that the customer is more satisfied by what is obtained in exchange with X than Y. In this way, organizations and their customers enact narratives of buying and selling. In addition to purchases, external stakeholders hold negative or positive opinions of personae of companies, which in turn affect business transactions and decisions that depend on the degree to which corporate behavior is believed to be ethical. A third category of stakes consists of public policy positions—the support or opposition of policy positions that have regulatory and legislative outcomes.

Central to this analysis is the realization that companies do more than respond to their environments in a cybernetic way. They try to define their environment. If they do so appropriately, they increase their chances of receiving stakes in competition with other companies. However, companies can make a serious mistake by adopting a communication stance that Gaudino, Fritsch, and Haynes (1989) captured this way: "If you knew what I know, you'd make the same decision" (p. 299). Companies become more successful when they adapt their enactment to that of their publics. The key is to achieve a joint enactment, one that is based on a shared principle (O) satisfying to both parties. To avoid appearing to be too obvious and aggressive, companies can employ narratives. They create narratives of buying behavior. They reinforce or alter narratives. They portray themselves as conforming to prevailing narratives.

Capturing the spirit of this enactment, Sproule (1989) reasoned that "organizations try to privatize public space by privatizing public opinions; that is, skillfully (one-sidely) turning opinion in directions favorable to the corporation" (p. 264). If that observation strikes you as "mind control," rest assured that messages from many companies and other organizations, such as environmentalists or consumer groups, compete in the opinion marketplace. In such matters, external stakeholders have the final say as they allot their stakes of agreement in support of one idea as opposed to another. For this reason, effective companies strive to be approachable, to enact agreeable narratives.

Through its enactment, each company provides information about itself. If what a company does disagrees with what it says or what publics expect, a legitimacy gap occurs (Sethi, 1977). Audiences base their expectations on messages they have received from many sources. Interpretative frames that they use to evaluate companies reflect zones of meaning—terministic screens—to which they subscribe; for that reason, a person who employs an environmentalist interpretative frame is likely to see issues related to timber companies or chemical companies differently than do audiences with different interpretative frames. Some of the information each person uses to judge companies is generated through direct encounter. For that reason, the quality of a product or service, or the attractiveness of a clear-cut hillside, is not based solely on assertions by a company but also on what people think based on their encounters with a product, service, or environmental condition.

External communication consists of statements and counterstatements, acts and counteracts. Typical of this dialectic is the survey finding that a majority of the U.S. public favors requiring alcohol and tobacco products to carry warning labels. Sixty percent of the sample would require equal time for public health commercials. Fifty-four percent believed cigarette ads should be banned from newspapers and magazines (Freedman, 1989). Findings such as these exemplify the fact that products and services survive or fail in an opinion environment that often extends beyond judgments about products (such as individual brands of cigarettes) or services (such as legal services).

The character of this discourse is revealed by Sproule's (1988) analysis of 20th-century rhetoric, the nature of which changed once large organizations displaced persons as dominant speakers or rhetors. In contrast to personal rhetoric, organizational rhetoric often recommends conclusions based on packaged ideology rather than reasoned arguments. It consists of self-contained slogans and seeks to advance images rather than ideas. It relies on identification and interpersonal attraction even though the source of attraction is a company—as in the case of a manufacturer of sports shoes that adopts the personae of popular sports figures. It creates facts rather than discovering and testing them. It employs entertainment as a persuasive medium. It segments society and speaks to each group as an individual entity that receives unique, tailor-made messages.

This chapter explains how messages are used to influence stakeholder views of a company, its persona, its products or services. External communication assists companies' efforts to build a favorable relationship—especially identification—with stakeholders and to gain their approval. Four terms are vital to this analysis: image, issue, value, and identity. As Cheney and Vibbert (1987) observed, "Issues point to values, values often become issues, the discussion of issues affects images, such changes are linked to identities" (p. 176). Through actions, words, and graphics, companies seek to have stakeholders identify with them in ways that foster relationships.

BUILDING RELATIONSHIPS

Relationships are everything. They are enacted by what employees do and say on behalf of their companies. Based on this principle, this section examines a range of means by which relationships are enacted, starting with what employees do.

True story: You set out to arrange to travel with a major airline weeks in advance of the scheduled flight to an academic convention. Using the 1-800 number provided in the academic association newsletter, you call to purchase your tickets from the convention agent. You arrange your flights and apply the cost to your credit card. The tickets, you are told, will arrive "by mail at your home in about 1 week. Thank you for flying X Airline." Two weeks later you call the same 1-800 number to announce that the tickets have not arrived. A courteous agent tells you that the airline has no record of your reservation, but the agent is solicitous and again makes the arrangements. One week later you call to say the tickets have not arrived. This time you get the agent's name, Chris, and are told that a slight problem has occurred in handling the tickets, but they will be sent immediately. Two days later your credit card statement arrives bearing the cost of the tickets, but the tickets do not arrive. The departure time is now so close that you cannot wait on mail delivery. You call the 1-800 number and ask for Chris. "Chris is busy but will call you shortly," you are told. Chris does not call. You call again. "Chris is away from his desk." Now you become desperate and renew the transaction with the agent on the line, Fred. He promises the tickets will be held for you at the ticketing area of your airport. Later, you call back to double check. Fred and Chris are unavailable, but Martha volunteers to help. "Nope, your tickets have not been issued, but I will take care of them immediately. Sorry for the inconvenience." Twenty-four hours later you arrive at the airport 2 hours early because you are convinced your tickets will not be available. Your worst fear is realized. After much pleading, an agent volunteers to help. (The line behind you is long, and others in line are angry at you for not having *your* "act" together.) The agent says, "I could lose my job for doing what I am about to do." Exhibiting extreme anxiety, the agent issues the tickets and you depart. The airline company has "spoken" to you. The Voice is discordant and confused. You vow to never do business with the company again. The relationship is strained or broken because of the failure to meet expectations of trust.

This story exemplifies, among other points, that people evaluate their relationships with businesses. Two well-established, interrelated lines of inquiry give insights into audiences' reactions to companies and their relationships with them. One line of analysis is captured in information integration, expectancy value theory (Ajzen & Fishbein, 1980; Fishbein & Ajzen, 1975, 1981) and the other involves cognitive processing (Wright, 1973, 1981). Fishbein and Ajzen contended that attitudes result when many subopinions (both negative and positive) work in concert. These opinions combine into an attitude toward something, in this case a company and its product or service. The expectancy value part of the theory postulates that people act based on interaction of two factors: (a) extent to which an action is predicted to produce positive or negative outcomes, and (b) desire to comply with established behavioral norms. Explaining cognitive theory, Wright concluded that receivers react to ad content by using refutation and counter and pro-opinion arguments. Wright's research demonstrates that audiences are not hollow vessels that companies "fill" with ad copy. Audiences approach communication about companies, products, and services with varying degrees of skepticism and are ready to refute statements companies make.

To enact their personae, companies flood the opinion marketplace using carefully designed statements about products and services, as well as profits, operations, and operating procedures. Even when they proudly proclaim products to be "new and improved," labels provide little information about ingredients to prove their point. Despite appearances of openness, companies keep secrets that have proprietary importance. Someone once said, in this regard, that a person is more likely to find out how to make an atomic bomb than to discover corporate recipes, such as that for Classic Coca-Cola. Despite appearances to the contrary, companies are notoriously bad about hiding information from curious publics, which often— because of ethical principles—deserve to have it.

As information is difficult for key publics to obtain from companies, it also may be slow and inaccurate when it flows from publics to companies where it may be misinterpreted. What do buying publics really want and like in a product? How typical and accurate are comments companies receive when they provide comment cards for customers to complete? What do buying publics truly think about quality, price, and value of an organization's goods and services? How angry have activist groups become and how likely are they to become active in their efforts to increase regulation to improve the quality or safety of products and services? Thousands of dollars are spent to answer these questions and many more like them.

In addition to considering flow of information between organizations and publics, we can examine the extent to which both entities operate out of similar principles or themes. Not only do businesses use rhetoric to influence judgments and actions of external audiences, but the fact that each company exists is an assertion—an argument—to justify its presence. Through their statements, companies—collectively and singly—assert their views regarding financial, consumer, economic, social, and political matters. This rhetoric shapes and exploits an opinion environment to achieve ends for which the business was created. The purpose of organizational rhetoric is to achieve efficacy as a business by creating favorable zones of opinion and taking advantage of premises that define and justify particular activities.

Companies assert themselves by getting publics to buy cars, garments, electronic equipment, houses, food products and such. The same is true of services provided by banks, investment companies, doctors, dentists, lawyers, and accountants. As these products and services become part of people's lives, an accompanying culture defines and rationalizes them into a lifestyle. By accepting (or rejecting) products and services, publics enact relationships with companies based on definitions of lifestyle. Perhaps no better evidence of this phenomenon exists than that revealed by the changes that redefined the automobile market in the past two decades. Detroit revolutionized U.S. society with the mass-produced automobile. Having become complacent with their definition of that relationship, U.S.

automakers have seen the public's definition of the preferred automobile change due to availability of foreign-designed and manufactured cars. The public supplanted its relationship with General Motors, Ford, and Chrysler with one with Toyota, Honda, and Volkswagen.

In ways that range from the blatant to the unobtrusive, companies have and continue to shape lifestyles. With highly polished and well-planned campaigns, they inform publics of the qualities of their goods and use motives to entice them to buy—to "vote" approval with their money. This litany of advertising and public relations messages creates scripts and expectations that give symbolic substance to lifestyle narratives, each episode of which is punctuated with purchases. Car companies, for example, advertise the joy of driving and thrill of automobile performance. For the most part, they do not remind audiences of the endless maintenance cost of owning a car, nor the aggravation of dealing with surly shop personnel, instead of the mythic "Mr. Goodwrench."

Companies can enact their relationship with key publics to the extent that both entities share narratives that contain compatible or complementary themes, *O*. Companies have harmonious relationships with stakeholders that share and enact the same central theme. For that reason, a new industry—such as inception of the automobile or the computer industry—needs to establish narratives that allow customers to make sense of it and to know how to interact with it. As innovation occurs, an existing narrative can be extended, as is the case when standard telephone service becomes mobile through handheld cellular phones or phones in automobiles. That new narrative, using car phones, gains impact when it is connected with other narratives such as ensuring that wives (self) or daughters are safe as they drive in places where they could be stranded and harmed; or the narrative is the expanded office, whereby a business person "takes the office phone" in a briefcase.

Narrative analysis considers how successfully companies adapt to narratives that their stakeholders believe. One striking example of this match of narratives can be found as the result of the environmental movement. The 1960s and 1970s created new narratives regarding environmental sensitivity. Despite companies' opposition, those narratives became well established; once they did industries jumped on them, tied their wagon to them, and said, "Us too!" Chevron's "People Do" campaign, for instance, attempts to show how a major petrochemical company loves nature. Texaco and Shell have used similar rhetorical appeals, to name only a few companies.

Similar events have occurred in the food industry. After ignoring pleas for more nutritious products, food companies now quickly join their product and company persona to health trends. One recent version involved "anti-cholesterol" narratives in which clogged arteries are the villain. Quaker Oats Company, for one, advertised that its Oat Bran could reduce serum cholesterol, as demonstrated by "27 years of research" by medical groups. The narrative of clogged arteries was intended to give way to a narrative of arteries cleansed of serum cholesterol by oat bran. The good health narrative had the same theme as the traditional Quaker Oats Bran narrative that has portrayed generations of people made healthy by the "Quaker character" who has prepared many meals for healthy people. Playing on the cholesterol narrative got food companies into trouble because if they were going to make medical claims—reduce serum cholesterol levels—their critics said they would have to meet standards of the "medicine narrative" by proving their claims and submitting data to more rigorous and demanding regulatory standards than would be required to substantiate advertising claims.

Despite appearances to the contrary, many advertising messages have little or no effect on individuals. Each day people ignore hundreds of ads because they are too focused on other issues to attend to every message that competes for their attention. They do not have time or inclination to cut through the clutter of ads to make sense of them all. Many ads that people remember are unlikely to influence their buying preferences. All of us can remember ads that have touted products that we did not buy. Nevertheless, the residual of all ads constitutes a potent statement about lifestyles that becomes so compelling that people do not think of living any other way. This meaning becomes the scene they enact with high degrees of narrative predictability.

Ever searching for ways to attract audiences, companies have begun to employ a new breed called infomercials. On television, these ads appear in 30-minute informative-entertainment segments. A typical TV infomercial is the "self-made" millionaire success story guy who often broadcasts from a spa or mansion. Other infomercials feature "slice-and-dice" equipment or miracle cures. In magazines, these ads address a range of topics from important features of foreign countries to health advice and product attributes. This kind of ad is designed to inform and sway opinions through friendly advice without appearing to be an ad, a tactic that has raised the hackles of critics and regulators because the ads can be deceptive. An aggressive infomercial effort occurred in 1991 when the Home Shopping Network initiated a 24-hour channel devoted to this advertising tactic.

Relationships between companies and external publics fall into one of four options: one-way asymmetrical, one-way symmetrical, two-way asymmetrical, and two-way symmetrical. The *one-way asymmetrical* model is characterized by public relations efforts to increase and place news items as though they objectively characterize company operations; in this way, for instance, newspapers have entire sections, such as those devoted to real estate, that are nothing more than placed advertisement. The *one-way symmetrical* model relies on public information flowing only from company to audiences. The *two-way asymmetrical* approach results when public information and persuasive campaigns use surveys to determine what audiences want to hear and predetermine the effect each message might have and did have on the target audience. The preferred model, *two-way symmetrical* communication, results when information flows into and out of companies with the goal of building harmony and negotiating differences with external publics (Grunig, 1989b, 1992; Grunig & Hunt, 1984).

Enactments related to this flow of information out of and into companies test each one's ability to cope with internal and external turbulence (Huber & Daft, 1987). Kinds of activists as well as regulatory agencies companies encounter can strain the business' ability to adapt and achieve the desired level of control. For instance, companies that deal with new regulatory agencies experience more uncertainty than do those that interact with established agencies (Ungson et al., 1985). Over time, the relationship between agency and company (or industry) stabilizes, resulting in less turbulence. The agency may eventually adopt so many standards recommended by the industry that it no longer truly regulates, but serves as an extension of the industry's effort to promulgate its zone of meaning. When regulatory environments are stable and certain, companies may succeed with one-way communication, but when turbulence soars, two-way relationships are more likely to help companies achieve their goals (Grunig, 1992; Grunig & Grunig, 1989).

Whether through activities of individual employees or via slick advertising campaigns or public relations activities, companies seek to develop relationships with external stakeholders. These relationships are not easily created and are constantly tested by those publics. These entities engage in social exchange, whereby stakes are negotiated. In this tug-of-war to define relationships, arguments are made and countered. The dialectic of act and counteract characterizes relationships between companies and their stakeholders.

ESTABLISHING PERSONA

Each company asserts a persona to which external publics react positively, negatively, or indifferently. That reaction can manifest itself in two kinds of identification. One is through symbols that bond company and individual, whether positively or negatively, and which may result from or lead to product or service preferences. Another depends on action such as membership (e.g., seeking employment) or financial support, such as buying behavior. People's identification also takes into consideration organizations they do not like and from which they disassociate. For instance, environmentalists may seek to disassociate themselves from companies that pollute by avoiding their products. Although environmentalists hate companies that pollute, a vital part of their identity is derived from such companies. Their identity is dialectic, a counterbalance to companies that pollute. Similar relationships exist when people believe that a company discriminates, operates unethically, sells undesirable products, or advocates repugnant policies and actions.

Persons' identities are related to the identifications they hold with companies (Burke, 1961). Who people think themselves to be is a product of and results in a variety of identifications with specific companies and industries. Cheney (1983a) concluded, "Identification—with organizations or anything else—is an active process by which individuals link themselves to elements in the social scene" (p. 342).

An important aspect of corporate persona is to be perceived as being effective and in charge. Organizations employ different tactics to impress on external audiences that they are able to solve problems, to produce quality products and services, and to make correct decisions. In this effort to assert efficacy, product and service advertising is a typical communication vehicle. Another means is the corporate annual report, which gives corporate managements the opportunity to assert their efficacy, especially to investors, brokers, and analysts.

In annual reports, when business outcomes are good and companies show profits, the management team tends to attribute success to itself, as in "we did it, we achieved success." But when financial outcomes are bad and companies suffer financial loss or plans fail, attributions in the annual report blame external forces, "an unfavorable turn of the economy" or "irresponsible federal environmental policies" (Conrad, 1992; see also Bettman & Weitz, 1983). Not only are those attributions made through words, but they also occur in the visual aspects of annual reports. When corporate performance is positive, visual attention is focused on product attributes giving the impression that these positive attributes are the reason for success. In bad financial times, visuals focus more on external references such as clients, or on charts and graphs that attribute reasons for poor financial performance of the company (Treadwell, 1991).

At first glance, these attributional orientations appear to be diametrically opposed. But Smilowitz and Pearson (1989) interpreted them as representing two metaphors: "hype and hoopla" routine of success or "it will be better next year" (p. 90). Both strategies fit the personae of corporate managements that attempt to attract and keep investors. In Wall Street parlance, the first statement advises investors to "hold," and the second is a "buy" recommendation. Either position is a statement affirming corporate efficacy.

One last comment on annual reports and a glance at corporate shareholder meetings further develops the issue of how companies enact their persona. Although annual reports tend today to feature fewer executives in corporate blue suits, that persona is still very much apparent. In that regard, annual reports are enactments of competence and control, even though the bottom line report is sometimes incongruent with the persona. In stark contrast is the corporate shareholder meeting of Ben & Jerry's Homemade Inc., which has featured live rock and roll, tie-dye T-shirts instead of corporate blue suits, and a mound of one billion rye grass seeds to demonstrate the billions of U.S. tax dollars spent on the military. The spirit of the 1960s entered the boardroom at this successful ice cream company, which has attempted to enact an honest, wholesome, and humane enterprise that is predicated on employee empowerment.

A company's persona does not only arise from its product and service advertising. As Herbert Schmertz (1986), former vice president of public relations for Mobil Oil observed, his company's opinion editorial (op-ed) and "Observations" campaigns affected the public's attitude toward Mobil and increased their willingness to do business with it. Its issue campaigns increased its name recognition, even for persons who did not agree with the issue stances taken by Mobil. Schmertz was pleased to find that 31% of the survey population preferred Mobil products to 16% for Exxon, 15% for Chevron, and 10% for Texaco. Schmertz described this approach as cause-related marketing and affinity-of-purpose marketing, a form of organizational identity building.

In a similar vein, Winters (1988) found that environmentalists preferred Chevron products because its "People Do" campaign explains that the company's actions help the environment—associating the company, its employees, and responsible environmental ideals translated into actions. The persona of Mobil was an aggressive and competent company, whereas Chevron's persona was care for the environment.

Mobil's "Observations" ads discussed technical, economic, policy, and financial aspects of the oil and gas industry in interesting and amusing ways. An entertainment format lured readers to the ads in order to educate them on these issues. Analyzing these ads, Crable and Vibbert (1983) invoked the Prometheus myth to disclose Mobil's rhetorical tactics. Mobil was embroiled in the oil embargo and knew from public opinion polls, as well as by reading the papers and listening to electronic news, that key segments of the public did not trust the oil industry. In the absence of information from the oil industry, people were relying on misinformation to judge the industry, so believed the advocates of the campaign.

According to Crable and Vibbert (1983), Mobil's discourse is epideictic, a form of speech used to praise and champion persons and to reinforce values and opinions. Messages could increase the intensity of an audience's feeling for that which is good, or increase its distaste for that which is bad. The ads laid out premises that could be used later to advocate subsequent claims. The persona of Mobil was, Crable and Vibbert argued, similar to that of Prometheus, the person who delivered fire to humankind, according to Greek mythology, despite the wishes of the gods. Mobil was struggling against great powers, namely the federal government and hostile media reporters, who were trying to keep truth from the people. This persona was enacted repeatedly during much of the 1970s and 1980s as Mobil attempted to assert its position on key technical, economic, financial, and policy issues. It requested that audiences take its side against that of regulators, legislators, and hostile reporters. Regulators and legislators where characterized as incompetent at anything other than formulating unwise policy and red tape; reporters were portrayed as being unwilling to play fair and wanting to hide behind First Amendment protection of free speech, no matter, Mobil asserted, how biased and ill-informed. Taking a different view of Mobil's persona, Simons (1983) interpreted its campaign as using democratic capitalism to dupe innocent publics. Mobil took a persona that it is "above the fray and has the ability to see what is good for the system as a whole" (p. 246).

Personae that companies present in their product and service advertisements speak volumes about their organizations, the impressions they seek to convey, and their view of the audiences who attend to these messages. Sometimes organizations communicate quite different messages than they intend, and even find customers turning away from, instead of being attracted to the business. For instance, at a time when the banking industry (along with the savings and loan industry) was in dire financial straits, one bank in Houston advertised that it was sensitive to what its customers wanted. To demonstrate that point in a series of television ads, that company portrayed customers driving through tollbooths. At each booth, customers were able to obtain handsful of money—gratis. In other ads, the company portrayed paperboys throwing money onto people's lawns, and pilots dumped bags of money from planes. At a time when the industry should have been characterizing itself as being fiscally sound and safe, this bank appeared to give money away. Viewers might wonder whether their deposits would be safe with a bank that gave away bundles of money.

In addition to organizations' efforts to create a favorable and differentiated identity of their products, services, and selves, we should be interested in an even broader issue. This issue is the effect corporations manage to achieve, not so much directly on buying behavior, but collectively on groups' sense of lifestyle. The key to understanding this issue is the discovery of major premises that guide choices and shape preferences.

Collectively, private sector organizations establish generic principles, such as "spend conspicuously," and product-specific principles, such as "Refresh yourself with...." Whether soft drinks are actually refreshing is not the essential issue in this regard. What is important is the fact that millions of dollars of advertising budgets have been spent to target our desire to be refreshed. Similarly, a nation that was "won by the sweat of brows" has become a population compulsively fearful of "perspiration wetness." The abundance of discretionary dollars that people enjoy is directed at purchases of larger "estate" houses, luxury automobiles, a vacation home, a backyard spa, a membership in a health club, fine food and drink, and stylish clothing.

In this sense, companies provide publics with scripts. Children love to learn commercials and jingles, with which they come to think about products and services. Buying behavior is an enactment of scripts provided partially by commercial advertising.

This influence does not mean that people's impressions do not change over time, even coming to disfavor products that once were alluring and enjoyable. Would cigarettes, for instance, have sold as well if they had not systematically been associated for decades with suave, sophisticated people? Ads portray smokers as rugged, commanding, and decisive. Female smokers are sultry, sophisticated, and liberated. When one kid offers that first cigarette to another, it is not merely a bunch of tobacco, a small piece of paper, and a filter. It is entry into adulthood, a time of sexual sophistication, ruggedness, freedom, or adventure. An afternoon spent looking at movies from the 1940s, 1950s, and 1960s would quickly impress on you how the tobacco industry established itself—enacted a persona and gave a persona to those who used its products. It created a market, reinforced that market, and so embedded itself into the mentality of the public that tobacco companies continue to be a good investment on the New York Stock Exchange despite the presence of health warnings on cigarette packages and their advertising. The assumption that messages presented on television were so powerful that children could not counter them led to cigarette ads being banned from television.

Personae of companies, governmental regulatory agencies, product identity, activists, and consumers come together as actors in communication arenas. An example is the battle waged over presentations of malt liquors in the early 1990s. G. Heileman Brewing Company wanted to name its brand of malt liquor PowerMaster. Foes of excessive drinking along with Black leaders charged the company with social irresponsibility. One problem was the high alcohol content of the drink. Another was the fact that Heileman, along with other malt liquor marketers, targeted low-income, inner-city Black consumers, who suffer high incidence of alcohol-related illnesses. Indeed, the product would not necessarily em*power* its consumers. It stood a good chance of doing the opposite.

This example demonstrates a dominant theme of marketplace advertising that entails the ability of companies, through their products, to empower their customers. Products increase peoples' self-efficacy by giving them dominance over insects (pesticides), weeds (herbicides), distance (air travel), colds (decongestants), and each other (cosmetics and toiletry items to say nothing of clothing and jewelry). Products increase the self-efficacy of the homemaker who wants to whisk away dirt and attract the neighbor's attention to a lovely yard and nicely painted house covered with long-lasting, nonfading paint.

Are companies mere image, a creation that exists only in the mind of the beholder, lacking substance? Addressing this issue, Cheney (1992) advised us to beware the "potential danger of an unreflective indulgence in corporate image-making." He worried that "we can come to elevate style over substance and lose ourselves in the process" and advised us to "spell out the arguments implicit in (or even suppressed by) corporate messages that are image-based. Even more importantly, audience members should examine their organizational memberships, associations and affinities for what they represent, what they mean in practice" (p. 181). Companies and their publics enact narrative rituals of buying and selling, of lifestyles and self-presentations. Corporate personae become interpreted through the substance and form of cultural narratives.

The best corporate advertising features each organization as a whole entity by combining product advertising, along with investor relations, employee relations, and marketing. Each audience is presented with the central theme of an identity campaign tailored to its particular interest and expectations. Ford Motor Company and General Telephone & Electronics (GTE) are classic examples. GTE repeats slogans about quality service, and Ford is proud to tell customers and potential investors that "At Ford, Quality Is Job One!" Slogans serve as a theme to invite customers and investors. The ads enact the corporate culture and present performance expectations that become real in the everyday work and communication activities of employees. The slogan constantly tells the employee to achieve "quality." Is that concept a factor in the self-concepts of Ford employees who believe they are special because they and their company are doing something to revitalize the domestic car market? Themes that capture corporate goals and performance commitments by Ford and GTE are stated and restated in employee publications, product advertisements, investor relations material, and other forms of corporate communication (MacEwen & Wuellner, 1987).

ZONES OF MEANING WITH EXTERNAL AUDIENCES

Businesses enact, with varying amounts of skill, their presence in the marketplace where they compete for profits, goodwill, and other stakes. To do so requires that they share zones of meaning with persons who approve of their behavior, buy their products and services, or agree with their public policy issue positions. In this regard, personae are a crucial part of what companies say to those who read about them and listen to their messages. Although companies contribute to this dialogue through advertisements, interpersonal channels and media reports are full of messages about products, services, and public policy issues important to companies.

For instance, as savings and loan scandals continued to unfold in the 1980s, members of the industry used print and electronic channels to reestablish trust with the public. Some messages were conveyed as customers encountered employees, such as tellers and customer service personnel, of the companies. In addition to these channels, messages were provided through conversations (interpersonal channels) whereby persons, perhaps potential customers, conversed about the industry's performance. A plethora of news stories and feature articles exposed the scandals and the persons who created them, and gave information about trials and massive fines industry executives suffered as a consequence of their violation of federal laws. In such cases, affected companies attempted to clarify, create, change, and associate with favorable zones of meaning.

Concerns such as these demonstrate that zones of meaning, interests, and expectations clash or overlap between companies and their stakeholders. Advertising and other communication efforts are employed to create zones of meaning to increase audience identification with products, services, companies, or issues. When favorable zones exist, companies attempt to show how their products and actions conform to them. When unfavorable zones exist, companies attempt to change them or dissociate from them.

Mission statements are some of the powerful tools managements have available to generate and disseminate meaning about their companies. Examining Fortune 500 companies' use of mission statements, Cochran and David (1986) concluded that they need to be more readable and their tones should be more positive if they are to enhance organizational images. Only half of such statements were found to convey an inspiring and positive tone.

Closely related to mission statements, annual reports are used to assert companies' missions, their strategic plans for accomplishing them, and annual assessments of how well they did in that regard. Despite their ability to reach vital audiences, especially shareholders, brokers, and analysts, annual reports are difficult to read and often hedge or obscure points rather than reveal information key publics would like to have (Heath & Phelps, 1984).

To define products and services is a goal of organizational rhetoric, but not just any names will do. Names are often selected to associate with well-established zones of meaning. For instance, naming weaponry of modern warfare constitutes an enactment of myths and narratives that favor the good guys and dishonor the bad ones. In this way, weapons manufacturers and government officials attempt to define situations in which these weapons are appropriate to use. Of significance in this regard are names such as the Flying Fortress, Minuteman (reminiscent of the patriots of the American war for independence), and Peacemaker. Some weapons are named in ways that belie their true purpose, such as Polaris, Poseidon, Tomahawk, Pershing, or Davy Crockett (Kauffman, 1989). Those who remember the military drama in the Persian Gulf region in the winter of 1991 recall the battle of SCUDs versus Patriots.

Other products are named in ways that characterize them in dramatic and enticing ways. For instance, car security systems are described with lethal names, such as Scorpion and Viper. One radar detection system is called Cobra. A casual review of the names of fragrance products adds examples to this list.

To achieve its objectives, product and service advertisements contain information designed to create and support zones of meaning. The amount of information provided in product or service advertising is likely to be greater for major products and services such as life insurance and automobiles. Ads for routine purchases (such as cleansers, perfumes, or greeting cards) typically contain few informational copy points (Nelson, 1974; Vaughn, 1986). Consumers realize how little information is provided by typical product and service advertisements (Bucklin, 1965; Marquez, 1977; Norris, 1983) and expect televised ads, in particular, to contain low levels of information (Reid & Rotfeld, 1981; Resnik & Stern, 1977; Soley & Reid, 1983).

Not only does product and service advertising attempt to induce trial of products or services, but such trials also provide consumers with valuable information concerning their quality (Finn, 1984; Smith & Swinyard, 1982). That is, consumers test the accuracy of an advertiser's claim by using the product or service. For this reason, customers' direct experiences with goods and services play important roles in determining zones of meaning regarding them. In the creation of zones of meaning regarding products and services, words and visual images are important, but trial uses of products and services supply information people use to decide on the quality of a product or service. Trials and repeated use reveal positive and negative attributes about products or services. When attributes are predominantly positive, customers are likely to repeat their purchases. If attributes are negative, the opposite is likely to occur.

Whereas issue advertising is intended to create or reinforce meaning, the primary goal of product and service advertising is behavioral—to stimulate trial and adoption (Gibson, 1983; Pavlik, Blumenthal, & Cropper, 1984). Audiences verify the content of issue and product or service advertisements differently. In public policy situations, direct verification of ad content ordinarily is impossible. For instance, consumers have few direct ways to determine whether chemical plants are safe and do not emit toxic substances into adjacent neighborhoods. Information acquired from issue ads is tested indirectly by comparing it against prior opinions and information acquired from other sources, such as news reports, environmental group newsletters, and conversations. Thus, in contrast to product and service advertising, desired outcomes of issue advertising are primarily cognitive: reception, recall of information, attitude reinforcement and change, information integration, and subsequent public use of the information in support of an opinion position.

Information campaigns influence opinions on an array of issues of public importance such as mental retardation (Douglas, Westley, & Chaffee, 1970), potential dangers of asbestos (Freimuth & Van Nevel, 1981), invasion of privacy through computer databases (Jones & Saunders, 1977), effects of alcohol on driving, and social problems of Hispanics in Los Angeles (Mendelsohn, 1973). Issue ads influence opinions on corollary issues not discussed in the ads but relevant to the issue topic (Heath & Douglas, 1986). Effects of issue advertising are likely to be more pronounced when persons have little prior knowledge of an issue (Resnik & Stern, 1977). Tracking a campaign concerning mental retardation, Douglas et al. (1970) observed that people who were more willing to acquire information from advertising content had a positive attitude toward the mentally handicapped. This kind of campaign is likely to succeed when it does not have to overcome deep-seated, negative attitudes, such as those against the mentally retarded. Campaigns are more successful when the information is perceived to be related to the self-interest of the audience or to causes, such as environmentalism or animal rights, for which the audience has an altruistic interest.

Most issue ad campaigns deal with controversial topics about which persons have developed opinions so that the effects of issue advertising may be mediated by opinion positions that exist prior to initiation of a campaign. This is likely to be the case even when the opinions are not about the specific issues raised in a campaign. For example, although persons may not have developed an attitude toward use of nuclear energy as an alternative fuel resource (the specific topic of a campaign), they probably hold comparatively firm positions on other aspects of nuclear development (such as waste storage or military applications of nuclear energy). What is more, prior opinions are likely to influence both the extent to which persons accept and assimilate specific issue advertisement content (Wright, 1973, 1981) and the integrated sense they make of the campaign content (Ajzen & Fishbein, 1980; Fishbein & Ajzen, 1975, 1981). This approach to advertising research is holistic, realizing that people are exposed to many messages (Schmalensee, 1983).

Companies are not the only sources of information and judgment that external audiences receive and utilize when forming opinions and judgments. Other communicators, such as editorialists, provide views that may differ from those preferred by companies. For instance, consumer editorialists often comment on the quality of products and services. What happens when editorialists do not interpret the facts as a company believes they should?

Confrontation is a strategic option for resolving differences and conflict (Newell & Stutman, 1991). It brings specific issues into focus so that those engaged in conflict can examine them, as well as the evidence and reasoning that support them. Confrontation has been used successfully by public relations practitioners who believe that reporters and editorialists are presenting incorrect opinions on crucial issues. In one case, for example, public relations practitioners realized that editors of automotive magazines doubted claims that Petrolon, Inc. made as it introduced an engine oil additive, "Slick 50," into the retail market. Carefully monitoring what editors wrote about the product, public relations specialists confronted claims they believed were misleading or misinformed. This campaign led to favorable reporting on the product, based on fact rather than false assumptions, and contributed to a marked increase in customer acceptance of the product. In a similar way, Mobil Oil Company confronted journalists who were making what it believed were false or misinformed statements (Schmertz, 1986).

Each company is an actor—asserting itself—and a reactor—responding to others' assertions and counterassertions. Businesses enact roles that they and others define. Companies operate on the premise that if we listen to them and accept their views on which product or service is best then our uncertainty is reduced and we can happily go about *our* business—or perhaps about *their* business. However, the relationship is strongest when it is based on mutual benefit, when people share a zone of meaning with companies that favor the interest of both. Without supportive zones of meaning, however, companies are not permitted to do business as they wish.

ISSUE ADVERTISING: ORGANIZATIONAL VOICES ON PUBLIC POLICY

One means companies use to create favorable zones of meaning is issue advertising. Although it accounts for a fraction of all advertising expenditures, issue advertising is an important part of companies' efforts to establish zones of meaning favorable to their public policy interests. Such ads occur in cycles that coincide with periods of reform, during which critics seek to redefine and constrain business practices. Approximately $2 billion is spent each year on issue advertisements, based on an estimate that $1.6 billion was spent in 1984 (Sethi, 1986, 1987a), a sum that grows approximately 10% annually (Sethi, 1987b).

Issue advertising is intended to influence public policy by advocating, mitigating, or defeating legislation or regulation. As Buchholz (1988) observed, "public policy is a specific course of action taken collectively by society or by a legitimate representative of society, addressing a specific problem of public concern, that reflects the interests of society or particular segments of society "(p. 53). This communication effort has implications for the formulation of public policy and an opinion environment that can permeate the health, safety, and lifestyles of millions of people.

For over a century, thousands of issue ads have been published in the print media. During the last years of the Great Depression and throughout World War II, for instance, issue ads championed the American capitalist system and countered extreme unionism, as well as communism and fascism. The great era of issue advertising began in the 1960s when corporations became beleaguered from all sides. Most of these ads are sponsored by corporations to advocate their public opinion/policy stances, but ads are also used by trade associations, public information organizations, labor unions, governments, and activist groups (Heath & Nelson, 1986; Sethi, 1987a). Several organizations routinely employ them. Some of the most visible issue advertisers have been Mobil Oil Corporation, the U.S. Council for Energy Awareness (a public information organization promoting the use of nuclear energy to generate electricity), United Technologies, tobacco companies such as R. J. Reynolds, and the American Association of Railroads.

Some issue ads have appeared on television. Most of those are sponsored by the U.S. Council for Energy Awareness, but TV ads have also been used by W. R. Grace to advocate a drastic reduction of the federal budget deficit. Several years ago, Getty Oil ran innocuous television ads calling for increased freedom. In the midst of a referendum or legislative battle, corporations, trade associations, and activist groups employ televised issue ads to make their point of view public. Television and radio campaigns are most likely to occur when referendum or initiative ballot issues are put to the public; in circumstances of that kind, organizations, especially corporations, are less likely to be inhibited in their public communication efforts by program directors fearful of Fairness Doctrine challenges by other voices that would be heard during the political campaign.

Most issue ads appear in print, either in newspapers, news magazines, or special interest and trade publications. One special interest outlet is *National Geographic*, in which environmental issues are discussed by companies who have had trouble with them, or organizations who can use premises current in environmentalism to advocate conclusions such as energy savings through the use of nuclear fuel to generate electricity. Trade publications, such as *The Columbia Journalism Review* and *The Washington Journalism Review*, are popular outlets for issue ads.

Including issue advertising in their discussion of organizational rhetoric, Cheney and Dionisopolous (1989) observed that "corporate communication (in practice and in theory) is fundamentally rhetorical and symbolic in responding to and in exercising power (in public discourse), and in shaping various identities (corporate and individual)" (p. 140). Those who design and place issue ads often employ research findings regarding product and service advertising; such practice makes assumptions that may be inappropriate to issue advertising (D. S. Solomon, 1989). Decisions regarding the design and placement of these ads are best when they are sensitive to audiences' efforts to reduce uncertainty (Berger & Calabrese, 1975), integrate information into attitudes and estimate reward outcomes (Ajzen & Fishbein, 1980), obtain information related to issues of self-interest (Petty & Cacioppo, 1986), and acquire useful information (Atkin, 1973). Responses to such ads range from awareness of them, through liking their content, comprehending them, to remembering and retrieving them, and finally to acting on their content (McGuire, 1989).

The potency of organizational discourse is its ability to establish, affirm, and employ premises that become part of people's thinking and behavior. "Such hegemony does not refer to simple or outright domination but rather to control over the (value) premises that shape basic and applied policy decisions. In essence, corporate discourse seeks to establish public frames of reference for interpreting information concerning issues deemed important by Corporate America" (Cheney & Dionisopolous, 1989, p. 144).

Because of the potential impact of these ads, studies have addressed two broad issues: (a) hegemonic presence of such messages in dialogues on commercial, social, economic, and political issues; and (b) regulatory and legislative control of such advertising to avert domination by sources that have the deep pockets potential to influence disproportionately the public policy dialogue. Attempts have been made to capture the historical and sociopolitical significance of such ads, as well as categorize and analyze them (Ewing, 1982, 1987; Garbett, 1981; Heath & Nelson, 1986; Marchand, 1987; Meadow, 1981; Raucher, 1968; Sethi, 1977, 1987a; Stridsberg, 1977; Waltzer, 1988). Scholars have discussed the rhetorical tactics employed by corporations, especially Mobil Oil (Crable & Vibbert, 1983; Simons, 1983) and public information organizations advocating the use of nuclear power to generate electricity (Dionisopoulos, 1986; Dionisopoulos & Crable, 1988; Heath, 1988b). Congressional hearings have been held to decide how they should be regulated by the Federal Trade Commission, Federal Communications Commission, and Internal Revenue Service.

Perhaps the best-known study of an issue campaign is Schmertz's (1986) self-examination of the rationale, execution, and results of the op-ed and "Observations" campaign utilized by Mobil Oil Corporation. Another insider account described how the American Bankers Association (ABA) campaign was designed and why it decisively defeated President Reagan's 10% withholding tax provision. Fritz Elmendorf (1988), the advertising manager of the ABA campaign, claimed that it generated more mail to Congress and to the president than occurred during the Vietnam War and defeated a tax provision promoted by Reagan at the height of his popularity. Another success story: Pincus (1980) pointed out that the American Forest Institute's "trees are the renewable resource" ad campaign changed the proportion of persons who believed forests were being wisely managed from 34% in 1974 to 55% in 1980.

Critics seek to constrain corporate use of communication, including product and service advertisements, because of the apprehension that businesses can engage in deep pockets spending and therefore dominate the informational marketplace to impose a view of products and services, as well as images of companies that may be detrimental to people's interests (Gandy, 1982; Meadow, 1981; Parenti, 1986). Efforts to distinguish between image and issue advertisements encounter resistance, particularly by critics who believe that all actions by corporations are inherently political.

Writers such as Gandy (1982), Parenti (1986), and Meadow (1981) have argued that issue ads are one of several means by which the private sector holds the public hostage to a capitalistic society. Critics such as these indict the media–business connection, which they contend is maintained through advertising revenue (including—or especially—product advertising), bonding the media to corporations and stifling alternative economic views. Not only do issue and image messages maintain a capitalistic view of society, but advertising dollars prevent media reporters from disclosing the weaknesses of businesses. A view that both contrasts with and complements this one has been advanced by Olasky (1987) who contended that public relations has been instrumental in stifling competition because it champions monopolistic control by key industry leaders.

Because of such criticisms, issue advertising is regulated (Heath & Nelson, 1985; Sethi, 1979). Recently issue advertising has become subject to Federal Trade

Commission (FTC) regulation, even though it had been treated as political speech, typically immune to regulation. If ads that once were considered issue or political are construed as commercial speech, they become subject to FTC considerations of deception and factuality. The Commission has, at least twice, become involved in the adjudication of the factual accuracy of issue ads. *National Commission on Egg Nutrition V. FTC*, F. 2d. (1978) upheld an FTC ruling that challenged the factuality of an ad that concluded that no scientific evidence supported the claim that eating eggs increases risk of heart disease. Based on that case, the FTC subsequently ruled that an ad by R. J. Reynolds Tobacco Company incorrectly reported findings that cigarette smoking is not linked to health problems. A by-product of this ruling was the clarification and broadening of the concept of commercial speech (thereby allowing FTC jurisdiction). The FTC ruling is that any form of speech from which a company could benefit financially from the presentation about or defense of services or products is commercial speech and not protected political communication. This ruling further blurs distinctions between issue and corporate image ads and substantiates the claims that such ads express the self-interest of the company and should not be placed if they do not have potential commercial value.

Although with caution, the general public approves of corporate use of issue advertising (Sethi, 1986). The Opinion Research Corporation, in 1981, reported favorable public acceptance of issue advertising. Of the 90% of the national sample that reported having read or viewed issue ads, two thirds claimed that such ads were fairly believable and had helped them form opinions on major issues. What they learned had prompted the survey respondents to form opinions, change their opinions, and participate in a campaign by voting, contributing money, or writing letters. Two Roper studies, in 1982 and 1984, found that only 38% of the public had read or viewed an issue advertisement. However, awareness was positively related to level of education and income, suggesting that such ads are most likely to influence opinion makers. Of related interest, Heath and Douglas (1986) found that when people read or view an issue ad, their attitude toward the use of this communication option becomes more positive and they feel that such ads contribute valuable content and insight to public policy debates. Nevertheless, people are apprehensive that companies have a deep pockets advantage over other participants in public debate.

Rhetorical study focuses on concepts such as hegemony and identification and deal with contestable interpretations of fact as well as social, economic, and political realities. This symbolism is often the product of contests between many competing interests, each of which has its unique perspectives. This study "directs our critical awareness to the practices and assumptions of organizational actors (in particular) and organized society (in general), many of which *are taken for granted*" (Cheney & Dionisopolous, 1989, p. 138). Such studies, concentrating on the symbolism that *is* organizations, are confronted with at least three kinds of issues: the organizational challenge (creators of structure and senders of messages) or the individual challenge (receiver confronted with managing self and organizational identity and persons attempting to achieve discourse with companies that are primarily symbolism), the rhetorical challenge (corporate and individual), and the ethical challenge (corporate and individual) (Cheney & Dionisopolous, 1989).

Revealed in these studies is the fact that issue advertising is important not only because it is part of the boundary spanning efforts of public relations but also "[b]ecause of the creative and evocative power of language, the very 'essence' and 'boundaries' of the organization are things to be managed symbolically" (Cheney & Vibbert, 1987, p. 176). Dionisopolous and Crable (1988) concluded that many organizational "rhetors will attempt to secure a desired outcome by aiming their messages toward leading and dominating the terminological parameters of emergent issues" (p. 143). To define something is to lead people to act toward it in a particular way. "When rhetorical agents assert definitions, they imply motives. To the extent the motives are appealing, the definitions may be acceptable; conversely, to the extent definitions are appealing, the motives may be acceptable" (p. 135). For this reason, if something is needed—electricity generated by nuclear power or chemical products—it is good, so good that any harms are offset by the good. Because facts are interpretable, the real action of corporate enactment is in the definition of those facts.

Wrestling with the contribution made by these ads, Sethi (1987b) observed, "Advocacy advertising, ultimately, is an educational tool and a political tool designed to play an active role in influencing a society's priorities." For that reason, "its legitimacy and effectiveness will also be judged in political terms, by the public's perception that its practitioners are using it responsibly and, in addition to their self-interest, are also serving some larger public purpose" (pp. 280–281). Issue campaigns not only provide information but also indicate to readers the information they have not been receiving and hint at what they should receive. "The managerial context of advocacy advertising," Sethi continued, "is that of defending or promoting the sponsor's activities, modus operandi and position on controversial issues of public policy" (p. 281).

Waltzer (1988) examined the placement of issue ads in *The New York Times, The Columbia Journalism Review,* and *The Washington Journalism Review.* These favorite outlets for such ads are likely to reach and influence leaders and journalists whose views on issues can be shaped by such ads. Approximately 64% of the issues contain ads, a publication rate far above other newspapers and journals. Seventy percent of the ads focus on image, whereas the remaining 30% discuss issues. Most of those (25% of all ads) take a policy position. Only 1% (and only in *The New York Times*) appeal to people to get involved in legislative battles.

Addressing issues related to the personae presented by ad sponsors, Sethi (1987b) reasoned that three concepts are central to advocacy communication: "identification of the sponsor's interest, intensity of advocacy and specificity in identifying the adversary" (p. 285). The personae include the following archetypes: disinterested sponsor, benevolent sponsor, acknowledged self-interested sponsor, participation sponsor, and elusive sponsor. Each of these personae can be predicted to advance unique themes and to view the adversary targeted in the ad content in different ways. Intensity of appeals ranges from dispassionate presentation of factual information to more inflaming appeals to emotions, and perhaps to a sense of morality and indignation against adversaries—a polarization tactic where interests are pitted against one another, perhaps to the paucity of fact and calculated analysis. Adversaries include the general public, governmental agencies, competitors, and public interest or social activist groups.

Cheney and Vibbert (1987) argued that three functions underpin corporate public discourse: (a) a rhetorical function *"designed to influence both internal and external publics, and therefore function as multifaceted rhetorical acts"* (p. 182); (b) an identity-management function, which refers to organizations' efforts to *"develop a distinct identity while at the same time being recognized as part of the cultural 'crowd' "* (p. 185); and (c) a political function, which entails political actions by corporations to influence specific policies and engage in political campaigns instead of deal with premises as is typical of the rhetorical function.

As companies enact their personae and those of stakeholding audiences, they have several message options. A fundamental characteristic of these ads is the degree to which they draw from a zone of meaning shared with the targeted audiences. The enactment of an image or issue position assumes that either a central theme (O) shared with the audience will support the issue discussion, or the campaign is designed to justify a theme and thereby to redefine the zone. A review of the ad types suggests the rhetorical options available to companies as the seek to reach targeted stakeholders.

Images

Corporate image ads are used to express attitudes about ordinary and usual business activities, differentiate between the identities of companies, create awareness of and present a favorable impression of products, services, or companies. This kind of ad presents facts about an organization's or industry's operations and demonstrates how its personnel, products, services, and policies satisfy or exceed public expectations. Such ads may reveal a company's charitable and community service activities, and thereby create goodwill with key publics. These ads often contain statements that associate companies with traditional values.

Although image ads employ tactics specifically deployed to affect *differentiation, association, identity*, and *goodwill*, issue ads also use tactics to achieve these functions. For that reason, these functions become focal points in the effort to determine whether an issue ad makes statements, uses graphics, or otherwise takes a rhetorical stance that can achieve any or all of these functions. For instance, a company that takes aggressive pro-environmental stances, challenging other members of its industry to do so, can be thought of more favorably (differentiated) from its competitors. Part of differentiation arises from the issue positions with which the company associates itself, the identity it asserts, and whether it makes claims that are couched to achieve or enhance goodwill with its publics.

Differentiation occurs when a product, service, or company can be distinguished from another based on its attributes. Associations result from the values, actions, or favorable traits attributed to the company, such as being a champion of safe driving (opposed to drunk driving) or pro-environmental ("green"). Identity is the metaphoric residue of the archetypal persona that is enacted in the ad, such as defender of freedom, aggressive advocate, technical advisor, or defender of national security. Identity personalizes the organization and its relationship with key publics that also have identities that complement companies they like and conflict with companies they dislike (Black, 1970). Goodwill occurs when ad content reveals that the sponsor takes a stand in the interest of the targeted audience.

Issue Ads That Use Widely Accepted Premises

These ads discuss issues of public concern by applying accepted premises that for much of society are beyond question. This kind of ad takes stands on social, economic, or financial issues by favoring a noncontroversial, popular point of view or by demonstrating that a controversial issue is supported by widely accepted premises. Image components of these ads result from *association* of the company with widely accepted premises. For example, whereas oil companies opposed environmental premises a decade ago, they now embrace them (at least in broad detail) as appropriate standards of corporate responsibility. Ad content reinforces these premises by applauding their veracity given the circumstances and expectancy value (reward–cost) ratios of competing issue positions. Although companies use established premises to justify contestable policy positions, this stance is the least controversial because the zone of meaning is shared by company and audience.

Issue Ads That Defend Premises

This kind of ad takes stands on issues that are being questioned by notable segments of the public or by governmental officials. If the premises are not successfully defended, operations of a company or industry will be required to change. How key publics' identities correspond to those of critics can be instrumental to the ways they access and respond to the ad message content. If premises become widely accepted, they can be used in future issue debates. These ads may be highly controversial because they not only require that basic premises be justified but also demand that reasoning and evidence be used to support conclusions based on those premises.

Issue Ads That Advocate New Premises

This kind of issue ad employs facts and arguments to advocate premises that are not widely accepted as true or thought to be important. This kind of ad brings issues to the attention of key audiences and, therefore, reasons that the issue messages are worthy of consideration. This kind of ad depends on cognitive involvement through perceptions of self-interest, uncertainty, and reward–cost ratios of a policy issue *as* policy.

Issue Ads That Champion or Challenge Policies

Many ads address propositions of fact or value, and imply policy positions that can be extrapolated from facts and values presented in conjunction with the persona of the sponsor. An important category of issue ad is that used to champion or challenge policies (based on reward–cost ratios). Policies are not just issue positions, what people believe to be appropriate, but entail actions thought to be in the public good (Buchholz, 1988). These ads use evidence, values, and premises, or perhaps defend premises, as they speak for or against policies implemented by legislative or regulatory bodies.

Issue Ads That Enlist Supporters to Take Action on Specific Policies

These ads call on groups (whether explicitly identified or merely implied by the ad) to participate in public issue debate and grass-roots pressure politics by taking a stand for or against pending policies by speaking or writing on behalf of the position advocated by the sponsor.

Each of these kinds of ads helps or detracts from the image or identity of the sponsoring company. Likewise, certain identity attributes may be controversial as key publics doubt the appropriateness of certain activities or characteristics of the sponsoring company. For instance, during the oil embargo days, large, diversified, integrated oil companies were criticized for their size and for a while risked being forced to divest key units.

Issue advertising is a vital part of external enactments, especially to create and adapt to zones of meaning. Companies help create these zones. For instance, insurance companies, in an attempt to lower the costs and human suffering that result from automobile accidents, joined their interest to that of the public by demanding that automobile manufacturers produce safer cars. The automobile industry opposed such measures, in an effort to demonstrate its efficacy over its zones of meaning. Then something happened, as exemplified by Chrysler Corporation's Lee Iacocca, who did a flip-flop on the air bag issue and went from staunch opponent to proud innovator. In a 1991 identity ad, Iacocca addressed readers through a personal persona proclaiming that "Safety should be our first priority. The auto industry has dragged its feet long enough." He continued, "We aren't crusaders. We're car builders. But we've discovered something wonderful. Drivers' air bags save lives." That take-charge guy empowered those who drove his cars to be able to save their lives.

Issue communication supports corporate strategic plans by helping companies to gain acceptance for principles required to accomplish those plans (Arrington & Sawaya, 1984; Buchholz, 1985; Ewing, 1987; Heath & Nelson, 1986). Companies utilize issues management and advertising because issue campaigns can affect public opinion (Adkins, 1978; Buchholz, 1982; Welty, 1981), in part because the public accepts issue advertising as being informative and useful in deciding the wisdom of policy positions (Ewing, 1982).

COMPLIANCE STRATEGIES AND EXTERNAL AUDIENCES

As well as interpersonal settings, compliance-gaining strategies are commonly employed by companies in public communication campaigns. Environmental groups, for instance, use such strategies in their efforts to guide judgments and get audiences to comply with recommended actions. These groups prefer to use prosocial strategies that explain the rewards to be achieved by holding environmentally responsible opinions and by taking actions recommended by environmentalists. They draw on their expertise on environmental issues to recommend opinions and actions, and they make moral appeals. In addition to positive appeals, these groups forecast negative outcomes that would result from irresponsible environmental behavior (Baglan, Lalumia, & Bayless, 1986). This tactic can be synthesized by the following statement: "Trust us and comply with our requests because we are experts who seek positive answers to questions and concerns you have."

Corporations also use compliance-gaining strategies in public communication campaigns. One instance is Mobil Oil's issue advertising program that began in the early 1970s. Portraying itself as a champion of the public interest, Mobil presented a persona that is friendly toward those of similar mind and assertively willing to challenge those who are neither well informed nor caring of the public's interest, at least in Mobil's view. More often than other compliance-gaining strategies, Mobil employed moral appeal and drew on its expertise to predict positive consequences for compliance and negative ones for noncompliance (Smith & Heath, 1990).

Use of moral appeal includes attempts to gain compliance by convincing the target audience that it is morally wrong if it does not comply. An example of this strategy occurred in a May 21, 1984 advertisement, in which Mobil discussed the issue of the freedom of the press: "The press (like any other segment of society) must be held accountable if the lies they print harm an individual's reputation. What else is left in this society if an honorable man's reputation is destroyed in the name of another's freedom?" This ad might assure readers that Mobil is speaking out on behalf of their interest. Furthermore, the advertisement contains traditional American values. This tactic is justified by Burke's (1969b) argument that persuasion occurs when entities identify with one another by sharing values and motives. By identifying with positive ideals, Mobil may overcome negative stigmas associated with the oil industry.

Mobil ads used positive and negative expertise as compliance-gaining strategies. They advised audiences to take actions that would lead to positive outcomes, avoiding those that result in negative consequences. As Mobil Oil engaged in dialogue, it presented a persona of a sensitive corporation that enjoys challenging ideas and public policy issues. It did this in ways that appear to be in the enlightened self-interest of those who would be likely to read op-ed pages. If a major task of corporations is to narrow the legitimacy gap, moral appeals and expertise are useful tactics of compliance gaining tactics.

FOCAL POINTS OF ANALYSIS

- What meaning is used to describe and evaluate the relationship between a company and its stakeholders? Does that meaning contribute to the allotment of stakes on behalf of the company?
- What meaning is used to describe and evaluate the persona of a company and its stakeholders? Does that meaning contribute to the allotment of stakes on behalf of the company and the enactment of personae favorable to the company *and* its stakeholders?
- Do the symbols used in external communication result in a harmonious identification and a symmetrical relationship between organization and audience?
- What symbols dominate external discourse? Do they foster all parties' interests?
- What facts, premises, and values constitute the substance of issue ads?
- What narratives join or frustrate the enactments of a company and its stakeholders?

CONCLUSION

Product, service, image, and issue ads reinforce, create, or draw on premises fundamental to the persona and purpose of each company. Debates that surround such ads relate to accuracy of differentiation claims and cultural assumptions from which the company draws its legitimacy. Even when ads are controversial with some groups or segments of the population, they have an effect on personal identities of stakeholders—persons who identify positively or negatively with the sponsor and the position advocated in the ad. How participants view their relationship becomes part of the boundary, the zone of meaning, defined by the ad.

Corporations play monumental roles in the political economy of this country. How and what they communicate becomes part of private norms as well as supports public policy guidelines that promote and constrain their efforts. Regardless of the specific roles that society allows and expects them to play, companies naturally engage in the dialogue of what those roles should be as part of their assertion of their views of what is required for them to be a productive part of society.

10

External Communication with Public Policy Stakeholders

If disharmony occurs between organizations and their external stakeholders, the result may be a loss of business or increased effort to force companies to act according to ethical standards the stakeholders prefer. Efforts to prevent or allay disharmony are the featured topics of this chapter that extend Smircich's (1983a) contention: "The fundamental task of strategic management then is mediating the relationship between environment and organization toward a fit; that is, managers align organizational and environmental forces to a desired state of congruence" (p. 227). For this reason, Freeman (1984) challenged managers to "*see external groups for the stake that they, in fact, have*" (p. 225). Failure to achieve harmony with external interests may lead companies to have less autonomy and control over their operations. One test of that failure is the extent to which audiences do not identify supportively with a company and its issue positions. External publics may enact a different narrative than the one enacted by companies; or they enact the narratives of conflict and power.

Organizations not only consist of networks, but they are also part of even larger networks, all of which constitute zones of meaning. These interorganizational networks are a source of power and can assist companies' surveillance activities. Each company's position in such networks will affect its influence on the discussion of issues and implementation of policies. For instance, an industry such as food production may be dominated by General Mills, Nabisco, or Quaker Oats; other organizations enact their personae in reaction to major players. Because networks receive and process information (surveillance), members use them "to reduce their environmental uncertainty in order to maintain stability in their internal structures and in environmental conditions affecting them" (Danowski, Barnett, & Fiedland, 1987, p. 812). If a company is central in interorganizational networks, it is more likely to get media coverage in business-oriented publications and to enjoy a favorable public image, or to be used as the negative example of the industry.

This chapter considers the surveillance and adaptive activities needed to understand what stakeholders are saying and attempting to do to constrain companies.

Typical stakeholders would be legislators, regulators, and special-interest groups, such as environmentalists or consumer activists. This chapter focuses on effective two-way flow of communication as a means for managing issues and managing responses to them (Grunig, 1992). Communication and strategic planning can assist companies' efforts to build harmony with stakeholders, who hold an array of opinions and subscribe to various public policy positions that can affect how companies operate.

Following themes established in previous chapters, this chapter is interested in dominant narratives, shared meaning, interlocking interests, and stakeholder negotiation. Control is a central factor in this discussion, set in the context of stakeholder negotiation (Freeman, 1984) and efforts to maximize rewards and minimize losses in these negotiations (Stanley, 1985). Companies seek to achieve a credible persona of control; they not only want to speak with a coherent Voice, but they also want to enact a single Voice with other members of their industry and with their stakeholders. Achieving that is not easy given the variety of stakeholders and voices. The management team becomes a focal point in this analysis because it is primarily responsible for obtaining and interpreting information, although savvy executives involve key members of the entire company. Moreover, the culture—especially standards of responsibility—that organizational members enact reflects the opinions and policies preferred by and implemented by management.

Public opinion does not merely occur, as the result of what media, government, or organizations say. It is enacted. Making this point, Noelle-Neumann (1991), concluded that "it is constant interactions among people, due to their social nature, that account for the transformation of the sum of individual opinions into public opinion" (p. 280). This crucial awareness extends the principle of enactment that is central to this book.

CORPORATE CULTURE AND EXTERNAL RELATIONS

One important aspect of corporate adjustment to external stakeholders is the culture that is used to define and evaluate their activities. Activism, for instance, changed the business culture of this country so that standards of corporate responsibility that are used to guide and evaluate company performance today differ markedly from those of the late 1950s. Companies make statements that become part of the business culture of our society; so do activist critics. If the culture of a company is similar to and compatible with that of its stakeholders, then harmony is likely to exist.

Because the fit of these two cultures is so important, companies need to assess their similarity. In such efforts, the culture that dominates the thinking of management of each company can stifle the adaptive efforts of its strategic planners, operations managers, industrial hygienists, and issue monitors, as was case for the asbestos industry, leading it to the brink of bankruptcy. Its culture led key members of the industry to fail to foresee courts beginning to apply new standards of product liability. The industry rendered itself unable to reposition itself and suffered intrusion by federal courts, demanding that a massive trust fund be set aside to pay damages to persons whose health had been harmed by exposure to the product.

Once praised for its product's fire retardant ability, the industry slipped in public regard as illustrated by one of its leaders, Manville Corporation. Ranked 181 on Fortune's 500 list in 1982, Manville slipped in 1985 to last out of 250 companies in terms of community and environmental responsibility, and in 1988 it was ranked at 248. In parallel fashion, after its Valdez catastrophe, Exxon dropped from 8 to 110 on Fortune's list of most admired companies. Cleanup costs reduced its rank among the wealthiest companies. Despite effects of these costs on earnings and the number of people who tore up credit cards, Exxon increased its dividend and issued four times more new cards than were reported to have been destroyed.

Management rhetoric is misguided when it produces a corporate culture that stifles the kinds of enactments needed to prosper. Corporate culture is "a pattern of basic assumptions—invented, discovered, or developed by a given group as it learns to cope with its problems of external adaptation and internal integration— that has worked well enough to be considered valid and, therefore, to be taught to new members as the correct way to perceive, think, and feel in relation to those problems" (Schein, 1985, p. 9). The power of corporate culture is its ability to stabilize organizational members' thoughts. It is "the organization's system of values, norms, beliefs, and structures that persist *over time*" (Falcione & Kaplan, 1984, p. 301). The social reality embedded in each culture influences what its managers use to decide which issues are important and what response options are feasible (Davis, 1984). Each culture involves "a process of reality construction that allows people to see and understand particular events, actions, objects, utterances, or situations in distinctive ways" (Morgan, 1986, p. 128).

Corporate culture contains value judgments, such as ethics in marketing, product design, employee relations, quality of work, and competition; it is vital to matters regarding how each company treats people: its customers, neighbors, and employees (Drake & Drake, 1988). In this way, each company's culture helps or fails to address questions of fact, value, or policy. Because culture expresses operating assumptions, it offers unique ways to understand how a company's history influences its present and guides it into the future (Smircich & Calas, 1987).

Culture constitutes terministic screens that filter how people view reality (Burke, 1966b). It not only indicates what data are believed to be important, but it also suggests how employees of the company should acquire information about its circumstances. Corporate adaptation to internal and external environments requires the ability to read and interpret information. Reading these environments with the wrong terministic screens can produce the false conclusion that all is well or that troubles abound that actually do not. Cybernetic adjustments must include making dynamic alterations, establishing new goals, developing new criteria for evaluating success, and being sensitive to change and turbulence in internal and external environments (Morgan, 1982, 1986).

Cultural differences affect how companies, airlines for instance, respond to crises—their personae under crisis. The president of Japanese Airlines was publicly involved in his airline's apology to victims and survivors when one of its planes crashed in 1985; a senior maintenance technician with the company committed suicide, an act more likely to occur in a Japanese company than one located in the United States. In contrast, airline executives did not personally appear at the scenes of crashes, such as the Pan Am catastrophe in Lockerbie, Scotland or United's crash near Sioux City, Iowa. Differences of culture and language also explain why crises occur, such as the Avianca crash during approach to Kennedy Airport in 1990 (Pinsdorf, 1991).

In each case, Voice becomes crucial to explaining the causes and reactions to these crises. It also brings to mind the culture of the airline industry, which asserts its efficiency, caring attitude toward customers, safety record, and willingness to advance technical and human safety features. Reports of crashes and pictures of torn fuselages compete against the cultural fabric the industry tries to maintain and applies in times of crisis. Culture accounts for where spokespersons place blame. Some accept it. Others point to devious terrorists who sabotage planes—rather than to the lack of security that could prevent terrorist acts. Other explanations rely on technical aspects such as weather variations and instrument error, human factors such as pilot judgment or difficulties of cross-cultural communication, or economic conditions such as those that lead to companies keeping planes longer than they should.

Turbulence is a key factor in organizations' effort to achieve and enact a persona of control and competence. Writers (for instance, Dutton & Duncan, 1987; Dutton & Ottensmeyer, 1987; Huber & Daft, 1987; Markley, 1988) have discussed factors that influence how managers make sense of turbulent environments. Turbulence results from instability or frequency of change in a company's environment and the randomness of change. During high turbulence, organizations tend to protect the basis of their business by increasing their means for adapting to their environment (Huber & Daft, 1987). The greater the uncertainty, the more likely a company will attempt to make sense of its environment. In this regard, the asbestos industry conducted many studies over the years, but none of them served as that triggering mechanism that Dutton and Duncan (1987) contended is necessary to prompt companies to change their policy. Companies can be blinded to emerging and changing issues by their own rhetoric, which supplies incorrect or inappropriate readings of information they receive (Krippendorff & Eleey, 1986). Information does not come to a company packaged; it must be discovered and interpreted.

Cultures serve to provide coherence by preferring some themes or principles. As warrants, these themes influence how managers process information, analyze problems and opportunities, and plan strategically (Mason & Mitroff, 1981; Toulmin, Rieke, & Janik, 1979). Warrants that exist in a corporate culture provide managers with a sense of interconnectedness among problems, the completedness of their thinking (ability to account for relationships among entities, situations, or ideas), uncertainty, ambiguity, conflict, and social constraints. For this reason, warrants constitute a diagnostic focal point at which to look for evidence, raise questions about issues, make information and its assumptions explicit, and attempt to formulate solutions. Failing to make proper decisions, the asbestos industry adhered too long to the warrant that "reasonable" health risks must be tolerated to produce needed products. This premise is a version of the cultural archetype, "You can't make an omelette without breaking an egg" (Heath, 1988b; Mitroff, 1983).

The search for which warrants managers of a company prefer begins by looking for terms that affect how they think and act. For instance, key changes in how managements think about their operations have occurred in the past two decades because of increased salience and new definitions of four terms: equality, security, esthetics, and fairness (Heath, 1988a). These terms serve as propositions to guide thoughts, plans, policies, and operations. How a management team defines these terms, for instance, will shape its organization's sense of its corporate responsibility. In the past two decades, those key terms have come to mean the following: Companies are expected to treat people *equally* and *fairly*; they are expected to not harm the *esthetics* of the environment, and may even be expected to enhance it. They are expected to not endanger the *security* or *safety* of those whom they contact—and of the environment. If companies define these key terms differently than their stakeholders do, a clash of cultures results.

Evidence of how changes in the meanings of these terms can affect a company and even an industry can be found in the experience of the asbestos industry. A change in tort laws and mounting evidence of health problems led to the landmark liability case *Borel v. Fibreboard* (1973), which established that the asbestos industry was liable for health-related problems of people who had come into contact with asbestos. This was one of many cases that brought public attention to evidence that refuted the industry's claim that it had acted responsibly and was ignorant of health hazards of its product. Applying the concept of *incremental erosion* to the analysis of the tobacco industry, Condit and Condit (1992) demonstrated how critics of a company or industry challenge one premise at a time, eventually eroding the support for the organization's operations.

Legal cases involving the asbestos industry uncovered four themes that its leaders had persuaded themselves to apply in their decision making and operations; these themes tell a great deal about how ill prepared they were to accommodate to a new era. First, industry leaders had come to believe that no conclusive evidence affirmed the relationship between asbestos and health hazards. They believed that evidence linking asbestos and health problems had to be overwhelming before they could conclude that the data warranted more than passing concern. In contrast, experts testified for plaintiffs that hundreds of reputable articles had been published by the mid-1960s claiming that asbestos caused health problems. Asbestos company leaders weakened their position on this issue by testifying in court that they had not commissioned studies to determine the relationship between health and asbestos or to establish safe levels (parts per million) of asbestos exposure. Counter testimony indicated that such tests had been conducted, but the results were not used proactively to reduce standards that had been set too high and not achieved. Second, companies had operated on the state-of-the-art liability standard that said they were responsible for their products only to the extent they could "reasonably foresee" their harm. Third, the industry relied on the warrant that liability would be shared (if liability were established). Believing that interpretations of liability would always favor them, asbestos companies claimed that workers were partially negligent (contributory negligence) because they had known that workman's compensation had applied to asbestos related problems since the 1920s. Asbestos companies argued that contractors were responsible for the health of their workers who installed asbestos. Finally, asbestos leaders had convinced themselves that minimal efforts to protect the lives and well-being of workers would be sufficient. Some efforts had been made to have asbestos workers use protective respirators, but health hazards were not fully and dramatically explained to workers and they were not required to wear respirators. The prevailing standard applied to health issues was that life is cheap (Brodeur, 1985).

Culture and organizational rhetoric are interdependent; they can affirm one another rather than foster critical examination. For this reason, it is axiomatic to prefer a culture and rhetoric that foster an open climate, one in which persons in a company aggressively seek information from as many sources as possible in their attempts to reduce uncertainty about facts, values, and policy positions. This is true for internal and external environments (Grunig, 1985). Books, such as that by Coates, Coates, Jarratt, and Heinz (1986), explore methods and philosophies of issue monitoring and analysis. To foster the appropriate kind of thinking, Stanley (1985) recommended applying a decision model predicated on maximizing wins and minimizing losses for assessing how and when to respond to conflict and risk.

Such perspectives and analytical tactics can be used to keep culture and organizational rhetoric from leading key personnel to think that warrants are truths rather than decision-making premises subject to reconsideration and incremental erosion. Each organization's culture should emphasize change rather than take a static view of its relationship with stakeholders. Organizational rhetoric, in terms of internal stakeholders, can convince management that employees are valuable resources to be groomed and utilized as part of the decision-making processes; or it can convince management of the opposite point of view, leading, in all probability, to an unproductive and contentious relationship with employees, as well as external stakeholders.

Organizational rhetoric can be devoted to creating and maintaining a high degree of belief consensus or certainty. If consensus is too high, no uncertainty exists—or uncertainty is resolved by finding evidence to support a foregone conclusion rather than searching for ways to determine which conclusion is appropriate given the evidence. Culture is more likely to foster constructive adaptation if it is predicated on constant reassessment of the implications of data and value alternatives. *What if* assumptions embedded in corporate culture can help personnel address scenarios and project consequences that can result from environmental changes. Thinking "what if" is not designed to increase information equivocality, but rather to serve as a means for being alert to events, facts, and value shifts that can alter planning, operations, and personnel management. Lessons learned in this regard have led some companies in recent years to create internal advocates (especially on health, safety, consumer, and environmental issues) who report to CEOs and are responsible for spotting and aggressively pointing to weaknesses in corporate performance standards.

What if extrapolations should have permeated the thinking of the asbestos industry in two obvious ways. *What if* asbestos is related to health problems? *What if* the liability rules change to the extent that companies can become increasingly responsible for their products? Data showing the connection between health and asbestos—coupled with workman's compensation claims—demonstrate the importance of the first question. A steady shift in liability interpretations beginning shortly after the turn of the century, particularly with increased policing of food, drugs, and cosmetics, should have been the basis for extrapolations by the leaders of the asbestos industry that liability standards would continue to become more restrictive. To foster *what-if* thinking, studies should have been conducted to challenge rather than confirm corporate assumptions.

Some companies have learned the rhetorical value of scenario analysis, whereby they attempt to build into planning and operating philosophies estimates of the consequences of actions and assumptions. Such extrapolations can forecast public policy changes and business opportunities. This tactic suggests how platforms of fact can be built by communicating to correct misinformation and provide missing information. This model suggests that companies can change the warrants on which they operate, attempt to change the warrants of various stakeholders, or advocate specific policy outcomes given the data and warrants at play in each situation. This rhetorical stance can lend dynamism to corporate efforts to compare the argument structure present in its culture to that held by key stakeholders. This analysis substantiates the belief that companies operate in an internal and external social reality that is subject to persuasive influence (Cheney & Vibbert, 1987).

Culture affects organizational climate. It gives each employee a sense of the key persons with whom to communicate and what to communicate. It prescribes the content and meaning of the communication because it contains dominant metaphors that have rhetorical potency and can reduce ambiguity. In this way, employees obtain a sense of where they fit in the structure of the company and its relationship to its environment (Falcione, Sussman, & Herden, 1987). If a company's climate is open to issue analysis, personnel can challenge assumptions and suggest that policies and procedures be changed. If management creates a climate that closes discussion, employees are likely to ignore issues, which then go unheeded until they explode.

CRISIS COMMUNICATION: ENACTMENTS DURING EXTRAORDINARY EVENTS

Companies work hard, some more than others, to enact the persona that they are in charge of their destinies. Crises strain the appearance of control. When a crisis occurs, a spokesperson is expected to explain publicly and quickly why it happened and what will be done to correct operations and protect people from further disaster, as well as to repay and comfort those who have been harmed. Crisis communication is the enactment of control (at least its appearance) in the face of high uncertainty in an effort to win external audiences' confidence, in ways that are ethical.

Crises come in all kinds, shapes, and forms. Some involve loss of life or property, or both. Others result from events such as bankruptcy, loss of a senior officer, or scandal. Some result from actions by the company itself, such as a major change in policy, sudden closure or relocation, or a violation of law or regulation. Crises can include accidents and actions arising from poor judgment such as a plant explosion or a spill of toxic materials into the environment. They result because of actions of others, such as saboteurs who placed cyanide in Johnson & Johnson's Tylenol capsules or marketers who embarrassed Kraft USA, the giant food company.

Kraft suffered a crisis at the hands of marketing persons who created a contest designed to increase product visibility and buying preferences of Kraft cheese slices. On Sunday, June 12, 1989, a promotional contest was launched in the Chicago and Houston markets. The plan was that persons who bought Kraft cheese slices automatically competed to see who would win one of the following prizes: a 1990 Dodge Caravan van valued at $17,000, 100 Roadmaster bicycles, 500 Leapfrog skateboards, and 8,000 packages of Kraft cheese. This typical promotion became a crisis when hundreds of people jammed Kraft's phone circuits to claim prizes. A printing error in the contest materials resulted in hundreds more customers having winning game pieces than had been planned. More than 10,000 people called to claim the van. Kraft responded by canceling the ad and trying to change the contest rules. Instead of giving prizes it had promised to winners, Kraft offered them nominal amounts of cash. That decision led to a class-action lawsuit.

Other crises include spills by companies transporting crude oil, dramatized by the Exxon Valdez spill, with damage to Prince William Sound in Alaska starting on March 24, 1989. Another crisis surfaced when the Selikoff study, concluded in 1964, linked asbestos to health problems and the first case, *Borel v. Fibreboard*, was decided against the asbestos industry in 1978. Plants blow up. Nuts enter fast food establishments and kill dozens of innocent patrons, including children.

How should companies respond to such crises? Rowland and Rademacher (1990) observed that a crisis can be approached passively by spokespersons who reaffirm the values that are relevant to the crisis situation and publicly recommit themselves to those values, for instance a proclamation by a plant manager whose plant blew up that the company remains committed to worker safety, or one that allowed a toxic release is committed to environmental responsibility. In such situations, blame can be placed on someone (perhaps a subordinate) or something (environmental factors—act of God or regulatory agency). In such situations, no actions are announced that are likely to result in actual changes, but the appearance of change may be part of the symbolic response to the crisis. Passive response is possible if an adversarial atmosphere does not occur and if reporters are unable to challenge the characterization presented by the spokesperson. Given what is typical of many crises, different media are likely to assume an adversarial role and different reports can result from news services' agendas (Dyer, Miller, & Boone, 1991). In any event, the company's account for the crisis is judged by the standards of narratives: a credible and ethical accounting for the event given the persons involved and the values that guided their actions.

Crisis communication often entails strategies of apologizing to harmed publics. Narratives are essential for such efforts that require that the offending company be able to tell a credible story, one that has factual fidelity. Such stories consist of efforts to shape details in ways that give a focus as favorable to the company as possible. This effort is strongest when it is sincere. Subsequent story accounts of the crisis events must be consonant with early accounts if crisis communication is to have the desired narrative impact (Hobbs, 1991). Inconsistencies in stories suggest the presence of deceit and falsehood.

Companies want very much to determine who will speak in their behalf if a crisis occurs, although many have no communication plan in place and therefore allow reporters to sort out the spokespersons based on those who make the most quotable statements and are easiest to contact. Even when a communication plan calls for executives and skilled public relations practitioners to act as spokespersons, reporters do not limit themselves to those sources. As public relations expert Judith A. Ressler (1982) concluded, "Local media often know and trust local management; and comments from that person are more believable and create confidence that local leaders are in charge" (p. 8). Operations personnel may understand technical processes and be able to explain them and answer technical questions more credibly than can executives or professional communicators. Even after a crisis, operations people are likely to be contacted by reporters because they were eyewitnesses and may be able to give newsworthy details about events and operations. They often give a more believable story of events that seem to be authentic rather than manufactured by slick public relations personnel, executives, and company lawyers.

For that reason, personnel on the scene of crises are prime targets for reporters who know that those personnel are likely to be less polished in media relations and more capable of providing authoritative comments that may even question the wisdom of company practices that led to the crisis. Those persons may speak with a voice that differs from that of management, leading to a discordant organizational Voice. Such persons may blame management policies, such as safety violations or budget cutbacks that led to personnel working under less than optimally safe conditions, including those that violate regulations. People working in plants or field operations where a crisis happens are unlikely to know reporters, reporting methods, and the best way to communicate on behalf of the company. Implicit in this realization is the fact that employees are part of the corporate communication network whether management wants them to be and trains them to effectively represent the company or not.

Awareness that plant personnel and eyewitnesses are prime targets of reporters has led some companies and a group of crisis management experts to recommend getting the highest company official to the scene of the crisis as soon as possible. Critics of Exxon's handling of the Valdez crisis pointed out that the number one person, Lawrence Rawl, was tardy in getting to the scene of the cleanup where he was needed to enact the persona of a concerned company. Some skeptics doubt the usefulness of chief executive officers showing up and seeming to be involved; others say that gesture is crucial. Herbert Schmertz, formerly vice president of public affairs of Mobil Oil Company, said that under Exxon Valdez circumstances he would have sent his CEO immediately and would have included a group of prominent environmentalists charged with the task of advising the cleanup. Regardless of whether the CEO goes to the scene of the crisis, the CEO is responsible for enacting the company's response narrative (Small, 1991).

Such responses require planning. A crisis plan includes procedures for internal and external communication in the event of a crisis. The effort is to create a single Voice that achieves credibility and timely response. Members of the company are expected to provide a credible story of events. It is expected to fit the narratives relevant to the event, the company, the industry, and most importantly, the community.

An effective crisis plan requires executives who are trained to deal with reporters and other publics under crisis conditions, and who are willing to share with employees the responsibility for dealing with crises and to train them to do so. Each company needs internal communication specialists internal to it who are skilled at meeting with the press and other publics in crisis circumstances. It needs a culture that supports effective crisis response, exuding openness, candor, and honesty.

The crisis communication plan sets the tone, specifies in advance who will be the players in the event of a crisis, and establishes the roles each of these persons will play. Such plans are often frustrated by the advice of legal counsel that recommends against open and full communication, whereas ethical professional public relations counsel prefers open and candid presentation of information. Decisions need to be made to determine the kinds of statements unique to this company that can be made without breaching what legal counsel believes to be corporate liability.

Those who design a crisis communication plan must realize that the court of public opinion plays by quite different ethical and evidentiary standards than does a court of law. The public no longer believes there is such a thing as an industrial accident. Faith in engineering and operations expertise abounds. Accidents are blamed on carelessness and cutbacks, all of which smacks of corporate irresponsibility, which carries with it dire implications for corporate and industry reputations and images. Unwillingness to make statements, so believes the public, is admission of guilt.

A crisis plan should be tailored to each specific industry and business. An effective plan cannot be generic. Circumstances of operations at a food manufacturing or processing organization differ dramatically, for instance, from those of a chemical plant or a gas transmission company. A crisis plan should name the communication team and establish its communication network in the event a crisis occurs. It should prescribe how to communicate with reporters, as well as specify crisis team members, command center location, 1-800 numbers, investigative procedures to avert additional crisis, and policies to demonstrate open and honest displays of concern for the persons who are affected by the crisis. For instance, a company may plan to provide counselors for victims' families, methods to redress damages, and other enactments of public apology.

Crisis communication training is like preparation for a theatrical performance. It can be highly scripted on the assumption that misstatements do no good for the company or the people whose lives it has affected. Such training includes practicing with case study scenarios, during which personnel respond to questions by people who enact the role of reporters. Training explains how reporters develop stories and indicates the kinds of comments they like to include in news stories. Training describes deadlines and constraints under which reporters work. It reminds personnel that reporters are human beings, doing their job, attempting to advance their careers, trying to earn a living and take care of a family, and serving a profit-making interest.

Bringing employees into the crisis communication system means sharing power and responsibility with them. For some managers, that is hard to do. But this sharing empowers the employees and makes crisis prevention, management, and communication something for which they are responsible, rather than something for which others are responsible. Such gestures should empower personnel and strengthen the team spirit while fostering a culture of crisis avoidance, because this discussion and training reminds employees to avoid crisis rather than allow them to happen and have to deal with the media—and investigators from regulatory agencies.

Done effectively, crisis planning, management, and communication add to the company's ability to enact a coherent and credible Voice. Efforts to prevent crisis become paramount in employees' minds as they think about having to deal with them. This culture lays a foundation for looking for problems that may result in crises and prepares employees and executives to enact a persona of candor and caring if a crisis occurs.

RISK COMMUNICATION: INFORMATION, RHETORIC, AND POWER

Few communication problems loom as ominously for coming decades as do those related to how risk levels will be successfully discussed in public by companies, governmental agencies, trade associations, unions, environmentalists, health specialists, journalists, and advocates of the public interest. A revolution in environmentalism as well as personal and public health is requiring efforts to change personal and collective behaviors and to create and promulgate legislation and regulation.

Widely discussed risks include those related to toxic substances such as chemicals in working and living environments, electromagnetic fields, AIDS, drunk driving, alcohol abuse, tobacco products, and crime, whether in the streets or at home. Two broad but overlapping categories of risk communication exist. One attempts to alert people to risks over which they have personal control, such as driving without fastened seat belts or eating high-cholesterol foods. A second involves efforts to help people understand and agree to regulated levels of risk— such as those created by chemical companies. Because that kind of risk depends on some entity's caution and goodwill, its grave sociopolitical implications lead to public policy discussions, whereby harmed parties seek to regulate those who are liable.

Risk communication requires that narratives of thought and behavior be changed. It involves attempts to manage different zones of meaning, a complex mixture of technical risk assessments, values, and self-interests. Illustrative of these zones, a survey conducted at 26 locations in the U.S. and Canada by Arthur D. Little, Inc. found that plant personnel, community response personnel, and community officials and representatives had different interpretations of the risks associated with toxic fume releases and general environmental pollution. Plant personnel thought all of the risks included in the survey were less significant than did either of the other groups (Young, 1990). Policymakers' attitudes tend to be more favorable toward risk conditions than are opinions of the general public (Thomas, Swaton, Fishbein, & Otway, 1980).

Differences of opinion are not easily remedied. For that reason, policy that results is often not the product of shared points of view, but negotiated resolution of conflicting opinions. Such outcomes may leave all parties feeling dissatisfied. Conflicting interests and epistemologies unique to the battlefield of risk often prevent communicators from finding "common ground between the social world of risk perceptions guided by human experience and the scientists' rational ideal of decisionmaking based on probabilistic thinking" (Plough & Krimsky, 1987, p. 5). Risk messages often suffer from "deficiencies in scientific understanding, data, models, and methods, which result in large uncertainties in risk estimates" (Davies, Covello, & Allen, 1987, p. 110).

Environmental risk communication was codified in the Superfund Amendment Reauthorization Act of 1986 (SARA), which requires chemical companies to inform key publics regarding chemical emissions. The Environmental Protection Agency, along with other organizations, established risk communication as a subdiscipline committed to open, responsible, informed, and reasonable discussion of risks associated with personal health practices, as well as those involved in living and working in proximity to harmful activities and toxic substances. Reflecting on right-to-know legislation, the Environmental Protection Agency (1988a) characterized risk communication in noble terms: "The Emergency Planning and Community Right-to-Know Act creates a new relationship among government at all levels, business and community leaders, environmental and other public-interest organizations, and individual citizens. For the first time, the law makes citizens full partners in preparing for emergencies and managing chemical risks" (p. 3).

Risk communication can be defined as "any purposeful exchange of information about health or environmental risks between interested parties." It involves "the act of conveying or transmitting information between interested parties about levels of health or environmental risks; the significance or meanings of such risks; or decisions, actions, or policies aimed at managing or controlling such risks" (Davies et al., 1987, p. 112). A similar view was offered by the National Research Council (1989), which defined risk communication as *an interactive process of exchange of information and opinion among individuals, groups, and institutions. It involves multiple messages about the nature of risk and other messages, not strictly about risk, that express concerns, opinions, or reactions to risk messages or to legal and institutional arrangements for risk management.*" It is "successful only to the extent that it raises the level of understanding of relevant issues or actions and satisfies those involved that they are adequately informed within the limits of available knowledge" (p. 21). However insightful these definitions are, neither reveals the frustration, lack of trust, rage, politics, and conflicting zones of meaning that make risk communication so difficult.

To be avoided are definitions of risk communication that feature "dissemination" not "communication" (Schultz, 1989, pp. 13–14) and fail to recognize the political realities related to risk estimates and solutions. The best view of risk communication avoids casting the public in a passive role based on the following false assumption: If the public only understood our side of the story as we do, then confidence regarding risk would increase and the problem would go away (Gaudino et al., 1989). That model is particularly weak because the amount of factual knowledge individuals possess does not predict how much risk they will tolerate (Baird, 1986).

Risk communicators often lack trust because risks may be unseen and their messages reflect disagreement among scientific experts. Media reporters who comment on risk suffer selective perceptions and biases. News reports are often overly dramatic, simplistic, and distorted. Receivers of risk communication often lack objectivity needed to appreciate competing points of view. They are disinterested in complex discussions and often over- or underestimate their ability to cope with harm. They exaggerate or are skeptical of the effectiveness of regulation and legislation.

Many prescriptions have been developed to guide risk communicators. For instance, in its "seven cardinal rules of risk communication," the Environmental Protection Agency (1988b) advised risk communicators to tailor their messages to audiences and to use "simple, non-technical language. Be sensitive to local norms, such as speech and dress. Use vivid, concrete images that communicate on a personal level. Use examples and anecdotes that make technical risk data come alive. Avoid distant, abstract, unfeeling language about deaths, injuries, and illnesses" (p. 4). This advice assumes that "if people are sufficiently motivated, they are quite capable of understanding complex information, even if they may not agree with you" (p. 5).

Extending the EPA list of "cardinal" principles, the Chemical Manufacturers Association (1989) added four items: "Run a safe operation," "Reduce [toxic chemical] releases," "Find out the concerns of the community so you can decide what kinds of community outreach activities will be successful," and "Get involved in the community; establish a speakers bureau and join service organizations to make industry's presence known and to 'de-mystify' the chemical industry for local citizens." Worth noting is the fact that two of these recommendations point to the need for improved operations, one calls for refined issue monitoring, and one recommends additional external communication. This advice assumed that chemical companies' enactment has to meet public expectations before communication can be effective.

Reviewing the Right-to-Know provision of SARA Title III for the Public Relations Society of America, Newman (1988) concluded, "The theory behind these toxic laws is that this information will not only help answer citizen questions about releases, but will also assist them in pressuring government and industry to correct practices that threaten their health and environment" (p. 8). This observation suggests that understanding is not the only factor involved in risk assessment, management, and communication. Another prominent factor is power—a rhetorical struggle by parties engaged in negotiating the levels of risk and standards of regulative or legislative control.

This power struggle requires that risk communication accommodate *rhetorical and political influence* (getting audiences—corporate, governmental, and public— to comply with judgments and recommendations), *uncertainty* (seeking and processing information), *evaluation* (judging what is equitable, fair, safe, and aesthetic), and *involvement* (expressing self-interest or altruism). This approach to risk communication assumes that narratives change over time and organizational activities must conform to narratives of risk believed by activist publics. Efforts to alter risk perception and behaviors related to risk entail the negotiation of stakes. Risk communication is rhetorical and political. One risk communication model predicts that if people receive credible and clear information regarding assessed risk levels they will accept the conclusions and recommendations of risk assessors. Although idealistic, this model overassumes the power of information and fails to acknowledge power struggles between parties that employ political pressure to impose operating standards on one another. Such influence occurs because risk experts do not have truly objective standards to assess risk levels. Therefore, decisions regarding acceptable risks are subject to value judgments regarding the point at which a risk is assumed to need regulation .

Groups that assess risks not only try to control risk decisions but the availability and interpretation of risk information as well. Experience led Ellen Silbergeld, Senior Scientist with the Environmental Defense Fund, to conclude, "Equal access to resources is needed to understand the issues, to go behind the presentation being made by the communicator—to reassess the risks, if you will, to reevaluate the grounds for decisions and discussions" (Davies et al., 1987, p. 34). When publics believe they lack access to information, they are prone to seek it and interpret it. Failing that, they assume the worst. Key publics realize that if they accept risk communicators' assessments of risk, they are obliged to concur with the consequent recommendations. In this regard, publics are at the mercy of risk assessors; their recourse is to refuse to accept those evaluations. Reflecting on this strategy, Covello, Sandman, and Slovic (1988) claimed, "A risk that the parties at risk have some control over is more acceptable than a risk that is beyond their control. A risk that the parties at risk assess and *decide* to accept is more acceptable than a risk that is imposed on them" (p. 6). In the face of unknown or unacceptably high risks, noncompliance by key publics forces risk assessors to strive toward zero risk or to bear the burden of justifying any level higher.

Critics of companies that create risks have influenced governmental agencies and officials for two decades. Such actions, William Ruckelshaus reasoned, reflect this principle: "Ours is a government of the people in this country, and it derives, as we have been told since we were children, its just powers from the consent of the governed. If the governed withhold that consent or take a portion of it back, it simply means that the government has been forced to once again share the power to govern with those who had earlier given their consent" (Davies et al., 1987, p. 4). Passage of SARA Title III is powerful evidence of key publics' desire to control risk discussion and decision making.

Critics are unwilling to be cut out of decision making even if the only thing they can eventually do is agree, based on facts presented, that a risk decision is correct. People are likely to become active in their efforts to constrain companies if they detect a problem that should be solved, see minimal constraints to their activism, and believe the problem affects their self-interests (Grunig, 1989a). Recognizing these new politics, EPA administrator Lee Thomas observed that "we will never return to the days when we were content to let people in white coats make soothing noises. Citizens must share directly in decisions that affect them, and we must ensure that they do so with a fuller understanding of the inevitable trade-offs involved in the management of risk" (Davies et al., 1987, p. 25).

Risk communication is cloaked in the principle that people want to be involved in decisions that affect their health and well-being (National Research Council, 1989). "Power in this motivational sense refers to an intrinsic need for self-determination" (Conger & Kanungo, 1988, p. 473). People can be self- or other-empowered. They can be granted the opportunity to participate in decision making or they can assert their right to be involved. Perhaps this recognition led the Chemical Manufacturers Association to advise chemical plant managers to "involve all parties that have an interest or a stake in the particular risk in question" (Covello et al., 1988, p. 2). This advice acknowledged that "people and communities have a right to participate in decisions that affect their lives, their property, and the things they value" (p. 2). Moreover, the decision regarding what level is acceptable "*is not a technical question but a value question*" (p. 6).

The enactment of risk communication is a response to the uncertainty key audiences experience about risks. Frank Press, as President of the National Academy of Sciences, said that "an uncertainty principle operates in science and the communication of risk" (Davies et al., 1987, p. 12). Risk implies uncertainty, "a combined measure of the probability and magnitude of undesirable effects" (Hadden, 1988, p. 137). Audiences are interested in any information that will reduce their uncertainty about the impact of hazardous processes and toxic materials on their health, that of persons for whom they are responsible, and the environment for which they have an altruistic interest. People may seek to reduce uncertainty by controlling sources of risk.

Trust is a multidimensional construct that results from the amount of control an audience believes it can exert over sources of risk information and assessment. As a hazard assessment expert, Roger Kasperson concluded, "There is not a single risk communication problem; there is not a single social trust problem. There are many problems, and they are different" (Davies et al., 1987, p. 45). Trust is affected by vulnerability, predictability, and reward dependability. Party A is vulnerable (at risk) to party B if A's interests can be harmed or enhanced by what B decides to do. If B can enhance rather than harm A, the trust relationship is different than if no prediction can be made, or if B can be predicted to harm A. Emphasizing the multidimensionality of trust, Joanne Kauffman observed, "Government, in particular, suffers from a loss of credibility; it is often perceived to have a hidden agenda rather than to facilitate a process" (Davies et al., 1987, p. 74).

Members of the public are faced with self-interested decisions where risks—especially those under the control of someone else—may conflict. For instance, the public may be asked to choose between tolerating a chemical risk level in a community or risk losing a plant as a source of wages and taxes. A homemaker must balance the risk of serving foods that contain preservatives against the risk of serving spoiled food. Companies have a different choice to make than do other parties—upgrade operations and lessen public criticism—which means increased costs and lowered ability to compete and attract investors, unless all members of an industry adopt the same standards. Each person, whether a member of the public or an executive of a company, has to weigh competing beliefs and evaluations to estimate rewards and losses. In this sense, beliefs (degrees of certainty that one or more attribute is associated with an object or situation) interact with evaluations (positive or negative judgments). Each party in such decisions weighs different estimates of their actions in terms of positive or negative outcomes (Ajzen & Fishbein, 1980).

Risk evaluation requires that values be imposed on risk estimations. Enactment of risk communication should not assume that understanding and agreement are the same. They are not. As variables, they may interact or be independent of one another. Two parties may understand one another, but disagree. Information becomes meaningful when it is evaluated. Persons may differ in the way they evaluate it. "Information to be communicated must fit into the frameworks of the receivers: because they will interpret the information according to these frameworks, we must be aware of what they are rather than bemoan their existence" (Davies et al., 1987, p. 81).

Risk assessment is a judgment call no matter how scientifically precise. Evaluation requires understanding, but even more importantly, it depends on agreement. Evaluative criteria used by each party in risk assessment will shape their estimates of what is unacceptable. Emphasizing this point, Sandman (1986) observed that "experts and managers are coming to recognize that how people perceive a risk determines how they respond to it, which in turn sets the context for public policy." For this reason, he continued, "It is hard to have decent policies when the public ignores serious risks and recoils in terror from less serious ones. The task of risk communication, then, isn't just conveying information, though that alone is a challenge; it is to alert people when they ought to be alerted and reassure them when they ought to be reassured" (p. 1).

How people assess risk depends on criteria that grow out of their self- or altruistic interests. Sandman (1986) reasoned that even though "risk assessments are intrinsically complex and uncertain" they are doubly difficult "because audiences cling tenaciously to their safe-or-dangerous dichotomy." Audiences are frustrated when they are confronted by offsetting risks, and for this reason, lay publics resist "risk–cost or risk–risk" analysis. And Sandman concluded, "Trading risks against benefits is especially offensive when the risks raise moral issues and the 'victims' are not the ones making the choice" (pp. 22–23).

Parties involved in assessing risks often employ different criteria. Technical experts try to depersonalize scientific investigation and think of percentages of risk spread across large populations. In contrast, journalists downplay the general and personalize issues; they believe that risk is newsworthy whereas safety is not, and often operate with limited expertise and under time constraints. Reflecting on these different approaches to risk assessment, Sandman (1986) concluded, "For science, objectivity is tentativeness and adherence to evidence in the search for truth. For journalism, on the other hand, objectivity is balance. In the epistemology of journalism, there is no truth (or at least no way to determine truth); there are only conflicting claims, to be covered as fairly as possible, thus tossing the hot potato of truth into the lap of the audience" (p. 6). Of all parties that voice risk assessments, "the media see environmental risk as a dichotomy; either the situation is hazardous or it is safe" (Sandman, 1986, p. 8).

Although reporters are expected to provide impartial and balanced reporting, they are biased in their reports of risk. Using a 4-month content analysis of media outlets, Singer and Endreny (1987) found a dearth of information about the benefits of complex technologies and discovered that news stories focused more on hazards and harms of risk and did not mention the ratio of benefits to costs. The implied ratio, based on the relative space given to harms versus benefits, suggests that risks outweigh benefits.

When protecting its well-being, the public distinguishes between legal and ethical issues by relying more on what is "right" (interpreted as self-interest) than what is legal. People believe laws can be changed to correspond to what is right. The rightness of decisions depends on whatever version of their self-interests key audiences believe needs to be advanced (seeking rewards and avoiding losses). Public relations practitioners make a grave mistake when they miss this point, arguing that some action is legal—as though that will satisfy the public's sense of ethics and security.

Risk communicators must realize that self-interest or altruistic values predict that audiences will be involved with public policy issues leading them to recognize which arguments are relevant, to have more knowledge of a topic, and to communicate about it (Heath & Douglas, 1991). Persons whose self-interests are involved are more thoughtful in their analysis of message content. Persons who are less involved with a topic are likely to be less thoughtful and rely more on source credibility. Involved persons can be reached with information and argument even though they may resist them, whereas less involved persons are likely to ignore discussions of the topic. Involved persons are more critical of arguments than are the less involved (Petty & Cacioppo, 1981, 1986). Persons who are frightened, angry, and powerless resist information that says that their risk is modest, whereas those who are optimistic and overconfident deny that their risk is substantial (Sandman, 1986).

Reflecting on the difficulties of incorporating risk assessments into policy, the National Research Council (1989) concluded, "To remain democratic, a society must find ways to put specialized knowledge into the service of public choice and keep it from becoming the basis of power for an elite" (p. 15). Resolution of risk controversies requires more than clear, candid, and honest communication. Risk discussions fail when they ignore the fact that risk is a power issue that depends on agreement, evaluation, and compliance. Rather than blunting disagreement and differences regarding risk issues, the answer may be to make them public and explicit as a first step toward resolving them (Cannell & Otway, 1988).

Companies engaged in risk communication face a difficult task if they are to form, change, or reinforce opinions and behavior. Some companies need to do this to protect themselves by creating harmony with external stakeholders. Zones of meaning contain themes and principles that reflect competing self-interests of companies, regulatory agencies, and activist publics. Efforts to affect risk assessments and policy entail the enactment of control. Narratives feature mistakes and dread outcomes, such as the Exxon Valdez, Bhopal, or Three Mile Island. Archetypal disasters keep alive concerns regarding acceptable risks. Stories companies tell key publics about risks are evaluated against prevailing narratives. Companies, regulators, and activist publics often employ different narratives. Enactment of processes that make publics feel at risk challenges companies to achieve harmony of mutual interest and agreement as to tolerable levels of risk.

ISSUES MANAGEMENT: FROM STRATEGIC PLANNING TO EXTERNAL COMMUNICATION

Companies try hard to enact a persona that they are competent and in control. Excellent companies achieve that goal. The public, even members of large, influential activist groups, believe that companies dominate issues and policies. Executives and other policy-oriented boundary spanners feel that they have very little control and complain that they are buffeted by opinions expressed and policies advocated by other companies, activists, and media reporters. Recognizing the need for special ways of thinking about their presence in communities, companies have adopted strategies they believe will help them respond to and manage issues. This activity has evolved into a discipline called *issues management*, a response to critics of business policies and practices who gained influence during the tumultuous 1960s and 1970s by challenging standards of business operations thereby creating "the great era of reform." During that era, smug corporate giants learned that they could not dominate employment, environmental, and business policies.

To maximize their self-control and build harmony with their stakeholders requires that companies understand and remain sensitive to the performance expectations others hold of them. This requirement, however, does not deny companies the privilege of seeking to shape expectations that they believe are incorrect, either too high or too low. Companies' efforts to enact a narrative of harmony with stakeholders should be based on a commitment to community.

Companies come closer to achieving self-control and harmony when they are genuinely concerned about their place in the community (Kruckeberg & Starck, 1988).

During the past three decades, organizations have come under increasing legislative and regulatory scrutiny, despite the deregulatory years of the Reagan and Bush administrations. Leaders in most industries recognize the value regulation and legislation have for the orderly conduct of business. Indeed, a great deal of legislation is enacted at the request of businesses or is shaped by them. Key members of one industry may, in fact, attempt to create regulatory constraints that help them by shifting responsibilities to other industries, as insurance companies promoted legislation to force automobile manufacturers to increase the design of safe automobiles.

From strategic planning to improved operations, companies have responded with varying degrees of savviness to these changes. Some have blundered into situations that were mishandled, thereby leading to increased and perhaps unnecessary regulation. Adjustments to the public policy arena have made demands on companies as have the challenges to increase quality and productivity.

One response to these strains has been the creation of issues management programs. The Special Committee on Terminology of the Public Relations Society of America reported in 1987 that issues management is a public relations function entailing "systematic identification and action regarding public policy matters of concern to an organization" (p. 9). Issues management recognizes corporations' need to harmonize their interests with those of their stakeholders; as Ewing (1987) concluded, issues management "developed within the business community as an educational task aimed at preserving the proper balance between the legitimate goals and rights of the free enterprise system and those of society" (p. 5). Only by becoming part of executive management (the dominant coalition) can external communication experts help improve their companies' enactment in ways that lessen criticism of their policies and actions.

Public relations experts and issues managers only become part of these dominant coalitions (Grunig & Grunig, 1989) when they can meaningfully contribute to strategic business planning and management in ways that affect the bottom line (Ewing, 1987; D. B. Thompson, 1981; Wartick & Rude, 1986). This challenge is made more difficult by the lack of consensus regarding the range of activities of issues management. As Miller (1987) observed: "Issue management isn't quite public relations. Neither is it government relations, nor public affairs, nor lobbying, nor crisis management, nor futurism, nor strategic planning. It embraces all of these disciplines, and maybe a few more" (p. 125).

Capturing the spirit of this activity as early as 1978, the Public Affairs Council proclaimed, "Public affairs has increasingly come to mean not merely a response to change, but a positive role in the management of change itself—in the shaping of public policies and programs, and in the development of corporate activities to implement change constructively" (p. 2). Discussion of what companies do in the face of changing social issues has increased managers' sensitivity to changing standards of corporate responsibility (Heath, 1988a). Commitment to issues management led companies such as Prudential Insurance Company of America (Mac-Naughton, 1976) to institutionalize standards of corporate responsibility, especially in their governmental relations programs (Bradt, 1972).

In 1977, W. Howard Chase coined the term *issue management*, which he designated as the new science. To recommend a new kind of corporate communication response to critics of business activities, Chase drew on his experience at American Can Company and the lead of John E. O'Toole (1975) who may have been the first to use the term *advocacy advertising*. In accord with this trend, Bateman (1975) advised companies "to move from an information base to an advocacy position" (p. 5). This stance, he rationalized, was needed because "companies should not be the silent children of society" (p. 3). By 1976, terms such as *issue advertising* and *advocacy advertising* were being used in business publication discussions of the aggressive op-ed campaign made famous by Mobil Oil Corporation (Ross, 1976).

Although a communication bias has dominated discussions of how companies should handle their critics, farsighted executives went so far as to incorporate issues analysis into their strategic business planning. For instance, William S. Sneath (1977), President of Union Carbide Corporation, said that his company was using "scenario evaluation" as a means for projecting its business planning efforts 20 years into the future. Public policy issues, such as environmentalism, were vital to Union Carbide's planning effort. Sneath said that only time could judge "our legacy not only in terms of the economic accuracy of our business planning but in the way we committed our best minds and our best intentions to meet the needs and aspirations of a free society in an increasingly interdependent world" (p. 199). This model of issues management recognized that slick issue advertising was not the way to manage issues.

Another farsighted executive was Archie R. Boe (1979), CEO of Allstate Insurance Companies (1972–1982) and President of Sears (1982–1984), who created a Strategic Planning Committee in 1977 and an Issues Management Committee in 1978. He arranged the two groups to have interlocking memberships. The Issues Management Committee was chaired by a vice president who was a member of the Strategic Planning Committee.

As these examples demonstrate, issues management in its early years was based primarily on a communication model and a commitment to high ethical standards, but leaders in the discipline recognized the need to integrate strategic planning, public policy analysis, and communication (Marx, 1986). One of the leaders, Monsanto Corporation, has used issues management to determine which product lines are advisable in light of public policy trends (Fleming, 1980; Stroup, 1988). Describing Monsanto's contingency approach, Stroup (1988) observed: "Early knowledge of these trends would give the company more time to change negative attitudes toward business or to adapt business practices proactively if attitudes and expectations could not be swayed from the identified path" (p. 89).

A 1978 publication of the Public Affairs Council entitled, *The Fundamentals of Issue Management*, was an early expression of a comprehensive approach to issues management as "a program which a company uses to increase its knowledge of the public policy process and enhance the sophistication and effectiveness of its involvement in that process" (p. 1). What principle guides this activity? Answering that question, J. K. Brown (1979) reasoned that "if management should accustom itself routinely to ask the full range of questions that ought to be asked about vital corporate decisions, taking into account all the relevant external environments as well as the internal environment, this business of issues would become, properly, a non-issue" (p. 74). The heart of that process is commitment to strategic planning process and requires that it be supported by personnel who are expert in spotting, analyzing, and knowing what can and *cannot* (should and should not) be done to communicate on public policy issues and how to adjust products and services to hostile environments as well as to take advantage of favorable ones.

Issues management is a comprehensive program of planning, management, and communication functions. It is a creative and constructive attempt to lessen the unwise or harmful effects of activism as well as increase or decrease intra- and interindustry pressures to define and implement standards of corporate responsibility. It includes the option of debating in public what those standards should be. The program assumes that corporations must create harmony by influencing or accommodating to public policy (Ackerman & Bauer, 1976; MacNaughton, 1976).

Extending this viewpoint, Arrington and Sawaya (1984) claimed that the heart of issues management "is reconciliation of conflicting internal interests on public policy issues of strategic importance in order to make a coherent external advocacy" (p. 150). This activity requires analysis and planning of public affairs options, which "should be viewed as analogous to corporate planning and research and development—as a strategic process to help realize the basic objectives of a company" (p. 158). Viewing issues management this way is important, according to Wartick and Rude (1986), because it loses its identity and credibility when it is located in departments that are not positioned to implement comprehensive issues management programs. Issues management is most useful when it interlocks with strategic information management and when corporate culture fosters the acquisition and utilization of information in strategic planning (Ansoff, 1980).

A survey by Post, Murray, Dickie, and Mahon (1982) discovered that a critical phase in a company's effort to adjust to its environment is its decision to integrate a public affairs perspective into corporate planning and management. Of 400 public affairs personnel surveyed, 66% of the respondents reported that they assisted in issue identification, monitoring, and analysis. The respondents provided information for the strategic business planning group and reviewed strategic plans to determine whether they were sensitive enough to social and political trends.

FUNCTIONS OF ISSUES MANAGEMENT

Issues management has become a means to integrate strategic business planning, assessment of corporate culture, analysis of public policy trends, improvement of standards of corporate responsibility, and assertive communication on key issues. The functions of issues management can be viewed from three levels of generality.

First-Order Topics

This level of analysis focuses on the interaction between variables in three contexts: macrosocial, linking, and intra-individual. Analysis of the macrosocial level, for instance, addresses questions related to strategic reduction of uncertainty by executive management as it attempts to plan and manage. An understanding of the links enacted between departments involved in the issues management process gives insight into which organizational culture, structure, and interpersonal relationships foster or hinder issues management. Intra-individual issues refer to the scripts and narratives individuals use as they observe, comprehend, analyze, evaluate, and adjust to the public policy environment (Heath, 1990). At this level of analysis, issues management focuses on what is required for companies to achieve identification between themselves and key publics; it entails coping with involvement, reducing uncertainty, evaluating, planning actions, employing useful scripts, presenting a positive persona, solving relationship problems, and exercising control.

Second-Order Topics

The second order of topics consists of activities that are essential for organizations to manage issues and adapt to public policy changes.

"Smart" Planning and Operations. What must be done to integrate public policy analysis into strategic business planning and operations management? If issues managers are doing a good job of capturing critical changes in public policy, then that information should be integrated into the strategic business plan and corporate management strategies. This kind of information can offer business opportunities, justify the curtailment or change of business activities, and guide standards by which the company operates. According to Wartick and Rude (1986), "IM can positively affect corporate performance by enhancing the firm's responsiveness to environmental change" (p. 125).

Issues management requires constant surveillance of opinions that can mature into public policy positions. The goal is to identify issues that could affect the company business plan—both as constraints and opportunities. How a company creates its business plan reflects its planning assumptions and its assessment of data about market and policy forces. Market forces are influenced by public policy issues. Therefore, to do the best job of planning requires that issues managers obtain data about trends and analyze issues to determine their potential effects on the strategic business plan (Stroup, 1988). In this way, issues management is not merely the institutionalization of corporate responsibility, but is also a thoughtful and systematic use of information to increase the likelihood that the strategic business plan will succeed. It takes advantage of business opportunities created by public policy changes and avoids collisions with unfavorable conditions created by public policy (Ewing, 1987; Stroup, 1988; Wartick & Rude, 1986).

Advancing this point, Ewing (1987) reasoned, "This new management technique is to corporate public policy/public affairs planning and operations as strategic planning is to corporate business planning and operations. Issues management and strategic planning together give senior officers, especially CEOs, an enhanced capability to manage their enterprises in the present and near-term future—1 to 3, 5, 10 or more years out" (p. 2). In this way, Ewing continued, "Issues management is about power. It is about the power that controls the new bottom line of all American corporations—optimal profits *and* public acceptance" (p. 1). Both can be adapted to and influenced most effectively if they are foretold sufficiently well.

Tough Defense and Smart Offense. What needs to be said to whom and with what intended effect to exert influence in the public policy arena? One way of thinking about issues management is that it offers rationale, tools, and incentives for early intervention in the public discussion of policy issues. If companies get involved before key publics have solidified their opinions on issues, communication campaigns are more likely to succeed (Chase, 1984; Crable & Vibbert, 1985). If issues are discussed openly, publics are empowered to adjudicate policy positions of fact, value, definition, and policy (Lesly, 1984; Schmertz, 1986).

Getting the House in Order. What is required to be a responsible corporation? Market forces alone do not shape the fate of companies; public policy plays a major role (Anshen, 1974; Buchholz, 1985; Sethi, 1977). For this reason, departments such as public affairs must be sensitive to public policy forces and assist in corporate planning and formulating business ethics (Post, 1979). Reflecting on the learning curve that has characterized the maturation of public affairs, Post and Kelley (1988) concluded:

> The public affairs management field has undergone tremendous change over the past five years. Change will continue as the field moves toward professionalization and legitimization within the corporate world. This trend should help organizations move from coping with external demands to anticipating how demands can best be met within the technical and economic context of the organization. This is the essence of being a responsive corporation in the modern world. For the central institution of our age, that is neither too much nor too little to ask. (p. 365)

The learning curve has matured to the point where people believe that prevention of issues entails honest and candid commentary on opinion positions, but also acknowledges that companies may have to change policies and operations to lessen the legitimate outcries of their critics.

Scouting the Terrain. What functions are needed to discover and make sense of changing issues in the public policy environment? Companies operate in environments that exhibit various degrees of turbulence. What they believe to be the nature of the marketplace is likely to influence their strategic business plans.

The same can be said of issues monitoring to assess the public policy environment. Over the past decade, strategic management information systems have become increasingly sophisticated. Efforts to obtain information consist of much more than surveys of key publics' opinions on issues. Futurists such as Joseph Coates and his associates (1986) used sophisticated social scientific techniques to obtain valuable insights into how issues can be identified, monitored, and analyzed. The effectiveness of this activity depends on each corporation's culture and its organizational and political structures (Huber & Daft, 1987).

Third-Order Topics

Questions of the third order entail specific issues management functions a company needs to take to foster harmony with its stakeholders in its public policy environment:

- Integrating critical public policy issues analysis and audits into corporate strategic planning to support the corporate business plan.
- Assuring that corporate strategic planning incorporates stakeholder group public policy issue stances and perceptions of corporate social responsibility.
- Obtaining input from all levels (executive, staff, and operations) of personnel regarding the implications of public policy changes on business plans and corporate communication.
- Assuring that management, staff, and operating personnel are aware of and comply with established standards of corporate social responsibility.
- Scanning and monitoring (tracking) the public policy environment to determine internal and external stakeholder groups' standards of corporate social responsibility (expectations of how businesses should operate in the public interest).
- Developing and implementing standards of corporate social responsibility (corporate ethics).
- Identifying, analyzing, forecasting, and prioritizing issues based on their impact on the organization.
- Developing a public policy plan designed to balance corporate and public interests.
- Communicating in regard to issues important to key publics with the intention of producing informed opinions and constructive evaluations regarding issues crucial to the implementation of the corporate strategic plan.

Issues management can improve business plans and enhance harmony between company operating standards and key publics' expectations. It is a means for engaging in communication that brings external messages inside and uses them persuasively to affect organizational culture. This communication can be turned externally. Therein is the power of issues communication, Cheney and Dionisopolous (1989) concluded, "for public relations statements and issue management campaigns do not only reflect the society of which they are part, they also help to create and recreate it" (p. 144).

FOCAL POINTS OF ANALYSIS

- How compatible is a company's culture and that of its stakeholders?
- Does the company's culture blind its managers to problems and opportunities?
- What needs to be done to strengthen identification between external publics and a company?
- Does the company have a crisis communication culture and plan that will lead to satisfactory resolution of a crisis, open and candid communication, and concern for those harmed by company actions?
- Does the crisis plan foster a culture of crisis prevention, one that empowers employees to seek ways to prevent crises but be prepared to communicate responsibly in the event one occurs?
- Is the company prepared to look for risk conditions, assess and manage them, and communicate with key publics to foster open, two-way communication?
- Does the company adapt to the rhetorical and political dimensions of risk assessment, management, and communication?
- Does issues management improve corporate enactment by bringing company performance closer to the expectations held by key publics?

CONCLUSION

Whereas crisis communication is the enactment of control in a situation of high uncertainty, issues management is a comprehensive monitoring, planning, and communication effort designed to give companies as much control over their destinies as possible. In either sense, companies may have to assess, manage, and publicly address risk levels of concern to key publics.

These challenges have helped public relations practitioners to understand that they are expected to play increasingly complex and involved roles in promoting the bottom line and protecting their company in ways that are sensitive to the needs of a variety of external interests. Issues management is a maturing program to assist companies' efforts to present a coherent and trustworthy enactment to external publics. It acknowledges that companies need to negotiate their relationships with these publics to achieve harmony. Narratives, created by stakeholders and companies, constitute the operating frameworks and standards of corporate responsibility companies need to meet or alter. These efforts are intended to result in internal and external enactments that increase the amount of control companies have over their destinies without diminishing the level of control sought by key publics. This synergy is the key to successful enactment by companies.

References

Ackerman, R. W., & Bauer, R. A. (1976). *Corporate social responsiveness: The modern dilemma.* Reston, VA: Reston.

Adkins, L. (1978, June). How good are advocacy ads? *Dun's Review, 111,* 76–77.

Ajzen, I., & Fishbein, M. (1980). *Understanding attitudes and predicting social behavior.* Englewood Cliffs, NJ: Prentice-Hall.

Albrecht, T. L. (1984). Managerial communication and work perception. In R. N. Bostrom & B. H. Westley (Eds.), *Communication yearbook 8* (pp. 538–557). Newbury Park, CA: Sage.

Albrecht, T. L. (1988). Communication and personal control in empowering organizations. In J. A. Anderson (Ed.), *Communication yearbook 11* (pp. 380–390). Newbury Park, CA: Sage.

Albrecht, T. L., & Hall, B. (1991). Relational and content differences between elites and outsiders in innovation networks. *Human Communication Research, 17,* 535–561.

Altman, I., Vinsel, A., & Brown, B. B. (1981). Dialectic conceptions in social psychology: An application to social penetration and privacy regulation. In L. Berkowitz (Ed.), *Advances in experimental social psychology* (Vol. 14, pp. 107–160). New York: Academic Press.

Anderson, C. W. (1960). The relation between speaking times and decision in the employment interview. *Journal of Applied Psychology, 44,* 267–268.

Anshen, M. (Ed.). (1974). *Managing the socially responsible corporation.* New York: Macmillan.

Ansoff, H. I. (1980). Strategic issue management. *Strategic Management Journal, 1*(2), 131–148.

Arrington, C. B., Jr., & Sawaya, R. N. (1984). Managing public affairs: Issues management in an uncertain environment. *California Management Review, 26*(4), 148–160.

Ashforth, B. E., & Fried, Y. (1988). The mindlessness of organizational behaviors. *Human Relations, 41,* 305–329.

Atkin, C. K. (1973). Instrumental utilities and information seeking. In P. Clarke (Ed.), *New models for communication research* (pp. 205–239). Newbury Park, CA: Sage.

Backman, C. W. (1988). The self: A dialectical approach. In L. Berkowitz (Ed.), *Advances in experimental social psychology* (Vol. 21, pp. 229–260). New York: Academic Press.

Baglan, T., Lalumia, J., & Bayless, O. L. (1986). Utilization of compliance-gaining strategies: A research note. *Communication Monographs, 53,* 289–293.

Baird, B. (1986). Tolerance for environmental health risks: The influence of knowledge benefits, voluntariness and environmental attitudes. *Risk Analysis, 6*(4), 425–435.

Bandura, A. (1977). *Social learning theory.* Englewood Cliffs, NJ: Prentice-Hall.

Bantz, C. R. (1983). Naturalistic research traditions. In L. L. Putnam & M. E. Pacanowsky (Eds.), *Communication and organizations: An interpretive approach* (pp. 55–71). Newbury Park, CA: Sage.

Bantz, C. R. (1989). Organizing and The Social Psychology of Organizing. *Communication Studies, 40,* 231–240.

Bantz, C. R. (1990). Organizing and enactment: Karl Weick and the production of news. In S. R. Corman, S. P. Banks, C. R. Bantz, & M. E. Mayer (Eds.), *Foundations of organizational communication: A reader* (pp. 133–141). New York: Longman.

Bateman, D. N. (1975). Corporate communications as advocacy: Practical perspectives and procedures. *Journal of Business Communication, 13*(1), 3–11.

Beatty, M. J. (1989). Group members' decision rule orientations and consensus. *Human Communication Research, 16,* 279–296.

Befu, H. (1980). Structural and motivational approaches to social exchange. In K. J. Gergen, M. S. Greenberg, & R. H. Wills (Eds.), *Social exchange: Advances in theory and research* (pp. 197–214). New York: Plenum.

Bem, D. (1972). *Beliefs, attitudes and human affairs.* Belmont, CA: Brooks-Cole.

Benson, J. K. (1977). Organizations: A dialectical view. *Administrative Science Quarterly, 22,* 1–20.

Benson, J. K. (1983). Paradigm and praxis in organizational analysis. In L. L. Cummings & B. M. Staw (Eds.), *Research in organizational behavior* (Vol. 5, pp. 33–56). Greenwich, CT: JAI.

Berger, C. R. (1987). Communicating under uncertainty. In M. E. Roloff & G. R. Miller (Eds.), *Interpersonal processes: New directions in communication research* (pp. 39–62). Newbury Park, CA: Sage.

Berger, C. R., & Calabrese, R. J. (1975). Some explorations in initial interaction and beyond: Toward a developmental theory of interpersonal communication. *Human Communication Research, 1,* 99–112.

Berger, C. R., Weber, M. D., Munley, M. E., & Dixon, J. T. (1977). Interpersonal relationship levels and interpersonal attraction. In B. D. Ruben (Ed.), *Communication yearbook 1* (pp. 245–261). New Brunswick, NJ: Transaction Books.

Berlo, D. K. (1977). Communication as process: Review and commentary. In B. D. Ruben (Ed.), *Communication yearbook 1* (pp. 11–27). New Brunswick, NJ: Transaction Books.

Bettman, J., & Weitz, B. (1983). Attributions in the board room. *Administrative Science Quarterly, 28,* 165–183.

Bingham, S. G., & Burleson, B. R. (1989). Multiple effects of messages with multiple goals: Some perceived outcomes of responses to sexual harassment. *Human Communication Research, 16,* 184–216.

Black, E. (1970). The second persona. *Quarterly Journal of Speech, 56,* 109–119.

Boe, A. R. (1979). Fitting the corporation to the future. *Public Relations Quarterly, 24*(4), 4–5.

Boland, R. J., & Hoffman, R. (1983). Humor in a machine shop: An interpretation of symbolic action. In L. R. Pondy, P. J. Frost, G. Morgan, & T. C. Dandridge (Eds.), *Organizational symbolism* (pp. 187–198). Greenwich, CT: JAI.

Bormann, E. G. (1983). Symbolic convergence: Organizational communication and culture. In L. L. Putnam & M. E. Pacanowsky (Eds.), *Communication and organizations: An interpretive approach* (pp. 99–122). Newbury Park, CA: Sage.

Bormann, E. G. (1988). "Empowering" as a heuristic concept in organizational communication. In J. A. Anderson (Ed.). *Communication yearbook 11* (pp. 391–404). Newbury Park, CA: Sage.

Bradt, W. R. (1972). *Current trends in public affairs.* New York: Conference Board.

Brodeur, P. (1985). *Outrageous misconduct: The asbestos industry on trial.* New York: Pantheon.

Brown, J. K. (1979). *The business of issues: Coping with the company's environments.* New York: Conference Board.

Brown, M. E. (1969). Identification and some conditions of organizational involvement. *Administrative Science Quarterly, 14,* 346–355.

Brown, M. H. (1990). Defining stories in organizations. In J. A. Anderson (Ed.), *Communication yearbook 13* (pp. 107–113). Newbury Park, CA: Sage.

Browning, L. D., & Hawes, L. C. (1991). Style, process, surface, context: Consulting as postmodern art. *Journal of Applied Communication Research, 19,* 32–54.

Buchholz, R. A. (1982). Education for public issues management: Key insights from a survey of top practitioners. *Public Affairs Review, 3,* 65–76.

Buchholz, R. A. (1985). *Essentials of public policy for management*. Englewood Cliffs, NJ: Prentice-Hall.

Buchholz, R. A. (1988). Adjusting corporations to the realities of public interests and policies. In R. L. Heath (Ed.), *Strategic issues management* (pp. 51–72). San Francisco: Jossey-Bass.

Bucklin, L. P. (1965). The informative role of advertising. *Journal of Advertising Research, 5*(4), 11–15.

Buller, D. B., Strzyewski, K. D., & Comstock, J. (1991). Interpersonal deception: I. Deceivers' reactions to receivers' suspicions and probing. *Communication Monographs, 58*, 1–24.

Bullis, C. A., & Bach, B. W. (1991). An explication and test of communication network content and multiplexity as predictors of organizational identification. *Western Journal of Speech Communication, 55*, 180–197.

Bullis, C. A., & Tompkins, P. K. (1989). The forest ranger revisited: A study of control practices and identification. *Communication Monographs, 56*, 287–306.

Burgoon, J. K. (1985). Nonverbal signals. In M. L. Knapp & G. R. Miller (Eds.), *Handbook of interpersonal communication* (pp. 344–390). Newbury Park, CA: Sage.

Burgoon, J. K., & Hale, J. L. (1984). The fundamental topoi of relational communication. *Communication Monographs, 51*, 193–214.

Burgoon, J. K., & Hale, J. L. (1988). Nonverbal expectancy violations: Model elaboration and application to immediacy behaviors. *Communication Monographs, 55*, 58–79.

Burke, K. (1934, May 2). The meaning of C. K. Ogden. *New Republic*, pp. 328–331.

Burke, K. (1942). The study of symbolic action. *Chimera, 1*, 7–16.

Burke, K. (1955). Linguistic approach to problems of education. In N. B. Henry (Ed.), *Modern philosophies and education*, Part 1 of *National Society for the Study of Education fifty-fourth yearbook* (pp. 259–303). Chicago, IL: University of Chicago Press.

Burke, K. (1961). *Attitudes toward history*. Boston: Beacon.

Burke, K. (1965). *Permanence and change* (2nd. revised ed.). Indianapolis: Bobbs-Merrill.

Burke, K. (1966a). Dramatic form—and: Tracking down implications. *Tulane Drama Review, 10*, 54–63.

Burke, K. (1966b). *Language as symbolic action*. Berkeley: University of California Press.

Burke, K. (1967). Dramatism. In L. Thayer (Ed.), *Communication: Concepts and perspectives* (pp. 327–352). Washington, DC: Spartan Books.

Burke, K. (1968). *Counter-statement*. Berkeley: University of California Press.

Burke, K. (1969a). *A grammar of motives*. Berkeley: University of California Press.

Burke, K. (1969b). *A rhetoric of motives*. Berkeley: University of California Press.

Burke, K. (1970). *The rhetoric of religion: Studies in logology*. Berkeley: University of California Press.

Burke, K. (1973). *The philosophy of literary form* (3rd. ed.). Berkeley: University of California Press.

Burke, K. (1976). The party line. *Quarterly Journal of Speech, 62*, 62–68.

Burke, K. (1983a). Counter-gridlock: An interview with Kenneth Burke. *All Area*, 4–35.

Burke, K. (1983b). Dramatism and logology. *Times Literary Supplement*, p. 859.

Burleson, B. R., & Levine, B. J., & Samter, W. (1984). Decision-making procedure and decision quality. *Human Communication Research, 10*, 557–574.

Burrell, G., & Morgan, G. (1979). *Sociological paradigms and organizational analysis*. London: Heinemann.

Burt, R. S. (1980). *Toward a theory of action*. New York: Academic Press.

Camden, C. T., & Kennedy, C. W. (1986). Manager communicative style and nurse morale. *Human Communication Research, 12*, 551–563.

Campbell, K. K. (1970). The ontological foundations of rhetorical theory. *Philosophy & Rhetoric, 3*, 97–107.

Campbell, K. K., & Jamieson, K. H. (1978). *Form and genre: Shaping rhetorical action*. Falls Church, VA: Speech Communication Association.

Cannell, W., & Otway, H. (1988). Audience perspectives in the communication of technological risks. *Futures, 20*, 519–532.

Cappella, J. N., & Greene, J. O. (1982). A discrepancy-arousal explanation of mutual influence in expressive behavior for adult–adult and infant–adult interaction. *Communication Monographs, 49*, 89–114.

Chase, W. H. (1977). Public issue management: The new science. *Public Relations Journal, 32*(10), 25–26.

Chase, W. H. (1984). *Issue management: Origins of the future.* Stamford, CT: Issue Action.

Chemical Manufacturers Association. (1989). *Title III: One year later.* Washington, DC: Chemical Manufacturers Association.

Cheney, G. (1983a). On the various and changing meanings of organizational membership: A field study of organizational identification. *Communication Monographs, 50,* 342–362.

Cheney, G. (1983b). The rhetoric of identification and the study of organizational communication. *Quarterly Journal of Speech, 69,* 143–158.

Cheney, G. (1991). *Rhetoric in an organizational society: Managing multiple identities.* Columbia, SC: University of South Carolina Press.

Cheney, G. (1992). The corporate person (re)presents itself. In E. L. Toth & R. L. Heath (Eds.), *Rhetorical and critical approaches to public relations* (pp. 165–183). Hillsdale, NJ: Lawrence Erlbaum Associates.

Cheney, G., & Dionisopoulos, G. N. (1989). Public relations? No, relations with publics: A rhetorical-organizational approach to contemporary corporate communications. In C. H. Botan & V. Hazleton, Jr. (Eds.), *Public relations theory* (pp. 135–157). Hillsdale, NJ: Lawrence Erlbaum Associates.

Cheney, G., & Vibbert, S. L. (1987). Corporate discourse: Public relations and issue management. In F. M. Jablin, L. L. Putnam, K. H. Roberts, & L. W. Porter (Eds.), *Handbook of organizational communication: An interdisciplinary perspective* (pp. 165–194). Newbury Park, CA: Sage.

Coates, J. F., Coates, V. T., Jarratt, J., & Heinz, L. (1986). *Issues management: How you can plan, organize and manage for the future.* Mt. Airy, MD: Lomond Publications.

Cochran, D. S., & David, F. R. (1986). Communication effectiveness of organizational mission statements. *Journal of Applied Communication Research, 14*(2), 108–118.

Cody, M. J., Greene, J. O., Marston, P. J., O'Hair, H. D., Baaske, K. T., & Schneider, M. J. (1986). Situation perception and message strategy selection. In M. L. McLaughlin (Ed.), *Communication yearbook 9* (pp. 390–420). Newbury Park, CA: Sage.

Coffman, S. L., & Eblen, A. L. (1987). Metaphor use and perceived managerial effectiveness. *Journal of Applied Communication Research, 15*(1–2), 53–66.

Conant, R. C. (1979). A vector theory of information. In D. Nimmo (Ed.), *Communication yearbook 3* (pp. 177–194). New Brunswick, NJ: Transaction Books.

Condit, C. M., & Condit, D. M. (1992). Smoking OR health: Incremental erosion as a public interest group strategy. In E. L. Toth & R. L. Heath (Eds.), *Rhetorical and critical approaches to public relations* (pp. 241–256). Hillsdale, NJ: Lawrence Erlbaum Associates.

Conger, J. A., & Kanungo, R. N. (1988). The empowerment process: Integrating theory and practice. *Academy of Management Review, 13,* 471–482.

Conrad, C. (1983). Organizational power: Faces and symbolic forms. In L. L. Putnam & M. E. Pacanowsky (Eds.), *Communication and organizations: An interpretive approach* (pp. 173–194). Newbury Park, CA: Sage.

Conrad, C. (1992). Corporate communication and control. In E. L. Toth & R. L. Heath (Eds.), *Rhetorical and critical approaches to public relations* (pp. 187–204). Hillsdale, NJ: Lawrence Erlbaum Associates.

Conrad, C., & Ryan, M. (1985). Power, praxis, and self in organizational communication theory. In R. McPhee & P. Tompkins (Eds.), *Organizational communication: Traditional themes and new directions* (pp. 235–257). Newbury Park, CA: Sage.

Corman, S. R. (1990). A model of perceived communication in collective networks. *Human Communication Research, 16,* 582–602.

Corporate culture: The hard-to-change values that spell success or failure. (1980, October 27). *Business Week,* pp. 148–160.

Covello, V. T., Sandman, P. M., & Slovic, P. (1988). *Risk communication, risk statistics, and risk comparisons: A manual for plant managers.* Washington, DC: Chemical Manufacturers Association.

Crable, R. E., & Vibbert, S. L. (1983). Mobil's epideictic advocacy: "Observations" of Prometheus-Bound. *Communication Monographs, 50,* 380–394.

Crable, R. E., & Vibbert, S. L. (1985). Managing issues and influencing public policy. *Public Relations Review*, *11*(2), 3–16.

Cronen, V. E., Pearce, W. B., & Harris, L. M. (1982). The coordinated management of *meaning: A theory of communication*. In F. E. X. Dance (Ed.), *Human communication theory: Comparative essays* (pp. 61–89). New York: Harper & Row.

Cude, R. L. (1991, May). *The development of communication competence during organizational assimilation*. Paper presented at the International Communication Association, Chicago, IL.

Cusella, L. P. (1982). The effects of source expertise and feedback valence on intrinsic motivation. *Human Communication Research*, *9*, 17–32.

Daft, R. L., & Weick, K. E. (1984). Toward a model of organizations as interpretation systems. *Academy of Management Review, 9*, 284–295.

Daniels, T. D., & Spiker, B. K. (1987). *Perspectives on organizational communication*. Dubuque, IA: Brown.

Danowski, J. A., Barnett, G. A., & Fiedland, M. H. (1987). Interorganizational networks via shared public relations firms' centrality, diversification, media coverage, and public's images. In M. L. McLaughlin (Ed.), *Communication yearbook 10* (pp. 808–830). Newbury Park, CA: Sage.

Davies, J. C., Covello, V. T., & Allen, F. W. (Eds.). (1987). *Risk communication*. Washington, DC: The Conservation Foundation.

Davis, S. (1984). *Managing corporate culture*. Cambridge, MA: Ballinger.

Deetz, S. A. (1982). Critical interpretive research in organizational communication. *Western Journal of Speech Communication, 46*, 131–149.

Deetz, S. A. (1988). Cultural studies: Studying meaning and action in organizations. In J. A. Anderson (Ed.). *Communication yearbook 11* (pp. 335–355). Newbury Park, CA: Sage.

Deetz, S. A., & Mumby, D. K. (1985). Metaphors, information, and power. In B. D. Ruben (Ed.), *Information and behavior* (Vol. 1, pp. 369–386). New Brunswick, NJ: Transaction Books.

deTurk, M. A. (1985). A transactional analysis of compliance-gaining behavior: Effects of noncompliance, relational contexts, and actors' gender. *Human Communication Research, 12*, 54–78.

DeWine, S. (1988). The cultural perspective: New wave, old problems. In J. A. Anderson (Ed.). *Communication yearbook 11* (pp. 346–379). Newbury Park, CA: Sage.

Dillard, J. P., Segrin, C., & Harden, J. M. (1989). Primary and secondary goals in the production of interpersonal influence messages. *Communication Monographs, 56*, 19–38

Dionisopoulos, G. N. (1986). Corporate advocacy advertising as political communication. In L. L. Kaid, D. Nimmo, & K. R. Sanders (Eds.), *New perspectives on political advertising* (pp. 82–106). Carbondale, IL: Southern Illinois University Press.

Dionisopoulos, G. N., & Crable, R. E. (1988). Definitional hegemony as a public relations strategy: The rhetoric of the nuclear power industry after Three Mile Island. *Central States Speech Journal, 39*, 134–145.

Donohue, W. A., & Diez, M. E. (1985). Directive use of negotiation interaction. *Communication Monographs, 52*, 305–318.

Douglas, D. F., Westley, B. N., & Chaffee, S. H. (1970). An information campaign that changed community attitudes. *Journalism Quarterly, 47*, 479–487, 492.

Downs, T. M. (1990). Predictors of communication satisfaction during performance appraisal interviews. *Management Communication Quarterly, 3*, 334–354.

Drake, B. H., & Drake, E. (1988). Ethical and legal aspects of managing corporate cultures. *California Management Review, 30*(2), 107–123.

Duck, S. (1985). How to lose friends without influencing people. In M. E. Roloff & G. Miller (Eds). *Interpersonal processes: New directions in communication research* (pp. 278–298). Newbury Park, CA: Sage.

Dutton, J. E., & Duncan, R. B. (1987). The creation of momentum for change through the process of strategic issue diagnosis. *Strategic Management Review, 8*, 279–295.

Dutton, J. E., & Ottensmeyer, E. (1987). Strategic issue management systems: Forms, functions, and contexts. *Academy of Management Review, 12*(2), 355–365.

Dyer, S. C., Jr., Miller, M. M., & Boone, J. (1991). Wire service coverage of the Exxon Valdez crisis. *Public Relations Review, 17*(1), 27–36.

Eisenberg, E. M. (1984). Ambiguity as strategy in organizational communication. *Communication Monographs, 51*, 227–242.

Eisenberg, E. M. (1986). Meaning and interpretation in organizations. *Quarterly Journal of Speech, 72*, 88–113.

Eisenberg, E. M., Monge, P. R., & Farace, R. V. (1984). Coorientation on communication rules in managerial dyads. *Human Communication Research, 11*, 261–271.

Eisenberg, E. M., Monge, P. R., & Miller, K. I. (1984). Involvement in communication networks as a predictor of organizational commitment. *Human Communication Research, 10*, 179–201.

Elmendorf, F. M. (1988). Generating grass-roots campaigns and public involvement. In R.. L. Heath (Ed.), *Strategic issues management* (pp. 306–320). San Francisco: Jossey-Bass.

Engel, S. (1988). Metaphors: How are they different for the poet, the child and the everyday adult? *Metaphor and Symbolic Activity, 2*, 239–250.

Environmental Protection Agency. (1988a, September). *Chemicals in your community.* Washington, DC: Environmental Protection Agency.

Environmental Protection Agency. (1988b, April). *Seven cardinal rules of risk communication.* Washington, DC: Environmental Protection Agency.

Eoyang, C. K. (1983). Symbolic transformation of belief systems. In L. R. Pondy, P. J. Frost, G. Morgan, & T. C. Dandridge (Eds.), *Organizational symbolism* (pp. 109–121). Greenwich, CT: JAI.

Evered, R. (1983). The language of organizations: The case of the Navy. In L. R. Pondy, P. J. Frost, G. Morgan, & T. C. Dandridge (Eds.), *Organizational symbolism* (pp. 125–143). Greenwich, CT: JAI.

Ewing, R. P. (1982). Advocacy advertising: The voice of business in public policy debate. *Public Affairs Review, 3*, 23–29.

Ewing, R. P. (1987). *Managing the new bottom line: Issues management for senior executives.* Homewood, IL: Dow Jones-Irwin.

Fainsilber, L., & Ortony, A. (1987). Metaphorical uses of language in the expression of emotions. *Metaphor and Symbolic Activity, 2*, 239–250.

Fairhurst, G. T. (1986). Male–female communication on the job: Literature review and commentary. In M. L. McLaughlin (Ed.), *Communication yearbook 9* (pp. 83–116). Newbury Park, CA: Sage.

Fairhurst, G. T., Green, S. G., & Snavely, B. K. (1984). Face support in controlling poor performance. *Human Communication Research, 11*, 273–295.

Fairhurst, G. T., Rogers, L. E., & Sarr, R. A. (1987). Manager–subordinate control patterns and judgments about the relationship. In M. L. McLaughlin (Ed.), *Communication yearbook 10* (pp. 395–415). Newbury Park, CA: Sage.

Falcione, R. L., & Kaplan, E. A. (1984). Organizational climate, communication, and culture. In R. N. Bostrom & B. H. Westley (Eds.), *Communication yearbook 8* (pp. 285–309). Newbury Park, CA: Sage.

Falcione, R. L., Sussman, L., & Herden, R. P. (1987). Communication climate in organizations. In F. M. Jablin, L. L. Putnam, K. H. Roberts, & L. W. Porter (Eds.), *Handbook of organizational communication: An interdisciplinary perspective* (pp. 195–227). Newbury Park, CA: Sage.

Farace, R. V., Monge, P. R., & Russell, H. M. (1977). *Communicating and organizing.* Reading, MA: Addison-Wesley.

Feldman, D. C. (1981). The multiple socialization of organization members. *Academy of Management Review, 6*, 309–318.

Fine, H. J., & Lockwood, B. R. (1986). Figurative language production as a function of cognitive style. *Metaphor and Symbolic Activity, 1*, 139–152.

Finn, D. W. (1984). The integrated information response model. *Journal of Advertising, 13*, 24–33.

Fischoff, B. (1976). Attribution theory and judgement under uncertainty. In J. H. Harvey, W. J. Ickes, & R. F. Kidd (Eds.), *New directions in attribution research* (Vol. 1, pp. 421–452). Hillsdale, NJ: Lawrence Erlbaum Associates.

Fishbein, M., & Ajzen, I. (1975). *Belief, attitude, intention, and behavior*. Reading, MA: Addison-Wesley.

Fishbein, M., & Ajzen, I. (1981). Acceptance, yielding and impact: Cognitive processes in persuasion. In R. E. Petty, T. M. Ostrom, & T. C. Brock (Eds.), *Cognitive responses in persuasion* (pp. 339–359). Hillsdale, NJ: Lawrence Erlbaum Associates.

Fisher, B. A. (1978). Information systems theory and research: An overview. In B. D. Ruben (Ed.), *Communication yearbook 2* (pp. 81–108). New Brunswick, NJ: Transaction Books.

Fisher, B. A. (1982). The pragmatic perspective of human communication: A view from system theory. In F. E. X. Dance (Ed.), *Human communication theory: Comparative essays* (pp. 192–219). New York: Harper & Row.

Fisher, W. R. (1985). The narrative paradigm: An elaboration. *Communication Monographs, 52*, 347–367.

Fisher, W. R. (1987). *Human communication as narration: Toward a philosophy of reason, value, and action*. Columbia: University of South Carolina Press.

Fisher, W. R. (1989). Clarifying the narrative paradigm. *Communication Monographs, 56*, 55–58.

Fleming, J. E. (1980). Linking public affairs with corporate planning. *California Management Review, 23*(2), 35–43.

Freedman, A. M. (1989, November 14). Rebelling against alcohol, tobacco ads. *Wall Street Journal*, pp. B1, 12.

Freeman, R.E. (1984). *Strategic management: A stakeholder approach*. Boston: Pitman.

Freimuth, V. S., & Van Nevel, J. P. (1981). Reaching the public: The asbestos awareness campaign. *Journal of Communication, 31*(2), 155–167.

Fulk, J., & Mani, S. (1986). Distortion of communication in hierarchical relationships. In M. L. McLaughlin (Ed.), *Communication yearbook 9* (pp. 483–510). Newbury Park, CA: Sage.

Gandy, O. H., Jr. (1982). *Beyond agenda setting: Information subsidies and public policy*. Norwood, NJ: Ablex.

Garbett, T. (1981). *Corporate advertising: The what, the why, and the how*. New York: McGraw-Hill.

Gaudino, J. L., Fritsch, J., & Haynes, B. (1989). "If you knew what I knew, you'd make the same decision": A common misperception underlying public relations campaigns? In C. H. Botan & V. Hazleton, Jr. (Eds.), *Public relations theory* (pp. 299–308). Hillsdale, NJ: Lawrence Erlbaum Associates.

Gerbner, G. (1967). An institutional approach to mass communications research. In L. Thayer (Ed.), *Communication: Theory and research* (pp. 429–445). Springfield, IL: Thomas.

Gergen, K. J., & Gergen, M. M. (1988). Narrative and the self as relationship. In L. Berkowitz (Ed.), *Advances in experimental social psychology* (Vol. 21, pp. 17–56). New York: Academic Press.

Gibson, L D. (1983). If the question is copy testing, the answer is . . . "not recall." *Journal of Advertising Research, 23*(1), 39–46.

Glaser, S. R., & Eblen, A. (1986). Organizational communication effectiveness: The view of corporate administrators. *Journal of Applied Communication Research, 14*(2), 119–132.

Glaser, S. R., Zamanou, S., & Hacker, K. (1987). Measuring and interpreting organizational culture. *Management Communication Quarterly, 1*, 173–198.

Goffman, E. (1959). *The presentation of self in everyday life*. Garden City, NY: Anchor Doubleday.

Goldberg, A. A., Cavanaugh, M. S., & Larson, C. E. (1983). The meaning of "power." *Journal of Applied Communication Research, 11*, 89–108.

Goodall, H. L., Jr. (1989). *Casing a promised land*. Carbondale, IL: Southern Illinois University Press.

Goodall, H. L., Jr. (1990). A theater of motives and the "meaningful orders of persons and things." In J. A. Anderson (Ed.), *Communication yearbook 13* (pp. 69–94). Newbury Park, CA: Sage.

Goodall, H. L., Jr., Wilson, G. L., & Waagen, C. L. (1986). The performance appraisal interview: An interpretive reassessment. *Quarterly Journal of Speech, 72*, 74–87.

Gorden, W. I., & Nevins, R. I. (1987). The language and rhetoric of quality: Made in the U.S.A. *Journal of Applied Communication Research, 15*(1–2), 19–34.

Greenberg, M. S. (1980). A theory of indebtedness. In K. J. Gergen, M. S. Greenberg, & R. H. Wills (Eds.), *Social exchange: Advances in theory and research* (pp. 3–26). New York: Plenum Press.

Greene, C. N. (1978). Identification modes of professionals: Relationship with formalization, role strain, and alienation. *Academy of Management Journal, 21,* 486–492.

Grunig, J. E. (1985, May). *A structural reconceptualization of the organizational communication audit, with application to a State Department of Education.* Paper presented at the International Communication Association, Honolulu, HI.

Grunig, J. E. (1989a). Sierra Club study shows who become activists. *Public Relations Review, 15*(3), 3–15.

Grunig, J. E. (1989b). Symmetrical presuppositions as a framework for public relations theory. In C. H. Botan & V. Hazleton, Jr. (Eds.), *Public relations theory* (pp. 17–44). Hillsdale, NJ: Lawrence Erlbaum Associates.

Grunig, J. E. (Ed.). (1992). *Excellence in public relations and communication management.* Hillsdale, NJ: Lawrence Erlbaum Associates.

Grunig, J. E., & Grunig, L. A. (1989). Toward a theory of the public relations behavior of organizations: Review of a program of research. In J. E. Grunig & L. A. Grunig (Eds.), *Public relations research annual* (Vol. 1, pp. 27–63). Hillsdale, NJ: Lawrence Erlbaum Associates.

Grunig, J. E., & Hunt, T. (1984). *Managing public relations.* New York: Holt, Rinehart & Winston.

Guerro, L. K., & Dionisopoulos, G. N. (1990). Enthymematic solutions to the Lockshin defection story: A case study in the repair of a problematic narrative. *Communication Studies, 41,* 299–310.

Guinan, P. J., & Scudder, J. N. (1989). Client-oriented interactional behaviors for professional–client settings. *Human Communication Research, 15,* 444–462.

Hadden, S. G. (1988). *A citizen's right to know: Risk communication and public policy.* Boulder, CO: Westview.

Hartman, R. L., & Johnson, J. D. (1989). Social contagion and multiplexity: Communication networks as predictors of commitment and role ambiguity. *Human Communication Research, 15,* 523–548.

Heath, R. L. (1979). Kenneth Burke on form. *Quarterly Journal of Speech, 65,* 392–404.

Heath, R. L. (1986). *Realism and relativism: A perspective on Kenneth Burke.* Macon, GA: Mercer University Press.

Heath, R. L. (1988a). *Strategic issues management: How organizations influence and respond to public interests and policies.* San Francisco: Jossey-Bass.

Heath, R. L. (1988b). The rhetoric of issue advertising: A rationale, a case study, a critical perspective— and more. *Central States Speech Journal, 39,* 99–109.

Heath, R. L. (1990). Corporate issues management: Theoretical underpinnings and research foundations. In J. E. Grunig & L. A. Grunig (Eds.), *Publication relations research annual* (Vol. 2, pp. 29–65). Hillsdale, NJ: Lawrence Erlbaum Associates.

Heath, R. L. (1991). Effects of internal rhetoric on management response to external issues: How corporate culture failed the asbestos industry. *Journal of Applied Communication, 18*(2), 153–167 .

Heath, R. L., & Douglas, W. (1986). Issues advertising and its effect on public opinion recall. *Public Relations Review, 12*(2), 47–56.

Heath, R. L., & Douglas, W. (1991). Effects of involvement on reactions to sources of messages and to message clusters. In L. A. Grunig & J. E. Grunig (Eds.), *Public relations research annual* (Vol. 3, pp. 179–193). Hillsdale, NJ: Lawrence Erlbaum Associates.

Heath, R. L., & Nelson, R. A. (1985). Image and issue advertising: A corporate and public policy perspective. *Journal of Marketing, 49,* 58–68.

Heath, R. L., & Nelson, R. A. (1986). *Issues management: Corporate public policymaking in an information society.* Newbury Park, CA: Sage.

Heath, R. L., & Phelps, G. (1984). Readability of annual reports: No matter how hard I try, I don't understand. *Public Relations Review, 10,* 56–62.

Hewes, D. E., & Planalp, S. (1987). The individual's place in communication science. In C. R. Berger & S. H. Chaffee (Eds.), *Handbook of communication science* (pp. 146–183). Newbury Park, CA: Sage.

Hickson, D. J., Astley, W. G., Butler, R. J., & Wilson, D. C. (1981). Organization as power. In B. M. Staw & L. L. Cummings (Eds.), *Research in organizational behavior* (Vol. 3, pp. 151–196). Greenwich, CT: JAI.

Hill, L. B., & Cummings, H. W. (1981). Job performance assessment for public affairs officers in the U.S. Air Force. *Journal of Applied Communication Research, 9,* 16–29.

Hirokawa, R.Y. (1985). Discussion procedures and decision-making performance: A test of a functional perspective. *Human Communication Research, 12,* 203–224.

Hirokawa, R. Y. (1988). Group communication and decision-making performance: A continued test of the functional perspective. *Human Communication Research, 14,* 487–515.

Hirsch, P. M., & Andrews, J. A. Y. (1983). Ambushes, shootouts, and knights of the roundtable: The language of corporate takeovers. In L. R. Pondy, P. J. Frost, G. Morgan, & T. C. Dandridge (Eds.), *Organizational symbolism* (pp. 145–155). Greenwich, CT: JAI.

Hobbs, J. D. (1991, November). *"Treachery by any other name": A case study of the Toshiba public relations crisis.* Paper presented at the meeting of the Speech Communication Association, Atlanta, GA.

Hollander, E. P. (1980). Leadership and social exchange processes. In K. J. Gergen, M. S. Greenberg, & R. H. Wills (Eds.), *Social exchange: Advances in theory and research* (pp. 103–118). New York: Plenum.

Holt, G. R. (1989). Talk about acting and constraint in stories about organizations. *Western Journal of Speech Communication, 53,* 374–397.

Huber, G. P., & Daft, R. L. (1987). The information environments of organizations. In F. M. Jablin, L. L. Putnam, K. H. Roberts, & L. W. Porter (Eds.), *Handbook of organizational communication: An interdisciplinary perspective* (pp. 130–164). Newbury Park, CA: Sage.

Infante, D. A., & Gorden, W. I. (1985). Superiors' argumentativeness and verbal aggressiveness as predictors of subordinates' satisfaction. *Human Communication Research, 12,* 117–125.

Jablin, F. M. (1982a). Formal structural characteristics of organizations and superior–subordinate communication. *Human Communication Research, 8,* 338–347.

Jablin, F. M. (1982b). Organizational communication: An assimilation theory. In M. E. Roloff & C. R. Berger (Eds.), *Social cognition and communication* (pp. 255–286). Newbury Park, CA: Sage.

Jablin, F. M. (1984). Assimilating new members into organizations. In R. N. Bostrom & B. H. Westley (Eds.), *Communication yearbook 8* (pp. 594–626). Newbury Park, CA: Sage.

Jablin, F. M. (1985). Task/work relationships: A life-span perspective. In M. L. Knapp & G. R. Miller (Eds.), *Handbook of interpersonal communication* (pp. 615–654). Newbury Park, CA: Sage.

Jablin, F. M., Putnam, L. L., Roberts, K. H., & Porter, L. W. (Eds.). (1987). *Handbook of organizational communication: An interdisciplinary perspective.* Newbury Park, CA: Sage.

Janis, I. (1972). *Victims of groupthink: A psychological study of foreign policy decisions and fiascos.* Boston: Houghton Mifflin.

Jarboe, S. (1988). A comparison of input–output, process–output, and input–process–output models of small group problem-solving effectiveness. *Communication Monographs, 55,* 121–142.

Jones, E. T., & Saunders, J. (1977). Persuading an urban public: The St. Louis Privacy Campaign. *Journalism Quarterly, 54,* 669–673.

Jones, G. R. (1986). Socialization tactics, self-efficacy, and newcomers' adjustments to organizations. *Academy of Management Journal, 29,* 262–279.

Jordan, J. M., & Roloff, M. E. (1990). Acquiring assistance from others: The effective of indirect requests and relational intimacy on verbal compliance. *Human Communication Research, 16,* 519–555.

Kauffman, C. (1989). Names and weapons. *Communication Monographs, 56,* 273–284.

Kelley, H. H. (1972). Attribution in social interaction. In E. E. Jones, H. H. Kanouse, H. H. Kelley, R. E. Nisbett, S. Valins, & B. Weiner (Eds.), *Attribution: Perceiving the causes of behavior* (pp. 1–26). Morristown, NJ: General Learning Press.

Kelley, H. H. (1973). The processes of causal attribution. *American Psychologist, 28,* 107–128.

Kelly, J. W. (1985). Storytelling in high tech organizations: A medium for sharing culture. *Journal of Applied Communication Research, 13*(1), 45–58.

Koch, S., & Deetz, S. (1981). Metaphor analysis of social reality in organizations. *Journal of Applied Communication Research, 9,* 1–15.

Kramer, M. W. (1989). Communication during intraorganization job transfers. *Management Communication Quarterly, 3*, 219–248.

Krefting, L. A., & Frost, P. J. (1985). Untangling webs, surfing waves, and wildcatting: A multiple-metaphor perspective of managing organizational culture. In P. J. Frost, L. F. Moore, M. R. Louis, C. C. Lundberg, & J. Martin (Eds.), *Organizational culture* (pp. 155–168). Newbury Park, CA: Sage.

Kreps, G. L. (1990). Stories are repositories of organizational intelligence: Implications for organizational development. In J. A. Anderson (Ed.), *Communication yearbook 13* (pp. 191–202). Newbury Park, CA: Sage.

Krippendorff, K. (1975). Information theory. In G. J. Hanneman & W. J. McEwen (Eds.), *Communication and behavior* (pp. 351–389). Reading, MA: Addison-Wesley.

Krippendorff, K. (1977). Information systems theory and research: An overview. In B. D. Ruben (Ed.), *Communication yearbook 1* (pp. 149–171). New Brunswick, NJ: Transaction Books.

Krippendorff, K., & Eleey, M. L. (1986). Monitoring a group's symbolic environment. *Public Relations Review, 12*(1), 13–36.

Kruckeberg, D., & Starck, K. (1988). *Public relations and community: A reconstructed theory.* New York: Praeger.

Lakoff, G., & Johnson, M. (1980). *Metaphors we live by.* Chicago: University of Chicago Press.

Lesly, P. (1984). *Overcoming opposition: A survival manual for executives.* Englewood Cliffs, NJ: Prentice-Hall.

Leventhal, G. S. (1980). What should be done with equity theory? New approaches to the study of fairness in social relationships. In K. J. Gergen, M. S. Greenberg, & R. H. Wills (Eds.), *Social exchange: Advances in theory and research* (pp. 27–55). New York: Plenum.

Likert, R. (1961). *New patterns of management.* New York: McGraw-Hill.

Lincoln, J. R., & Miller, J. (1979). Work and friendship ties in organizations; A comparative analysis of relational networks. *Administrative Science Quarterly, 24*, 181–199.

Lundberg, C. (1978). The unreported leadership research of Dr. G. Hypothetical: Six variables in need of recognition. In M. W. McCall, Jr. & M. M. Lombardo (Eds.), *Leadership: Where else can we go?* (pp. 65–83). Durham, NC: Duke University Press.

MacEwen, E. C., & Wuellner, F. (1987, June). *Corporate communications and marketing: An integrated effort.* Paper presented at the A. N. A. Corporate Advertising Workshop, New York, NY.

MacNaughton, D. S. (1976). Managing social responsiveness. *Business Horizons, 19*, 19–24.

Mangham, I. L., & Overington, M. A. (1987). *Organizations as theatre: A social psychology of dramatic appearances.* New York: Wiley.

Marchand, R. (1987). The fitful career of advocacy advertising: Political protection, client cultivation, and corporate morale. *California Management Review, 29*, 128–156.

Markley, O. W. (1988). Conducting a situation audit: A case study. In R. L. Heath (Ed.), *Strategic issues management: How organizations influence and respond to public interests and policies* (pp. 137–154). San Francisco: Jossey-Bass.

Marquez, F. T. (1977). Advertising content: Persuasion, information or intimidation? *Journalism Quarterly, 54*, 482–491.

Martin, J., & Powers, M. (1983). Organizational stories: More vivid and persuasive than quantitative data. In B. Staw (Ed.), *Psychological foundations of organizational behavior* (pp. 161–168). Glenview, IL: Scott, Foresman.

Martin, J., Sitkin, S. B., & Boehm, M. (1985). Founders and the elusiveness of a cultural legacy. In P. J. Frost, L. F. Moore, M. R. Louis, C. C. Lundberg, & J. Martin (Eds.), *Organizational culture* (pp. 99–124). Newbury Park, CA: Sage.

Marx, T. G. (1986). Integrating public affairs and strategic planning. *California Management Review, 29*(1), 141–147.

Mason, R. O., & Mitroff, I. I. (1981). *Challenging strategic planning assumptions: Theory, cases, and techniques.* New York: Wiley.

Mayo, E. (1949). *The social problems of an industrial civilization.* London: Routledge & Kegan Paul.

McCabe, A. (1988). Effect of different contexts on memory for metaphor. *Metaphor and Symbolic Activity, 3,* 105–132.

McCornack, S. A., & Parks, M. R. (1986). Deception detection and relationship development: The other side of trust. In M. L. McLaughlin (Ed.), *Communication yearbook 9* (pp. 377–389). Newbury Park, CA: Sage.

McGregor, D. (1960). *The human side of enterprise.* New York: McGraw-Hill.

McGregor, D. (1968). Theory X and theory Y. In D. R. Hampton, C. E. Summer, & R. A. Webber (Eds.), *Organizational behavior and the practice of management* (pp. 132–137). Glenview, IL: Scott, Foresman.

McGuire, W. J. (1989). Theoretical foundations of campaigns. In R. E. Rice & C. K. Atkin (Eds.), *Public communication campaigns* (2nd ed., pp. 43–65). Newbury Park, CA: Sage.

McLeod, J. M., & Chaffee, S. H. (1973). Interpersonal approaches to communication research. *American Behavioral Scientist, 16,* 469–499.

McPhee, R. D. (1989). Organizational communication: A structurational exemplar. In B. Dervin, L. Grossberg, B. J. O'Keefe, & E. Wartella (Eds.), *Rethinking communication: Particular exemplars* (Vol. 2, pp. 199–212). Newbury Park, CA: Sage.

Meadow, R. G. (1981). The political dimensions of nonproduct advertising. *Journal of Communication, 31*(3), 69–82.

Mendelsohn, H. (1973). Some reasons why information campaigns can succeed. *Public Opinion Quarterly, 37,* 50–61.

Meyers, R. A., Seibold, D. R., & Brashers, D. (1991). Argument in initial group decision-making discussions: Refinement of a coding scheme and a descriptive quantitative analysis. *Western Journal of Speech Communication, 55,* 47–68.

Millar, F. E., & Rogers, L. E. (1976). A relational approach. In G. Miller (Ed.), *Explorations in interpersonal communication* (pp. 87–103). Newbury Park, CA: Sage.

Miller, V. D., & Jablin, F. M. (1991a, May). *A longitudinal investigation of newcomers' information seeking behaviors during organizational entry.* Paper presented at the International Communication Association, Chicago, IL.

Miller, V. D., & Jablin, F. M. (1991b). Information seeking during organizational entry: Influences, tactics, and a model of the process. *Academy of Management Review, 16,* 92–120.

Miller, W. H. (1987, November 2). Issue management: "No longer a sideshow." *Industry Week, 235,* 125–129.

Mintzberg, G. H. (1973). *The nature of managerial work.* New York: Harper & Row.

Mitroff, I. I. (1983). *Stakeholders of the organizational mind: Toward a new view of organizational policy making.* San Francisco: Jossey-Bass.

Monge, P. R. (1987). The network level of analysis. In C. R. Berger & S. H. Chaffee (Eds.), *Handbook of communication science* (pp. 239–270). Newbury Park, CA: Sage.

Monge, P. R., & Eisenberg, E. M. (1987). Emergent communication networks. In F. M. Jablin, L. L. Putnam, K. H. Roberts, & L. W. Porter (Eds.), *Handbook of organizational communication: An interdisciplinary perspective* (pp. 304–342). Newbury Park, CA: Sage.

Monge, P. R., & Miller, G. R. (1985). Communication networks. In A. Kuper & J. Kuper (Eds.), *The social science encyclopedia* (pp. 130–131). London: Routledge & Kegan Paul.

Morgan, G. (1982). Cybernetics and organization theory: Epistemology of technique? *Human Relations, 35,* 521–537.

Morgan, G. (1986). *Images of organization.* Newbury Park, CA: Sage.

Morgan, G., Frost, P. J., & Pondy, L. R. (1983). Organizational symbolism. In L. R. Pondy, P. J. Frost, G. Morgan, & T. C. Dandridge (Eds.), *Organizational symbolism* (pp. 3–35). Greenwich, CT: JAI.

Morris, G. H., Gaveras, S. C., Baker, W. L., & Coursey, M. L. (1990). Aligning actions at work: How managers confront problems of employee performance. *Management Communication Quarterly, 3,* 303–333.

Morse, B. W., & Piland, R. N. (1981). An assessment of communication competencies needed by intermediate-level health care providers: A study of nurse–patient, nurse–doctor, and nurse communication relationships. *Journal of Applied Communication Research, 9,* 30–41.

Mumby, D. K. (1987). The political function of narrative in organizations. *Communication Monographs, 54,* 113–127.

Mumby, D. K. (1988). *Communication and power in organizations: Discourse, ideology, and domination.* Norwood, NJ: Ablex.

National Research Council. (1989). *Improving risk communication.* Washington, DC: National Academy Press.

Nelson, P. (1974). Advertising as information. *Journal of Political Economy, 82,* 729–754.

Newell, S. E., & Stutman, R. K. (1991). The episodic nature of social confrontation. In J. A. Anderson (Ed.), *Communication yearbook 14* (pp. 359–392). Newbury Park, CA: Sage.

Newman, K. M. (1988). *Toxic chemical disclosures: An overview of new problems, new opportunities for the professional communicator.* New York: Public Relations Society of America.

Noelle-Neumann, E. (1991). The theory of public opinion: The concept of the spiral of silence. In J. A. Anderson (Ed.), *Communication yearbook 14* (pp. 256–287). Newbury Park, CA: Sage.

Norris, V. P. (1983). Consumer valuation of national ads. *Journalism Quarterly, 60,* 262–268.

O'Keefe, B. J. (1988). The logic of message design: Individual differences in reasoning about communication. *Communication Monographs, 55,* 80–103.

O'Keefe, B. J., & McCornack, S. A. (1987). Message design logic and message goal structures. *Human Communication Research, 14,* 68–92.

O'Keefe, B. J., & Shepherd, G. J. (1987). The pursuit of multiple objectives in face-to-face persuasive interaction: Effects of construct differentiation on message organization. *Communication Monographs, 54,* 396–419.

Olasky, M. N. (1987). *Corporate public relations: A new historical perspective.* Hillsdale, NJ: Lawrence Erlbaum Associates.

O'Reilly, C. (1989). Corporations, culture, and commitment: Motivation and social control in organizations. *California Management Review, 31*(4), 9–25.

Ornstein, S. (1986). Organizational symbols: A study of their meanings and influences on perceived psychological climate. *Organizational Behavior and Human Decision Processes, 38,* 207–229.

Orton, J. D., & Weick, K. E. (1990). Loosely coupled systems: A reconceptualization. *Academy of Management Review, 15,* 203–223.

O'Toole, J. E. (1975). Advocacy advertising shows the flag. *Public Relations Journal, 31*(11), 14–16.

Owen, W. F. (1990). Delimiting relational metaphors. *Communication Studies, 41,* 35–53.

Pacanowsky, M. E. (1988a). Communicating in the empowering organization. In J. A. Anderson (Ed.), *Communication yearbook 11* (pp. 356–379). Newbury Park, CA: Sage.

Pacanowsky, M. E. (1988b). Slouching towards Chicago. *Quarterly Journal of Speech, 74,* 453–467.

Pacanowsky, M. E., & O'Donnell-Trujillo, N. (1982). Communication and organizational cultures. *Western Journal of Speech Communication, 46,* 115–130.

Pacanowsky, M. E., & O'Donnell-Trujillo, N. (1983). Organizational communication as cultural performance. *Communication Monographs, 50,* 126–147.

Palmer, M. T. (1989). Controlling conversations: Turns, topics and interpersonal control. *Communication Monographs, 56,* 1–18.

Parenti, M. (1986). *Inventing reality: The politics of the mass media.* New York: St. Martin's Press.

Pavitt, C., & Haight, L. (1986). Implicit theories of communicative competence: Situational and competence level differences in judgments of prototype and target. *Communication Monographs, 53,* 221–235.

Pavlik, J. V., Blumenthal, L. E., & Cropper, J. J. (1984). Reconceptualizing the information-processing paradigm: A Guttman Scalogram Analysis. In D. R. Glover (Ed.), *Proceedings of the 1984 Convention of the American Academy of Advertising* (pp. 133–137). Lincoln: School of Journalism, University of Nebraska.

Pearce, W. B., & Cronen, V. E. (1980). *Communication, action, and meaning.* New York: Praeger.

Penley, L. E. (1982). An investigation of the information processing framework of organizational communication. *Human Communication Research, 8,* 348–365.

Petronio, S., Martin, J., & Littlefield, R. (1984). Prerequisite conditions for self-disclosing: A gender issue. *Communication Monographs, 51*, 268–273.

Pettegrew, L. S. (1988). Theoretical plurality in health communication. In J. A. Anderson (Ed.), *Communication yearbook 11* (pp. 298–308). Newbury Park, CA: Sage.

Petty, R. E., & Cacioppo, J. T. (1981). *Attitudes and persuasion: Classic and contemporary approaches.* Dubuque, IA: Brown.

Petty, R. E., & Cacioppo, J. T. (1986). *Communication and persuasion: Central and peripheral routes to attitude change.* New York: Springer-Verlag.

Pfeffer, J. (1978). The ambiguity of leadership. In M. W. McCall, Jr. & M. M. Lombardo (Eds.), *Leadership: Where else can we go?* (pp. 13–34). Durham, NC: Duke University Press.

Pfeffer, J. (1981). Management as symbolic action: The creation and maintenance of organizational paradigms. In B. M. Staw & L. L. Cummings (Eds.), *Research in organizational behavior* (Vol. 3, pp. 1–53). Greenwich, CT: JAI.

Pilotta, J. J., Widman, T., & Jasko, S. A. (1988). Meaning and action in the organizational setting: An interpretive approach. In J. A. Anderson (Ed.), *Communication yearbook 11* (pp. 310–334). Newbury Park, CA: Sage.

Pincus, J. D. (1980). Taking a stand on the issues through advertising. *Association Management, 32*, 58–63.

Pincus, J. D. (1986). Communication satisfaction, job satisfaction, and job performance. *Human Communication Research, 12*, 395–419.

Pincus, J. D., Rayfield, R. E., & Cozzens, M. D. (1991). The chief executive officer's internal communication role: A benchmark program of research. In L. A. Grunig & J. E. Grunig (Eds.), *Public relations research annual* (Vol. 3, pp. 1–35). Hillsdale, NJ: Lawrence Erlbaum Associates.

Pinsdorf, M. K. (1991). Flying different skies: How cultures respond to airline disasters. *Public Relations Review, 17*(1), 37–56.

Plough, A., & Krimsky, S. (1987). The emergence of risk communication studies: Social and political context. *Science, Technology, & Human Values, 12*(3–4), 4–10.

Pondy, L. R. (1978). Leadership is a language game. In M. M. Lombardo & M. W. McCall, Jr. (Eds.), *Leadership: Where else can we go?* (pp. 87–99). Durham, NC: Duke University Press.

Pondy, L. R. (1983). The role of metaphors and myths in organization and in the facilitation of change. In L. Pondy, P. Frost, G. Morgan, & T. Dandridge (Eds.), *Organizational symbolism* (pp. 157–166). Greenwich, CT: JAI.

Pondy, L. R., & Boje, D. M. (1980). Bringing mind back in. In W. M. Evan (Ed.), *Frontiers in organization and management* (pp. 83–101). New York: Wiley.

Poole, M. S., & McPhee, R. D. (1983). A structural analysis of organizational climate. In L. L. Putnam & M. E. Pacanowsky (Eds.), *Communication and organizations: An interpretive approach* (pp. 195–219). Newbury Park, CA: Sage.

Poole, M. S., & Roth, J. (1989a). Decision development in small groups IV: A typology of group decision paths. *Human Communication Research, 15*, 323–356.

Poole, M. S., & Roth, J. (1989b). Decision development in small groups V: Test of a contingency model. *Human Communication Research, 15*, 549–589.

Porter, L. W., Allen, R. W., & Angle, H. L. (1981). The politics of upward influence in organizations. In B. M. Staw & L. L. Cummings (Eds.), *Research in organizational behavior* (Vol. 3, pp. 109–149). Greenwich, CT: JAI.

Post, J. E. (1979). *Corporate behavior and social change.* Reston, VA: Reston.

Post, J. E., & Kelley, P. C. (1988). Lessons from the learning curve: The past, present, and future of issues management. In R. L. Heath (Ed.), *Strategic issues management: How organizations influence and respond to public interests and policies* (pp. 345–365). San Francisco: Jossey-Bass.

Post, J. E., Murray, E. A., Jr., Dickie, R. B., & Mahon, J. F. (1982). The public affairs function in American corporations: Development and relations with corporate planning. *Long Range Planning, 15*(2), 12–21.

Pratt, K., & Kleiner, B. (1989). Towards managing by a richer set of organizational values. *Leadership and Organization, 10*, 10–16.

Public Affairs Council. (1978). *The fundamentals of issue management.* Washington, DC: Author.

Public Relations Society of America. (1987). Report of Special Committee on Terminology. *International Public Relations Review, 11*(2), 6–11.

Putnam, L. L. (1982). Paradigms for organizational communication research: An overview and synthesis. *Western Journal of Speech Communication, 46,* 192–206.

Putnam, L. L. (1983). The interpretive perspective: An alternative to functionalism. In L. L. Putnam & M. E. Pacanowsky (Eds.), *Communication and organizations: An interpretive approach* (pp. 31–54). Newbury Park, CA: Sage.

Putnam, L. L. (1989). Negotiation and organizing: Two levels of analysis within the Weickian model. *Communication Studies, 40,* 249–257.

Putnam, L. L., & Jones, T. S. (1982). Reciprocity in negotiations: An analysis of bargaining interaction. *Communication Monographs, 49,* 171–191.

Putnam, L. L., Van Hoeven, S. A., & Bullis, C. A. (1991). The role of rituals and fantasy themes in teachers' bargaining. *Western Journal of Speech Communication, 55,* 85–103.

Raucher, A. R. (1968). *Public relations and business: 1900–1929.* Baltimore: Johns Hopkins University Press.

Ray, C. A. (1986). Corporate culture: The last frontier of control. *Journal of Management Studies, 23,* 287–297.

Ray, E. B. (1991). The relationship among communication network roles, job stress, and burnout in educational organizations. *Communication Quarterly, 39,* 91–102.

Redding, W. C. (1985). Stumbling toward identity. In R. McPhee & P. Tompkins (Eds.), *Organizational communication: Traditional themes and new directions* (pp. 15–54). Newbury Park, CA: Sage.

Reid, L. N., & Rotfeld, H. J. (1981). How informative are ads on children's TV shows? *Journalism Quarterly, 58,* 108–111.

Resnik, A., & Stern, B. L. (1977). An analysis of information content in television advertising. *Journal of Marketing, 41,* 50–53.

Ressler, J. A. (1982). Crisis communications. *Public Relations Quarterly, 27*(3), 8–10.

Richetto, G. M. (1977). Organizational communication theory and research: An overview. In B. D. Ruben (Ed.), *Communication yearbook 1* (pp. 331–346). New Brunswick, NJ: Transaction Books.

Roberts, K. H., & O'Reilly, C. A. (1974). Measuring organizational communications. *Journal of Applied Psychology, 59,* 321–326.

Rogers, E. M., & Kincaid, D. L. (1981). *Communication networks: Toward a new paradigm for research.* New York: Free Press.

Roloff, M. E. (1981). *Interpersonal communication: The social exchange approach.* Newbury Park, CA: Sage.

Roloff, M. E. (1987). Communication and reciprocity within intimate relationships. In M. E. Roloff & G. R. Miller (Eds.), *Interpersonal processes: New directions in communication research* (pp. 11–38). Newbury Park, CA: Sage.

Rose, R. A. (1988). Organizations as multiple cultures: A rules theory analysis. *Human Relations, 41,* 139–170.

Ross, I. (1976, September). Public relations isn't kid-glove stuff at Mobil. *Fortune, 94,* 106–111, 196–202.

Rotondi, T., Jr. (1975). Organizational identification and group involvement. *Academy of Management Journal, 18,* 892–897.

Rowland, R. C. (1989). On limiting the narrative paradigm: Three case studies. *Communication Monographs, 56,* 39–54.

Rowland, R. C., & Rademacher, T. (1990). The passive style of rhetorical crisis management: A case study of the Superfund controversy. *Communication Studies, 41,* 327–343.

Sackmann, S. A. (1990). Managing organizational culture: Dreams and possibilities. In J. A. Anderson (Ed.), *Communication yearbook 13* (pp. 114–148). Newbury Park, CA: Sage.

Salem, P., & Williams, M. L. (1984). Uncertainty and satisfaction: The importance of information in hospital communication. *Journal of Applied Communication Research, 12,* 75–89.

Sandman, P. M. (1986, November). *Explaining environmental risk: Some notes on environmental risk communication*. Washington, DC: Environmental Protection Agency.

Sanford, S. (1990). A view from within: An insider's reflection on the effect of relocation. In J. A. Anderson (Ed.), *Communication yearbook 13* (pp. 107–113). Newbury Park, CA: Sage.

Schein, E. H. (1985). *Organizational cultures and leadership*. San Francisco: Jossey-Bass.

Schlueter, D. W., Barge, J. K., & Blankenship, D. (1990). A comparative analysis of influence strategies used by upper and lower-level male and female managers. *Western Journal of Speech Communication, 54*, 42–65.

Schmalensee, D. H. (1983). Today's top priority advertising research questions. *Journal of Advertising Research, 23*(2), 49–60.

Schmertz, H. (1986). *Good-bye to the low profile: The art of creative confrontation*. Boston: Little, Brown.

Schultz, D. L. (1989). Toxic chemical disclosure: Companies tackle the challenge. *Public Relations Journal, 45*(1), 13–19.

Seibold, D. R., & Spitzberg, B. H. (1982). Attribution theory and research: Review and implications for communication. In B. Dervin & M. J. Voigt (Eds.), *Progress in communication sciences* (Vol. 3, pp. 85–125). Norwood, NJ: Ablex.

Sethi, S. P. (1977). *Advocacy advertising and large corporations: Social conflict, big business image, the news media, and public policy*. Lexington, MA: Heath.

Sethi, S. P. (1979). Institutional/image advertising and idea/issue advertising as marketing tools: Some public policy issues. *Journal of Marketing, 43*, 68–78.

Sethi, S. P. (1986, August 10). Beyond the fairness doctrine: A new war on corporate "propaganda." *The New York Times*, p. F3.

Sethi, S. P. (1987a). *Handbook of advocacy advertising: Concepts, strategies and applications*. Cambridge, MA: Ballinger.

Sethi, S. P. (1987b). A novel communications approach to building effective relations with external constituencies. *International Journal of Advertising, 6*, 279–298.

Shannon, C. E., & Weaver, W. (1949). *The mathematical theory of communication*. Urbana: University of Illinois Press.

Shrivastava, P., Mitroff, I. I., & Alvesson, M. (1987). Nonrationality in organizational actions. *International Studies of Management & Organizations, 17*, 90–109.

Shrivastava, P., & Schneider, S. (1984). Organizational frames of reference. *Human Relations, 37*, 795–809.

Siehl, C. (1985). After the founder: An opportunity to manage culture. In P. J. Frost, L. F. Moore, M. R. Louis, C. C. Lundberg, & J. Martin (Eds.), *Organizational culture* (pp. 125–140). Newbury Park, CA: Sage.

Sillars, A. L. (1982). Attribution and communication: Are people "naive scientists" or just naive? In M. E. Roloff & C. R. Berger (Eds.), *Social cognition and communication* (pp. 73–106). Newbury Park, CA: Sage.

Simon, H. A. (1957). *Administrative behavior* (2nd ed.). New York: Macmillan.

Simons, H. W. (1983). Mobil's system-oriented conflict rhetoric: A generic analysis. *Southern Speech Communication Journal, 48*, 243–254.

Singer, E., & Endreny, P. (1987). Reporting hazards: Their benefits and costs. *Journal of Communication, 37*(3), 10–25.

Small, W. J. (1991). Exxon Valdez: How to spend billions and still get a black eye. *Public Relations Review, 17*(1), 9–25.

Smeltzer, L. R., & Kedia, B. L. (1985). Knowing the ropes: Organizational requirements for quality circles. *Business Horizons, 28*, 30–34.

Smilowitz, M., & Pearson, R. (1989). Traditional, enlightened, and interpretive perspectives on corporate annual reporting. In C. H. Botan & V. Hazleton, Jr. (Eds.), *Public relations theory* (pp. 83–97). Hillsdale, NJ: Lawrence Erlbaum Associates.

Smircich, L. (1983a). Implications for management theory. In L. L. Putnam & M. E. Pacanowsky (Eds.), *Communication and organizations: An interpretive approach* (pp. 221–241). Newbury Park, CA: Sage.

Smircich, L. (1983b). Organizations as shared meanings. In L. R. Pondy, P. J. Frost, G. Morgan, & T. C. Dandridge (Eds.), *Organizational symbolism* (pp. 55–65). Greenwich, CT: JAI.

Smircich, L., & Calas, M. B. (1987). Organizational culture: A critical assessment. In F. M. Jablin, L. L. Putnam, K. H. Roberts, & L. W. Porter (Eds.), *Handbook of organizational communication: An interdisciplinary perspective* (pp. 228–263). Newbury Park, CA: Sage.

Smircich, L., & Morgan, G. (1982). Leadership: The management of meaning. *The Journal of Applied Behavioral Science, 18,* 257–273.

Smith, G., & Heath, R. L. (1990). Moral appeals in Mobil Oil's op-ed campaign. *Public Relations Review, 16,* 48–54.

Smith, R. C., & Eisenberg, E. M. (1987). Conflict at Disneyland: A root metaphor analysis. *Communication Monographs, 54,* 367–379.

Smith, R. E., & Swinyard, W. R. (1982). Information response models: An integrated approach. *Journal of Marketing, 46,* 81–93.

Snavely, W. B., & Walters, E. V. (1983). Differences in communication competence among administrator social styles. *Journal of Applied Communication Research, 11,* 120–135.

Sneath, W. S. (1977). Managing for an uncertain future. *Vital Speeches, 43*(7), 196–199.

Soley, L. C., & Reid, L. W. (1983). Satisfaction with the informational value of magazine and television advertising. *Journal of Advertising, 12,* 27–31.

Solomon, D. S. (1989). A social marketing perspective on communication campaigns. In R. E. Rice & W. J. Paisley (Eds.), *Public communication campaigns* (2nd ed., pp. 87–104). Newbury Park, CA: Sage.

Solomon, J. (1989, June 12). Managing. *The Wall Street Journal,* p. B1.

Spitzberg, B. H. (1991). An examination of trait measures of interpersonal competence. *Communication Reports, 4,* 22–29.

Sproule, J. M. (1988). The new managerial rhetoric and the old criticism. *Quarterly Journal of Speech, 74,* 468–486.

Sproule, J. M. (1989). Organizational rhetoric and the public sphere. *Communication Studies, 40,* 258–265.

Srivastva, S., & Barrett, F. J. (1988). The transforming nature of metaphors in group development: A study in group theory. *Human Relations, 41,* 31–64.

Stanley, G. D. D. (1985). *Managing external issues: Theory and practice.* Greenwich, CT: JAI.

Stinchcombe, A. L. (1990). *Information and organizations.* Berkeley: University of California Press.

Stohl, C. (1986). Quality circles and changing patterns of communication. In M. L. McLaughlin (Ed.), *Communication yearbook 9* (pp. 511–531). Newbury Park, CA: Sage.

Stohl, C. (1987). Bridging the parallel organization: A study of quality circle effectiveness. In M. L. McLaughlin (Ed.), *Communication yearbook 10* (pp. 416–430). Newbury Park, CA: Sage.

Stone, D. L., & Stone, E. F. (1985). The effects of feedback consistency and feedback favorability on self-perceived task competence and perceived feedback accuracy. *Organizational Behavior and Human Decision Processes, 36,* 167–185.

Street, R. L., Jr. (1986). Interaction processes and outcomes in interviews. In M. L. McLaughlin (Ed.), *Communication yearbook 9* (pp. 215–250). Newbury Park, CA: Sage.

Street, R. L., Jr., & Giles, H. (1982). Speech accommodation theory: A social-cognitive approach to language and speech behavior. In M. E. Roloff & C. R. Berger (Eds.), *Social cognition and communication* (pp. 193–226). Newbury Park, CA: Sage.

Stridsberg, A. B. (1977). *Corporate advertising: How advertisers present points of view in public affairs.* New York: Hastings House.

Stroup, M. A. (1988). Identifying critical issues for better corporate planning. In R. L. Heath (Ed.), *Strategic issues management: How organizations influence and respond to public interests and policies* (pp. 87–97). San Francisco: Jossey-Bass.

Sullivan, J. J. (1988). Three roles of language in motivation theory. *Academy of Management Review*, *13*, 104–115.

Switzer, D. E., & Switzer, J. Y. (1989). Strategies for managerial and employee intervention in the idealization–frustration–demoralization cycle. *Management Communication Quarterly*, *3*, 249–262.

Sypher, B. D., & Zorn, T. E., Jr. (1986). Communication-related abilities and upward mobility: A longitudinal investigation. *Human Communication Research*, *12*, 420–431.

Taylor, S. E., & Thompson, S. C. (1982). Stalking the elusive "vividness" effect. *Psychological Review*, *89*, 155–181.

Tengler, C. D., & Jablin, F. M. (1983). Effects of question type, orientation, and sequencing in the employment screening interview. *Communication Monographs*, *50*, 245–263.

Tenneco. (1984). *Annual Report*. Houston, TX: Author.

Theberge, L. J. (1981). *Crooks, conmen, and clowns: Businessmen in TV entertainment*. Washington, DC: The Media Institute.

Theus, K. T. (1991). Organizational ideology, structure, and communication efficacy: A causal analysis. In L. A. Grunig & J. E. Grunig (Eds.), *Public relations research annual* (Vol. 3, pp. 133–149). Hillsdale, NJ: Lawrence Erlbaum Associates.

Thomas, K., Swaton, E., Fishbein, M., & Otway, H. J. (1980). Nuclear energy: The accuracy of policy makers' perceptions of public beliefs. *Behavioral Science*, *25*, 332–344.

Thompson, D. B. (1981, February 23). Issue management: New key to corporate survival. *Industry Week*, *208*, 77–80.

Thompson, S. C. (1981). Will it hurt less if I can control it? A complex answer to a simple question. *Psychological Bulletin*, *90*, 89–101.

Tompkins, P. K. (1987). Translating organizational theory: Symbolism over substance. In F. M. Jablin, L. L. Putnam, K. H. Roberts, & L. W. Porter (Eds.), *Handbook of organizational communication: An interdisciplinary perspective* (pp. 70–96). Newbury Park, CA: Sage.

Tompkins, P. K., & Cheney, G. (1983). Account analysis of organizations: Decision making and identification. In L. L. Putnam & M. E. Pacanowsky (Eds.), *Communication and organizations: An interpretive approach* (pp. 123–146). Newbury Park, CA: Sage.

Tompkins, P. K., & Cheney, G. (1985). Communication and unobtrusive control in contemporary organizations. In R. D. McPhee & P. K. Tompkins (Eds.), *Organizational communication: Traditional themes and new directions* (pp. 179–210). Newbury Park, CA: Sage.

Toulmin, S., Rieke, R., & Janik, A. (1979). *An introduction to reasoning*. New York: Macmillan.

Tracy, K. (1984). The effect of multiple goals on conversational relevance and topic shift. *Communication Monographs*, *51*, 274–287.

Treadwell, D. F. (1991, May). *Performance correlates of visual appeals in corporate annual reports*. Paper presented at the meeting of the International Communication Association, Chicago, IL.

Trujillo, N. (1983). "Performing" Mintzberg's roles: The nature of managerial communication. In L. L. Putnam & M. E. Pacanowsky (Eds.), *Communication and organizations: An interpretive approach* (pp. 73–97). Newbury Park, CA: Sage.

Turner, D. B. (1990). Intraorganizational bargaining: The effect of goal congruence and trust on negotiator strategy use. *Communication Studies*, *41*, 54–75.

Ungson, G. R., James, C., & Spicer, B. H. (1985). The effects of regulatory agencies on organizations in wood products and high technology/electronic industries. *Academy of Management Journal*, *28*, 426–445.

Vaill, P. B. (1978). Toward a behavioral description of high-performing systems. In M. W. McCall, Jr. & M. M. Lombardo (Eds.), *Leadership: Where else can we go?* (pp. 103–125). Durham, NC: Duke University Press.

Van Maanen, J., & Barley, S. R. (1985). Cultural organization: Fragments of a theory. In P. J. Frost, L. F. Moore, M. R. Louis, C. C. Lundberg, & J. Martin (Eds.), *Organizational culture* (pp. 31–53). Newbury Park, CA: Sage.

Vaughn, R. (1986). How advertising works: A planning model revisited. *Journal of Advertising Research*, *26*(2), 57–66.

Vielhaber, M. E. (1983). Communication and attitudes toward work-related change. *Journal of Applied Communication Research, 11*, 1–16.

Waltzer, H. (1988). Corporate advocacy advertising and political influence. *Public Relations Review, 14*(1), 41–55.

Wartick, S. L., & Rude, R. E. (1986). Issues management: Corporate fad or corporate function? *California Management Review, 24*(1), 124–140.

Weaver, P. H. (1988). The self-destructive corporation. *California Management Review, 30*(3), 128–143.

Weber, M. (1947). *The theory of social and economic organization* (T. Parsons, Ed., M. Henderson & T. Parsons, Trans). New York: The Free Press.

Weick, K. E. (1979a). Cognitive processes in organizations. In B. M. Staw (Ed.), *Research in organizational behavior* (Vol. 1, pp. 41–74). Greenwich, CT: JAI.

Weick, K. E. (1979b). *The social psychology of organizing* (2nd ed.). Reading, MA: Addison-Wesley.

Weick, K. E. (1983). Organizational communication: Toward a research agenda. In L. L. Putnam & M. E. Pacanowsky (Eds.), *Communication and organizations: An interpretive approach* (pp. 13–29). Newbury Park, CA: Sage.

Weick, K. E. (1987). Theorizing about organizational communication. In F. M. Jablin, L. L. Putnam, K. H. Roberts, & L. W. Porter (Eds.), *Handbook of organizational communication: An interdisciplinary perspective* (pp. 97–122). Newbury Park, CA: Sage.

Weick, K. E., & Browning, L. D. (1986). Argument and narration in organizational communication. *Journal of Management, 12*, 243–259.

Weiss, H. M. (1977). Subordinate imitation of supervisor behavior: The role of modeling in organizational socialization. *Organizational Behavior and Human Performance, 19*, 89–105.

Welty, W. (1981). Is issue advertising working? *Public Relations Journal, 37* (11), 29.

Wilkins, A. L. (1984). The creation of company cultures: The role of stories and human systems. *Human Resource Management, 23*, 41–60.

Wilkins, A. L., & Dyer, W. G., Jr. (1988). Toward culturally sensitive theories of culture change. *Academy of Management Review, 13*, 522–533.

Winters, L. C. (1988). Does it pay to advertise to hostile audiences with corporate advertising? *Journal of Advertising Research, 28*(3), 11–18.

Wood, R., & Bandura, A. (1989). Social cognitive theory of organizational management. *Academy of Management Review, 14*, 361–384.

Wright, P. L. (1973). The cognitive processes mediating acceptance of advertising. *Journal of Marketing Research, 10*(2), 53–62.

Wright, P. L. (1981). Cognitive responses to mass media advocacy. In R. E. Petty, T. M. Ostrom, & T. C. Brock (Eds.), *Cognitive responses in persuasion* (pp. 263–282). Hillsdale, NJ: Lawrence Erlbaum Associates.

Young, S. (1990). Combatting NIMBY with risk communication. *Public Relations Quarterly, 35*(2), 22–26.

Author Index

Subject Index